THE ENCYCLOPEDIA OF
MASS MURDER

Also by Brian Lane

The Murder Club Guides (6 vols.)
The Murder Guide to Great Britain
The Murder Guide to London
The Butchers
Murder Update
The Encyclopedia of Forensic Science
The Encyclopedia of Cruel and Unusual Punishment
The Murder Yearbook
The Murder Yearbook: 1994 Edition
Chronicle of Twentieth Century Murder
The Encyclopedia of Women Killers

with Wilfred Gregg

The Encyclopedia of Serial Killers
The New Encyclopedia of Serial Killers

BRIAN LANE AND WILFRED GREGG

THE ENCYCLOPEDIA OF

MASS MURDER

ROBINSON
London

Constable & Robinson Ltd
3 The Lanchesters
162 Fulham Palace Road
London W6 9ER
www.constablerobinson.com

First published in hardback in the UK by
Headline Book Publishing 1994

This revised and updated paperback edition published in the UK
by Robinson, an imprint of Constable & Robinson Ltd 2004

A copy of the British Library Cataloguing in
Publication Data is available from the British Library.

ISBN 1–84119–770–X

Printed and bound in the EU

10 9 8 7 6 5 4 3 2 1

Contents

Acknowledgements

It is becoming increasingly difficult to think of new things to write by way of acknowledgement; the fact is, having been lucky enough to find a winning combination of willing talents, we have hung on to them gratefully. With the exception of a few minor alterations the major players in the cast-list for *The Encyclopedia of Mass Murder* are identical to that for its companion volume, *The Encyclopedia of Serial Killers*, and for many other books from the 'pens' of Lane and Gregg. Once again, although the words contained between these covers are our own, we have inevitably relied in great part on the efforts of a multitude of previous authorities as well as on our own first-hand researches. In practical terms our most valuable assets have been Wilf Gregg's exhaustive true-crime library and archive and the cuttings collection assembled with help from members of the former Murder Club. These resources were supplemented, as ever, by the unfailing expertise and courtesy of the staffs of the British Library Reading Room and Newspaper Library. Of the individuals who have proved invaluable in the research and development of this study we would like to single out for special mention columnist and fellow crime-writer Frank Jones, whose regular despatches on derring-do in Canada have been most welcome. Our thanks go to Natasha McCoy for keeping us supplied with American newspapers and magazines. A new face across the desk on this venture has been John Bevis who, apart from adding his own special viewpoint to a number of the individual texts, gallantly came to the rescue when our computer dumped half the manuscript.

Brian Lane
Wilfred Gregg
London, 1994

Picture credits
Some of the illustrations contained in this volume are from the authors' personal collections; where photographs derive from picture agencies these have been acknowledged in the appropriate place. If we have failed to trace any copyright then may we apologize in advance.

Introduction

One of the most important considerations in compiling a broadly thematic collection of cases such as this is to ensure that the contents are not only representative of the wider study – in this instance Mass Murder – but representative also of the many aspects of that subject. At the same time, one of the constraints is acknowledging the sheer scale of the undertaking and recognizing that the 'encyclopedia' will never be truly encyclopedic. For example, even as the manuscript was being delivered to our publisher, news arrived that Mamoru Takuma had been sentenced to death in Japan for the murder of eight children in a frenzied attack at a primary school. By the time that manuscript is transformed into the book you hold in your hands there will inevitably have occurred other significant cases of multicide. Consequently, this book does not, cannot, contain references to *all* those killers who have gone on sprees resulting in multiple victims – to have done so would require several volumes. Instead, we have adopted a format which will present an overview embracing as many of the types of motive, method and *modus operandi* as possible and taking examples from countries around the globe and from different periods of history. For this reason we have necessarily made subjective decisions on which cases to include and which to exclude; inevitably readers will occasionally be surprised or disappointed to find their own particular 'favourites' missing from the cast list. Above all we have tried to assemble a book which, although it pivots on a subject, tells the stories of individual personalities – some, it is true, quite mad, some sad, others downright bad, but all human beings, in many ways not unlike ourselves with our pleasures and problems, our passions and dislikes, successes and failures. The awful fascination lies in the fact that these human beings, by committing the one ultimate and unforgivable crime have severed their link with humankind. From **Barend Strydom** who didn't like blacks to **Mark Essex** who didn't like whites, and **Brenda Spencer** who didn't like Mondays, these are the lives of those human beings who became, often in one brief moment, monsters.

But before embarking on this voyage into darkness, let us try to find some rules by which we might begin to understand and measure the threat of the mass killer. First a definition would be useful. We can say that mass killers all conform to one or more of the following characteristics:

1. A number of victims are slain over a comparatively short span of time, usually hours, less often, days.
2. If the killings are committed in more than one location they are part of a 'continuous' action.
3. Victims are typically either selected at random and attacked or not on the momentary whim of the killer; or form part of a target group – again often arbitrarily chosen as 'scapegoats'.
4. The killer frequently concludes his spree by taking his own life (though this may take the less obvious form of behaving so recklessly that armed law enforcement officers are obliged to shoot to kill).

Due to the nature of their crime, mass murderers do not bask for long in the glare of their media notoriety, nor do they endure sufficiently to be awarded the lurid *noms de guerre* coined for the serial killers. They are, perhaps, best described as the commandos of homicide – striking swiftly, fatally and unexpectedly; indeed, this comparison is more truth than mere metaphor, because many mass killers do have a fascination with military, paramilitary or survivalist activities, and frequently dress in combat uniform to commit their murders.

However, despite the fact that law enforcement agencies and the medical professions have made enormous strides in understanding the motivation of multicides, we are still a long way from being able to identify the threat before it becomes a reality. The problem inherent in any attempt to anticipate the mass killer is his unpredictability. In the case of the serial killer a pattern does begin to emerge – a victim trait, perhaps, or a locational preference. But the one-off multicide is the most dangerous killer on earth; the location for his crime could be anywhere that people congregate in numbers – including his own home – and the victims anybody who happens to be congregating there – including his own family.

'Un'safety in numbers

Some killers have deliberately maximized their death count by selecting situations where an unusually large number of potential victims are confined in a limited area. One of the worst cases of mass murder in the United States occurred when **Julio Gonzalez** set fire to the crowded Happy Land social club in New York; Gonzalez claimed the lives of eighty-seven people. An English equivalent took place in 1980 when **John Thompson** set fire to two Soho drinking clubs with a loss of life of thirty-seven. Restaurants also attract the potential mass killer; in 1991 **George Hennard** carried out his massacre of twenty-two people in the busy branch of Luby's cafeterias at Killeen, Texas – the worst multiple shooting in recent American criminal history. The Australian **Wade Frankum** chose to begin his killing spree in the crowded Coffee Pot restaurant in Sydney's Strathfield Plaza, before turning his attention to the shopping mall outside.

Other killers simply stalk the streets picking off randomly anybody who comes within sight and range. In one of Britain's worst mass shootings, **Michael Ryan** inflicted a reign of terror on the small Berkshire village of Hungerford in August 1987. Dressed in army combat uniform and armed with an arsenal of deadly weapons, Ryan claimed the lives of fourteen victims, including his own mother, before turning the gun on himself. It is a baffling and alarming fact that killers such as Ryan (and one can also call to mind the names of **Charles Manson** and Peter Sutcliffe) seem to attract a kind of cult following, some of whom go on to commit their own copycat murders. Michael Ryan's number one fan, for example, was a disturbed youth called **Robert Sartin** (though he usually left the 'r' out of his surname so that it sounded like 'Satan'). Just days before embarking on his own murderous shooting spree around the sleepy seaside suburb of Monkseaton, Sartin paid a visit of homage to Hungerford.

There is another category of mass killers, less universally dangerous, but just as deadly. They include those multicides who have pre-selected specific targets, such as families, or places of employment or education.

Keeping it in the family

It is within the family circle that the greatest degree of psychological tension exists, with its jealousies, frustrations and rivalries; and it is within and between families that we find the greatest incidence of multiple murder (as well as the more prosaic one-off killings). The rivalries within the hierarchy of the **Schlaepfer** family of New Zealand, for example, resulted in typically tragic consequences, and the frustration and anger generated by a broken marriage provoked **Vernon Reynolds** into attempting familicide before killing himself and three innocent people in a horrific head-on car crash. The most notorious British familicide of recent times is **Jeremy Bamber**. In August 1985 the bodies of five members of the Bamber family were found shot dead in their farmhouse at Tolleshunt D'Arcy. Suspicion at first fell upon the daughter, twenty-seven-year-old Sheila Caffell. Bamber, who had throughout the investigation presented such a dramatic and convincing demonstration of grief over his parents' deaths only came under suspicion when his ex-girlfriend, Julie Mugford, betrayed him. Jeremy had, according to her testimony, decided to go ahead with the killings after testing his nerve by strangling farmyard rats with his bare hands.

There is no shortage of contenders for the worst family massacre in the United States, but one that has become a household name after a series of films was based on the case is the murder of his family by **Ronald DeFeo** at their home in Amityville, Long Island. On 13 November 1974, twenty-two-year-old Ronald called the police claiming that his mother and father had been killed. When detectives arrived they also discovered the bodies of Ronald's two brothers and two sisters. While he was in custody DeFeo admitted that he had shot dead his whole family out of hatred. What is significant about the statements he made at this time is that they conform closely to one of the psychological 'profiles' of mass murderers. For example, he told detectives: 'Once I got started I just couldn't stop. I went so fast'; and at his trial DeFeo claimed: 'When I get a gun in my hand there's no doubt who I am. I am God.'

Family feuds can also have devastating consequences such as that which erupted near Bogotá on the first day of 1994. Five armed men arrived at a family's home in the village of El Paramo demanding to speak to two young women. The family complied with the gunmen's wishes and all twelve members were shot dead including a five-year-old boy. It transpired that a broken love affair between the two women and two of the killers was the cause of the massacre.

Death in the workplace

In many practical respects the workplace represents a macrocosm of the family home, with managers and supervisors cast in a 'parental' – or sometimes 'spouse' – role, and workmates as 'siblings'. Because we spend almost as many of our waking hours at work as we do with our families, it is understandable that these relationships are prone to similar tensions as those found in the home. A domineering overseer will provoke the same secret resentments as a bullying father or husband; and petty jealousies and dislikes will develop between colleagues as they will between brothers and sisters. The recent history of mass murder provides numerous examples of disgruntled employees (or former employees) returning to their place of work to carry out acts of revenge. **Edward Allaway**, a janitor at the Library of the California State University killed seven of his colleagues who, he claimed, had been responsible for his separation from his wife; and **Bryan Dyer** combined revenge with robbery when he shot the manager and three former colleagues at the Brighton Bowl, Boston, in 1980 – the manager had refused to re-employ him following dismissal.

A curious phenomenon has been the apparently bitter relationship between employees and supervisors of the United States Postal Service which has resulted in several major incidents of multicide committed by postal workers (see, for example, **Joseph Harris** and **Thomas McIlvane**). Dr James A. Fox, Dean of the College of Criminal Justice at North-Eastern University, and a leading authority on the phenomenon of mass murder, told the *New York Times*: 'These [post office incidents] are not indiscriminate shootings. They are very well planned and orchestrated, and the killer only wants to get certain people, not others. It's not that these guys suddenly snap and go berserk and kill everything that moves. It's that they want to get even, get revenge, before they end their lives.' Asked why it should be so prevalent among postal workers, Dr Fox explained that 'as far as public employees go, they are down low on the totem pole when it comes to prestige.'

Not only American postmen get disgruntled. In Besançon, France, in July 1992, a sacked machine tool worker opened fire at the Bourgeois Découpage plant killing six; and in the same year Swiss butcher **Erminio Criscione** went on the rampage and killed six people who were on a wholesale meat suppliers course with him. Even the long-term *un*-employed can resort to outbursts of violence in the *non*-workplace; at the end of 1993 Alan Winterbourne, an engineer who had been out of work for eight years, shot dead three people and wounded another six in a Californian unemployment office, then shot a police officer in the head before in turn being gunned down by police marksmen.

Some killers have combined the targets of home *and* workplace, and the most dramatic of these incidents occurred during the Christmas period of 1987 in Russelville,

Arkansas. On 28 December **Ronald Gene Simmons** went on a forty-five-minute spree during which he shot six former workmates; but when police made a routine search of Simmons' home they found that no fewer than fourteen members of his family had earlier fallen victim to his madness. In the same year, 1987, a parallel spree killing took place in Bristol, in the west of England. **Kevin Weaver** – in common with many mass killers a gun fanatic – took a 12-bore pump-action shotgun capable of rapid fire from his collection of firearms, shot dead his mother and sister and then shot up two employees at the office where his ex-girlfriend worked. It is not without significance in the light of mass killer profiles, that police officers searching Weaver's room at the family home found collections not only of weapons but of survival magazines and police surveillance literature.

School and university sprees
Partly because, like restaurants and workplaces, schools and universities present the mass killer with a maximum possible body-count, they have been the scenes of some of the world's worst multicides. But it is not only the concentration of potential victims that is relevant here, but often some other, more deeply personal motivation. In 1989 **Marc Lepine** opened fire on a class of female students at the University of Montreal because, so he explained in a suicide note, he hated 'feminists'; it was also significant that the same university had, earlier in the year, turned down Lepine's application for a place as an engineering student. Internal disputes have also led to campus carnage – such as when Chinese research fellow **Gang Lu** shot dead colleagues at the physics faculty of the University of Iowa because he had been overlooked for a much-coveted prize; and the killing of three fellow lecturers by Professor **Valery Fabrikant** at the inappropriately named Concordia University, Montreal, after a long-running and bitter feud over educational ethics.

Schools have not infrequently been selected as targets for attacks on groups of children and there have been several notable incidents, particularly in the United States. Among these have been **Laurie Dann** – one of the rare female mass killers who went on a shooting rampage in Winnetka, Illinois and **Patrick Purdy**, who shot dead five children and wounded thirty others in Stockton, California. The worst American school killing to date occurred at the **Columbine High School** in Littleton, Colorado in 1999, when two maddened teenagers killed twelve pupils and a teacher.

The dilemma of politically motivated murder

In addressing the question of politically motivated murder, the recurrent dilemma is how, if at all, to treat those instances of mass killing which would best be described as 'crimes motivated by the state or committed by or on behalf of world-wide terrorist organizations' – as distinct from multicides which result from the private prejudices of an individual or group of individuals. Readers will note that while the pub bombings at **Guildford** and **Birmingham** in England, and the airport massacre carried out by members of the Japanese Red Army Brigade at Tel Aviv Airport (see page 259) have been included, the massive extermination plans resulting from atrocities committed during times of armed conflict or by world-wide terrorist organizations have been excluded. Our yardstick, then, has been the degree of *individual* responsibility, and where responsibility for those crimes can be laid at the door of a country, state or world-wide terrorist organization (Germany's Auschwitz and September 11 for example) then they have been felt to be more properly the subject for a different book.

Profile of a mass killer

As to the mass killer *him*self (for the female of the type is uncommon), there are a number of surprisingly uniform factors which combine to create the stereotype. He is white and approaching middle-age; he is a loner, and has been since childhood, when an unhappy or disrupted home life or sense of rejection bred a suspicion of relationships and an inability to form lasting friendships – and he knows it.

Consequently the loner, lacking in the social skills with which to integrate, surrounds himself with the trappings of what he sees as 'power'. It is no coincidence that the majority of mass killers become obsessed with the machismo of martial arts, body building and military activities, often adopting combat uniform as a mode of dress, plus an unhealthy preoccupation with firearms. Because such weapons are capable of inflicting the greatest damage in the shortest time, guns (and explosives as an extension of this concept) are favoured by the mass killer. It is no coincidence that in the nation where there is almost unlimited access to weapons with which to feed the murderer's fantasies – the United States – there is the worst problem with multicide. The potential killer will also have developed his own personal scapegoats, people or groups of people whom he can blame for the real or imagined ills and rejections that he has suffered. They may be government officials, women, employers, members of other ethnic groups, indeed any conveniently identifiable set of people.

Thus armed, and comforted by his fantasies, the mass killer can temporarily mask his feelings of isolation and underachievement. Sadly, one day he *will* achieve; for a short period of time at least everybody will know his name. It is impossible to predict what will trigger this final separation from reality, what the final straw will be. He may have been reprimanded at work, or short-changed at the corner store; a neighbour's child may have kicked a ball at his car, or his advances been rejected by a woman; he may have been served cold food or warm beer. Whatever it is, it acts as the finger which presses the self-destruct button. This is the point at which the potential killer sees through the fantasies and into his own emptiness, where the anger and frustration of years erupts into an uncontrollable destructive force (many survivors have described mass killers as acting like 'zombies'). Having made his final statement, exacted his final revenge, it is common for the mass murderer to turn his weapon on himself. In his study of modern multicides, Dr Elliott Leyton (*Hunting Humans*, 1989) describes this phenomenon as 'the mass killer, who no longer wishes to live, and whose murders constitute his *suicide note*'.

In the case studies which comprise the rest of this book, some or all of these characteristics will be encountered in the individual mass murderer. There will, however, be those who do not conform; this unpredictability is what makes the spree killer the most dangerous of all.

Mass Murder A-Z

A

ACQUIN, Lorne J. People living in Cedar Hill Drive, Prospect, Connecticut, were awoken from their sleep in the early hours of Friday 22 July 1977, by the smell of smoke and the crackling of fire. Looking out, they saw the house occupied by the Beaudoin family was a blazing inferno. The fire brigade were called and doused the flames with their hoses, but despite their best efforts the house was gutted. When firefighters entered the still smouldering ruins they found the charred remains of human corpses everywhere.

They came upon twenty-nine-year-old Mrs Cheryl Beaudoin dead on the kitchen floor, her clothes burned from her body. The bodies of three children were discovered in a bedroom to the right of the hall and two others in a bedroom to the left. Another child was dead in the master bedroom and two more in the bathroom. Investigators later noticed that Mrs Beaudoin and several of the children had their hands tied behind their backs and the two in the bathroom had their feet bound together; all the children appeared to have head wounds.

The victims, apart from Mrs Beaudoin, were her own seven children Frederick (twelve), Sharon Lee (ten), Debra Ann (nine), Paul (eight), Roderick (six), Holly Lyn (five) and Mary Lou (four). The ninth victim was Mrs Beaudoin's niece Jennifer Santoro (six), who had been staying with the family.

Police immediately launched the largest murder investigation in Connecticut's criminal history. Post-mortems established that Mrs Beaudoin died from head injuries and a stab wound in the chest. Paul also died from head injuries, while the others perished from a combination of head injuries and smoke inhalation. Within twenty-four hours detectives had interviewed more than a hundred potential witnesses, including the bereaved husband and his foster brother Lorne J. Acquin, who turned out to have been at the house playing with the Beaudoin children on the night before the fire. A witness later confirmed that a man had been seen in the area sitting in his car on the day before the murders.

The police investigation now concentrated on twenty-seven-year-old Acquin, who, according to the criminal records had a previous conviction for burglary plus an additional sentence for an attempted jail break. On Saturday 23 July, Acquin was detained for questioning. On the Sunday morning, he agreed to make a statement in which he admitted attacking his sister-in-law with a tyre lever, after which he did the same to the children before spreading petrol round the house and setting it on fire. Later that day Lorne Acquin was charged with nine counts of murder and one of arson.

Acquin eventually went on trial at Waterbury on Monday 16 July 1979, after jury selection had taken more than a month. The prosecution emphasized that in his confession, Acquin said he 'might' have sexually molested ten-year-old Sharon Beaudoin but that the post-mortem examinations had confirmed there were signs of sexual injury in her case. On Friday 19 October 1979, after three days' deliberation the jury convicted Acquin on all nine counts of murder and the charge of arson. He was subsequently sentenced to twenty-five years to life on each of the murder convictions and twenty for arson.

ALLAWAY, Edward Charles Ed Allaway, employed as a janitor in the Library of the California State University at Fullerton, was regarded by neighbours and fellow workers alike as Mr Nice Guy. In 1976 Ed was thirty-seven years old and into his third marriage; in this case third time was far from lucky and the marriage was in trouble. Arguments between Allaway and his twenty-two-year-old wife Bonnie had become so violent that on occasion neighbours had been obliged to call the police just to restore a bit of peace. On Memorial Day weekend Allaway packed a case and left home.

Unfortunately the separation triggered serious emotional stress in the once popular janitor, and living alone he had become moody and argumentative. If his colleagues had known that a week after leaving his wife Allaway had bought himself a .22-calibre semi automatic rifle, they would have been even more alarmed. In July 1976 Edward Allaway took his gun to work with him in the campus library. Striding through the basement and first floor of the building he shot nine of his fellow workers, killing seven and wounding two, within the space of a few minutes. Then he surrendered to the police, explaining that he had only shot the people he blamed for the separation from his wife.

Allaway was indicted on seven counts of murder and two of assault with a deadly weapon; the jury convicted him of six counts of first-degree murder, one of second-degree murder and the two assault charges. There had been, of course, no doubt that Allaway was guilty – he had made a confession; and anyway, there were eye-witnesses to the shootings. The jury was, however, deadlocked – six to six – on the question of his sanity. The hung jury resulted in a further hearing after which it was the judge's responsibility to rule on Allaway's sanity; he committed him to the Atascadero State Hospital. This effectively erased all penalties for the crime and means that should Allaway ever regain his sanity to the satisfaction of psychiatrists and the court, he would have to be freed.

ALLEN, Floyd, *et al.* The Allen family, headed by Floyd, had been a thorn in the side of law enforcement officers in the Blue Ridge Mountains area of Virginia for as long as anyone could remember. They considered themselves above the law and openly practised the traditional mountainfolk's pastime of moonshining; needless to add, they also refused to pay taxes. In many ways this kind of naughtiness was at least containable, but on 14 March 1912 in the Carroll County Courthouse at Hillsville, Floyd Allen escalated the scale of their activities into a bloody battle. Allen had been convicted of assaulting a peace officer and preventing the arrest of another member of the clan. The court was packed with members of the Allen family and as Judge Massie pronounced the relatively modest sentence of one year's jail on Floyd Allen, he announced plainly: 'I don't aim to go.' And he and the other members of the family produced guns and began firing. It was later estimated that at least seventy-five shots were fired during the shoot-out, including those fired by the heavily armed representatives of law and order. When the smoke cleared, six people lay dead – the judge, Sheriff Lew Webb, Prosecuting Attorney W. M. Foster, a juror named C. C. Fowler, a witness named Betty Ayers and an innocent spectator; eight others were wounded. Floyd Allen was so badly injured that he was unable to escape from town, and was arrested the following day at a nearby hotel. The other members of the Allen family scattered. Floyd Allen, his son Claude and brother Sidna became the main focus of the subsequent manhunt, and the mischievous Allens were gradually hunted down, leaving the Blue Ridge Mountains a wholly more peaceable place.

Floyd and Claude were convicted of murder, and following unsuccessful appeals were sent to the electric chair on 28 March 1913. Sidna Allen received two terms of fifteen years and one of five, and the other members of the family, who claimed they only loosed off their guns to create a diversion, were given various lesser prison sentences. Sidna Allen was released in 1926 through a pardon from the state governor. He later wrote his memoirs which were published in 1929 and in which he claimed the shootings were unpremeditated and only intended as an attempt to free Floyd.

ANDREWS, Lowell Lee   Andrews, a bespectacled, overweight honours student at the University of Kansas, had been flatteringly described in his home town newspaper as 'The Nicest Boy in Wolcott'. The problem was that in reality eighteen-year-old Andrews was far from being the gentle, sweet-natured boy portrayed; and it would have been a nasty shock to his unsuspecting family had they known that he entertained ideas first of poisoning them, and then becoming a Chicago gangster. The fact was, young Lowell had quite a few such fantasies, and he was relying on the not inconsiderable wealth that his father had derived from farming to finance them.

Lowell Andrews and his sister were both at the family home for the Thanksgiving holiday in 1958. On the evening of 28 November, Jennie Marie was watching television with her parents, while upstairs Lowell was dipping into Dostoevsky's celebrated classic *The Brothers Karamazov*. He finished reading, shaved, put on his best suit and went downstairs carrying a .22-calibre rifle in his hands and a revolver in his hip pocket. Walking into the room where the family were watching TV, crazy Lowell switched on the light and opened fire with the rifle. He shot his sister between the eyes killing her instantly. Without the slightest hesitation he next turned the gun on his parents, shooting his mother three times and his father twice. Mrs Andrews made a brave effort to stagger towards him, and caught another three bullets; Mr Andrews tried to crawl into the kitchen and was shot several times with the revolver – in all, Lowell fired seventeen shots into his father. Then he went through the house, opening a window to make it appear the premises had been burgled, before driving to the town of Lawrence, throwing his weapons into the Kansas River on the way. In town, Lowell Andrews went to his college apartment and told the landlady that it had taken him two hours to drive from Wolcott because of the bad road conditions. Later he went to a cinema where he was uncharacteristically friendly with the staff. When the movie finished Andrews drove home, fed the dog, and telephoned the police to report a robbery.

When officers arrived at the house they found Lowell Andrews sitting on the porch with the dog. Although the police were suspicious at Andrews' apparent unconcern at the death of his family (when asked by the coroner about funeral arrangements, he replied: 'I don't care what you do with them'), his insistence on his own innocence was unshakeable. It was only the intervention of the family's Baptist minister that finally squeezed a confession out of Lowell.

At his trial Andrews pleaded not guilty by reason of insanity, and it is true that he was a very odd lad. However, the jury preferred to think of him as more bad than mad, and decided to accept his confession. Thus Lowell Andrews was convicted and sentenced to hang.

While he was on Death Row in Kansas State Prison, Andrews was in an adjoining cell to the Clutter killers, Perry Smith and Richard Hickock. The Kansas Supreme Court confirmed the conviction and in spite of two appeals to the US Supreme Court, Andrews went to the gallows on Friday 30 November 1962.

ANDREWS, William, and **PIERRE, Dale Selby** It happened that in one of the most controversial cases in recent American criminal history, William Andrews was not even at the scene of the crime when his accomplice Dale Selby Pierre shot dead three white people during a robbery in 1977. However, Andrews, a black man like his associate, did admit that during the raid he tortured five people by forcing them to drink Drano, a caustic drain cleaner. Two of the victims survived, though one has permanent brain damage. As for the other three victims, the medical examiner stated in court that the Drano would have killed them within twelve hours anyway – if Pierre had not shot them first. The murders became known as the 'Hi-Fi Killings' because they took place at Ogden's Hi-Fi shop, Salt Lake City. So brutal and unnecessary were the attacks that the predominantly white local population began to fear an anti-white movement existed among the area's one per cent black citizens.

Indeed, it was the racial issue which created the controversy in the case, with a legal representative of the NAACP Legal Defense and Educational Fund going on record as saying: 'I've never seen such a raw case of racism;

the entire case was infected with racism.' There is no denying that the jury in the Andrews trial was composed of all whites, most of them Mormons. And it was also true that during sentencing a note was passed to the jury reading 'Hang the Niggers'. However, invoking racism as a ground for appeal against the capital sentence has a long history in the courts of the United States, and it is frequently advanced by lawyers representing black clients. It has also been consistently unsuccessful. In the case of William Andrews, his attorney claimed: 'During the trial people in Utah looked at Bill Andrews and only saw a scary looking black guy; they didn't see a scared nineteen-year-old kid.'

Following their trial, Pierre and Andrews were sentenced to death, and the lengthy process of appeals began. After a decade of legal wrangling Dale Selby Pierre was executed on 28 August 1987. For Andrews the wait was longer.

In all, eighteen appeals were made, eighteen appeals rejected. Days before his execution date the last hope failed when the Utah Board of Pardons turned down Andrews' plea. On 30 July 1992 he died by lethal injection at Utah State Prison; his last words were: 'Thank all those who have tried so hard to keep me alive. I hope they continue to fight for equal justice after I'm gone.'

ARCHIBEQUE, Gilbert   At two-thirty on the morning of 18 May 1986, Gilbert Archibeque burst into a bar in the resort town of Colorado Springs and demanded money from the four people present. Without bothering to wait for a response, Archibeque simply opened fire killing two women and a man. A second man staggered from the bar despite a serious head wound and managed to escape.

Archibeque then set fire to the bar and proceeded next door to a grocery store where he shot and killed two young sisters before making off. Having identified the twenty-nine-year-old plumber as the gunman, armed police officers laid siege to Archibeque's home, calling on him to surrender. Although after some negotiation he agreed to give himself up, before anything could be arranged a shot was heard in the house and when police forced a cautious entry, Gilbert Archibeque lay dead by his own hand, a bullet through his head.

With uncharacteristic understatement, a police spokesman later said: 'We have never seen anything like this before. This is normally a very quiet town, everyone is very shocked.'

ARCHINA, Frank In Italy in 1952, two Italian-born brothers, Frank and Gene Archina, married two American sisters, Mary and Rose Macri. Only simple civil ceremonies were performed, but these were sufficient to enable the brothers to emigrate to the United States as the husbands of American citizens.

Frank and Gene took up residence in Denver, Colorado with their father-in-law, Frank Macri senior, who took it into his head that the marriages should not be consummated until they were fully solemnized in the Roman Catholic Church. The boys had no objection to this, but old Signor Macri was not finished with his demands; now he said the marriages could not go ahead until Frank and Gene had saved enough money for full-scale weddings, lavish receptions, home, furniture, and until they proved they had sufficient assets to keep his daughters in the manner to which he thought they should become accustomed.

As a consequence, there were continual squabbles between the brothers and their father-in-law. Matters reached a head on Sunday 24 January 1954, when a fight broke out between Frank Archina and Macri senior, who, having secured his wife and two daughters in a bedroom closet, armed himself with a shotgun and went to confront Frank Archina. Rose Macri later said she heard several shots and screams. The next thing they knew, Frank Archina, holding a shotgun, opened the closet door and shot Rose's mother and sister Mary twice. Rose Macri said that as she ran for her life she heard the shotgun click again.

When the police arrived they found Frank Macri, his wife

and son Frank junior dead. Mary Macri was seriously wounded and died later in hospital. Frank Archina was arrested later in a bar and charged with four counts of murder. At his trial, Archina said his father-in-law had tried to kill him with a knife and that he blacked out when the old man pointed a shotgun at him and could remember nothing more. He was nevertheless found guilty of first-degree murder and sentenced to death.

On appeal, the Supreme Court of Colorado reversed the conviction and ordered a new trial. When he came before the second jury, they found Frank Archina not guilty by reason of insanity and he was ordered to be detained in a state hospital. After the re-trial, one of the jurors said: 'The evidence showed that Archina emptied double-barrel blasts into both his mother-in-law and sister-in-law while they cringed in a bedroom closet. A sane man would not have to pull a trigger twice at that range to kill somebody.' A strange decision indeed.

In 1958, Frank Archina was released from hospital being considered to have regained his sanity, and in August of that year he was deported back to his native Italy. There he was arrested and again charged with the same murders, this time under an old Italian law which bestowed on the country the right to try its own nationals for crimes committed abroad – regardless of a foreign court's decision. Frank Archina was confirmed sane and culpable for the murders of his mother-in-law and sister-in-law and of the attempted murder of his wife. The killings of his father-in-law and brother-in-law were classed as self-defence. Archina was sentenced to six years' imprisonment, but in 1963 an appeal court decided he should be released as time spent in custody in the United States could count towards the current sentence.

ARMANASCO, Raymond   Armanasco, a milkman, lived with his wife and six children in Perth, Australia. He frequently confided in friends that he was not getting on with his wife and that his marriage was miserable. Another great sorrow for him was that his children, with the exception of nine-year-old Elsie Rose, who had always been his favourite, were siding with his wife against him.

One day in October 1950, he took Elsie Rose to some friends and asked them to look after her for him. The next morning a visitor to the Armanasco home found Raymond's wife and the five other children dead – all had been viciously bludgeoned and then had their throats cut. There was no sign of any forced entry and no evidence of robbery; but some razors and a bloodstained hammer had been left at the scene of the massacre.

When detectives arrived to investigate they heard sounds coming from the attic and noticed that plaster was drifting down from the ceiling. In the attic they found Raymond Armanasco. He had gathered together a supply of food and blankets and had intended to hide in the attic until the investigation was scaled down and he could have made his escape.

Armanasco was charged with six counts of murder and at his trial was found guilty and sentenced to life imprisonment.

AUSTIN, Thomas Thomas Austin was born around the middle of the seventeenth century at Columpton, in Devonshire, of very honest parents, who at their death left him a farm worth about eighty pounds per annum. As his land was without encumbrances, and he had a good character at that time, he soon got a wife with a suitable fortune, she having no less than eight hundred pounds to her portion. But this increase of his riches, and the thought of having so much ready money, made him neglect the improvement of his living and to take an idle and extravagant course, by means of which, in less than four years, he had consumed all that his wife had brought and mortgaged his own estate. Being now reduced to pinching circumstances, and not knowing which way to turn for a livelihood, the devil got so far the upper hand of him as to excite Austin to all manner of unlawful acts for the support of himself and his family. He was detected in several frauds which his neighbours were good enough to forgive out of respect to his family and what he once had been. At last he was so desperate as to venture on the highway, where, assaulting Sir Zachary Wilmot on the road between Wellington and Taunton Dean, Austin murdered that unfortunate gentleman for making some attempt to save his money.

The booty he got from Sir Zachary was forty-six guineas and a silver-hilted sword, which he got home undiscovered and undetected. This sum did not, however, last him long, and he returned to his old riotous course. When it was all spent he went to visit an uncle of his who lived about a mile away, and it turned out to be one of the bloodiest visits that was ever made. When he came to the house he found nobody at home but his aunt and five small children, who informed Austin that his uncle had gone out on business and would not be home until evening; they invited him to stay and wait, and he consented to remain. However, he had not sat many minutes before he snatched up a hatchet that was at hand and cleaved the skull of his aunt in two; afterwards he cut the throats of all the children and laid the dead bodies in a heap, all weltering in their gore. Afterwards, he went upstairs and robbed the house of sixty pounds.

Thomas Austin then made haste home to his wife who, having perceived some drops of blood on his clothes, asked him how they came there. 'You bitch,' said he, 'I'll soon show you the manner of it!' at the same time pulling the bloody razor from his pocket and cutting her throat from ear to ear. When he had gone thus far he completed the tragedy by ripping out the bowels of his own two children, the elder of whom was not yet three years of age.

Scarcely had Austin finished all his butcheries before his uncle, whom he had been to visit, came unknowingly to call upon him on the way home. When he entered the house and beheld the horrid spectacle he was almost thunderstruck with the sight, though as yet he little thought that the same tragedy had been acted on all his family too. What he saw, however, was enough to point the finger at the offender, whom he immediately laid hands on and carried before a magistrate who put him in Exeter jail. In the month of August 1694, this inhuman wretch suffered the punishment of execution provided by the law, which appeared much too mild for such a black, unnatural monster.

(From *The Annals of Newgate*, London, 1776)

B

BALABAN, John In the early hours of 12 April 1953, screams were heard coming from the Sunshine Cafe in Adelaide followed by one of the cafe's waitresses hurtling twenty feet from an upstairs window on to the street below. Although seriously injured, the woman later recovered in hospital. Meanwhile, police had forced an entry into the premises and found three people, all of whom had been savagely bludgeoned. The victims were identified as thirty-year-old Mrs Thelma Balaban, who was lying dead in bed when the police arrived, her mother Mrs Susan Ackland, aged sixty-six, and Mrs Balaban's six-year-old son from a previous marriage, Philip Cadd. Both Mrs Ackland and the boy were still alive but died in hospital. Mrs Balaban's husband, John, was arrested outside the cafe.

Under questioning, Balaban made a statement admitting to the attack on his family and the waitress. He described how he had returned to the cafe and decided to kill his wife and mother-in-law, and because the boy had woken he killed him as well. Then he went into the room where the waitress was sleeping and hit her because, so he said, she had been stealing money and 'siding with his wife' against him. After beating the girl, Balaban had sex with her and then returned to batter the other victims again, just for good measure. It was not much of an excuse, but he said he had killed them because they deserved to be killed. In his statement, John Balaban also confessed that in December 1952 he had murdered a prostitute called Zora Kusic, by cutting her throat and slashing open her stomach. Balaban had in fact been arrested and charged with this murder, but was discharged by a magistrate who judged there was no *prima facie* case against him. Balaban, a Rumanian immigrant, also laid claim to having murdered another woman in Paris. Following enquiries by the French police which confirmed Balaban's confession, the Paris authorities closed their file on the previously unsolved killing. John Balaban was charged only with the murders of his wife and Zora Kusic.

At his trial in July 1953, Balaban's defence was insanity, and a psychiatrist stated that in his opinion Balaban was schizophrenic and was certifiable. The superintendent of government mental institutions, on the other hand, considered that despite an abnormal personality, John Balaban was not mentally disordered. He was eventually found guilty of murder and sentenced to death by Mr Justice Abbott. Balaban's appeal was dismissed and he was hanged on 26 August 1953.

BAMBER, Jeremy In the early hours of an August morning in 1985, the duty officer at Chelmsford police station received an agitated telephone call from a young man giving his name as Jeremy Bamber and claiming to be anxious about the safety of his parents. He told the policeman that a few minutes earlier his father had telephoned to say that his daughter Sheila – Jeremy's sister – was at their Essex farmhouse home going berserk with a semi-automatic rifle. Then there had been the sound of a shot and the line had gone dead.

When an investigation team arrived at White House Farm, they found the battered and shot bodies of Nevill and June Bamber, the 'insane' daughter Sheila, and her own twin children Daniel and Nicholas. From the state of the bodies and the stories of his sister's mental instability enthusiastically related by Jeremy, it looked like a clear case of murder followed by suicide – the young woman, a bullet through her brain, was still holding the .22 Anschutz.

This was the one insurmountable psychological disadvantage to the police inquiry – the 'killer' had already been named; and it was with this misinformation at the forefront of their minds that investigating officers found themselves, in effect, looking for clues to fit the story of the young woman's mad rampage, in the process misinterpreting what did not fit the murder/suicide theory.

Information was there for the finding, and even if no other suspect came immediately to mind, then at least all the evidence indicated that Sheila Caffell *could not* have committed the murders. It was later learned that she suffered impaired hand-eye coordination anyway, and had no experience whatever in handling firearms. Nevertheless, she is supposed to have fired twenty-five accurate shots into her family, stopping twice to reload the gun. It might have seemed inconsistent, even to the untrained eye, that such extensive ballistic activity could have been carried out without the slightest damage to the 'killer's' perfectly manicured fingernails, and leaving her hands free of oil and powder deposits. What was more, the soles of her feet were found to be as clean 'as though she had just stepped out of a bath' – despite having supposedly run around the house on a bloody massacre.

Nobody thought to ponder how this slim, 5ft 7in woman had bludgeoned her healthy, sturdily built, 6ft 4in father with the rifle butt, which broke under the impact, without suffering any injury herself. Incidentally, because of their assumption of her guilt, the real killer, Jeremy Bamber, who probably *was* bruised and marked in the struggle, was not examined by the police for four weeks.

The pathologist's report revealed that Sheila Caffell could not possibly have killed herself; either one of her wounds would have been instantly fatal, and besides, detailed examination had shown that while one of those wounds had been inflicted with the gun in its normal state, a silencer had been used during the other shot – even the most inexperienced officer might have felt that this represented an unusual extravagance for a suicide. Besides, she would have needed much longer arms to have shot herself in the head with a gun lengthened by a silencer.

Ignoring the clues offered by this victim's body was not

the only area of the investigation that proved wanting. Fingerprinting procedure was, by all reports, rather lack-adaisical, and many were surprised when experienced scenes-of-crime officers moved the murder weapon with their bare hands. Not all of the bodies were fingerprinted at the time, and the cremation of the victims so soon after the crime rendered the situation unsalvageable. Ironically, the police took the real killer's fingerprints *six weeks* after the shooting. By now Jeremy had developed an almost thea-trical display of filial grief. Blood was obligingly washed off the farmhouse walls, and bloodstained bedding and carpets removed and burned.

One week later the inquest on the victims opened before the deputy coroner, and in evidence a detective inspector outlined the scenario as seen by the police, and emphasized once again that the official view was to regard the young woman as guilty of the murders.

Rather less happy with the outcome were the surviving members of the Bamber family, in particular two of Sheila's cousins. David Boutflour and Christine Eaton were con-vinced that she was incapable of killing anybody, least of all the twins she adored. In more practical terms they knew that Sheila's bad coordination made pouring a cup of tea without spilling it difficult enough – so how could she manage to kill her whole family? Adding a certain 'Miss Marple factor' to this already bizarre investigation, the amateur detectives visited the farmhouse and retraced the movements of the police search. They entered the study where, as the investigation team had done before them, they found the gun cabinet. To the police it had contained nothing significant; to David Boutflour and Christine Ea-ton it contained a bloodstained gun silencer of a type that fitted the murder weapon. They lost no time in alerting the police to this vital piece of evidence that they had already missed the first time round. And vital it most certainly was, for the silencer provided indisputable proof that their suspect could not have shot herself; the blood that had seeped into the silencer's baffles was her own – which made it rather difficult to explain how it got into the gun cupboard if she, the last to die, had killed herself. Although the information was not revealed until the trial, the silencer, when it came into police possession, had a single grey hair attaching to it. This hair, presumably from the head of either of the elder victims, was lost by the police while in transit to the forensic laboratory for testing.

The true perpetrator of this brutal and cynical act of familicide turned out to be none other than the young man who had so unashamedly pointed the accusing finger at his own sister. But when Jeremy Bamber stood in the dock he was not the only person to find himself on trial. Fairly or not, the whole of the initial police inquiry came under scrutiny in court. The judge himself remarked that the examination by officers at the scene of the crime 'left a lot to be desired'; and the Deputy Chief Constable of the force concerned added that 'with the benefit of that perfect science, hindsight, the judgement made at the scene of the crime . . . was misdirected'. Finally, the then Home Secretary called for an urgent report on police handling of the murder inquiry. As for Bamber, having been found guilty of multiple murder at Chelmsford Crown Court, he began five concurrent life sentences on 28 October 1986.

Bamber has made two appeals against his conviction, the second one being a referral by the Criminal Cases Review Commission, a statutory body which reviews cases where there could be a miscarriage of justice, but both have been dismissed. He continues to protest his innocence mainly through his website, www.jeremybamber.com. At the time of writing he is launching a High Court action, claiming over one million pounds from his surviving relatives. He claims this money is due to him under his grandmother's will.

BARRETO, Miguel On 6 October 1991, Miguel Barreto, without warning or apparent reason and armed with a machete, attacked and killed his brother Emilio in the tin-roofed wooden shack they called home in Hatillo, a small town west of the Puerto Rican capital of San Juan. Barreto then turned his attention on a neighbouring house where he burst in through the frail door, killed two children at play in the living area and then slaughtered their thirty-eight-year-old mother Gloria Arroyo Vazquez in her own bedroom, and Gloria's sixty-two-year-old mother out on the patio.

By now, as you might expect, quite a crowd had gathered; among them was Miguel Barreto's aunt, an elderly woman in her late sixties who was nevertheless singled out for the most brutal of treatment; and when he tried to stop the rain of blows from Barreto's vicious blade, Gloria Vazquez' father was cut down without a second thought and seriously injured.

But neighbours, rather like neighbours everywhere, were anxious not to be seen to interfere in family matters; and so they sent for Darwin Melendez Delgado, Gloria Vazquez' common-law husband. It was the infuriated Darwin Delgado who ended the massacre; when he stormed the house in which many of his family lay dead; when he broke through the door, wrestled the machete from Barreto's crazed grip and cut the assassin down with his own weapon. Despite a spirited investigation by the local police, no motive was ever discovered for Miguel Barreto's murderous rampage.

BARTHOLOMEW, Clifford Cecil Forty-year-old labourer Clifford Bartholomew lived with his wife Heather and their seven children, aged between four and nineteen, in a run-down farm-house at Hope Forest, near Adelaide. In 1971 the Bartholomews took in a lodger, a Vietnam veteran in his twenties.

It was around this time that Cliff Bartholomew was laid off from his job, which – as happens in many families facing the same problem – resulted in stress being put on his relationship with his wife; not helped by the mutual attraction which was developing between Heather and the lodger. Clifford and Heather Bartholomew soon took to spending lengths of time apart, visiting relatives. In Heather's case she was occasionally accompanied by the lodger. In July 1971 she went to Sydney to visit her sister Winnis Keane, and while she was away wrote a passionate letter to the lodger. Clifford Bartholomew opened the letter; the lodger left.

Heather returned to the marital home shortly afterwards, followed by her sister and her two-year-old nephew Danny. The state of affairs between Mr and Mrs Bartholomew could now best be described as open warfare, the letter had seen to that; the letter had pushed things beyond mere marital strife. The result was that it was Clifford who left home this time, to stay with his stepmother.

On Sunday 5 September 1971, Cliff Bartholomew drove out to the farm with presents for the children on Father's Day; they included a .22-calibre rifle for his eldest son. Despite a frosty reception and an opening skirmish, Bartholomew seems to have calmed down a bit and during the conversation pleaded with his wife for a reconciliation. By way of an answer Heather told him she was taking the children to Adelaide where their former lodger was arranging accommodation for them. Dejected and rejected, Clifford Bartholomew left the farmhouse and returned to his stepmother's. That night he couldn't sleep; his mind just refused to accept it, refused to accept the loss of his wife and family to a younger man. In the early hours of the following morning, Monday 6 September, Bartholomew came to a decision. The plan was this: with all the upset of the previous day he had forgotten to give his children their presents. The gun was still in the trunk of the car. He would drive up to Hope Forest, knock his wife unconscious with a rubber-headed mallet, drag her into the shed and shoot her. This way he would not disturb the rest of the family.

And that, more or less, is what he did. When he arrived at the farmhouse, Bartholomew loaded the rifle, put on a pair of gloves and crept up to his wife's bedroom. It may have been nerves, it may be that he found it difficult to hurt the person he once shared his life with, but Cliff Bartholomew didn't bring the mallet down nearly hard enough; that first blow simply made his wife scream, so he hit her again, harder, and she fell back on the pillow. Bartholomew later wrote: 'All of a sudden things seemed to be dead quiet.'

What happened next we may never know; probably the screams had woken the rest of the household and Bartholomew panicked and killed them. All he remembered was standing in the kitchen with the rifle in his hand; his wife, seven children, sister-in-law and her young son were lying dead around the house, shot and battered. He telephoned to tell his stepmother, and she rang the police. When the squad car arrived Clifford Bartholomew was sitting drunk in the kitchen.

At his trial in the Adelaide Supreme Court, Bartholomew pleaded guilty and was sentenced to death, though that was later commuted to life imprisonment. He was a model prisoner, and in spite of a public outcry he was paroled on 10 December 1979.

BATES, Clyde, *et al.* On a late evening in April 1957, four drunken men staggered into the Mecca Cafe, a sleazy bar in downtown Los Angeles. One of them, Oscar Brenhaug, was so many over the eight that he was incapable of doing any more than slump helplessly at the bar. The other three, Clyde Bates, Manuel Chavez and Manuel Hernandez pestered female patrons to dance with them, and when they were rejected, retaliated by cursing the women roundly and in such foul terms that the offended barman felt constrained to throw them out, enthusiastically helped by another male customer. As they hit the street, Bates, Chavez and Hernandez, screamed loud threats of revenge before driving away.

As they motored around, Bates, Chavez and Hernandez concocted a dreadful plan. They obtained a five-gallon drum, filled it with petrol and drove back to the Mecca where they double-parked and left the engine running with Hernandez remaining in the driver's seat. Brenhaug was still sprawled in a semi-stupor in the back of the car. Bates took the drum of petrol and hurled it into the bar while Chavez lit a book of matches and tossed it on to the spilled fuel; with hideous results. In less than five minutes, six people sitting in the cafe were burned to death and two others suffered horrific burns.

Bates and Chavez ran back to the car, and together with Hernandez, spent the rest of the night drinking, leaving Oscar Brenhaug still sleeping it off on the back seat. Police enquiries following the arson attack identified Bates' car from licence-plate details supplied by witnesses at the scene. The four men were picked up over the next couple of days and under questioning Brenhaug and Hernandez admitted their involvement in the petrol bombing; Bates and Chavez denied everything.

Charges against Brenhaug were dropped when he turned state's evidence and appeared as a witness for the prosecution. Bates, Chavez and Hernandez were charged with six counts under two special categories of first-degree murder – murder during arson and murder with torture for the purpose of revenge. The trial concluded with unanimous guilty verdicts in August 1957. Manuel Hernandez was sentenced to life imprisonment without possibility of parole and Bates and Chavez were given death sentences.

While they were on San Quentin's Death Row, Bates, Chavez and four other condemned men made an attempt to break out of the prison. They took guards as hostages but were eventually persuaded by the Warden to surrender. The capital sentences on Bates and Chavez were commuted to life imprisonment by state Governor Brown in what turned out to be the last days of his administration.

BECKETT, Henry (aka Henry Perry)   On the evening of Monday 28 April 1919, Mr Walter Cornish was found covered in blood trying to climb over the back fence of his house in Stukeley Road, Forest Gate, London. Cornish, who had a deep wound to the head and another to his hand, was taken to hospital in a very serious condition. He was still conscious and told police the soldier who had been staying with them for some weeks had attacked him.

Police officers went to the house in order to search the premises, and in a shed at the bottom of the garden, discovered the body of forty-three-year-old Alice Cornish. She had been struck several severe blows to the head and face and a three-pronged carving fork had been stuck into her throat; in addition, her wedding ring finger had been hacked from her hand. The Cornishes' two children, fifteen-year-old Alice and six-year-old Marie, were found battered to death in the cellar, where they appeared to have been thrown.

Witnesses were quickly traced, one of whom had called at the house earlier in the afternoon and had been told by a soldier she knew was staying there that Mrs Cornish was out shopping. A young girl said she had seen a man dressed in khaki running from the direction of the Cornish home with his hands and face covered with blood. The house showed signs of having been searched and some loose money which was normally kept in the house for emergencies was missing.

As the investigation proceeded, Walter Cornish's condition worsened and he died in the early hours of Wednesday 30 April.

Enquiries had established the identity of the soldier who had been staying at the house, and a description was issued under the name of Henry Beckett, aged thirty-eight. Beckett was arrested in East Ham on 2 May, thanks to the sharp eyes of a local shopkeeper who, realizing he matched the description of the wanted man, followed him until they passed East Ham Police Station where he was able to alert the police.

Questioned by detectives, Henry Beckett made a statement, which in effect was a full confession to the murders. He appeared to be quite unmoved by the enormity of his crime, only showing any agitation when he heard the large hostile crowd baying for his blood outside the police station. Beckett was charged with the murders of the Cornish family and in due course committed for trial. He came up at the Old Bailey before Mr Justice Darling on 27 May. The defence claimed that Beckett was insane at the time he committed the crimes but the jury, after a retirement of only ten minutes, found him guilty and he was sentenced to death.

Beckett appealed against his conviction but this was dismissed on 23 June 1919. The Home Secretary ordered the customary inquiry under the Criminal Lunatics Act, which speedily reported that Henry Beckett was not insane within the legal definition of the word, and he was hanged on Thursday 10 July at Pentonville Prison.

BELACHHEB, Abdelkrim   In the early hours of Friday 29 June 1984, patrons and dancers were enjoying themselves at Ianni's Club in Dallas, Texas. Thirty-two-year-old Marcelle Ford was dancing with a dark-haired man named Abdelkrim Belachheb, thirty-nine years old and a Moroccan by birth. Quite what the row was about we do not know, but at one point in the revelry Marcelle pushed her partner roughly away, glaring at him in a decidedly unfriendly manner; at the time Belachheb simply blew her a kiss and walked off.

Minutes later a shot was heard in the crowded room and Marcelle Ford fell to the floor, where her prostrate body received several more slugs as Belachheb fired again and again with the 9mm automatic pistol. When the gun was empty he rushed out to his car to reload before returning to the club and systematically shooting six more patrons, killing five of them instantly. Marcelle Ford was still alive when the paramedic team arrived, but died on the way to hospital; the other victims were Frank Parker, Joseph Minasi, Janice Smith, Linda Lowe and Ligia Kozlowski.

Police launched an immediate search for Abdelkrim Belachheb and found his car abandoned close to where he lived. In the meantime, the police received a telephone call from Belachheb, saying he wanted to give himself up. When officers arrived at the friend's address which he had given them Belachheb submitted without any resistance. Apparently he had spent the intervening period since the shootings celebrating the last day of Ramadan during which Muslims must observe fasting and, ironically, refrain from violence.

Abdelkrim Belachheb was indicated on six counts of murder and one of attempted murder, and on 15 November 1984 he was found guilty and sentenced to life imprisonment.

BENAVIDES, Guillermo, et al. At the height of a left-wing rebel offensive against the US-backed armed forces in El Salvador, six Jesuit priests, their housekeeper and her fifteen-year-old daughter were shot dead by an armed gang who forced their way into the cleric's home at the University of Central America. The university was under the control of the government's forces and on the night of the murders, 16 November 1989, the local commander was Colonel Guillermo Benavides. Prior to the killings, leading members of the government had accused the priests of links with the guerrillas.

In January 1990, Colonel Benavides and eight soldiers under his command were charged with murder, and because the government was anxious to prove to international observers that there would be no military interference in the judicial process, an examining magistrate was appointed to prepare the prosecution case.

The trial opened in the country's capital, San Salvador, on 26 September 1991. Colonel Benavides, three lieutenants and four soldiers were in the dock – a fifth soldier had fled the country. The five-man jury sat behind a large wooden screen protecting them from being seen by the defendants and the public.

It was the prosecution case that although the junior ranks committed the murders, they had not planned the attack. Alleged confessions by several of the defendants were read out in court, which described in detail how the priests were dragged from their beds, taken to a campus garden and forced to lie on the ground before being shot. The housekeeper and her daughter appeared to have been killed in order to eliminate witnesses. The trial ended on 28 September with Colonel Benavides being convicted on all eight counts of murder and Lieutenant Yusshy Mendoza being found guilty on one count. The remainder of the defendants were acquitted of the murder charges but three soldiers were convicted of participation in an attempted military cover-up of the killings. The prosecution accepted the verdicts, which it agreed placed greater importance on those who ordered the murders rather than those who carried them out.

On 24 January 1992, Colonel Benavides and Lieutenant Mendoza were given the maximum jail sentences of thirty years. The soldiers convicted of assisting in the attempted cover-up received suspended sentences. On 1 April 1993, Benavides and Mendoza were freed under a controversial amnesty for El Salvador's war criminals after serving just fifteen months.

BERTUCCI, Clarence   In 1945, with the end of the war in Europe and the revelations of the full horrors of the Nazi death-camps, a tidal wave of anti-German sentiment flooded the United States. Although feeling was running high, the general common sense and dignity of the American people prevented any greater excess than a few bricks being thrown through the windows of property owned by German-Americans; many of whom, ironically, may have had relatives fighting in the Allied cause. The most extreme reaction was by a twenty-three-year-old private in the US Army who indulged in a multiple murder spree of German prisoners of war.

Clarence Bertucci could claim a far from distinguished service record, having faced several charges for military offences, including desertion. He had recently returned from a tour of duty in Europe, though he had not been involved in combat action; rather, he had been assigned to the relatively comfortable posting as a guard at the German prisoner-of-war camp at Salina some 150 miles south of Salt Lake City, Utah. The regime was comparatively relaxed both for the guards and their prisoners. The Germans slept in tents overlooked by gun towers sited at strategic points throughout the camp. During the day the prisoners (who were mostly awaiting repatriation) were escorted to local farms where they helped out on the land.

On 8 July 1945, Bertucci had been drinking with the local residents of Salina during the evening, and reported for duty at the camp's Tower One at midnight. On taking over the tower, he loaded 250 rounds of ammunition into the 30-calibre machine gun and opened fire on the tents below. Panic-stricken detainees, violently woken from their sleep, ran for cover as the tents were ripped to shreds by bullets. When fellow-guards climbed the tower to detain Bertucci, they found the machine-gun empty; eight German prisoners had been killed and twenty wounded. Bertucci never gave any explanation for his murder spree other than to say that he hated Germans and in his opinion they should all be killed. In August, he was examined by a board of psychiatrists and certified mentally ill. Clarence Bertucci was discharged from the army and ordered to be confined in a mental institution.

BIRMINGHAM PUB BOMBINGS The events of the evening of Thursday 21 November 1974 will live in the memory of everyone who was in the city at that time. The first intimation of trouble was a telephone message called in to the *Birmingham Post* newspaper at 8.11 p.m. by a man speaking with an Irish accent. He gave a recognized code word and added: 'There is a bomb planted in the Rotunda and there is a bomb in New Street.'

The warning was immediately relayed to the police, and the first officers arrived at the Rotunda around 8.15 p.m., only to realize the search would be difficult. The Rotunda was a twenty-storey block of glass and concrete which dominated the Birmingham skyline; it was also a rabbit warren of corridors and offices, virtually impossible to make safe in a short time. As it turned out, the problem was purely theoretical, because at 8.17 the officers felt the building tremble and heard a huge explosion. The bomb had devastated the Mulberry Bush, a pub occupying two storeys at the base of the building. Glass, concrete and debris had been blasted across the street. At the Tavern in the Town in New Street, a few minutes' walk away, patrons heard the explosion and shortly afterwards this building too was rocked, by a second blast. It was a scene of unbelievable horror, particularly for the emergency services and volunteers, all of whom worked so hard to free victims from the wreckage in both locations. Later, when the situation could be assessed, it was learned that twenty-one people were dead and 162 injured. About an hour after the two explosions had rocked the city centre a third bomb was found in the suburb of Ladywood but this was rendered harmless with a controlled explosion.

Police launched an immediate and massive hunt for the bombers. Checks were ordered on all passengers leaving on boats and aircraft for Northern Ireland and the Irish Republic. During the investigation, British Transport Police put in a report to the coordinators in Birmingham that they had observed a party of Irish men apparently travelling from the Midlands to Heysham on the boat train. They were said to be laughing and joking and playing cards to while away the journey. West Midlands police asked their colleagues in Lancashire to arrest the men on their arrival at Heysham, and four men, William Power, John Walker, Richard McIlkenny and Gerard Hunter were detained; another Irishman, Patrick Joseph Hill, was arrested on board the ferry. Police sources reported that all five men had known James McDade, a member of the IRA, who had been killed in Coventry when a bomb he was carrying exploded prematurely; it was believed that they were going to Ireland to attend his funeral.

An expert from the North West Forensic Laboratory, Dr Frank Skuse, was brought in to administer the so-called Greiss test to the detained men. Many scientists at that time believed this test to be a foolproof method of determining whether a person had handled explosives. The procedure involved swabbing the hands with ether and testing the swabs with reagents. The tests on McIlkenny and Hunter were negative, those on Power and Hill positive and Walker's result was inconclusive. Officers from the West Midlands Serious Crimes Squad travelled to Lancashire to interview the men, and they were eventually transferred to Birmingham for further interrogation. Under intensive questioning, which the men later claimed was accompanied by violence, statements were made admitting their parts in the bombings. William Power and Patrick Hill also named Hugh Callaghan as an accomplice, and he too was detained for questioning.

All six men were subsequently charged with murder and when they appeared in court on 25 November complained publicly of police brutality while in custody. They were remanded to Winson Green Prison and, as if to confirm their allegations, when they returned to court for a second time each appeared visibly marked and scarred.

The trial of the men the press had labelled the 'Birmingham Bombers' took place at Lancaster Crown Court and lasted for forty-two days closing on 15 August 1975. They denied all the charges and claimed that their confessions had been made under the threat of police brutality. All six men were, nevertheless, found guilty on twenty-one counts of murder. Mr Justice Bridge in passing life sentences told them: 'You all stand convicted on each of twenty-one counts, on the clearest and most overwhelming evidence I have ever heard of the crime of murder.'

The convicted men's applications for leave to appeal were dismissed by the Court of Appeal on 30 March 1976. On 15 July 1976, fourteen prison officers were acquitted of charges alleging they had assaulted the six men in Winson Green Prison.

From prison, the 'Birmingham Six' continued to protest their innocence. They took civil action against Lancashire and West Midlands police forces, for assault, but the case was struck out by Lord Denning. However, strong doubts were being raised elsewhere about the convictions. The Granada television programme 'World in Action' and journalist (later Labour MP), Chris Mullin unearthed much new supporting evidence. In October 1985, 'World in Action' broadcast a programme discrediting the forensic evidence and claiming that the confessions had indeed been obtained by force. Chris Mullin in his book *Error of Judgement* claimed to have interviewed those actually responsible for the bombing.

On 20 January 1987, the then Home Secretary, Douglas Hurd, announced that he was referring the case of the Birmingham Six to the Court of Appeal in order for it to consider new evidence relating to challenges made to the forensic evidence given at the original trial, plus claims that the men were intimidated after their arrest. The Devon and Cornwall Constabulary were invited to carry out an inquiry into allegations that the six had been beaten while in custody. The results of this inquiry would, however, not be published.

The Court of Appeal hearing, held at the Old Bailey for security reasons, lasted from 2 November to 9 December 1987, when judgement was reserved. On 28 January 1988, the Lord Chief Justice, Lord Lane, delivered judgement that the original trial verdict was 'safe and satisfactory'. Lord Lane said that the longer the hearing had gone on 'the more convinced this court has become that the verdict of the jury was the correct one'. In other words, the Court did not accept the evidence of the new witnesses that the men had been beaten while in police custody, and it still remained convinced by the scientific evidence given at the trial.

Notwithstanding this setback, the pressure continued and Granada television broadcast a further programme 'Who Bombed Birmingham?' in March 1990, in which they named four other Irishmen as the actual bombers. The Home Office set up another inquiry, also conducted by the Devon and Cornwall police, and on 29 August 1990, a new Home Secretary, David Waddington, announced that he was referring the case to the Court of Appeal for a second time.

On 25 February 1991, the Director of Public Prosecutions announced that his office would no longer be contending that the convictions were 'safe and satisfactory'. The Court of Appeal hearing opened on 4 March 1991, and on the 14th Lord Justice Lloyd announced that the appeals were allowed. After sixteen years in prison the Birmingham Six were free men.

Following internal police inquiries, three members of the original investigation team, including ex-Detective Superintendent George Reade, who led the inquiry, were charged with perjury and conspiracy to pervert the course of justice. When they appeared for trial at the Old Bailey in October 1993, the judge Mr Justice Garland accepted defence submissions that a fair trial was not possible and discharged the jury.

BODKIN, John, *et al.*   John Bodkin, a native of Tuam in Ireland, was sent by his father to study law in Dublin. Instead of pursuing his studies he followed a dissolute lifestyle in the capital and soon gave up the law and returned to live near Tuam on an allowance from his parent. When this proved insufficient for his tastes he demanded more; and being refused, decided to take revenge against his father and other members of the family – which would result in his death on the gallows in 1742.

In this diabolical plan he enlisted the help of his cousin Dominick Bodkin and his father's shepherd John Hogan. Together they went to the home of Oliver Bodkin, where they found the family at supper. They murdered Oliver, his wife, a younger son and a guest named Lynch, who was staying with them at the time. The next victims were three serving maids whom the assassins found in the kitchen; they also killed four male servants whom they found in different parts of the house.

On the following morning a visitor to the house discovered the scene of carnage. The bodies of Oliver Bodkin, his wife, young son and Mr Lynch were found hacked and with their throats cut. The servants had been treated in the same barbarous manner, and in a final gesture of brutality even the cats and dogs in the house had been slaughtered. Because of his generally dissipated lifestyle and bad reputation, suspicion immediately fell on John Bodkin and he was arrested. Under interrogation, Bodkin confessed and named his accomplices. Dominick Bodkin later admitted that he had committed five of the murders and Hogan confessed to two.

All three men were brought to trial at Tuam, and all three pleaded guilty and were sentenced to death. They were executed at Tuam on 26 March 1742. Hogan's head was fixed on Tuam market-house and the other two were gibbeted within sight of the house where the murders had been committed.

BOLOGNA RAILWAY STATION MASSACRE Eighty-five people died and 200 were injured when a terrorist bomb exploded at Bologna railway station on Saturday 2 August 1980. The explosion demolished a large part of the station burying dozens of passengers under piles of rubble, and sections of the roof fell on to the Rome to Basle express which had just arrived. A subsequent recorded telephone message from an extreme neo-Fascist organization, the Armed Revolutionary Nuclei (NRA), claimed responsibility for the attack. The call linked the bombing to the arrest of a right-wing militant on a charge of derailing the Italicus Express between Bologna and Florence six years earlier, in which twelve people died. The NRA also claimed in the call that they were responsible for the earlier destruction of an Italian airliner with the loss of eighty-one lives.

Police investigations concentrated on known Fascist sympathizers and by the end of the month they had arrested twenty-eight right-wing extremists to join four other suspects who were in jail at the time of the station bombing. The inquiry was later extended to include the powerful Masonic Lodge P.2, notorious for its involvement in the Banco Ambrosiano scandal. The police, while accepting that the Bologna attack had been the work of neo-Fascists considered they had established links from P.2, via the secret service to right-wing terrorists, with the aim of destabilizing Italy and thus paving the way for a right-wing government.

State prosecutors took six years to draw up indictments which eventually saw twenty-one defendants facing charges including causing a massacre, multiple homicide, attempting to mislead investigators and membership of an armed band.

The trial was held at Bologna assizes and lasted for sixteen months ending on 11 July 1988. The jury was out for eighteen days considering its verdicts. Four defendants, Francesca Mambro, Valerio Fioravaranti, Sergio Picciafuocco and Massimiliano Fachini were convicted of causing a massacre and aggravated multiple murder and jailed for life. Mambro and Fioravaranti had married in

1985, while in prison awaiting trial. Mambro admitted taking part in other terrorist plots but denied any involvement in the Bologna bombing. She also insisted that Fioravaranti was innocent. Licio Gelli, the sixty-nine-year-old former leader of Masonic Lodge P.2, was jailed for five years for trying to mislead investigators. Eight defendants received sentences ranging from six to sixteen years for membership of an armed band and attempting to mislead investigators. Eight defendants were acquitted. The trial failed to place the blame for the bombing on any organization.

On 18 July 1990, an appeal court overturned the convictions and acquitted all the defendants, resulting in a claim by the families of those killed and injured in the bombing that the victims' right to justice had been denied.

BOOHER, Vernon   At around 8.30 p.m. on 9 July 1928, Dr Heaslip, a prominent physician in Mannville, Alberta, received a telephone call from Vernon Booher, the younger son of a local farmer, pleading with him to come quickly because 'something terrible has happened'. The doctor drove to the farm and met Vernon Booher outside the house, trembling and gibbering that murder had been done; he claimed that a short while earlier he had gone to the house to investigate the sound of gunshots and found his mother and brother dead.

Entering the house, they came upon Mrs Eunice Booher, sitting in a chair in the living room, shot several times in the head. In the kitchen was the body of the elder brother Frederick Booher, also shot in the head. In an outhouse lay the body of a hired hand, Gabriel Goromby, shot twice through the head and once in the chest. Later that same night, Vernon Booher remembered another hired man, Bill Rosyk, was missing. At Vernon's suggestion, a barn was searched and Rosyk's body was found, shot through the head and stomach.

Police specialists established that all the victims had been shot with a .303 rifle. Just such a weapon had been stolen from a nearby farm on the previous Sunday, and it was known that Vernon Booher had been hanging around the farm at the time. On 17 July the police were confident enough to arrest Booher and charge him with the murders. While in prison Booher was interviewed by a visiting Viennese criminologist Dr Langsner; several days later, at Dr Langsner's suggestion, police searched an area near to the Booher farm and discovered a rifle resembling the one stolen. The rifle was shown to Booher in his cell, who promptly confessed to the killings, complaining that his mother had been nagging him about a girl he was seeing.

Vernon Booher stood trial at Edmonton, where his counsel fought to have the confession ruled out on the grounds that he had been hypnotized by Dr Langsner at the time, and on this point the judge ruled in favour of the defence. However, the evidence was still strong enough to persuade the jury to return a verdict of guilty, and Chief Justice Simmons to sentence him to death. On appeal to the Supreme Court of Alberta Booher was granted a new trial on technical grounds. This second trial opened on 21 January 1929 before Mr Justice Walsh. It largely followed the pattern of the earlier trial with additional evidence from the Warden of Alberta Gaol who testified that Booher had admitted his guilt to him in the previous September, before the trial began. There could be no objection that this statement had been made under hypnotic influence, and following a five-hour retirement, the jury again found Booher guilty and again he was sentenced to death. Vernon Booher was hanged in Fort Saskatchewan Jail.

BOSTON MASSACRE By early March 1770, rioting and fighting between visiting British troops and elements of the Boston, Massachusetts, population had become one of local life's regular features. But on the 5th of the month matters came to a head when a group of around 300–400 faced a British troop of just eight soldiers under the command of Captain Thomas Preston. A drunk named Samuel Gray, with more bravado than common sense, began to urge the mob on, saying the soldiers would not fire. The crowd, by no means as sure as Gray, responded by gently taunting the soldiers and throwing a few snowballs; the troopers did not open fire. Emboldened by their apparent strength the mob began to flex their muscles, and somebody threw a heavy club which hit a soldier named Hugh Montgomery, knocking him to the ground. Montgomery fired his musket at no one in particular, whereupon another member of the rabble hit Montgomery and, most unwisely, Captain Preston himself. And when another man charged the soldiers he met the business ends of a bristle of bayonets. Things were now getting out of control, and when a crowd of thirty sailors led by one Crispus Attucks mounted an attack on the British, the soldiers opened fire, shooting dead the drunken Gray, Attucks, James Caldwell, Samuel Maverick and Patrick Carr. Captain Preston and twelve other men, military and civilian, were later charged with murder.

Captain Preston was the first to stand his trial, and the process took place between 24–30 October at the end of which he was acquitted. Eight of his soldiers were tried next, beginning on 27 November and closing on 5 December. Six of the soldiers were found not guilty. Hugh Montgomery, who fired the first shot, was found guilty of the manslaughter of Crispus Attucks, and Matthew Killroy was convicted of the manslaughter of Samuel Gray. Both men were allowed to plead 'benefit of clergy', were punished by being burned with a hot iron on the left thumb and discharged. The six other soldiers were acquitted. A third trial was held on 12 December, when four civilians who had been indicted for murder along with the soldiers appeared. As the men had earlier been cleared by the magistrates, the judge directed an acquittal in their case also.

BRAM, Thomas Mead Chambers   It was in July 1896, after a delay caused by the deep New England fog, that the three-masted sailing vessel *Herbert Fuller* put out from Boston, Massachusetts, bound for Rosario with its cargo of lumber. The ship's master, Captain Charles I. Nash, was accompanied on the voyage by his wife Laura, and the first mate was Thomas Bram, whose first voyage on the *Herbert Fuller* this was.

On 13 July, when the ship was well out into the Atlantic, a

passenger called Lester Monks was resting in his cabin when he heard what he described as a 'gurgling noise' coming from the chart room. Monks took the precaution of first loading his revolver, and then went to the chart room where he found Captain Nash lying on the floor close to death. Outside the room Monks caught a glimpse of the first mate and called out 'Mister Bram'; whereupon the mate inexplicably threw a plank of wood at him. Then Bram entered the chart room, saw the captain and muttered something about a mutiny – explaining to Mr Monks that the second mate, Blomberg, was conspiring with the crew. For no very good reason, first mate Bram next summoned the steward and sent him off to Blomberg's cabin, where the unfortunate man was discovered lying on his bunk with his head severed from his body. The steward hastened back to Bram and Monks and announced: 'Mr Blomberg is dead – murdered.' Further investigation revealed that Mrs Nash too had been murdered in her bed.

Bram, Monks and the steward now made their way along to the wheelhouse, where Bram asked the man at the wheel if he had heard anything untoward; he had not, but Bram's next move was a puzzle. The mate, as if he had some prior knowledge of its whereabouts, suddenly pointed to an axe half-hidden beneath a plank. The small group of men had only time enough to notice that the implement was covered with blood before Bram hurled it overboard into the sea. In a clumsy attempt to conceal this obviously suspicious action, Bram now began to advance the most fanciful theory to explain the recent deaths. Suppose, he said, that Captain Nash and his second mate had quarrelled over Mrs Nash, fought, killed her and then each other. It was in all a most bewildering performance by the first mate.

In the meantime, according to maritime tradition, the bodies of the three victims had been sewn up in sailcloth and placed in a rowing boat which was towed behind the ship. This served the double purpose of showing some respect for the dead and preventing aboard ship the kinds of pestilence which might be occasioned by decomposing corpses. Thomas Bram enthusiastically took command of the vessel, and for good measure had a Swedish seaman called Charlie Brown clapped in irons as the suspected murderer. Later in the voyage the steward, who had long suspected Bram, had *him* put in irons. When the *Herbert Fuller* dropped anchor off Halifax, Nova Scotia, on 21 July the prisoners were returned to Boston.

As expected, the grand jury cleared Charlie Brown of the murders of which he was so clearly innocent, and returned an indictment against Thomas Bram who was equally clearly guilty. Bram stood his trial before the US Circuit Court on 14 December 1896. On 2 January the following year, after a retirement of longer than twenty-six hours, the jury found him guilty of murder and he was sentenced to hang.

An appeal to the Supreme Court surprisingly resulted in this verdict being set aside, and a new trial was ordered. The second process opened on 16 March 1898, and dragged on until 20 April, when the jury again found Bram guilty. However, under a recently passed Act of Congress they were able to add the modifying phrase 'without capital punishment'. On 12 July Thomas Bram was sentenced to life imprisonment; he was released on parole in 1913 and granted a full pardon by President Woodrow Wilson on 22 April 1919.

BREITLER, Richard   Richard Breitler was a jeweller by trade, but his earnest endeavours never quite managed to match his financial requirements, and 1990 found him in serious debt to a number of financial institutions. On 30 August, Breitler invited four bankers to dine with him at Zurich's chic five-star Strohof restaurant in order to discuss the inconvenient problem of their demands for repayment. When they had seated themselves, Richard Breitler offered his solution; it was as simple as it was swift – he pulled a pistol from beneath his jacket and fired shots into three of his creditors, killing one outright and seriously wounding the others. In trying to effect his escape Breitler also shot and wounded the restaurant's outraged manager in the hands and stomach before fleeing on a motor-cycle.

But this was not the full horror of the Breitler tragedy, for in visiting the family's Zurich home, the Austrian police found Frau Breitler and her teenaged children shot dead, and in Breitler's jewellery shop his loyal secretary also lay on the floor in a pool of her own blood. And Breitler? He was later found outside the city beside his motor-cycle, a bullet in his brain. He had at least made some effort to explain; in a letter and a taped confession to the newspaper *Blick*, Richard Breitler spoke of his 'hatred for banks', on whom he blamed all his financial and personal problems. But despite the killer's grandiose aspirations to get even with 'them', it was, as so often, his family who had to pay for Breitler's personal madness.

BRIGHTON BOMBING The IRA bombing of the Grand Hotel, Brighton remains arguably the most audacious act of that organization's mainland terror campaign. In October 1984, the Conservative party faithful had gathered in Brighton for their annual party conference still buoyant following their victory in the 1983 General Election. The Grand Hotel had been chosen to be the conference home for Prime Minister Margaret Thatcher and most of the leading members of her Cabinet.

At 2.54 a.m. on Friday 12 October 1984, the Grand Hotel was rocked by an explosion. After the dust had settled, a gaping hole could be seen in the front of the hotel and rubble and debris had been hurled across the road on to the promenade. Six rooms had collapsed downwards to the ground. The main force of the explosion appeared to have centred on rooms 528, 529, 628 and 629. The Prime Minister's escape had been providential as she was in room 128, directly below the blast. Masonry had crashed through Mrs Thatcher's bathroom ceiling where she had been a short time before. Four people died in the explosion, and another died later in hospital; thirty-two were seriously injured.

Within hours of the explosion, the Provisional IRA issued a statement in Dublin claiming to have exploded a one hundred-pound bomb 'against the British Cabinet and Tory warmongers'. Police enquiries commenced immediately, concentrating on all those who had been in the hotel on the night of the blast, and all staff who had been employed there in the past three months. The enquiry was subsequently extended to include all residents of rooms 528, 529, 628 and 629 over the same three-month period. Experts established that the bomb had been planted under the bath of room 629. By sheer hard work, police investigators succeeded in tracing all residents of the rooms except one – Roy Walsh who had occupied 629 for three days from Saturday 15 September 1984. The address given by Walsh was genuine, but no one of that name was known there. However, a fingerprint expert managed to recover a right palm, and a little-finger print from the hotel registration card completed by Walsh; Scotland Yard subsequently matched these with Patrick Joseph Magee, aged thirty-five, a known IRA man who was already wanted in connection with earlier terrorist offences in London.

In June 1985, security forces identified Magee as living in a block of flats in a Glasgow suburb. Armed police raided the flat and arrested not only Magee, but also Gerald McDonnell, aged thirty-four, an escapee from the Maze Prison in Belfast and three others, Peter Sherry (thirty), Martina Anderson (twenty-three) and Ella O'Dwyer (twenty-six). They were transferred to London where Magee was charged with the murders of the five Grand Hotel victims, and with planting the bomb and causing it to explode. All five were charged jointly with conspiracy to cause explosions.

Following a six-week trial at the Old Bailey ending on 23 June 1986, they were convicted on all charges. Magee was given eight life sentences and Mr Justice Boreham recommended he should serve at least thirty-five years. Sherry, McDonnell, Anderson and O'Dwyer were all jailed for life.

BROOKS, Andrew   In the early hours of Sunday 13 October 1991, a wedding party celebrating at Little Neck, New York City, was leaving the synagogue when they were horrified to see a man stagger from a nearby house, badly wounded. Police were summoned and made a search of the building from which the victim had emerged. In a tool shed in the back garden, they discovered the bodies of Andrew Brooks senior, the seventy-five-year-old owner of the house, and a neighbour, twenty-nine-year-old Brian Ducker. In the house itself, two friends of Ducker's, Daniel Gantovnick and Michael Zarabi were also found dead – Gantovnick in the lounge and Zarabi in the kitchen. Another man was discovered wounded and rushed to hospital where he joined the man who had staggered from the house into the street. Of the main occupants of the house two were missing, Andrew Brooks senior's wife Marion, and their forty-seven-year-old son Andrew Brooks junior. Although a 12-gauge shotgun was found at the house, forensic examination of the numerous shell casings at the scene indicated that the victims had been killed with shots from a .22-calibre rifle, of which there was no sign.

An all-points bulletin was issued for the apprehension of Andrew Brooks junior, and information already collected established that he was known locally as an eccentric and a peeping tom, who would sometimes prowl the streets taking practice golf shots on his neighbours' lawns. He did not have a regular job but apparently made a few dollars dealing in pornographic videos. Called by some locals 'Stench' because of his body odour, Andrew Brooks had lately taken to telling neighbours that he was ill and the treatment he was receiving was killing him. Although they had been warned about his peculiar behaviour, Andrew's parents had claimed he was not as bad as all that. 'Just stay away from him when there's a full moon,' his father warned.

On the day following the mass killing, a visitor calling at the house of an elderly doctor and his wife in Lake Success, Long Island, was greeted with a fusillade of shots from inside. When the police were called it became apparent that Brooks junior was holed up in the building and had taken the couple hostage. Officers surrounded the house and began the delicate process of negotiating with Brooks who, to give him some credit for humanity, did eventually agree to release the doctor because he was suffering from a severe heart condition – presumably not improved by looking down the barrel of a .22. But that was as far as it went; Brooks adamantly refused to release the woman, and during the day continued to amuse himself sniping at the police while using his hostage as a shield. Late on in the afternoon Brooks, either through over-confidence, boredom or sheer stupidity, decided to take a nap allowing his hostage the opportunity to creep out of the house to freedom.

The siege continued through the night with Andrew Brooks periodically loosing off a few rounds into the dark over towards the police lines. On the Monday afternoon, after a period of silence, a SWAT team made their way into the house where they found Brooks lying on a bedroom floor, dead from a self-inflicted gunshot wound.

Police continued the search for seventy-three-year-old Marion Brooks, but it was not until 21 November that she was found in the basement of the Brooks house. She had been shot in the back and stuffed into a three-foot deep sump hole, which had been covered over with a metal plate weighted with old car tyres.

BROUGH, Mary Ann   Mary Ann Brough had been married to her husband George for some twenty years, and though she always claimed her marriage was unhappy she had nevertheless become the mother of seven children. George Brough was a servant in the royal household where he was highly regarded. Mary Ann had been on the staff at Clarence House before her marriage and for one short period had been wet nurse to one of the sovereign's children.

In June 1854, Brough told his wife that he was leaving her and would no longer be living at their home in Esher, Surrey, as he suspected her of being unfaithful. On 9 June, Brough called at the house in company with a friend and told Mary Ann that he would be seeing a lawyer with a view to taking action against her for adultery and removing the children from her custody.

Early on the morning of the following day, 10 June, a

man walking past the Brough house noticed a pillow hanging from one of the windows and saw that it was bloodstained. Neighbours were called and entered the house to find Mary Ann Brough in a bedroom, with a wound in her throat and seemingly unable to talk. In other rooms they came upon the six youngest children (the eldest child was away at the time), all of whom appeared to have had their throats cut. Doctors treated Mrs Brough for her wound and she recovered but the children were beyond all earthly hope. Mrs Brough was detained pending an inquest.

The inquest was held on Monday 12 June, and ended in a verdict of wilful murder against Mary Ann Brough.

Mrs Brough came up for trial at Surrey Assizes on 8 August 1854. Her lengthy statement was read out to the court, in which she described how she had got a razor and gone to the children's bedrooms. The statement continued: 'I went to Georgiana and I cut her first; I did not look at her. I then came to Carry and cut her, then to Harry. He said "Don't mother", I said "I must" and did cut him. Then I went to Bill. He was fast asleep. I turned him over. He never woke. I served him the same. I nearly tumbled into this room. The two children here, Harriet and George, were awake. George made no resistance at all. Harriet struggled very much after I cut her and gurgled for some time. Then I lay down and did myself.' Mental health experts including the noted Dr Forbes Winslow were unanimous in stating that they believed Mary Ann was insane at the time of the murders.

Despite the judge's evident disapproval of the insanity defence the jury returned a verdict of not guilty on the grounds of insanity and Mary Ann Brough was ordered to be detained during Her Majesty's pleasure.

BRYANT, Martin On Sunday, 28 April 1996, Martin Bryant killed thirty-five people in the popular and one-time Tasmanian convict settlement of Port Arthur. One of the comparatively rare mass murderers who survived the massacre, he has never offered any explanation for his actions. Prior to the killings, he had reportedly said, 'Nobody listens to me. I'm getting fed up. I'll think of something and everybody will remember me.'

Bryant had always evinced signs of being difficult and a loner but his lifestyle improved dramatically when, at the age of twenty, he was given work clearing up the garden of a wealthy middle-aged spinster, who seemingly took a shine to him. When the woman was killed in a car accident she left her entire estate to him. There were some suspicions about the accident as Bryant, who was in the car at the time, was known to pull on the steering wheel to frighten his benefactress. However, this good fortune allowed him to indulge himself in new cars and widespread travelling.

On the fateful Sunday, he had driven ninety-three kilometres to Port Arthur, calling first at a guest house run by an elderly couple, Sally and David Martin, with whom he had a dispute. They became his first victims and were later found stabbed and beaten to death.

He then drove to a popular tourist haunt, the Broad Arrow Café, entered the restaurant armed with a semi-automatic rifle and immediately opened fire on the patrons. The initial attack was very quick – survivors said that he laughed as he fired. Police later estimated he had killed twelve people inside fifteen seconds.

Bryant then left the cafe and returned to his car to get a second rifle, he then walked around the streets firing at random at anyone he saw. One of the most horrific killings during this period was the shooting of a mother and her two daughters aged just six and three-years old. He ordered the mother to kneel and then shot her and the youngest child before pursuing the other girl and despatching her with a shot to the back of her neck.

The killings continued – by now thirty-two people where dead and twenty were wounded in central Port Arthur. Bryant took a man hostage and returned to the guest house where the killings had begun. His final victim was the hostage who was despatched with a bullet to the head.

Bryant then took refuge in the guest house and fired an estimated 250 rounds at the police surrounding the building. The siege continued until the following morning when the house was seen to be on fire. Bryant then ran from the building tearing his clothes off and, badly burnt, he was arrested.

Initially, Bryant pleaded not guilty to all charges against him but at a special hearing he changed his plea to guilty.

On 22 November 1966, he was sentenced to life imprisonment on each of the thirty-five charges of murder and to twenty-one years on each of twenty counts of attempted murder, three of causing grevious bodily harm, eight of wounding, four of aggravated assault, one of arson and one of unlawfully setting fire to property. The judge ruled that he should never be eligible for parole.

BUQUET, James   Nineteen-year-old James Buquet was a dedicated weightlifter and, like many committed bodybuilders, had been devastated by a serious knee injury which needed surgery and prevented him from pumping his regular dose of iron in the local health centre; in his case at El Cajon near San Diego. Buquet, a former drug addict, had been an enthusiastic member of the health centre for some three months.

On Thursday 14 October 1993, Buquet drove to the centre in his Datsun car. He circled the car park for some minutes before jumping out and shooting dead a man standing outside the building, then blasted his way in through a window. In the gymnasium, James Buquet fired wildly in all directions with a 12-bore shotgun. Witnesses described his actions as 'crazy', shooting people in the head and all the time laughing; as terrified bystanders were screaming and begging for mercy, Buquet just kept on shooting. At one point he stood over a victim's body, reloaded his gun and fired repeatedly into the corpse. Three women died in the gymnasium and two elderly men were injured.

Suddenly, James Buquet stopped firing; he left the club, got in his car, put the barrel of the shotgun under his chin and pulled the trigger. Police investigating the quadruple killing were unable to come up with any motive, though they were able to discount rumours that Buquet had been involved with one of the slain women.

And that, as it stood, was the unremarkable and brief if bloody life of James Buquet. It was what emerged in the aftermath that would grip the imagination.

During the investigation into Buquet's background it was discovered he had once written a thirteen-page essay about a fictional mass murderer as part of a creative writing course at a college in El Cajon. The piece described the activities of a character named Natas (Satan spelt backwards!) A. Bishop, who believed that he could give some meaning to his own life by robbing others of theirs. In the essay, Buquet wrote: 'Natas had these thoughts a lot. They would come and go along with his depressions. God, how many times had he thought about this? At night it was the last thought he had. The one that put him to sleep. In fact, he didn't feel right at night unless he thought about killing.' The reality was that the fiction had an uncomfortably consistent similarity with Buquet's own killing spree: Natas uses a 12-gauge shotgun to kill at least ten people in a fast-food restaurant. The essay describes Natas preparing for the killings 'with the ice of a serial killer going in for the prey', and sets out the murders in detail, particularly describing how one woman was shot in the face: 'The pellets hit her face and it became nothing more but a red pile of glob with thin hair and blood drops rinsed through it.' This reference was chillingly reminiscent of Buquet standing over one of his own victims and firing shot after shot into the body. Buquet's piece of fiction concluded by insisting that society was full of 'robots', and that he would one day show the world what life was really all about by murdering them.

In a curious postscript, two weeks after James Buquet's killing spree, sixty-two-year-old Gordon Newman, a recluse and long-time resident of El Cajon opened fire on people in the street below his second-floor apartment window; a woman and a nine-year-old child died and five others were wounded. The shooting ended when Newman's apartment inexplicably burst into flames and he was found dead inside. The reason for the spree? None really, except that Newman was known to hate children and noise.

BURGESS, Richard, *et al.* Four men, Felix Mathieu, John Kempthorne, James Dudley and an American, James de Pontius, left Pelorus Bridge, New Zealand on Wednesday 13 June 1866 with the intention of prospecting for gold in the area of Maungatapu, called the 'Sacred Mountain' by the natives of the region.

As they departed, the men were unaware that they had been marked out by four hardened criminals who planned to hold up the prospectors at gun point, tie them up and lead them away into the bush to be robbed and murdered. The robbers were Richard Burgess (aka Hill), Thomas Kelly, Philip Levy and Joseph Sullivan. The four gold-hunters were intercepted as planned, bound and gagged, and taken into the bush where they were stabbed to death. The assassins were then able to rob them at leisure, stealing cash, gold and other valuables from their pockets. A search of the prospectors' baggage yielded a little more gold, but the total value of their haul was far less than they had hoped for, amounting to around £300. It was while they were plundering their victims' belongings that the robbers saw a horseman approaching from the summit of Maungatapu, but as they watched the rider headed off in another direction. For the purpose of confusing future investigations, Richard Burgess fired shots into the bodies of Mathieu, Kempthorne and Dudley in order to try to create the impression that de Pontius had killed and robbed them. To reinforce this scenario, the body of James de Pontius was buried out of sight, while the others were left to the elements.

Burgess and his murderous band then travelled on to Nelson where they took a week out to spend some of their loot. It was not for them to know that Mathieu had arranged to meet another man in the same town, and that therefore when the gold prospector failed to arrive, an alarm was raised. The finger of suspicion immediately pointed in the direction of Philip Levy and his companions, well known in the area as criminals. A systematic search of the Maungatapu area was put in hand and a dead pack-horse, a shotgun and other signs of the missing men were found. A reward of £200 was offered for information on the missing men, who were described as 'presumed murdered'. The four suspects were detained, and with minimum persuasion, the treacherous Sullivan offered to make a full statement on condition he was pardoned. In his statement Sullivan confessed his part in the murders of the missing prospectors, and implicated Burgess and Kelly in the earlier murder of an old man named James Battle. Acting on Sullivan's directions, the corpses of Mathieu, Kempthorne, Dudley and de Pontius were recovered. Burgess, Kelly and Levy were charged with the murders of the four men, and it was announced that Sullivan would give evidence against them. While on remand Burgess, in a revengeful mood, made a statement implicating Sullivan not only in the murders of the four prospectors, for which he would be pardoned, but also in those of James Battle and another man called George Dobson.

On Wednesday 12 September 1866, the trial of Burgess, Kelly and Levy opened at the Supreme Court in Nelson before Mr Justice Alexander Johnston. Sullivan gave evidence against them and they, in their turn, railed at him for *his* part in the murders. The trial ended on Tuesday 18 September with verdicts of guilty against all three men, who were sentenced to death.

The following day, Sullivan was put on trial for the murder of James Battle and he too was found guilty and sentenced to death.

Two weeks later, the death sentences on Burgess, Kelly and Levy were confirmed but that on Sullivan was commuted to life imprisonment. On Friday 5 October 1866, Richard Burgess, Thomas Kelly and Philip Levy were hanged.

BURKE, David　The Pacific Southwest Airlines flight took off from Los Angeles airport on 7 December 1987 on its regular scheduled run to San Francisco; of the forty-three passengers and crew aboard, not one would reach their destination. As the BAe 146 commuter jet flew over the craggy San Luis Obispo area it began to lose height, then to drop rapidly, plunging 22,000 feet into a mountainside.

Among the first reports to reach the crash investigation team was that a man named David Burke, a former employee of the airline who had recently been dismissed, had been among the passengers. One possibility that could not be ignored was that Burke went aboard with revenge in mind. The National Transportation Safety Board called in the FBI to assist in this part of the investigation, and they established that thirty-five-year-old Burke had been sacked following the theft of funds from the company's airport alcohol sales. Although nothing was ever proved, it was thought that Burke had also used his position with the airline to assist cocaine smugglers.

From among the thousands of fragments of wreckage from the plane, crash investigators at the site recovered a .44 Magnum from which six bullets had been fired. Ballistics tests established that shots had been fired in the cockpit, and this was confirmed by the sound of gunfire picked up on the aircraft's black box flight recorder. Further evidence came from the pilot of a light plane flying in the area at the time of the crash, who had received a radio message from the jet's captain that he had an emergency on board and there was shooting.

The reason for this tragic and pointless destruction of life was explained by a note which had been recovered from the wreckage. It was written by David Burke, and read: 'Hi Ray, I think it's sort of ironical that we ended up like this. I asked for some leniency for my family, remember? Well, I got none and you will get none.'

David Burke had also left a suicide note behind in which he wrote that he intended to smuggle a gun aboard the plane and kill Raymond Thompson, the supervisor who had sacked him and who was also on the flight's passenger list.

It is all but impossible to make airports and aircraft one hundred per cent secure, though the introduction of sophisticated safety procedures has made the crimes of skyjacking and sabotage more difficult. However, no amount of technology will ever eradicate human error; the kind of human error that led airport staff to wave David Burke through security without a check – because they knew his face!

BURNS, Joseph In the early hours of 23 October 1847, the Royal Navy ship *Dido* lay at anchor off Auckland, New Zealand. The watchman's attention was attracted by something bursting into flames in the area of the naval base, and closer examination through a telescope showed that it was the cottage occupied by the local naval commander, Lieutenant Robert Snow, his wife Hannah and their two small daughters.

A party was sent ashore to deal with the fire, but by the time they arrived the cottage was gutted. In the ruins the sailors found three burned and mutilated bodies later identified as Snow, his wife and their baby daughter Mary. The other daughter had mercifully been away from home that night.

At an inquest the remains were identified by Able Seaman Thomas Duder, and medical evidence was given that the bodies bore severe wounds possibly inflicted by an axe. The coroner's jury returned the only verdict available to them: 'wilful murder by some person or persons unknown'.

Enquiries at first concentrated on the possibility of involvement by discontented Maoris, but this line of inquiry was dropped, and there were no further developments until after the trial of a man named Joseph Burns in March 1848. Burns appeared before the court charged with attempting to murder and/or causing grievous bodily harm to Margaret Reardon, with whom he had previously been living. The result of the trial was Burns being sentenced to transportation for life on the lesser charge of causing grievous bodily harm.

Following his conviction, Joseph Burns made a statement confessing his involvement in the Snow murders. He said that Able Seaman Duder and a man named William Oliver had killed the Snows in an attempted robbery, while he, Burns, had remained outside as look-out. Duder was later arrested, and taken before the magistrates who cleared him of all suspicion. Meanwhile, Burns had retracted his confession, but was nevertheless charged with the Snow murders, and in due course committed for trial.

The trial of Joseph Burns was held in the Auckland Supreme Court on 1–2 June before Chief Justice Martin. Margaret Reardon testified that Burns had told her he killed the Snows. Burns, who defended himself, told the jury he was entirely innocent and the whole story had been concocted by Margaret Reardon out of spite and revenge. Following a short retirement, the jury was clearly inclined to believe Miss Reardon; they returned a verdict of guilty, and Burns was sentenced to death.

On Saturday 17 June 1848, Joseph Burns was taken in a cart to the site of the murders and there hanged on a specially built gallows. Before the execution he asked forgiveness of Able Seaman Duder for falsely accusing him, and Duder, who was present, told Burns that he had his forgiveness.

C

CASTIGADOR, Victor, *et al.* The carnage was discovered at 7.55 on the morning of Tuesday 3 April 1989, when the staff of an amusement arcade on the corner of London's Gerard Street and Wardour Street arrived for work and smelled burning and heard shouting from the basement. When police and firefighters made their way to the subterranean storeroom in the heart of the capital's Chinatown, they found four bodies lying on the floor. As officers moved through the acrid smoke and smouldering furnishings, it was clear that two of the victims were alive, but the fire damage to their bodies was so extensive that it was only afterwards in the burns unit at Queen Mary's Hospital that one was identified as a woman. This pair had been lucky. In the basement two more figures remained, burned beyond recognition and quite dead.

As police scientists examined the scene of what was clearly a murder of the kind the area had rarely seen, the arcade's security cameras were beginning to tell the story of how the horror began. It started as staff were closing the premises in the early morning; Yurev Gomez, the twenty-five-year-old manager, and cashier Debbie Alvarez were locking up and handing over to security guards Ambikaipahan Apapayan and Kandiahkanapathy Vinayagamoorthy. As they did so, the gang, who had been posing as customers, struck. Later testimony would complete the sequence of events and would identify the killers as Victor Castigador, Calvin Nelson and Paul Clinton; also along for the night's entertainment were Nelson and Clinton's girlfriends.

Castigador, armed with a plastic imitation gun, forced his four hostages down into the basement strongroom where Mr Gomez was ordered to open the safe. Then Gomez, Ms Alvarez and the two security guards were tied up and locked in a wire cage in the strongroom. Meanwhile, Castigador fetched a bottle of white spirit from the adjacent storeroom and poured it over the captives while Nelson lit matches and flicked them into the cage as the others watched.

'There was a ball of fire,' recalled Gomez. 'It was like an oven. There was nowhere to go. I undid my hands and kicked my way out of the cage. My skin was on fire, I could feel myself disintegrating. I rolled on to the floor and the wall and put myself out. I managed to get my mouth near the keyhole.' Thus Yurev Gomez survived in agony for almost eight hours on the little oxygen that could be sucked through his blistered mouth from the outside.

Almost as unbelievable was the survival of Debbie Alvarez who, with Gomez's help, managed to wriggle to the door and lay there, sustained by the small amount of air that filtered under it. Even so, both suffered terrible burns. The two Sri Lankan security guards fared far worse, being at the back of the cage, and succumbed to the most agonizing of deaths, sustaining dreadful burns before being asphyxiated by the smoke from their own burning flesh and clothing.

Given the location and circumstances of the attack there was initial speculation that the Triad gangs known to be operating in Chinatown were responsible. However, informed police teams were working on the theory that the motive had been robbery and the victims had been killed to prevent the thieves being identified. Within days of the murders a thirty-four-year-old Filipino named Victor Castigador had been arrested. On 7 April he appeared at Bow Street magistrates' court charged with murder and attempted murder. Castigador, whose name, appropriately enough, translates from the Spanish as 'The Enforcer', arrived in Britain from Manila in 1985, married an English woman and later worked as a security guard in the very amusement arcade where he committed robbery and murder. It was mainly due to his unpleasant and aggressive personality that Castigador was passed over for promotion; and when it was discovered that there was far less trouble at the arcade when he was not on duty, the small Filipino was given the sack; this was on 31 March, two days before his murderous revenge. For the person who boasted that he had previously been a hit-man for the late president Marcos in his native country, and had killed 'at least twenty people or more', his dismissal was an indignity not to be borne.

Within days of Castigador's arrest his accomplices were picked up and detained. At first all five defendants pleaded not guilty to the charges brought against them – murder, attempted murder, and in the cases of the two women, robbery. On the first day of their trial at the Old Bailey, 19 February 1990, Victor Castigador changed his plea to guilty and sentence on him was deferred until the end of his accomplices' trial.

Jean Southworth QC, for the Crown, described Castigador as 'the main villain of the piece . . . he is a Filipino who obviously sees himself as a tough guy and frequently bragged to his friends of his earlier life in the Philippines where he said he had been in the commandos and the secret police'. Even Castigador's own counsel, James Mulcahy, was obliged to admit to the judge: 'It would be very surprising if you had not come to the conclusion, having read the evidence and seen the witnesses, that Castigador was a ruthless, callous and inhuman monster.'

It was obviously a description which met with his Lordship's approval, for when the formality of conviction was complete, Mr Justice Rougier passed sentence on Victor Castigador using much the same terms of reference: 'I find it almost impossible to understand the workings of a mind as twisted and evil as yours. You condemned your victims to an agonizing death without one shred of mercy or pity. You have an uncontrollable murderous desire and you are a danger to everyone. You have forfeited the right to walk free. Some may say you have forfeited the right to live, but unlike you, we in this country do not go to those lengths.'

Castigador was sentenced to life imprisonment with

Mr Justice Rougier's recommendation that he should serve no less than twenty-five years. As for the rest of the gang, Calvin Nelson was sentenced to life imprisonment in a young offenders' unit; Paul Clinton to be detained during Her Majesty's pleasure; and the two women were sentenced one to three years' youth custody, the other to three and a half years' imprisonment, both for robbery.

CHARLES, Robert Charles had been born to slave parents in the deep South of America, and had lived quietly in New Orleans for six years. On the evening of Monday 23 July 1900, Robert Charles and a friend decided to visit two women friends who were maids in a white household. On the way they sat down in front of a house belonging to another white family. Three passing policemen challenged them, whereupon Charles drew a pistol and fired at the officers, one of whom he wounded. Charles escaped despite being wounded in the upper right leg when the police returned fire. The other man was detained and identified Robert Charles by his alias 'Curtis Robertson'.

Police officers went to Charles' address, and in the gun battle which followed, Captain John T. Day and Patrolman Peter J. Lamb were shot dead by Charles using a .38 Winchester rifle. The police laid siege to the building and when at around 5.00 a.m. they realized he was not returning their fire, they entered his room and discovered that he had escaped again.

With the news of his exploits spreading, demonstrations began to take place in the streets of New Orleans, and these soon escalated into full-scale race riots, partly in support of Robert Charles, but also against local authority plans to restrict the numbers of blacks living in the city. Police manpower and resources were at full stretch dealing not only with the riots, which resulted in several deaths, but also with the continuing hunt for Robert Charles.

On Friday 27 July, the police received a tip-off that Charles was in hiding at 1208 Saratoga Street. They entered the building and were surprised by Charles, who shot Sergeant Gabriel Porteous dead and fatally wounded

Corporal John F. Lally. Shortly afterwards, Charles fired from a window, killing nineteen-year-old Arthur Brumfield. Armed officers surrounded the building and poured shot after shot into the area where Charles was hiding. He fired back, fatally wounding two other men, Andrew Van Kuren and Howell H. Batte. During the course of this siege, Charles wounded nineteen other men, some seriously. Police set fire to a mattress at the foot of the stairs below Charles' hideout to try and smoke him out. Eventually, he made a break for it but was cut down by police guns before he could reach cover, and officers continued firing into his lifeless body, before dragging it into the street, where it was kicked, beaten and had even more shots fired into it before being taken away on a wagon.

The mutilated body of Robert Charles was put on display before being secretly buried. The riots were quelled, following which indictments for murder were filed against several people. Though one of the rioters was imprisoned for manslaughter, the remainder of the charges were eventually dropped.

CHAVVA, Karel A man arrived at the secretary's office of the school in Eppstein-Vockenhausen, near Frankfurt on 3 June 1983 and asked for an appointment with the headmaster; he said he also wished to see Adolf Gelhaar, a teacher of English at the school. The man, later identified as Karel Chavva was directed to a second-floor classroom.

Chavva burst into the classroom with a revolver in each hand and began shooting indiscriminately; two thirteen-year-old girls, a boy aged twelve and a thirty-six-year-old teacher died instantly. Herr Gelhaar was seriously wounded while attempting to protect some of his pupils. Two unarmed policemen instructing children in the school yard took the sounds to be explosions from the school laboratory but one, forty-five-year-old Gisbert Beck, went to investigate and was also shot dead. Altogether thirteen children were wounded in the shooting, five seriously. Karel Chavva, like so many mass murderers, then turned the gun on himself.

Detectives investigating the appalling incident were quite unable to establish any possible motive for the attack. Chavva, a Czech by birth, had been granted political asylum twelve years earlier, and although he had been a trainee psychologist, for the last few years he had been working as a taxi driver in Frankfurt.

CHICAGO RESTAURANT KILLINGS In the early hours of the morning of Saturday 9 January 1993, the parents of one of the kitchen workers at Brown's Chicken Restaurant grew anxious that their son had not returned home from his part-time night shift and telephoned the police.

Brown's is one of those single-storey fast-food places popular with travellers, and sat at the side of the busy four-lane highway that runs through Palatine, a suburb north-west of Chicago. When they arrived, the police found the restaurant manager's car parked in the lot at the side of the building, and as they approached, officers saw the back door to the restaurant was open. As they cautiously stepped inside, they found a trail of blood leading to the large walk-in refrigerator where four bodies were discovered; nearby lay three more. Among the victims were manager Dick Ehlenfeldt, his wife Lynn and the cook Guadalupe Maldonado; the other four were students employed part-time at the eating house. They had all been shot. It later emerged that on one employee the gods seemed to be smiling favourably – he was supposed to have been on duty at Brown's that night, but decided to take the shift off and put his feet up at home.

It was an educated guess that the gunman must have entered through the rear door of the restaurant while the staff were counting the takings and clearing up after Friday night's business. In January 2003 two men were charged and are currently awaiting trial. The so-called Chicago Restaurant Killings were yet another example of a massacre in an American fast-food outlet; the grim twist in this case was that the victims were not customers, but staff.

CHOW TSE-MING On 11 April 1955, an Air India Constellation suffered an explosion on board, burst into flames and plummeted into the sea off Sarawak. The plane had been chartered by the People's Republic of China to take delegates to the Afro-Asian conference at Bandung; of the eighteen passengers and crew aboard the flight only three survived, all of them members of the crew.

The Indonesian government set up a court of enquiry, at which survivors told of an explosion in the starboard wing followed by a fire resulting from a ruptured fuel tank, which spread thick smoke through the cabin. The majority of the wreckage was recovered from the sea and forensic tests were carried out, including some on the remains of a clockwork device. Taken together with the testimony from those rescued, the evidence left no doubt that the cause of the disaster was a time bomb.

Subsequent investigations were complicated by the involvement of no fewer than seven governments, and concentrated on all the people involved in servicing the aircraft at its last stopover in Hong Kong. One important revelation was that the Chinese authorities claimed that thirty-two hours before the bombing they had warned the British authorities in Hong Kong that there was a plot instigated by the Chinese in Formosa (now Taiwan) to sabotage the Chinese delegation.

On 13 June, the Hong Kong police offered a reward for information leading to the arrest of the saboteur. They had already attached suspicion to an aircraft cleaner, Chow Tse-Ming but had been unable to detain him because he had already stowed away on a plane to Formosa. Chow Tse-Ming was indicted for the murders in his absence, but the Formosan government refused to return him to Hong Kong for trial.

An official British enquiry published on 11 January 1956 stated that 'a Kuomintang intelligence organization' was to blame for the explosion, and had paid the saboteur to plant the bomb. Chow Tse-Ming, the report revealed, had boasted to friends that he was responsible and that he had been paid 600,000 Hong Kong dollars; and it was certainly true that before absconding he had been spending money at a rate far beyond his means. The British government enlisted the aid of the United States in an attempt to persuade Formosa to extradite Chow Tse-Ming back to Hong Kong for trial but without success.

CHUNGULI, Joseph In February 1949, Joseph Chunguli savagely beat a boy employed on his brother Livingstone Mudidi's farm at Majengo, Nyanza Province, Kenya. Mudidi reported Chunguli to the tribal chief, who did nothing. In March Mudidi took his brother to the African Court accusing him of damage to his farm, while the injured youth brought a case for assault.

Three days after the hearing, Joseph Chunguli went berserk and attacked Mudidi with a panga, wounding him, following which he killed Mudidi's wife and two children and set fire to his and several other huts. John Lango, who attempted to put out the fires and save the occupants also fell victim to Chunguli's panga and died en route to hospital.

Chunguli admitted the murders and arson, explaining that he had been in dispute with his brother over bananas planted on his farm. He claimed his brother told him the tribe had been ordered to kill him and that a magician had been ordered to arrest him. That morning he had gone to his farm and met a black hen which disappeared. This had frightened him, made him lose his temper and feel he did not value anybody. He went to look for Mudidi, saying to himself 'either he kills me or I kill him'. Arriving at his brother's hut, Chunguli took a box of matches and set fire to it. His brother's wife was inside crying bitterly and he said: 'You shall die and I shall also die.' Following this he set fire to six neighbouring houses before being taken into custody by the police.

At his trial, Joseph Chunguli was found guilty of murder and later hanged.

CIUCCI, Vincent At the time of his crime, Vincent Ciucci lived with his twenty-eight-year-old wife Anna and their three children, nine-year-old Vincent, eight-year-old

Virginia and four-year-old Angeline at their grocery store on West Harrison Street, Chicago.

On 5 December 1953, a fire broke out in the shop and Vincent was the only one to survive the blaze. As the firefighters arrived, he stumbled from the burning building claiming he had been initially overcome by the fumes, but managed to drag himself out. Autopsies carried out on the victims' bodies established that they had been chloroformed and then shot in the head with a rifle. It did not take the subsequent police investigators long to discover that Vincent Ciucci had a mistress, an eighteen-year-old named Carol Amora, who had recently had a baby by him. Ciucci was charged with the murder of his family and his reply was: 'I admit I'm a gambler and I like to fool around with women but I wouldn't do a thing like that . . . How could a man kill his own children? He would kill himself instead.'

At his trial Vincent Ciucci pleaded not guilty to the indictments, and insisted that somebody else must have entered the apartment and killed his family. The jury, perhaps not entirely surprisingly, found the story more difficult to believe than that Ciucci, in a tight spot, had killed them himself; so he was convicted and, on 11 January 1955, sentenced to death in the electric chair.

By dint of the American appeals procedure, Ciucci received several stays of execution and his lawyers kept him alive until Thursday 22 March 1962, when he held a press conference during which he told journalists a new and even more preposterous story; that he had seen his wife shoot the children. After this he had snatched the rifle away and shot her.

At around midnight Vincent Ciucci was strapped into the chair and pronounced dead at 12.09 a.m.

CLATTERBUCK, Thomas William   On 1 June 1943, a travelling salesman called at the homestead farmed by Morris Love, some eight miles from the town of Leesburg, Pennsylvania. Just prior to his stopping at the Love farm he had seen a car parked near the farm and a man closing the gate. When he saw the salesman, the man jumped into the car and hurriedly drove away. The salesman was unable to get any response to his calls at the farmhouse, but on a closer investigation found the body of fifty-eight-year-old Morris Love slumped in a chair on the porch, his head severely battered. The salesman rushed to a neighbouring house and called the sheriff.

When the law enforcement officers arrived and entered the farmhouse they discovered the bodies of Love's wife Ruby, and their twenty-one-year-old son James, lying in the dining room. Ruby Love had been shot through the heart and James had been shot and his skull battered. A .22 rifle lay across his body; a bloodstained croquet mallet was found near Morris Love's body. The officers then decided they had better look in on Walter Russell who, with his wife, occupied a tenant farm, a hundred yards from the Love house. Three deputies went to the Russell home and found the body of Mrs Russell lying shot between the kitchen and the dining room. A search of the grounds revealed the body of Walter Russell on the edge of a cornfield; he had been shot in the head and had a .22 rifle lying beside him. In Russell's pockets the officers found Morris Love's wallet. By this time the sheriff's men had been joined by the local coroner, who gave his opinion that Russell had not killed himself, based on the absence of powder burns around the entry wound, usually a sure indication of a close-range shot.

The sheriff set to work organizing his men to make a thorough search of the area around the Love and Russell farms, and himself drove to the house of another neighbour who had called to say she had information about the murders. The woman claimed that she had inadvertently overheard on her party-line telephone a violent argument between Morris Love and another local, Tom Clatterbuck. She said Love had told Clatterbuck that unless he 'straighthened out the business' he would have him arrested. Now the sheriff remembered that when the call had come through about Love being murdered, Tom Clatterbuck, a highly respected member of the local community, had been with him and appeared very shocked. But appearances are not always the best guide to the truth, and it was subsequently established that about a month earlier Morris Love had lent Clatterbuck $2,500. In the meantime, another neighbour who was known to dislike Morris Love and was observed to have several scratches on his face, had been detained. Tests on the rifles found at the murder scenes showed that neither of them had been used to fire the fatal shots.

In view of the new information and the matter of the outstanding loan, it was decided to question Tom Clatterbuck, even though it was a puzzle how he could possibly have been the killer *and* been in the sheriff's office when the call reporting the murders had come through. During questioning, Clatterbuck claimed he had paid off the loan to Morris Love in cash and, in the absence of any other incriminating evidence against him, he was released. On the following day, a state trooper found part of a .22 rifle on the outskirts of the Love farm. From markings it was identified as belonging to another farmer in the area, and he said he had sold it to Tom Clatterbuck. Interviewed again, Clatterbuck insisted that the rifle, by now identified as the murder weapon, had been stolen from his car some time ago.

It was quite by accident that a sheriff's deputy going about his more domestic office chores noticed some scraps of paper wedged into a small incinerator. When he freed and uncreased them it was clear that the documents were part of the note of the loan made by Love to Clatterbuck. The sheriff, not unreasonably, guessed that Clatterbuck must have tried to burn the note when he was at the office; just before the call came in about the murders.

On 4 June 1943, Tom Clatterbuck was taken into custody. Following three hours of sustained interrogation, he finally confessed to the murders. Morris Love, so Clatterbuck said, had discovered he had forged endorsements to the loan note and threatened to expose him. Clatterbuck said he lost his head and killed Love. Ruby Love and young James apparently had to die because they had seen Clatterbuck at the farm and knew he was attempting to blame the killings on Walter Russell. He said he had driven 'like all the bats out of hell' to get to the sheriff's office before the killings could be reported.

At his trial, Tom Clatterbuck pleaded insanity, a defence which was quickly rejected by the jury who found him guilty and recommended death in the electric chair; he was executed at Richmond penitentiary on 10 December 1943.

COLUMBINE HIGH SCHOOL KILLINGS Running through many mass murder cases are a killer's twisted desire to revenge perceived wrongs and, seemingly, a total acceptance that their actions will lead to their own death, more often than not by suicide. The Columbine killings were unusual in that they were committed by two teeangers acting together.

Eric Harris (18) and Dylan Klebold (17), schoolboys at Columbine High School, Littleton, Colorado, were founder members of a gang calling itself The Trenchcoat Mafia. They dressed in a uniform of black trench coats and, to the outsider, seemed to be comparatively harmless in their devotion to the music of the 'shock rocker', Marilyn Manson and to the constant playing of computer games. However, Harris seemingly a very strong personality, began to preach a weird doctrine involving both Satanism and neo-Nazism and he talked of killing their enemies. Aided by Klebold, who appeared to be more of a follower, these doctrines took them much farther than the remaining members wanted. Harris and Klebold set up a website featuring a poem entitled 'The written works of the Trenchcoats' which called for rage and the apocalypse.

On Tuesday, 18 April 1999, they put all this talk into violent action. Dressed in their black trench coats, armed to the teeth and carrying homemade pipe bombs they went to the school and began to systematically execute their schoolmates. Targeting black students and athletes, they moved around the school buildings, laughing as they fired. During the massacre, they kept shouting that they were taking revenge on those who had made fun of them. A particularly horrific murder was their shooting down of a young girl who was on her knees praying. In addition to the shooting they planted some of their pipe bombs around the school, obviously with the idea of causing further devastation. A total of twelve students and a teacher died at the hands of the maddened teenagers.

When the police arrived and began searching the buildings, Harris and Klebold were found shot dead in the library. Either sated by their blood lust or realizing the game was up they had committed suicide or as was suggested later, one shot the other and then killed himself.

COLUMBO, Patricia Ann, and **DeLUCA, Frank**　In May 1976 police discovered a Thunderbird car stripped of all its fittings and abandoned on Chicago's South Side. A registration check identified it as belonging to Frank Columbo, a resident of the prosperous suburb of Elk Grove Village. When police called at the Columbo home the front door was ajar, and on entering officers stumbled upon the bodies of Columbo, his wife Mary and their thirteen-year-old son Michael.

Frank Columbo's body lay in the living room; he had been repeatedly stabbed, shot four times, his skull had been crushed, and lighted cigarettes had been stubbed out on his bare chest. There were signs of a fierce struggle, with overturned furniture and blood splashed over the walls. Mary Columbo's body lay just outside the door of the bathroom. She had been shot, her throat cut, and she had been stabbed repeatedly and battered over the head. Mrs Columbo's nightgown and robe were ripped open and her panties were down around her ankles, but a subsequent autopsy revealed no evidence of rape or sexual assault. The boy was discovered in an upstairs bedroom; he had been shot and beaten around the head, and his body had nearly a hundred stab wounds, several of which had hardly pierced the skin. A knife, a bowling trophy and a pair of scissors, all heavily bloodstained, were found close to the victims' bodies and it was reasonably assumed these were the murder weapons. The Columbos' pet poodle was alive, cowering in a corner of the living room.

The only surviving member of the family was the Columbos' nineteen-year-old daughter Patricia Ann, who had left home two years previously to live with her married boyfriend, Frank DeLuca, a thirty-eight-year-old pharmacist. When she was contacted by police Patricia (known as Patty) seemed unusually calm and suggested that drug-crazed teenagers might have been responsible. Examination of the scene of the crime indicated that the motive was not robbery because, although the house had been ransacked, many items of value had been left. The pathologist who performed the autopsies offered his opinion that the high degree of overkill was consistent with the murderers being motivated by hatred.

Police enquiries uncovered a long-standing disagreement between Frank Columbo and his daughter over her liaison with DeLuca. The two men had come to blows on one occasion, and Patty had been cut out of her father's will. Then two men approached the police claiming that Patty had tried to hire them to kill her parents in exchange for sexual favours, and this was later confirmed by one of Patty's girlfriends.

On 15 May, Patricia Ann Columbo was arrested and charged with the murders of her parents and brother. DeLuca was arrested at the same time, but no charges were proferred at that stage. Two days after being charged Patty Columbo gave detectives a statement in which she described having had a 'vision' which implied that she 'might have been involved' in the murders. DeLuca took a lie-detector test but the results were inconclusive and he was released. A grand jury returned indictments for triple murder and conspiracy to murder against Patty. In July, another grand jury returned indictments against DeLuca and he was rearrested and charged.

At their trial, evidence was presented to prove that Frank DeLuca had described the murders to some of his employees. Patty Columbo did not give evidence in her own defence but DeLuca went into the witness box and denied all the allegations against him. On 1 August 1977, after a retirement of just two hours, the jury returned verdicts of guilty on all counts against both defendants.

On 8 August, after making final statements proclaiming their innocence, both Patty Columbo and Frank DeLuca were sentenced to from 200 to 300 years on the murder convictions, the sentences to run concurrently. The judge also ordered a twenty- to fifty-year prison term for Patty, and ten to fifty years for DeLuca, on the conspiracy to murder convictions.

COOK, Robert Raymond   Twenty-one-year-old Bobby Cook was arrested in Stettler, Alberta, on 27 June 1959 on a charge of using his father's identity card to obtain a car by fraud. Cook, who already had a previous record for auto theft insisted that his father had given him the ID in order to get the car. The following morning, Royal Canadian Mounted Police Sergeant Roach went to Cook senior's home to check on his son's story, but found nobody in. Returning the next day, the police decided to search the house and found in the garage, concealed in a grease pit, no fewer than seven bodies, all of which had been shot and bludgeoned. The victims were Ray Cook senior, his second wife Daisy Mae and their children, Gerald Rae (nine), Patrick William (eight), Christopher Frederick (six), Kathy Vern (four) and Linda Mae (three). Inside the house, officers noticed that attempts had been made to scrub the walls clean of bloodstains. Hidden beneath a mattress in the master bedroom was a bloodstained prison-issue blue suit and tie which had been allotted to Bobby Cook.

Cook was charged with his father's murder and remanded to a mental institution for psychiatric examination. When he was refused permission to attend his family's funeral, Cook escaped but was recaptured four days later, without any resistance, less than an hour's journey from the cemetery where his family had been buried.

Robert Cook's trial opened in Red Deer in November 1959 before Mr Justice Peter Greschuck. The prosecution presented a strong but circumstantial case. Cook's defence rested on his claim that he was not in Stettler at the time of the murders. After a ten-day trial, the jury found him guilty and he was sentenced to death.

Following an appeal to the Alberta Court of Appeal, the justices by a 3–2 majority ordered a new trial. The second trial opened in Edmonton on 20 June 1960, and followed a similar course to the first, except that the jury deliberated for less than half an hour before returning with their guilty verdict. Mr Justice Harold Riley passed sentence of death. A second appeal to the Alberta Court of Appeal was dismissed, and an application for leave of appeal to the Supreme Court of Canada was refused. Bobby Cook was hanged at the Fort Saskatchewan Correctional Institute on 14 November 1960.

In the intervening years many people have confessed to the Cook family murders but none convincingly enough to be believed. Nevertheless, despite a lack of evidence to support their claim, there are still some Canadians who are convinced of Robert Cook's innocence.

CORDERO, Jose Antonio, *et al.* In the early hours of Sunday 24 October 1975, fire broke out at the Puerto Rican Social Club in the Bronx, New York. The club was in one room on the second floor of the building with a single staircase leading up to it. There were windows along one side and a steel door giving on to a fire escape behind the bandstand. Twenty-five people died in the fire and twenty-four others were seriously injured, two of whom died later in hospital.

Fire investigators established that the blaze had been started deliberately with the use of flammable liquids which had been thrown on the stairway; when ignited, the fire had funnelled up the stairs into the club. Most of the survivors were people who had broken windows and jumped into the street. The majority of the dead had been found near the windows, where they had been trapped in their attempt to get out, and had died of asphyxiation, or in the toilets where they had fled to escape the fire.

A witness reported seeing a green car double parked outside the club at the time the building was torched, but was unable to recall the licence number. The witness agreed to be hypnotized, and although he still could not

remember the registration, he was able to add that he had
seen three men getting into the car.

The break in the case came when a man was arrested in a
stolen car, and in order to try and make a deal with the
police, claimed he could give them the name of somebody
involved in the Social Club fire. The name he volunteered
was that of Hector Lopez. Lopez, just seventeen years old,
was arrested and admitted to police that he and another
seventeen-year-old, Francisco Mendez, had started the fire
as a favour to an older man named Jose Antonio Cordero.
Cordero was picked up and, after a search lasting several
days, Mendez was located and detained in Puerto Rico and
returned to New York. All three were charged with murder
and arson.

At a pre-trial hearing Cordero was alleged to have
instigated the fire because of his jealousy over a young girl
who attended a dance at the club on the night of the fire
against his wishes. He claimed his confession had been
forced out of him by physical abuse on the part of the
police and fire investigators. However, at their trial in June
1977, Jose Cordero, Hector Lopez and Francisco Mendez
pleaded guilty. Cordero was sentenced to life imprisonment;
Lopez, who admitted lighting the fire, was also jailed for
life, and Mendez received twenty-five years to life for
spreading the fuel.

(*For an uncannily similar incident see GONZALEZ, Julio*,
page 135.)

CRABBE, Douglas John A man who had been refused
service drove a heavy articulated lorry (known in Australia
as a 'road train') through the bar of a motel at Ayers Rock
on 17 August 1983. Police said that of the estimated forty
people in the bar at the time twelve were seriously injured
and four were killed instantly; one of the injured died later
in hospital. An eye-witness said she had been saying good-
bye to some friends by the bar door when she heard an
engine start up. The next thing she knew a huge truck came
crashing through the wall and she found herself pinned

beneath the front wheels and covered in bricks and rubble. The woman continued: 'We all knew the driver of the truck. He used to make deliveries to the Rock every week or so, bringing food and so forth. He had been drinking in the bar when a row broke out and he was asked to leave.'

The driver escaped the crash but was arrested by the police on a building site about ten miles away. Thirty-six-year-old Douglas John Crabbe appeared in court at Alice Springs on 19 August indicted on four counts of murder, and was remanded in custody. A further charge of murder, that of the casualty who died in hospital, was added at a later hearing.

Crabbe's defence rested solely on the claim that he had no memory of the incident; on 21 March 1984, he was found guilty on all counts and jailed for life.

Crabbe appealed against his conviction and in November 1984, the Federal Court allowed the appeal by a majority of two-to-one and ordered a new trial.

At the re-trial in the Darwin Supreme Court in October 1985, Douglas John Crabbe was again convicted on all counts and again jailed for life. In evidence, Crabbe this time conceded that he was driving the truck, but that his judgement had been seriously impaired by alcohol.

CRISCIONE, Erminio Ironically, Erminio Criscione was not only a butcher by trade but, it transpired, by inclination as well. On 5 March 1992, during a bloodbath which lasted for two hours, Criscione shot and killed six people who had been on a wholesale meat suppliers training course with him, and seriously wounded a further half dozen.

Armed with the Kalashnikov automatic assault rifle so beloved of the modern multicide, the thirty-seven-year-old butcher tracked down his fellow students to the lakeside holiday resort of Lugano and shot them in the hallways of their homes when they answered his knock at their front door. The first victim was his best friend, who was blasted in both legs. Later, in the nearby village of Rivera-Soresina, Criscione shot four members of another family dead and wounded three more. Finally, he made his way to the home of the training course instructor, whose wife came to the door and told Criscione that her husband was not in; the gunman shot her in both legs and ran off, shouting over his shoulder: 'Tell him I'll be back.'

As he sat slumped, weeping, in his car, Erminio Criscione was surrounded by more than a hundred armed police officers. When he was arrested, he insisted that he could remember nothing of his murderous spree, still less could he account for it. Nor are we ever likely to be any wiser as to his motive; after two days in custody, the Butcher of Lugano hanged himself in his cell.

CRUMP, Daniel Eugene A house in Olathe, Kansas was rent by a tremendous explosion on the morning of 20 September 1980. The house, which had been occupied by the Post family, was completely destroyed by the blast and six members of the family died. The victims were fifty-one-year-old Robert Post, his wife, Norma Jean, aged forty-seven, and four of their children, Diane Crump (nineteen), Richard (twenty-one), Susan (twenty) and James (ten), who survived the initial blast but died later in hospital. Against tremendous odds, three other children who were in the house at the time survived, despite their injuries; they were Diane's four-month-old son Randy, an older son of the Posts, David, and a neighbouring boy, ten-year-old Craig Weber.

Forensic examination of the debris quickly established that the explosion had been caused by dynamite, probably contained in a box that had been detonated in the kitchen. A witness told police he had seen a box on the bonnet of the Posts' car parked in their driveway. The witness had also seen someone come out of the house, pick up the box and take it inside. Within a few minutes, the house erupted.

Enquiries into the background of the victims revealed that there had been several disputes between Diane Crump and her exhusband, Daniel Eugene Crump, over custody of their son Randy. When the court had awarded custody to Diane, Crump had vowed to get his son back. Two months earlier, Daniel Crump had been wounded by a sniper and accused Diane of having been involved. It was alleged that Crump had told a friend he had some dynamite and was going to take it to the Post house and put it in their car.

Daniel Eugene Crump was detained, and denied any knowledge of the explosion. He claimed he had been with his seventeen-year-old girlfriend at the time. When the girl was questioned she said they had driven to the Post home and Crump left a box on the bonnet of a car parked outside. Crump was questioned again and made a statement admitting he had placed a bomb on the car but insisted it was only to damage the car. Crump was arrested and charged with six counts of first-degree murder and three counts of arson and aggravated assault.

The trial opened on 13 April 1981. Crump gave evidence in his own defence and stated that a friend and his girlfriend had left the dynamite bomb on the car at the Post home, and that he had no reason to want to harm anyone in his ex-wife's family. On 17 April, after only a three-hour retirement, the jury found Daniel Crump guilty on all counts. At a sentencing hearing on 11 June 1981, he was given six concurrent life sentences on the murder charges with a further eighty years' jail on the other three counts.

D

DANN, Laurie Wasserman Although Laurie Dann's murder spree only resulted in one victim, her intention to kill many more was manifestly obvious.

By the time she embarked on her bid for notoriety in 1988, Dann already had a long history of mental instability. In 1982, she had married Russell Dann, but the marriage ended four years later in separation; during the subsequent divorce proceedings Russell Dann complained to the police that an intruder, who he thought was Laurie, had entered his room and stabbed him with an ice pick while he was sleeping. The case was not proceeded with due to lack of direct evidence, though Laurie later retaliated by alleging that her ex-husband had raped her. Another one-time boyfriend claimed he was receiving threatening letters from Laurie, and fellow students at university accused her of damaging their property. Indeed Laurie Dann's behaviour at university was so eccentric that she was eventually forced to leave and return to her parents' home. Here she collected criminal convictions for shoplifting and complaints were made about damage to homes where she worked as a baby-sitter.

In spite of this obvious mental deterioration, Laurie Dann was able to obtain several handguns, and early on 20 May 1988, she drove to a number of homes where she had been employed and left food containing arsenic on the front porches. She also attempted, unsuccessfully, to start fires at two of the houses. Then Laurie drove out to the Hubbard Woods Elementary School in Winnetka, Illinois, walked calmly through the entrance and took a pot-shot at a six-year-old boy; thankfully she missed. Laurie then entered one of the classrooms, and when the teacher attempted to disarm her opened fire with a .357 Magnum wounding five children, and killing eight-year-old Nicholas Corwin, after which she calmly left the school, got into her car, and drove off. A short distance away, Laurie Dann abandoned the vehicle and knocked on the door of a house where she told the occupants she had been raped, had shot the rapist, and was now being pursued by the police. When this obviously unbalanced woman was tackled by the houseowner's son, she shot and wounded him before shutting herself in a second-floor room.

When armed police officers had surrounded the house, siege negotiators brought Laurie Dann's father to appeal to his daughter to surrender. When it was obvious that no amount of reasoning was going to work, a twelve-man police squad stormed the house and found Laurie Dann lying face down, with a .32 revolver at her feet. She had shot herself through the mouth, sending a bullet into her brain.

DARE, Richard On the morning of Saturday 6 August 1960, police in Oklahoma City received a telephone call from a woman who said she was unable to raise her friend Mrs Virgie Albert, either on the phone or by calling at her home. It was a comparatively quiet day, so the police decided to send a couple of officers to the house; on arrival, they forced an entry and found four dead bodies inside.

The victims were Mrs Albert, aged fifty-eight, and her daughter Mrs Patricia Dare, who were both lying in a front bedroom; Mrs Albert's husband Edward and their grandson William McCormack were discovered in a back bedroom. All four had been covered over with bedspreads. The two men had been shot in the head and a cord was tied round McCormack's throat. The women had probably been strangled, and Mrs Dare appeared additionally to have been bludgeoned about the head.

The living room of the house showed all the signs of a fierce struggle. Investigating officers presumed that the murders had taken place in that room and that for some reason as yet unclear, the killer had then dragged the bodies into the bedrooms and covered them. A .22-calibre rifle standing in the corner of the living room appeared to have been fired recently. There was no money in the house and the men's wallets were missing; the women's handbags also seemed to have been ransacked, making robbery the most likely motive. More of a puzzle was the absence of any sign of a forced entry, which indicated that the killer was known to the victims.

Enquiries into the backgrounds of the Dare family were largely unhelpful, although it was reported that Patricia Dare was separated from her husband, Richard, and was said to be contemplating divorce. Richard Dare was traced to a local hotel, and when told, appeared shocked at the killings.

Post-mortems showed that the victims had been killed one by one over an eight-hour period on the day before the discovery of the bodies. Patricia Dare, who was pregnant, died first, by strangulation; her mother had died about four hours later, also by strangulation. William McCormack was next, shot in the head, and finally Edward Albert, again by shooting.

The police routinely detained Richard Dare for questioning and he claimed he had intended to go to see his wife on Friday 5th to try to persuade her to agree to a reconciliation. However, after talking to her on the telephone Dare realized there was no chance of this. His first thought had been to leave town and talk to a friend at Ardmore, a town about a hundred miles away, arriving around 5 p.m. on the Friday evening. On Saturday morning Richard Dare decided to return to Oklahoma City and face his difficulties. He said the problems he had been having with his wife arose from her infidelity with an apparently criminous man, currently on bail for armed robbery. The man was interviewed, proved unable to account for his movements on the Friday of the killings, and was detained. A check on Richard Dare's movements on the same night showed that he had not arrived in Ardmore until midnight and, more sinister still, had left a bloodstained shirt at his friend's house. When detectives went to the hotel to question him, Dare had already signed out. An all-points bulletin was broadcast, and Richard Dare turned himself in the following day.

Questioned by detectives, Dare confessed to the murders, saying he had quarrelled with his wife after she told him she was pregnant and would insist he support the child financially. They had fought and he had strangled her. When Patricia's mother came in, Dare told her what he had done and she, not unreasonably, became hysterical, so he strangled her too. He had shot the two men when they came home, his father-in-law because he believed the old man had turned Patricia against him, and young William McCormack because he was a witness. Dare admitted stealing money from the house and trying to incriminate Patricia's new boyfriend.

At his trial in May 1961, Richard Dare pleaded not guilty by reason of insanity to the charge of murdering Edward Albert, the only killing for which he was tried; he was nevertheless found guilty and sentenced to die in the electric chair. The State's Pardon and Parole Board recommended that Richard Dare's sentence be commuted to life imprisonment, a decision that was immediately overruled by the governor.

Richard Dare was electrocuted at 10 p.m. on Saturday 1 June 1963.

D'AUTREMONT BROTHERS   When they found a pair of greasy overalls, a pair of shoes and a gun at the scene of the crime, detectives from Ashland, Oregon, knew exactly what to do with them, exactly where to send them. Which is how the clues in question arrived in the laboratory of Edward O. Heinrich, a forensic polymath who had already earned the reputation of being 'the Edison of Crime Detection'. Heinrich was Professor of Criminology at the University of Berkeley, California, and, as the Ashland police would soon find out, the living embodiment of Conan Doyle's fictional hero Sherlock Holmes.

Edward Heinrich's first discovery when examining the overalls was to highlight an often overlooked function of forensic science – to prove suspects *innocent* as well as to prove them guilty. The police had already taken into custody a local motor mechanic because he was wearing similar oily overalls, and they were about to charge him with murder. But Heinrich's report was emphatic about one thing: '*You are holding the wrong man*; the grime on these overalls is not car grease, it is fir pitch. In the pocket I found fragments of Douglas fir needles. The man who wore these overalls is a left-handed lumberjack. He is between twenty-one and twenty-five years old, about five feet ten inches tall, and weighs about 165 lbs. His hair is medium light brown, his hands and feet are small, and he is a man of fastidious habits.'

So much for the hero of this story; for Heinrich went on to become the most distinguished forensic scientist of his generation. What of the villains? What of the fastidious left-handed lumber-jack?

On 11 October 1923, the Oregon to San Francisco train was stopped by a gang of robbers while it was half in and half out of the tunnel running through one of the peaks of the Siskiyou Mountains. While two of the gang forced the engineer and his fireman out of the cab, a third detonated a bomb close to the mail carriage. The problem now was that a fire created by the explosion was raging in the part of the train still inside the tunnel, defeating the bandits' plan to plunder the mail car. When the engineer failed to pull the rest of the carriages out of the tunnel both he and his fireman were shot dead. By now the whole train was ablaze and the three outlaws fled empty handed, leaving the mail clerk to burn to death in the inferno. They also left behind a pair of greasy overalls, a pair of shoes and a gun . . .

One other clue that had escaped the police examination of the greasy overalls but was recovered by the eagle eye of Edward Heinrich was a tiny folded piece of paper in the corner of one of the pockets. It was a receipt for a registered letter. Like all registered mail this package had been given an individual serial number, and through the US Mail Department it was possible to identify the item as having been sent by a man named Roy D'Autremont from Eugene, Oregon, to Ray D'Autremont in Lakewood, New Mexico. When the police paid a visit to the only D'Autremont they could find in Eugene, old Paul told them exactly what they needed to know: Roy and Ray were his twin sons, and they and their brother Hugh had been missing since the day of the train hold-up. Roy was a lumberjack; and he was left-handed.

Meanwhile, Edward Heinrich was at work on the gun found at the scene of the murders. The serial number led to a gunsmith in Seattle who had sold the weapon to a man giving the name William Elliott. Heinrich compared the purchase documents with Roy D'Autremont's handwriting and found that Roy and Elliott were one and the same.

Although it was not until the spring of 1927 that the three D'Autremont brothers were arrested, they were eventually put on trial, convicted and sentenced to life imprisonment.

So how was Professor Heinrich able to describe Roy D'Autremont just from an examination of his overalls?

He found chips of fir wood and needles in the right-hand pocket. Now a right-handed lumberjack would stand with his left side to the tree picking up debris as it scattered, a left-handed lumberjack would stand to the right side of the tree . . . besides, there was a greater degree of dirt and wear on the left-hand pockets, evidence of greater use. The bottoms of the trousers had been turned up to fit inside logging boots, which, with the position of the braces clip gave an idea of the height and build of the man who wore them. A hair caught in one of the buckles was put under a microscope and proved to belong to a Caucasian with medium light brown hair. Finally, the neatly cut nail clippings found in one of the pockets told Professor Heinrich that the police were looking for a man fastidious about his personal appearance. The size of the feet was an easy deduction – after all, Heinrich had his shoes; but he also knew that, anatomically, human hands are normally in proportion to the feet, therefore the man who wore the shoes almost certainly had small hands.

Elementary. As in similar circumstances Sherlock Holmes might have said.

DEAN, Douglas On 18 July 1971, Mrs Constance Schneider called at her mother's house in Sheboygan, Wisconsin, and was surprised to see the curtains still drawn even though it was the middle of the afternoon. Mrs Schneider let herself into the house and was horrified to find the body of Mrs Hildegarde Dean, shot in the head. Two spent .22-calibre cartridges lay where they had fallen, just outside the bedroom door. In the son's bedroom, ammunition and an empty gun box were found.

It was some hours later, when investigators were carrying out routine house to house enquiries that they reached the Rammer family home where more bodies were found. Mrs Naomi Rammer lay just inside the front door in a pool of blood. Her son Paul seemed to have crawled into the hall before dying after being shot in a bedroom. Sixteen-year-old John Rammer had been shot several times, with one fatal wound to the head, and his brother Tom was lying dead on the stairs. Spent .22-calibre cases lay all around the house and a gun found at the scene matched the serial number on the empty gun box found in the Dean house.

It did not require any great skill in detection to point the finger at Mrs Dean's nineteen-year-old son Douglas, who earlier in the day had been rushed to hospital having been found sitting on the steps of a church in an apparently drugged state. When he had sufficiently recovered, Douglas Dean was arrested and on 22 July was charged with murder. His defence attorney refused to let the police interview him.

Douglas Dean's trial opened on 1 November 1971. Among the key prosecution witnesses was a fellow prisoner, Kenneth Kregel, who claimed that Dean had described the killings to him while they were both in jail. Kregel testified that Dean said he shot the Rammer family because a child kept crying. In his own defence Dean not unnaturally denied ever talking to Kregel; however, he did admit that, while he was a non-violent person, he did enjoy shocking people with outrageous stories. Less convincingly Dean insisted that he did not intentionally take drugs, but the candy he ate on the night before the murders must have been tainted with LSD because he had hallucinated. In rebuttal the prosecution said LSD had been found embedded in candy discovered in Dean's possession, and a psychiatrist called to give evidence doubted whether LSD could have induced the state of amnesia being claimed by Dean.

On 9 November, after a retirement of only eighty minutes, the jury found Douglas Dean guilty on all five counts of murder. On 12 November Judge James Buchen sentenced him to five consecutive life sentences which would mean he would have to serve at least fifty-eight years and four months before he could be considered for parole.

The Wisconsin Supreme Court dismissed Dean's appeal on 10 April 1975, and subsequently the United States Supreme Court refused to hear the case. An appeal to the state governor to amend the life sentences to run concurrently rather than consecutively was also refused.

During his lengthy stay in prison, Douglas Dean has gained advanced degrees in psychology and has taken a leading role in counselling inmates and troubled teenagers.

DeFEO, Ronald Greguski was the first officer on the scene. The call had come through to the Amityville Village police department at 6.35 that evening of 13 November 1974: 'Hey, kid's just run into the bar. Says everyone in his family's been killed.' So in the autumnal gloom patrolman Kenneth Greguski was despatched to Ocean Avenue where a small crowd was beginning to assemble. The centre of attraction seemed to be the young man crouched down sobbing that they had got his mom and dad. It turned out that 'they' had got a lot more than that. When Greguski worked his way through the house he made the body count six; they were later identified as Ronald DeFeo senior, a wealthy motor trader, his wife Louise, their daughters Dawn and Allison, aged eighteen and thirteen respectively, and sons Mark, twelve years old, and John, seven. Still weeping on the porch was Ronald junior, twenty-three years old and the sole survivor of the DeFeo family massacre.

When he was finally settled in at the Amityville police station, Ronald 'call me Butch' DeFeo had a strange tale to tell. As the detectives listened, 'Butch' told them that his father had been involved with the Mafia, and in particular had crossed swords with one of the mob's hit-men named Louis Falini. A fortnight earlier there had been an armed hold-up when money was being transported from the DeFeo car showroom to the bank, during which Ronald junior had been obliged to part with the company's takings. According to his present narrative, Butch's father had accused him of inventing the robbery story and stealing the money for himself.

On the morning of the murders Ronald junior had got up early and driven to the showroom; several times during the morning he had tried to phone home but there had been no reply. At noon Ronald returned to Amityville where he spent the afternoon drinking with friends. In the early evening he left the bar for home, throwing over his shoulder the casual remark that he had forgotten his keys and would have to break in through a window.

While this interview was going on, other officers were checking out Butch's friends, and learned that he was a gun fanatic. What's more, the DeFeos had all been shot with a Marlin .35-calibre rifle – and there was a cardboard box which had contained a Marlin .35 in Butch's wardrobe. Understandably Ronald DeFeo found himself spending longer in police custody than he had bargained for. He whiled away the time inventing ever more preposterous accounts of the killings until at last he was detained on a holding charge of the second-degree murder of his brother Mark.

It was nearly a year later that DeFeo stood trial, and he had made good use of this time feigning insanity; truth to tell, he had made a pretty good job of it – at least, defence psychiatrist Dr Daniel Schwartz was prepared to give expert testimony that at the time he killed his family Butch was suffering from mental disease – 'paranoid delusions' the doctor said, a belief that if he did not kill them they would kill him. As if to add weight to his insanity plea, when Ronald was shown a photograph of his mother lying dead on her bed, he claimed: 'I have never seen this person before.' But Butch did not have it all his own way. Dr Harold Zola for the prosecution gave his opinion that the defendant was not a psychopath but a sociopath, who had so devalued human life that even his parents were expendable in Butch's drive to assert his superiority. And the jury obviously agreed, because they found Ronald DeFeo junior guilty on all six counts of murder. DeFeo was sentenced to twenty-five years to life on each count and confined to the Dannemora Correctional Facility, New York. As the six slayings are legally considered to be forming part of a single act, the sentences are being served concurrently.

And so a dreadful crime might have been forgotten. But that is to reckon without the power exerted when the supernatural meets Hollywood. The DeFeo home in Amityville, ironically called 'High Hopes', was subsequently sold to a family who, after only a year fled the house following a series of disturbances by what they called 'evil forces'. This phenomenon was first re-created as a best-selling book and then not one but several films in the 'Amityville Horror' sequence. It is just as well the media cashed in when they did – the present owners of 'High Hopes' find the place a very quiet and pleasant home.

DE LA ROCHE, Harry Eighteen-year-old Harry De La Roche had fallen decidedly short of his father's ambitions for him, though in fairness it would have been an all but impossible task for even the most gifted child – and Harry was far from that. De La Roche senior was a self-made man who, by dint of hard work and tireless energy, had raised himself up to a senior position with the Ford Motor Company. Nor had he neglected his social position, for the busy executive became a highly respected citizen involved in community work around his home town of Montvale, New Jersey. His father had enrolled Harry junior as a student in The Citadel, a military college in Charleston, South Carolina. Unfortunately young Harry hated discipline; and it was no surprise to anybody to discover that he was not suited to a military career.

On Sunday 21 November 1976, Harry junior flew home for the Thanksgiving holiday determined to tell his parents that he was not going back. His family, including his two younger brothers, fifteen-year-old Ronald and twelve-year-old Eric, welcomed him warmly, and when they asked about his progress at The Citadel he said he would tell them about it later. What they did not know was that Harry had already told the college authorities that he would not be returning. For dramatic emphasis he claimed his mother had terminal cancer.

The following Saturday night, the day before he was supposed to return to college, Harry De La Roche went out driving with a friend, returning home at about 2 a.m. Two hours later a police patrolman witnessed a car in downtown Montvale speed through a stop sign and pull up outside a bar. The patrolman was in the process of booking young Harry when the youth suddenly said: 'Quick – come up to my house. I've just found my parents and my younger brother dead and my middle brother missing.'

When police followed Harry's instructions and went to the house, they found fifty-one-year-old Mary Jane De La Roche shot dead in the main bedroom, and in an adjoining room her husband and youngest son Eric also shot dead. Harry told detectives he had come in from an evening out and found the bodies. He also mentioned that his father and brother Ronnie had earlier had a big row about Ronnie taking drugs. Soon after midday, the body of Ronnie De La Roche was discovered squashed into a trunk in the attic of the family home. Harry Jr then made a second statement to the police, this time admitting killing his family. Harry described in detail how twelve-year-old Eric had fought desperately for his life. That evening, Harry De La Roche junior was charged with murder. In early December, he made another statement, now he said Ronnie had killed his parents and Eric and he, Harry Jr, had shot Ronnie; it was all getting rather complicated.

At his trial, Harry De La Roche pleaded not guilty by reason of insanity. However, in view of his constantly changing and increasingly improbable accounts, this defence was not accepted by the jury who simply saw him for what he was – a killer, and a particularly brutal and cynical killer at that. Harry De La Roche was convicted on all four counts of murder, and sentenced to four concurrent life terms.

DE LEEUW, Huibrecht   Huibrecht de Leeuw was one of those individuals whose ambitious requirements are always frustrated by their slender wallets; however, de Leeuw was disgraced not by his lack of funds, but by the unworthy manner in which he sought to increase them.

De Leeuw was the town clerk of Dewetsdorp, in the Orange Free State, and had for some time been attempting to juggle to his own financial advantage the cash kept in the exchequer safe and the record of it kept in the accounts books. It was clearly not a state of affairs which could pass unnoticed for ever, and time was already running out. In brief, the books were in a mess and the mayor himself was demanding that a tally be made. Unable to raise any tangible token of sympathy from his friends, De Leeuw turned – as so many had done before him – to more desperate solutions.

On 8 April 1927, Mayor P. J. von Maltitz, accompanied by two representatives of the town's finance committee, arrived to conduct their own inspection of the accounts. As they pored with increasing bewilderment over the columns of incomplete and inaccurate figures, a tremendous explosion ripped through the building, tearing off the roof and setting the fabric ablaze, during which conflagration the mayor perished instantly and his financial advisers sustained fatal injuries.

An arrest was made not long afterwards, when a local tradesman told police how the improvident de Leeuw had been obliged to borrow a match from him to ignite the home-made contraption of dynamite and petrol.

With the simple message 'I am prepared to meet my Creator' on his lips, Huibrecht de Leeuw was hanged on 30 September 1927.

DELGADO, Campo Elias Delgado was an electronics engineer who had served with some distinction with the United States Air Force during the conflict in South-east Asia, and had returned to live in Bogotá, Colombia, with his mother. At the age of fifty-two, Delgado was becoming difficult to get on with, and had developed an irritating affectation of addressing people as though they were on a military parade ground. On 4 December 1986, he told friends: 'I have a problem. I don't love my mother.'

A few hours later, in his apartment, Campo Elias Delgado shot his mother dead, wrapped her body in newspapers and set it on fire. He then went to three other apartments in the building and shot at anyone who opened the door. Delgado left the building having killed six neighbours. Now he went to an expensive restaurant and ate a meal alone. A waiter remembered that: 'First he ate, then asked for the bill. Then he asked for two drinks and after paying the bill, he stood up and began shooting in all directions.' Twenty-one diners were killed including a six-year-old girl before the gunman was himself shot dead by police officers.

The authorities later said that Delgado had spent more than thirty minutes on the rampage, reaching into a brief-case to reload his gun from five boxes of ammunition. The examining magistrate, Judge Lucero Echeverri de Henao, said that Delgado 'handled his gun with chilling calmness', and had carefully and deliberately aimed at the heads of many of his victims.

DEL VALLE, Jose Alfredo On 9 May 1953, at the tiny airport outside the Mexican town of Mazatlan, baggage was being wheeled towards the main building prior to being loaded on to an aircraft scheduled for the flight to La Paz, when suddenly there was an explosion which killed two baggage handlers and the airport manager; fourteen other people were injured, some seriously. Examination of the wreckage disclosed pieces of a clock and evidence of dynamite. It was subsequently established from airport records that a package had been despatched to an address in La Paz, and was originally scheduled for direct flight across the Gulf of California. However, that aircraft was already carrying a full load and the package had been diverted to the longer route via Mazatlan. It was evident the bomber had intended to destroy the aircraft over the gulf.

A description was put together of the man who had shipped the package and it was found to match that of a would-be suicide who had been arrested in La Paz after attempting to hang himself in a public park. Jose Alfredo del Valle confessed that he had sent the bomb as part of a scheme to falsify his own death so that his 'widow' could collect 850,000 pesos life insurance. Del Valle had befriended a man whom he persuaded to travel with him from Mexico City, lending the man his own clothes and finally buying a plane ticket in his own name which he gave to the stranger. When del Valle saw the package had not been put aboard the direct flight he panicked and fled to La Paz. Del Valle claimed he had got the idea from a previous Mexican case in which thankfully the pilot had managed to land the plane after the bomb detonated. He had friends in military circles from whom he had obtained the dynamite and had spent many months practising making bombs.

Jose del Valle admitted charges of murder and was sentenced to thirty years in a penal colony. On 14 October 1956, after two previous unsuccessful attempts, he committed suicide by taking an overdose of sleeping tablets.

DHILLON, Harbhajan, and **APPLETON, Richard** The trial report which follows is based on contemporary accounts in the *Uxbridge Gazette* and the *Daily Telegraph* of 24 and 25 June 1982:

Accused security men deny murder of family

An Uxbridge security man told the Old Bailey that he had accepted £500 to help a workmate set fire to his house; however, he denied knowing about a murder plot.

Richard Appleton, aged twenty-four, of Myddleton Road, Uxbridge, and Harbhajan Dhillon of Granville Road, Hayes, denied murdering Mrs Lakhbir Dhillon and her children Rajinder, nine years old, Balwinder, eight, and Paramjit, six.

Appleton told the court that he had no idea that Dhillon's wife or children would be in the house. He said: 'It was only a plan to commit arson. We went into the house and Dhillon went to get an oil can. He told me to wait in the kitchen while he went upstairs to fetch £500 for me. While he was upstairs I heard some muffled sounds. Dhillon came in and gave me the money and told me if I went up and started splashing petrol around he would start smashing things up downstairs. When I went up I saw the body of a woman lying on the floor. I just felt deep panic and ran down again.'

He added: 'Dhillon stopped me and said: "You are fully involved no matter what you do."'

Appleton said he returned upstairs and started scattering petrol. Asked if he noticed there were children inside the house, Appleton claimed he had not. He continued: 'When the plan changed I was sickened by the thought of a woman's body burning. I deny it was a murder plan all along.'

Affair

The Old Bailey heard earlier that Dhillon denied arranging to kill his wife and three daughters, and claimed that he had offered his workmate money merely to beat up the man with whom he believed his wife had been having an affair.

Dhillon claimed his workmate went to the family home in Granville Road, strangled his wife and then set fire to the house while the children were sleeping.

In evidence, Dhillon told the court he let slip to Appleton that he suspected his wife of having an affair with another man. 'I asked him to scare him and we would beat him up.' According to Harbhajan Dhillon, Appleton asked if the man would be at Dhillon's home on the night of 22 November. Dhillon said he thought he might be. He added: 'I heard some noises and went upstairs and saw Appleton strangling my wife with some wire. I was pushed back and said, "I did not ask you to do this, I just wanted you to beat up the man."'

Dhillon alleged Appleton was in an angry mood and took £500 from him; he said he was very nervous and told Appleton: 'Let's go, let's not wake up the children.'

Dhillon said that Richard Appleton told him to carry on, because he wanted to go to the lavatory. Dhillon claimed he went back to the car outside. Appleton then joined him shortly afterwards, saying: 'Let's go, I have started a fire.' Asked what he did when he knew five children were still inside the house in bed, Dhillon replied: 'I tried to get out of the car but Appleton would not let me go; he threatened he would kill me as well.'

Two of the children were rescued from the fire.

Father jailed for 'horror' murders

Harbhajan Dhillon, a twenty-nine-year-old father was jailed for life at the Old Bailey for what the judge described as the 'horrifying' murders of his thirty-year-old wife and three of their five daughters. A workmate he enlisted to assist in the murders with a promise of a £500 'contract' was also sentenced to life imprisonment. Mr Justice Kenneth Jones told Harbhajan Dhillon: 'No words are adequate to describe the enormity of the crime you have committed.'

Twenty-four-year-old Richard Appleton, a security officer, of Myddleton Road, Uxbridge, was found guilty of helping Dhillon to murder his wife, manslaughter of the three children, arson and injuring the survivors. Mrs Dhillon was strangled with a length of wire and the house was set on fire. Neighbours managed to rescue two of the children who were badly burned.

DIPENDRA, Crown Prince Although the Royal Family of Nepal were regarded by their people as descendants of Vishnu, the Eton-educated heir to the throne, Crown Prince

Dipendra was hardly god-like with his addiction to alcohol and drugs. Add to these problems his love of guns and habit of walking around palace grounds shooting at any animals he came across – yet another recipe for disaster was in the making.

On Friday 1 June, 2001, he attended a reception at the Narayanhiti Palace in Kathmandu given by his parents King Barendra and Queen Aishwarya, got drunk and was carried back to his quarters to sleep it off. Seemingly, he came to, dressed and armed himself with a semi-automatic rifle and returned to the reception. He opened fire immediately on entering the room, his first target was his father, King Barendra, who collapsed dying with three bullet wounds. He continued to rake the room with bullets and the next to die were his younger brother, Prince Nirajan, and his sister, Princess Shrutti. Queen Aishwarya stood her ground against him but was quickly despatched with a bullet to the head. Surrounded by the dead, dying and wounded, he finally shot himself in the head.

When rescuers arrived, they found ten members of the Royal Family dead but Dipendra was still alive. He was removed to hospital, where according to Nepalese protocol, mass murderer or not, he was bizarrely proclaimed King. However, he avoided a constitutional crisis by dying soon after.

It was later reported that he had been told by his parents that his position as Crown Prince would be revoked if he went ahead with his intention to marry a girl they regarded as unsuitable. An ancient prophecy had said that the ruling Shah dynasty would be in danger of ending on the death of the tenth king, which was Birendra.

DOMINICI, Gaston In the summer of 1952, sixty-one-year-old Sir Jack Drummond, a distinguished English bio-chemist, took his wife and eleven-year-old daughter on a camping holiday to Southern France. On the night of 4 August, Sir Jack brought the Hillman station wagon to a halt at a picturesque spot by the river just outside the Provençal village of Lurs.

Early the following morning local police were alerted by Gustave Dominici, a thirty-three-year-old farmer, who had come across the dead bodies of the Drummond family at their camp-site. Sir Jack and his wife had been shot, Elizabeth had been bludgeoned to death.

The nearest habitation to the scene of the murders was a farm named Grand'Terre, some 150 yards away, owned by seventy-five-year-old Gaston Dominici and worked by his sons, one of whom was Gustave. Despite the police's deep suspicion that the Dominici family were involved in the killings, a search of Grand'Terre revealed nothing incriminating. It was not until several weeks had passed that investigating officers received their first promising lead. A railway worker told detectives that Gustave Dominici had admitted to him that young Elizabeth Drummond had still been alive when he found her. It was not much, but sufficient to have Gustave charged with the offence of failing to help a person in danger of dying. But still the police could not penetrate the smoke-screen of lies and deceits thrown up by the machinations of the unscrupulous Dominicis. Eventually the seriousness of the crime and the eminence of the victims resulted in no less an official than Commissaire Edmond Sebeille, Superintendent of the Marseilles police, being given charge of the inquiry.

For almost a year Commissaire Sebeille and his team worked away trying to undermine the resistance of the Dominicis, until finally Gustave and his forty-nine-year-old brother Clovis admitted they knew the identity of the killer – it was their father Gaston. Despite his loud accusations of treachery, old Gaston eventually made a confession. He had been on a nocturnal prowl around the area of the farm, carrying his rifle as always, when he stumbled upon the Drummonds' camp. As it was obvious that Sir Jack and his wife were undressing for bed the old farmer decided to hang around and watch. Unfortunately for them all, Jack Drummond caught Dominici at it, and during the ensuing struggle was shot dead. Fearing identification, Dominici then shot Ann Drummond and, as she tried to run away, bludgeoned Elizabeth about the head with the butt of his gun. Or so he said. Because over the course of the next several weeks Gaston Dominici retracted and confessed again with monotonous regularity. At one point he accused Gustave of the murders, which resulted in Gustave retracting his accusation of Gaston in favour of another assassin. The whole bizarre situation was crowned when, during one of those reconstructions of the crime so beloved of the French authorities, Gaston broke free from the police and tried to kill himself by jumping off a railway bridge.

Gaston Dominici was put on trial at the Digne Assizes in November 1954, and after an eleven-day hearing he was found guilty of murder. His advancing years saved Dominici from the guillotine, and he served only a brief period in prison before being released in 1960; he died of congestion of the lungs in 1965.

DONNELLY MURDERS   Members of the Donnelly clan had been feuding and fighting since their early days in Ireland, and had continued the tradition in a similar vein after emigrating to Canada and settling in Biddulph, Ontario. Convictions had regularly been recorded against the family over the years, the most serious of which was the case of James Donnelly senior, father of the present generation, who was found guilty in 1859 of the murder of Patrick Farrell two years earlier and sentenced to die on the gallows. Largely due to the efforts of his wife Johannah in organizing a petition for his reprieve, James Donnelly's sentence was commuted to seven years in the penitentiary. He was released after serving the full term (there was no remission of sentence in those days) and returned to his feuding and fighting family.

On the night of 4 February 1880, a mob arrived at the Donnelly home. What happened was later described by eleven-year-old Johnny O'Connor, who was staying with the Donnellys at the time: Constable James Carroll entered the house first and handcuffed Tom Donnelly, though there was some dispute as to the constable having a warrant for Tom's arrest. Then the mob burst in and began attacking the Donnellys with sticks. Young Johnny O'Connor had by this time hidden himself in terror but emerged when he realized the mob had sprayed kerosene around the house and set it on fire. As he escaped he saw the bodies of Johannah and Tom Donnelly, but not those of James and Bridget. After fleeing the burning house, the mob went on to the home of Will Donnelly, where they shot and killed John Donnelly.

Johnny O'Connor ran to a neighbour's house and raised the alarm. By the time help arrived, James Donnelly's home had been reduced to smouldering rubble and ashes, and all that was found were the incinerated remains of James, Johannah, Tom and Bridget. Thanks to the evidence of the boy and other witnesses, a large number of arrests were made, and Constable James Carroll, John Kennedy, Martin McLoughlin, James Ryder, Thomas Ryder and John Purtell were committed for trial at the next assizes charged with murder. Just prior to the committals, an inquest jury returned a verdict of murder by some persons unknown.

The trials were delayed until September 1880, when the Crown chose to put officer James Carroll on trial first. Johnny O'Connor gave evidence identifying Carroll and several of the other accused. After a protracted retirement, the jury failed to agree on a verdict.

Carroll's second trial began in January 1881 and was largely a repeat of the first. On Saturday 29 January the jury returned a verdict of not guilty. The remaining accused were released on bail, but no proceedings were ever taken against them.

DOODY, Jonathan, and **GARCIA, Alessandro**   The culmination of what the trial prosecutor called Arizona's 'biggest homicide case' came on Monday 12 July 1993, with verdicts of guilty by a Phoenix jury against a teenaged military fanatic on nine counts of murder, nine of armed robbery and one each of burglary and conspiracy to commit armed burglary.

The scene of the crime was the Wat Promkunaram Buddhist temple at Phoenix on 9 August 1991. The prosecution alleged that Doody (aged seventeen at the time) and his co-accused Garcia (then sixteen) had planned to rob the temple. They had ransacked the monks' quarters and taken cameras, electronic equipment and $2,790 in cash. In order to eliminate witnesses, Doody had herded six monks, an elderly nun and two male followers into a circle on the floor of the temple's living quarters and methodically shot them all in the head with a borrowed .22-calibre rifle. The bodies of the victims, who ranged in age between sixteen and seventy-one, were discovered the following day by would-be worshippers.

Garcia had entered into a plea bargain arrangement with the prosecution whereby he agreed to plead guilty to murder and give evidence against Doody in a deal to avoid the death sentence. Garcia testified that he had fired harmless shotgun shots between the victims while Doody did the killings.

Doody did not give evidence at his trial but his lawyer, no doubt to his embarrassment, was obliged to present his client's preposterous excuse for being at the temple waving a gun – he was playing a war game to test the building's security! In his defence, it was also suggested that the prosecutors were attempting to influence the jury by the persistent production of bloody autopsy photographs of the victims because they had no direct proof of Doody's guilt. The defence claimed that four men from Tucson who had originally been detained, or a friend, Roland Caratachea, who had lent Doody the rifle, may have been responsible for the killings. Caratachea was called as a witness, but refused to answer any questions, invoking his rights under the Fifth Amendment not to incriminate himself.

After two days of deliberations the jury convicted Doody on all counts; his defence attorney immediately gave notice of appeal, and the sentence hearing at which he could receive the death penalty was postponed.

DORNIER, Christian   A farmer living at Luxiol near the French border with Switzerland, Dornier had already acquired a local reputation as a surly and violent man when, on 12 July 1989, he went berserk with a double-barrelled shotgun killing fourteen and wounding eight. Thirty-one-year-old Christian Dornier first shot and wounded his father and killed a veterinary surgeon who had been called to the farm. He then shot his mother and recently married sister before rushing out into the village's main street, shooting indiscriminately at any of the 140 inhabitants who were unlucky enough to be in the firing line. One little girl playing in the garden and two young boys riding on a bicycle died in the space of three minutes; Dornier then got into his black Volkswagen Golf. A gendarme attempted to stop him but failed, and was wounded in the process. One of the villagers had slightly better luck when he shot and wounded Dornier, though this did not stop him; he killed another four people before driving off to the nearby village of Autechaux, where he continued firing on everyone he encountered; he killed a farmer on a tractor, and three motorists in their cars. Dornier then drove on to another village, Verne, where gendarmes finally succeeded in putting an end to the bloodbath by shooting and seriously wounding him.

Women in the villages later wept as they described how children had screamed as Dornier's car had driven recklessly through the streets with its occupant firing wildly at anyone and everyone: 'He seemed completely out of his mind,' said one woman.

Meanwhile, Dornier had been detained in hospital for treatment after which he was subjected to a thorough psychiatric examination. On 10 November 1989, it was announced that medical officers had certified Christian Dornier insane, and because he was not considered responsible for his actions, he could not be put on trial. Dornier was instead committed to a mental institution.

DREESMAN, Robert At a family reunion in Algona, Iowa, on New Year's Day 1988, a forty-year-old man with a history of mental instability shot dead six relatives and then committed suicide. Police found the blood-spattered bodies lying amidst the seasonal decorations when they broke into wealthy landowner John Dreesman's house when neighbours became alarmed and reported hearing shooting.

Robert Dreesman, described by neighbours as a loner and a recluse, had entered his parents' dining room where the family were sitting down to a meal and systematically shot each one dead with bullets to the head and chest before turning the gun on himself. The victims were his father, John Dreesman, aged seventy-nine, his mother Agnes Dreesman, aged seventy-four, his forty-eight-year-old sister Marilyn Chuang and her three children, Jason, aged twelve, Jennifer, eleven, and Joshua, eight. Mrs Chuang and her children had been visiting from Hawaii, and short of any other part-way rational motive there was speculation that Dreesman had been jealous of the attention that they had been getting from his parents and that this was the reason for the killing spree.

DROPPIN' WELL BOMBING   The Droppin' Well disco bar at Ballykelly, near Londonderry, was a popular haunt of off-duty army personnel from the nearby Shackleton barracks who took the opportunity to socialize with the local young people. On 6 December 1982, the disco was packed as usual with soldiers and local youngsters dancing and drinking, when without warning a huge explosion devastated the building. The walls and roof collapsed, trapping the dead and injured under piles of rubble and debris. Cries for help and screams of anguish could be heard half a mile away. Eleven soldiers, five civilian women and a teenaged boy lay dead and more than a hundred people were injured, many seriously. Forensic examination established that a 5lb bomb, hidden in a holdall, had been left under the stage.

Extensive police enquiries concentrated on members of the Irish National Liberation Army and their sympathizers. Five people were subsequently arrested and charged with murder: they were Anna Moore, aged forty, her sister Helena Semple, aged thirty-nine, her common-law husband Eamon Moore, aged twenty-five, her twenty-two-year-old daughter Jacqueline Moore, and the INLA's finance officer in Londonderry, Patrick Shorter. Police announced they were still looking for two other men in connection with the bombing – the organizer and another man who helped to plant the bomb.

The trial was held amid heavy security at Belfast Crown Court before Mr Justice Carswell. On 12 June 1986, after six days, Anna Moore, Helena Semple, Eamon Moore and Patrick Shorter changed their pleas to guilty of murder and the judge accepted Jacqueline Moore's plea of guilty to manslaughter.

In passing life sentences on those pleading guilty to murder, and ten years' imprisonment on Jacqueline Moore, Mr Justice Carswell told them that they had been bent on murdering any soldiers in the bar and that they were callously prepared to let anyone else there be killed or maimed in order that they could achieve that objective.

In March 1993, it was reported in the press that Anna Moore, who was still serving her sentence was to marry Bobby Corry, a Loyalist terrorist also serving life for murder, in a prison ceremony at Maghaberry gaol in County Antrim. Both bride and groom claim to be born-again Christians and have renounced paramilitary violence. Anna Moore's maid of honour at the wedding was Susan Christie, formerly of the Ulster Defence Regiment and serving nine years in Maghaberry for the manslaughter of Penny McAllister, wife of her lover Captain Duncan McAllister.

DURAND, Earl Earl Durand, from Powell, Wyoming, fancied himself as something of a latterday Robin Hood and would make periodic hunting trips, illegally shooting game and distributing some of the proceeds among friends. In September 1939, he was arrested for illegal elk hunting, jailed for six months and fined $100. This was the first time he had received any punishment for what he clearly saw as a noble cause, and Earl Durand was determined on revenge. When Deputy Riley brought him his supper in the town jail at 5.30 on the evening of 15 March 1939, Durand attacked and overpowered the officer and marched him to his office where Durand took a high-powered rifle and forced the deputy at gunpoint to drive him away in a police car.

The fugitive and his reluctant chauffeur drove to the Durand farm pursued by Deputy Baker and Marshal Charles Lewis. The officers challenged Durand, who turned his stolen gun on them, killing Baker instantly and mortally wounding Lewis. In the maelstrom, Deputy Riley managed to slip away and hide, while Durand drove off to the next farmhouse where he stole a rifle and a supply of ammunition.

Posses were formed and despatched out in several directions in search of Durand but without any success. His prowess as a hunter and woodsman enabled Earl Durand always to keep one step ahead of his pursuers and to live off the land. During this time he made regular raids on isolated farms where he mainly stole arms and ammunition to supplement his growing arsenal. At one of the farms Durand left a letter for Sheriff Blackburn in which he threatened to shoot any law officer he came in contact with. The letter was headed with the words: 'Earl Durand, Undertakers Office, Powell', and ended: 'When you kill me I suggest you have my head mounted and hung up in the courthouse for the sake of law and order.' The sheriff narrowly missed Durand on one of his thieving raids and no doubt this persuaded Durand to make a break out of the area. Durand broke in to the home of a Mr and Mrs Thornburg and forced them to drive him to Beartooth Mountain, where he courteously thanked his hostages and hiked off into the hills.

The police search now moved to the Beartooth Mountain area, and a select party of seventy-two experienced hunters and trackers fanned out to search for Durand. One small group picked up his trail early on, but came under fire and two of its members, Orville Linaberry and Art Argento, were shot dead. On Friday 24 September, three men out driving in the area were hailed by a man who claimed to be a member of the posse and asked for a lift to the search headquarters. As soon as he was in the car, the man pulled out a gun, announced he was Earl Durand and insisted they drive him to Deaver where he collected some more ammunition; then he commandeered the car and drove off alone in the direction of Powell.

Arriving in town, Earl Durand held up the First National Bank and fired on several different business establishments on Main Street. He robbed the bank of $3,000, and tied up bank employees Nelson and Knutson, before forcing cashier Gawthrope out of the bank as a human shield. As they stepped outside on to the pavement, a shout rang out: 'It's Durand' and a bullet hit Gawthrope, who fell forward exposing Durand. Another shot hit Durand, who crawled back into the bank and shot himself in the head. Cashier Nelson, who had managed to free himself and find a gun, fired a further shot into Durand just to make sure he was dead.

The final casualty was cashier Gawthrope who was rushed to hospital but died of his injuries a few minutes after arrival.

DYER, Bryan A.   Day staff at the Brighton Bowl, Boston, were always regular in arriving for work around 6.30 a.m. and Monday 22 September 1980 was no exception. The manager, Donald Doroni, met employees George Hagelstein and Brian and David Cobe in the parking lot and they entered the Bowl together, leaving the front doors open because a mechanic was expected at around 8 a.m. to check the automatic pinspotters.

However, when the mechanic arrived he saw the office safe was wide open and money scattered about on the floor. He immediately called the police who began a search of the building. An officer searching the rear of the bowling alleys opened the door of a workroom and found the four employees, bludgeoned and riddled with bullets, and blood splashed everywhere. Three of the men had been handcuffed behind their backs and the fourth, Doroni the manager, had his hands tied behind him with a belt. Brian Cobe was still alive when the police arrived, and he was rushed to hospital only to be found dead on arrival. The other three men were already dead.

Police investigations were based on the theory that the killer had handcuffed the three men and beaten Doroni until he had revealed the safe combination as there was no sign of it being forced. It was estimated that between $5,000 and $10,000 had been stolen. The medical examiner said that all the victims had been beaten about the head before being shot with a .38-calibre gun. Police checked on all known associates of the victims and present and former employees of the Brighton Bowl; the thinking was that the brutality of the killings may have stemmed from the fact that the killer was known to the dead men and may have been nursing a grievance.

These checks brought the name of Bryan A. Dyer, aged forty-one, to the top of the list. He had been employed at the Bowl in the 1970s and three days before the killings had enquired whether there was any chance of getting his old job back. In addition, it was discovered that Dyer had a previous conviction for assault with a deadly weapon.

On 1 October, Dyer was arrested at the YMCA in Somerville, where he had been living since his release from prison. In his car, police found a gun and an unspent .38-calibre bullet, bloodstained clothing and some coin-wrappers similar to those in use at the Brighton Bowl. Dyer appeared in court the following day, charged with four counts of first-degree murder, armed robbery and illegal possession of a firearm.

Dyer came up for trial in May 1981, when the prosecution produced a witness who identified him as the driver of a car swerving erratically near the Bowl around the time of the killings. A ballistics expert said that the gun found on Dyer had been used in the murders. On 27 May Dyer was found guilty on all counts. The following day, when asked if he had anything to say before sentence was passed, Dyer still professed his innocence. Judge Pierce handed down four consecutive life terms for murder, with a concurrent life sentence for armed robbery and five years for unlawful possession of a firearm, thus attempting to ensure that Dyer would never be given parole.

E

EARLY, David F.   In 1957, when David Early was serving a term in Leavenworth Penitentiary, he warned a prison psychiatrist that he would commit murder as soon as he was released. He said: 'I will get back at my landlady. I will get back there when I get out and I will stomp her over the head, tie her up and rape and finally kill her. I will make it to Death Row yet. I have an uncle-in-law who is a corporation lawyer. I have a scheme for holding him up for ransom money and I would kidnap his family and threaten to kill his children for ransom. Right now I am doing an illegal sentence and when I get out of this I am going to kill people to get money if necessary.' Not a great literary speech, but clear enough to anyone with half an ear that David F. Early needed watching. Instead, on 22 April 1958, they released him on parole. Early travelled back to Denver, Colorado, though he did not look for his former landlady; instead, on 25 April, he went to the home of his uncle-in-law, the lawyer, and walked in through an unlocked door. Once inside Early found a rifle and a pistol, and as the family arrived home separately, he held them up at gunpoint and bound all four – father, mother, son and daughter.

Originally Early had planned to leave the house with the money he had stolen but on a whim, he changed his mind and shot and killed the lawyer, his wife and fifteen-year-old daughter. The seventeen-year-old boy succeeded in freeing himself from his bonds and escaped. As he was running away, Early shot at him but missed.

David Early was captured while driving away from the

house, and when questioned later he said: 'I killed three people. I killed them with no compunction. It didn't mean any more for me to kill them than to turn off the lights.' He added that he had resented the family's wealth and respectability ever since he was a child. Early was tried and convicted on three counts of first-degree murder and sentenced to death. He was executed in the gas chamber at Colorado State Penitentiary on 11 August 1961.

EASBY, Thomas To hide or destroy all trace of their crime is frequently the first thought that runs through the mind of the murderer. Many have thought that fire is the best method of concealment; few realized quite how difficult it is to burn a human body. A classic Canadian case was the killing of the Easby family, although whether the murderer would have proceeded had he known how things would turn out is doubtful.

Thomas Easby, an early settler to the country, lived with his wife and five children in a log house in Drummond Township, Lanark County near Bathurst, Upper Canada. One night in early December 1828, Easby's house burned down and in the ruins the bodies of his wife and four of his children were found. An inquest jury decided they had perished from suffocation, and brought in a verdict of accidental death.

The surviving child, four-year-old Joseph, was adopted by a neighbouring family, who were horrified one day as they were building a fire, to hear Joseph say: 'That was what Daddy did to Mammy.' This was reported to the authorities who exhumed the bodies, and on closer examination it was discovered that their skulls had been beaten in. Easby was arrested and charged with the murder of his wife.

Thomas Easby was tried at Perth in August 1829. Evidence was presented of his confession to the murders while awaiting trial, and after a retirement of only a few minutes, the jury found him guilty and he was sentenced to death. A few days later Easby was hanged, apparently penitent but offering no explanation of his crimes. He was at first buried in a local cemetery but fearing reprisals by the local people his earthly remains were soon afterwards exhumed for dissection. Easby's body was skinned, the hide tanned and cut into small squares which were sold to the public for $2 each.

EAST HAM FIRE BOMBING   A dispute among Tamils in an East End of London pub was said to be the cause of a fire-bomb attack on a house in East Ham on 14 November 1986. Sam Kulasingham, thirty-one years old and believed to be a prominent member of the Tamil community, was alleged to have led the attack in which three men died to avenge a threat made to Kulasingham in a local pub. On the night of the fire there was an explosion, and the house in which nine people were sleeping burst into flames. Six people on the upper floors managed to escape through the windows but three Tamil students on the ground floor died from smoke inhalation. The dead were identified as Karunahatan Arithimoorthy, his brother Ganaharan and Nirmalan Selvanayagam, all aged in their twenties.

Following police enquiries five Tamils – Kulasingham, Nadarajah, Varathadasan, Ravi Ponnu, Gerald Nadarajah and Premaj Sivalingam – were arrested and charged with murder. After several appearances on remand the men were committed for trial at the Old Bailey.

The trial opened on 6 April 1988, when the prosecution alleged that the targets of the fire-bombing had survived and the three dead men were not party to the original dispute. A witness stated that Sivalingam had told him that the defendants had started the fire with a petrol bomb. Another witness alleged that Kulasingham had admitted the attack to him and threatened anyone who spoke about the incident. The defence claimed that witnesses and some of the defendants had been beaten by the police in order to make them give statements helpful to the prosecution case. On 14 April, the judge instructed the jury to return verdicts of not guilty in the cases of Nadarajah, Varathadasan and Ponnu as there was insufficient evidence to convict in their cases. The trial continued against Kulasingham and Sivalingam, and the jury finally returned guilty verdicts against them and the two men were each sentenced to life imprisonment.

Appeals by Kulasingham and Sivalingam were dismissed in February 1992, and a month later Kulasingham went on hunger strike in protest against his conviction. His condition worsened and after five weeks he was removed from prison to a hospital. After eight weeks Samuel Kulasingham abandoned the hunger strike when the Home Office agreed to look into his conviction. On 5 July 1993 the Home Secretary announced that after studying the papers in the case of Kulasingham and Sivalingam, he had decided to refer it back to the Court of Appeal.

The result of the new appeal was that on 27 May 1994 both the Tamil refugees had their convictions quashed. Announcing the verdicts Lord Justice McCowan said: 'This matter has left us with a distinct sense of unease about the verdicts and we cannot regard the convictions as safe or satisfactory'. Sam Kulasingham, released after five years, to a jubilant crowd of supporters outside the High Court: 'I'm shocked but very happy to be free.'

EASTBURN MURDERS   In May 1985, memories of the murders of the MacDonald family (see page 228) were revived for the inhabitants of Fayetteville, North Carolina, when another army officer's wife and her two small children were found brutally murdered.

On Mother's Day, 12 May, Kathryn Eastburn was found stabbed to death, naked and with her hands tied behind her back, in the master bedroom of her home at Fort Bragg Army Base. Mrs Eastburn's body had fifteen stab wounds in the chest and her throat had been cut. Lying next to her in the bedroom was the body of her three-year-old daughter Erin, who had also been repeatedly stabbed in the chest; her throat, too, had been cut. In another bedroom, five-year-old Kara Eastburn lay, killed in a similar manner. The Eastburn's youngest child, twenty-one-month-old Jana, was found in another bedroom, crying and very disturbed after she had been left alone for up to three days, but otherwise physically unharmed.

Police investigators contacted Captain Gary Eastburn, who had been away on army duties at the time of the murders. He was unable to offer any help other than to say that his wife had telephoned to let him know she had found a home for their dog, an English Setter, with a 'nice' man who had agreed to take the animal on a trial basis to see if it got along with his other dog. On Wednesday 15 May, a news release was issued asking the man who had taken the dog to contact the police. Following this, Army Staff Sergeant Timothy Hennis presented himself at the police station as the man who had adopted the dog. He was interrogated for six hours and put in a line-up where he was picked out by a man who had been in the neighbourhood of the Eastburn home in the early hours of Friday 10 May and had seen a man leave the house and drive away in a white Chevette car. The witness said that he was not entirely sure, but Hennis could have been the man and his car looked like the one he had seen.

Hennis cooperated with the police doctor who took samples of his blood and hair, and was then released. However, at one o'clock on the morning of Thursday 16 May 1985, he was arrested and charged with the murders of the Eastburn family. On 11 December Timothy Hennis was released again on bail after his attorney successfully argued that the state's case against him was weak and insubstantial.

The trial opened on 26 May 1986. In spite of defence objections, the prosecution was allowed to show the court enlarged slide projections of the victims. The previously uncertain identification witness was by now sure that it was Hennis whom he had seen. A surprise witness identified Hennis as the man she had seen drawing money from a cash dispenser at a time the bank records proved Kathryn Eastburn's bank card was being used. The defence countered with evidence that no traces of blood had been found on Hennis or on any of his clothing, and that his shoe size did not fit a footprint left in blood at the scene of the murders.

On Friday 4 July, after a deliberation lasting almost two

days, the jury found Timothy Hennis guilty on three counts of first-degree murder and one of first-degree rape. On 7 July following a penalty hearing, the jury fixed his penalty as death. Offered a choice of the gas chamber or lethal injection, Hennis chose the latter.

Timothy Hennis appealed against his conviction, and on 6 October 1988, the North Carolina State Supreme Court ordered a new trial, ruling that the 'grotesque and macabre' photographs shown to the jury had precluded a fair trial.

The re-trial was moved to Wilmington because of the adverse pre-trial publicity. At this second hearing the atmosphere was very different, and the identification witnesses less sure in their evidence. On 20 April 1989, the jury quickly returned a unanimous verdict of not guilty on all counts and Hennis was freed. Members of the jury speaking after the verdict said they came to a quick decision because they felt the state's case was weak. The lack of physical evidence linking Hennis to the murders and the frailty of the identification testimony had been their main consideration.

ESCUDERO, Hector, *et al.*   Labour disputes in America seem to have a history of provoking mass murder, and none worse than that which devastated the casino of the luxury Dupont Plaza Hotel in San Juan, Puerto Rico, on New Year's Eve 1986. The Teamsters' union planned to call a strike of its members to start at midnight, and earlier in the day an anonymous warning had been issued that guests should leave the hotel because a bomb was set to detonate. At midnight the ballroom and casino exploded in a sheet of flame, and the twenty-two-storey hotel was devastated. Firefighters succeeded in putting out the blaze, and when investigators entered the ballroom and casino area they found bodies piled on top of other bodies. Investigator Jose Luis Baaz reported that some corpses were 'plastered in an upright position against the walls. The piano in the corner of the room was completely charred and the pianist was seated by the instrument with his fingers in position, extended as though he were still playing. Other victims were seated like museum figures at tables, some with teeth hanging out and missing limbs. You could just see raw flesh and bones. Skulls were without flesh on them.' The death toll was ninety-seven. Forensic experts finally established that the fire had been started with a tin of cooking fuel.

Police and federal investigators arrested three former employees of the hotel, Hector Escudero, a maintenance worker aged thirty-five, and two former bar boys, Jose Rivera, aged forty and Armando Jiminez, aged twenty-eight, and charged them with murder and arson.

On 23 June 1987, the three men appeared first in a federal court, where Escudero received two concurrent sentences of ninety-nine years' jail for arson and the murder of Manuel de Jesus Marrero, an American secret service agent who had been in the casino checking for counterfeit currency. Rivera was jailed for ninety-nine years and Jiminez got seventy-five years for arson. A local court later sentenced Rivera to twenty-five years' jail on each of ninety-six second-degree murder charges plus eighteen years for arson, and Jiminez got twenty-four years on each charge.

ESSEX, Mark James Robert Twenty-four-year-old Mark Essex grew up in Emporia, Kansas, the son of hardworking parents. His early years were happy, and he graduated from high school, then tried college life before returning home to work in the local factory where his father was employed. In January 1969, Essex joined the navy and for the first few months everything appeared to go well. Then he began to change, becoming withdrawn because he felt that, as a black man, he was being discriminated against. He became a rebel, trying to organize his fellow black ratings to demand equal treatment and was disciplined several times. In early 1970, Mark Essex deserted and went home to his family in Emporia. They persuaded him to return to his posting, where he was court-martialled and discharged from the service. In August 1972, Essex left Emporia and travelled to New Orleans, where he became involved with various black militant groups. It was during this period that he received training in urban guerrilla warfare and started collecting a wide variety of firearms, including a Ruger carbine, a revolver and a large quantity of ammunition.

On New Year's Day 1973, a police cadet reporting for duty at headquarters was shot at and took cover. From his hiding place he saw another cadet, Alfred Harrell, collapse to the ground with a massive chest wound, from which he died within minutes. There was no sign of the gunman. Twenty minutes later two policemen, officers Harold Blappert and Edwin Hosli, were called to the scene of a burglary at a nearby warehouse, and waited there for the keyholder. After he arrived they were walking over to the building when a shot rang out, hitting Hosli in the chest. Two shots were then fired at Blappert, who took cover and called for reinforcements, but by the time they got there, there was no sign of the sniper and Hosli was dead. A search of the neighbourhood revealed nothing significant – only signs that the sniper, later identified as Mark Essex, had spent the night hiding in a church.

No further attacks were reported until the morning of Sunday 7 January, when Essex shot a grocer and escaped after commandeering a car. He drove to the Howard Johnson's Downtowner Motor Lodge, a motel on Loyola Avenue. Inside the building he came upon a honeymoon couple, Dr Richard Steagle and his wife Virginia. Dr Steagle confronted Essex who shot him during a struggle, after which he killed Mrs Steagle as she knelt hysterically by her dying husband's side. Before leaving Essex set fire to their room. He then went to the eleventh floor, where he met a coloured maid. Before setting another fire he said to the girl, 'This is a revolution. I'm only shooting whites. No blacks.' When the elevator doors opened and two motel employees stepped out, Essex shot and killed one of them. More fires were started by Essex before he encountered the motel's assistant manager, Walter Collins, who was trying to get guests out of the burning building. Essex shot Collins in the back.

Mark Essex now began to shoot at people in the street. He killed policeman Philip Coleman and wounded three other officers. As the fires spread, Essex made his way to the sixteenth floor and shot another officer, Paul Persigo, in the face. By 1 p.m., the fires had taken a strong hold but Essex nevertheless climbed to the seventeenth floor to set two more fires. At the same time a police assault team led by Deputy Superintendent Louis Sirgo made their way up the stairwell to the sixteenth floor where Essex was lying in wait for them. He shot Sirgo in the back.

The fires now forced Essex up to the roof of the building where he took cover. The police assault team stormed on to the roof but were forced back when Essex shot one of the officers in the stomach. Essex was now in a concrete cubicle on the roof and police marksmen directed a fusillade of gunfire at his hiding place. He could be heard shouting 'Come out and fight like a black man' and 'Power to the people'. The siege continued all day until 8.50 p.m. when, with a police helicopter hovering over the building, Essex charged out of hiding, shooting and shouting 'Come and get me'. Immediately the marksmen opened fire with a barrage that cut Essex down killing him instantly. The police kept up their fire, pouring shot after shot into his dead body. The police examination revealed that Essex had only two bullets left so his final assault had been an almost ritual suicide. Over a thirty-hour period the total death toll was ten, with another seventeen wounded.

F

FABRIKANT, Valery Professor Valery Fabrikant was a
disgruntled man. A specialist in mechanical engineering, he
had emigrated from what was the Soviet Union in 1979
and was currently on the staff of Concordia University,
Montreal. For reasons either real or imaginary, Professor
Fabrikant was convinced that his academic colleagues were
exploiting students and researchers by adding their own
names to scientific papers in which they had played no
material role. Professor Fabrikant had already taken out
lawsuits against two staff members, in which he insisted
both men withdraw their names from upwards of thirty
published papers and make a public admission that they
had made no contribution to them. The two accused
responded with counter lawsuits of their own. A storm,
indeed, was brewing over the groves of Academe.

Valery Fabrikant next made use of some truly twentieth-
century wizardry – a system of transmitting information
internationally through a computer network accessed by
most universities around the world. The professor's exposé
began: 'Dear Colleague, the events I will tell you about are
so outrageous that you will have to see it to believe it . . .';
he concluded: 'I have little time left, because on 25 August I
will be in jail for contempt of court and must do the mailing
fast . . . I cannot fight the battle without your help. Speak
up.' Far from arousing moral outrage on his behalf,
Fabrikant's electronic campaign, supported by copious
bundles of printed documentation, was greeted either with
knowing winks and taps on the forehead, or irritation. Thus

did the sword become mightier than the pen – or in this case the gun became mightier than the word processor.

On 24 August 1992 Professor Valery Fabrikant took a gun with him to the ninth floor of Concordia University where he opened fire on his colleagues; not, it should be added, with any great attention to target selection. Fabrikant killed three people and wounded two others, including a woman, and took a couple of hostages. One student later recalled: 'We were in my teacher's office talking, then we heard noises. I looked out and saw this man walking; my teacher said he had a gun.' When the final reckoning was made, when the hostages had been released and Professor Fabrikant taken into custody, it was revealed that of the five victims only one was even mentioned on his list of 'miscreants', and the two men who were the targets of his greatest venom (and lawsuits) were not harmed.

At his trial he was convicted on three counts of murder and sentenced to life imprisonment with a non-parole period of twenty-five years.

FERGUSON, Colin It was 5.33 on the evening of 7 December 1993; rush hour on the busy Long Island commuter rail system – the largest in the country. Nobody had paid much attention to the rather bulky black man who had boarded the express train at New York's Pennsylvania station carrying a paper bag; not until the train was just outside Garden City station, when the man later identified as thirty-five-year-old Colin Ferguson opened his paper bag and pulled out a Ruger 9mm semi-automatic handgun and opened fire, apparently randomly, on his fellow passengers. Ferguson walked up and down the third carriage of the train shooting and reloading as he went; screaming passengers in total panic tried desperately to escape – by crawling from that carriage to the next, or throwing themselves under seats; some simply knelt and prayed. Finally the gunman was overpowered by three passengers who wrestled him to the floor and snatched away the gun. In a spree which had lasted just over three minutes, four people lay dead, nineteen suffered bullet wounds, one of whom died later, and two passengers suffered crush injuries. A survivor later told journalists:

> I heard 'Pop, pop, pop!' My first thought was that someone outside the train was shooting . . . then I glanced up, and out of the corner of my eye I could see someone making a slow back and forth motion with his hand. That's when I realized there was actually someone in the train shooting people. I just crashed to the ground. I ducked down behind a partition. I didn't want to make eye-contact with him. He was standing at the door at the end of the carriage and was shooting. He was holding the gun waist-high – it looked as if he had both hands on it. He was shooting people point-blank. When he finally stopped, I ran the length of the car to the opposite end. People piled on top of each other trying to get to the door. Then he went into another round of shooting.

Although the killings had at first seemed random, it was observed later that Ferguson had only shot white or Asian people, no blacks; it was a fact that would prove significant in the light of what was later learned of Colin Ferguson's possible motive for such gratuitous violence. Notes found in Ferguson's pockets after his arrest, and others recovered from his Brooklyn bedsit revealed that he had nurtured an irrational hatred of white people, 'rich Chinese' and 'Uncle Tom Negroes and rich black attorneys'.

Colin Ferguson was born in Kingston, Jamaica, in 1958, and following the sudden death of his parents he emigrated to the United States. He married, but was divorced by his wife in 1988, a blow from which, according to friends, he never recovered. Subsequently bad grades forced him to quit New York's Adelphi University. Although Ferguson had never been arrested or had a record of mental illness, his oddball racial prejudices were well known. His landlord recalled Ferguson telling him: 'I shouldn't be living here; I should be living in a mansion.' Apparently he was convinced that the only thing holding him back from his rightful position at the top was white people. Not that he had much time for those blacks whom he considered 'non-militant', and after he had been mugged by two black men, Ferguson took to carrying a gun around in a paper bag. Things went from bad to worse; after an injury at work he was refused compensation, then his landlord asked him to vacate his room because he was sick of Ferguson taking five baths a day and keeping all the other residents in the building awake at night by chanting mantras about 'all the black people killing all the white people'. Ferguson thought he had suffered enough . . . next day he shot up the Long Island commuter express.

Colin Ferguson has been charged with four counts of murder in which it was said that he behaved with 'depraved indifference to life'. One of the prime exhibits at his forthcoming trial is certain to be the scrap of paper found in his pocket. Scribbled at the top is 'Reasons for this', followed by 'The sloppy running of the #2 train. It is racism by Caucasians and Uncle Tom Negroes. Also. The false allegations against me by the filthy Caucasian Racist female on the HI line.' This last reference was to an earlier incident when a woman complained to the police that Ferguson had harassed her on the subway. However, other observers have commented that far from being a victim of racism, Colin Ferguson is a 'paranoid madman'. The question of his sanity was not raised at the trial due to his intransigence.

On 17 February 1995, Ferguson was found guilty of six counts of first-degree murder, after a trial in which he refused to allow his lawyers to put forward a defence of insanity and took over his own case. The following month, he was sentenced to six consecutive terms of twenty-five years imprisonment. The judge said that this was to ensure he was never released.

FINCH, James, and **STUART, John** On 17 February 1988, James Finch flew home to Britain from Australia after being deported as part of his parole conditions from a life sentence imposed in 1973.

Finch and John Stuart had been convicted of manslaughter after being found responsible for a fire-bomb attack on the Whiskey-Au-Go-Go in Brisbane in which fifteen night-club patrons died. The prosecution alleged that Finch had been brought over from England to run a protection racket around the clubs, and that the two men had first bolted the Whiskey-Au-Go-Go's windows in order to prevent anybody escaping. Then two drums of petrol were thrown into the foyer and ignited with a petrol bomb. Grease had been smeared on a fence around the club making it harder for anybody to climb out to safety, and apart from the fatalities, many of the one hundred people in the club were dreadfully burned. Finch and Stuart insisted that the police had framed them, but were convicted of manslaughter and jailed for life.

John Stuart went on a hunger strike while he was in prison and successfully starved himself to death. Finch swallowed nails, safety pins and wire for the purpose of drawing attention to his campaign to be released. He too went on a hunger strike for thirty-five days and bit off half the little finger of his right hand.

On his arrival back in England, James Finch was still protesting his innocence, saying he was delighted to be home, but there would be no celebrations until he had cleared his name. However, in October 1988, a Brisbane newspaper printed a claim that Finch had admitted his part in fire-bombing the club, boasting: 'Fifteen years is cheap. I only hope the mothers, fathers, children and friends of those fifteen can forgive me.'

FORD, Priscilla   The fact that it was Thanksgiving Day, 1980, in Reno, Nevada, made no difference to the gamblers hurrying down the glitzy Casino Row on their way to see if Dame Fortune was about to smile on them. But for six people that day luck was well out.

The crowds thronging the sidewalk on North Virginia Street were suddenly shattered by a large black car smashing through them. Bodies flew in all directions – a passing police officer saw two people picked up by the impact and carried on the bonnet of the car before being thrown off into the street. The vehicle continued on its way crushing pedestrians and hurling them into the air. The first report to the authorities described the scene as being like a battlefield – severed limbs, dental plates and wigs lay scattered among the bodies. The car continued on its bloody way, striking another passer-by and flinging him into the air.

Tom Jaffe, a passing motorist, saw this latest killing and identified the car as a 1974 Lincoln and the driver as a black woman. Jaffe went in pursuit of the Lincoln and saw that the woman driver was staring straight ahead and seemed almost oblivious of everything around her. Jaffe accelerated and got in front of the Lincoln before pulling over and forcing it to stop. A patrolman who witnessed the incident drove up and took the woman into custody.

Back at the scene of the earlier carnage it had been established that six people were dead and twenty were injured, some seriously.

At the medical centre, the woman driving the car was asked for her name and she replied: 'Priscilla Joyce Ford. Sometimes I am called Jesus Christ.'

In accordance with the law, blood samples were taken from Priscilla Ford, who told the arresting officer:

'I'm a New York teacher, tired of life. I want attention. I'm sick of trouble. I deliberately planned to get as many as possible. A Lincoln Continental can do a lot of damage, can't it? In June I was in Boston. A voice told me to drive through a crowd at a theatre and kill as many as possible but another voice said she's too much of a lady to do that. I had wine today to blame it specifically on the accident. The more dead the better. That will keep the mortuaries busy. That's the American way. Did I get fifty? How many did I get? I hope I got seventy-five.'

The blood sample taken from Ford indicated that she was well above the Nevada level of intoxication; medical examination did not indicate any organic problems. Priscilla

Ford was held in custody on six charges of first-degree murder and twenty-three counts of attempted murder.

At her trial which commenced in October 1981, Priscilla Ford pleaded not guilty by reason of insanity. Giving evidence on her own behalf, Ford disagreed with the specialist's diagnosis of schizophrenia. She said she had no memory of running anyone down . . . the car must have gone out of control. After a thirteen-hour retirement the jury returned verdicts of guilty on all counts. At a separate penalty hearing the jury fixed her penalty as death.

FORD, William S. A fire broke out in the three-storey house at 9417 Nineteenth Avenue, Bensonhurst, Brooklyn, in the early hours of Monday 15 October 1923. The wood-frame house had been turned into separate apartments on the three floors, and the flames spread rapidly through the building. In spite of the efforts of the New York fire brigade who rushed to the scene, the house was gutted and six people died. Firefighters fought heroically to rescue survivors from the building and carried the bodies of the six who had perished to the street outside.

The dead were two boarders, George Keim and Francis P. Fowler; the seventeen-year-old son Charles, the daughter Marjorie, aged twelve, and the sister-in-law of the owner Lilian Andrews; and a maid Rosina Weishert. Investigations led by the New York Fire Department soon found evidence of traces of gasoline in the charred remains of the building and the fire was officially classified as arson.

Police concentrated their enquiries on the background of those in the building at the time of the blaze, since the indications were that the fire was not the work of an irrational pyromaniac but, rather, of someone with a specific victim in mind and little regard as to who else died as a result. There seemed to be no evidence that anyone had a grudge against the Andrews family or Francis Fowler, so investigations centred on George Keim. Although at first nothing irregular was discovered in Mr Keim's past, as enquiries progressed, witnesses began to speak of trouble between Keim and his son-in-law William S. Ford. At one time Keim and Ford had been in business together, but the partnership had been dissolved by George Keim because, so he claimed, Ford's fondness for drink led to him neglecting the business.

Investigators also received a tip-off that a Brooklyn youth named Arthur Jones knew something about the fire, and he was detained for questioning. During the interrogation Jones confessed that he and another man had driven William Ford to the house at Bensonhurst where he had poured petrol around the front and set it alight. Ford was taken into custody and later charged with murder and arson.

William S. Ford faced trial in March 1924, where his main defence was that Jones' testimony was uncorroborated and besides, he had been an accomplice. Despite these protestations the jury found Ford guilty after a retirement of less than an hour, and he was sentenced to die in the electric chair.

While awaiting execution in Sing Sing Prison, William Ford committed suicide by hanging himself in his cell.

FOUNTAIN TRAIN EXPLOSION   In the early hours of 14 May 1888, the Kansas City Express stopped at the village of Fountain, Colorado to take on water. A few miles away a freight train had also stopped, in this case to unload some horses which were in transit. While the conductor and brakeman were dealing with the horses they discovered to their surprise and dismay that the caboose and four cars had become detached from the train and were no longer in sight. One of the cars contained two passengers, one of them a one-legged man, and two of the freight cars were loaded with the inflammable oil naphtha and an explosive known as Giant's powder. Fearful of what could happen if the cars crashed at Fountain, the conductor tried, unsuccessfully, to contact the village on the dispatcher's telegraph wire.

The railwaymen decided to reverse what was left of the train back to Fountain but had only moved a short distance when they heard and were rocked by an explosion the force of which was felt in far distant towns. There had been no warning to the crew of the Kansas City Express still standing in Fountain. When the five lethal wagons smashed into the stationary train, the naphtha spilt from the freight car and caught fire in the heat from the express engine. The express train staff managed to avert a much greater loss of life by courageously unhooking the three passenger cars from the express and rolling them away from the flames.

Residents of Fountain were naturally awoken from their beds by the noise of the crash and rushed to the scene. Attempts were made to put out the fire, but it had taken such a hold that, after burning for half an hour, the flames reached the powder car which erupted in a tremendous explosion. The force blew apart large parts of both trains and totally devastated the village; the blast left a crater almost forty feet in diameter and fifteen feet deep.

Amazingly the loss of life was limited to four people, three local residents – Charles Smith, Henry Hutchins and Mrs Sarah Widrig, who had all come to the scene to help – and the one-legged passenger on the freight train whose identity at that stage was not known. However, at the subsequent inquest he was identified as Frank Shipman who had been travelling to visit his brother in Pueblo. The coroner's jury returned a verdict of death in an explosion, but was unable to give any indication as to where to lay the blame for the deaths.

It was an investigation instigated by a Colorado newspaper, *The Rocky Mountain News*, that established there had been a third passenger on the train who had had violent arguments with Frank Shipman, and that this third passenger had needed to be physically restrained from attacking the one-legged man. Following this revelation, Shipman's body was exhumed and it was discovered that he had suffered a skull wound apparently from a blunt instrument. A description of the third passenger, who it was believed had murdered Shipman and then released the cars in the hope of covering up the killing, was issued but despite various vague sightings nobody was ever apprehended for the crime.

FRANKUM, Wade The massacre began on the Saturday afternoon of 17 August 1991, at the Coffee Pot restaurant in Sydney's crowded Strathfield Plaza. Fifteen-year-old Roberta Armstrong and her schoolfriend, Katherine File, had been cheerfully chatting over soft drinks when they became aware of the unwelcome attention being paid to them by the man sitting in the next booth, his eyes fixed, unblinking, on them. Suddenly the stranger drew out a long-bladed knife and lunged at Roberta, slashing into her back. As Katherine began to scream, so the attacker began to laugh, at the same time pulling an SKS self-loading assault rifle seemingly from nowhere and firing wildly. The restaurant's manager was shot through the head and terrified diners threw themselves under anything that might offer cover. Then, as suddenly as it had started, the shooting stopped, and the madman with the gun walked with uncanny calm out of the Coffee Pot and up to the roof-top car park, shooting a bystander on the escalator as he passed.

Catherine Noyes was sitting in her car when the man levelled his gun at her head. She had already watched horrified as he had sent five bullets ripping into another car and was in no mind to argue when the gunman climbed in beside her and told her to drive. They reached the bottom of the ramps just as the first police cars, sirens screaming, arrived at the Plaza. As he jumped from the vehicle, the man turned to the driver and said simply: 'I'm really sorry'; he dropped down on one knee, put the rifle barrel beneath his chin and pulled the trigger. So ended thirty-three-year-old Wade Frankum's murderous spree during which, in just ten minutes, he left eight people dead and dozens injured.

At the inquest into the killings, on 22 November 1991, forensic psychiatrist Dr Rod Milton told the coroner: 'Frankum led a troubled and lonely life, full of simmering emotional and sexual frustration which finally exploded in an outpouring of rage.' Whether or not Dr Milton's claim that Wade Frankum's final spree was triggered by his 'well-thumbed' copy of the controversial novel *American Psycho*, by Bret Easton Ellis can be taken at face value, or whether, more realistically, it must be assumed that Frankum would have exploded into violence sooner or later books or not, is a hotly debated issue. However, there was no debating Dr Milton's final chilling words to the court: 'Guns make people like Frankum feel more powerful. If you want to have semi-automatic weapons you will have more killings; it's a simple equation.' The point was taken up by the New South Wales coroner, Mr Kevin Walker, as he summed up the seven-day hearing. Mr Walker expressed his alarm to learn that as many as 150,000 SKS semi-automatic rifles, identical to Wade Frankum's, were owned in Australia. He did, however, emphasise that as eighty per cent of murders were committed by people who were neither habitual criminals nor psychopaths, there would be little advantage in a system of psychological screening of applicants for gun licences.

G

GANG LU At about 3.40 on the chilly afternoon of 1 November 1991, a man wielding a .38-calibre revolver walked purposefully up to a group of professors and students in the University of Iowa's physics department. With a frightening calmness and detachment he shot four men dead. The assassin then ran to the main administration building where he critically wounded the assistant vice-president and her assistant. When armed campus police arrived on the scene and combed the administration building they found the gunman lying dead, a bullet in his brain fired by his own hand; beside the body lay the murder weapon, and in the killer's pocket was an unfired .22 handgun.

When the initial shock had passed, the killer was identified as a Chinese graduate student named Gang Lu. He was a doctoral candidate in physics, and apparently a brilliant scholar in the field of theoretical space physics. Unfortunately for him – and even more unfortunately for his victims – Gang Lu had not been quite brilliant enough to secure a coveted cash prize for his academic dissertation.

The four male victims were by no means random targets, but specially singled out as recipients of Gang Lu's revenge against the grove of Academe. The first victim had been the chairman of the Physics and Astronomy Department to which Gang Lu had been attached, then a professor in the same department fell dead from a bullet in the chest, and then a researcher. The fourth victim was a fellow graduate from the People's Republic of China, Linhua Shan. Shan's crime had been to win the $1,000 prize which his killer believed was rightly his.

By the following morning one of the two critically injured women had died at the university hospital, and a little more information had emerged about the murderous Gang Lu. It transpired that although rejection for the prize may have triggered his rampage, this was not Lu's only grievance. A whole catalogue of malcontent was revealed by a series of letters, some in English, one in Chinese, addressed to various international news agencies which Lu had entrusted to colleagues to post in the event of his death. Not only did the correspondence discuss plans for the shooting of those already dead, but it also contained a list of other names on Gang Lu's death list.

GARCIA, Joseph William Watkins, a thirty-seven-year-old farm labourer, lived with his wife Elizabeth and three of their five children in a farm cottage on the outskirts of the village of Llangibby, a few miles from Newport in Monmouthshire.

On the morning of Wednesday 16 July 1878, a boy who worked on the farm where Watkins was employed went to the cottage to find out why he had not turned up for work that morning. The lad was horrified when he walked through the front gate to find the bodies of Watkins and his wife sprawled on the garden path outside the cottage. The boy ran to fetch help, and neighbours heeding his cry saw that Elizabeth Watkins had been repeatedly stabbed in the chest and that her throat had been cut. Her husband had been battered about the head and also repeatedly stabbed in the chest and throat. The neighbours now noticed smoke pouring from an upstairs window of the cottage, and going inside they found the place smashed and ransacked. Upstairs in two of the bedrooms, four-year-old Alice Watkins lay dead from knife wounds to the chest and shoulders, six-year-old Frederick had his throat cut, and eight-year-old Charlotte had been repeatedly stabbed. The bodies of all three children had been slashed with a knife and in the cases of Alice and Frederick, their lower limbs were badly burned. It seemed clear that the murderer had attempted to conceal evidence of his crime by setting fire to their beds.

An alarm was raised and it was recalled that a man described as a 'foreigner' had been seen hanging around Llangibby the previous day. A mail-cart driver reported that he had been asked for a lift into Newport by this rough-looking man. The stranger was next sighted at the railway station. Police officers rushed to the station where they found the suspect and noticed that he had scratches on his face and hands. When he was arrested the man gave his name as Joseph Garcia, said he was twenty-one years old and that he had been released from Usk prison the previous day after serving a sentence for housebreaking. Parts of his clothing were wet as if they had been recently washed, and traces of what could have been bloodstains were found. In Garcia's possession were a knife, a pair of boots and other items which were later identified as having belonged to the Watkins family. Joseph Garcia was charged with murder and later committed for trial at the Monmouth Assizes.

When he stood trial before Baron Pollock, the judge agreed to a defence application to transfer the trial to Gloucester Assizes, in view of the strong local feeling against Garcia. It made little difference to the outcome. At Gloucester Assizes on 28 October 1878, Joseph Garcia was found guilty of murder and sentenced to death; he was executed at Usk Prison on 18 November 1878.

GARGANTUA NIGHTCLUB KILLINGS   The Gargantua, a sleazy haunt of Montreal's underworld, was the scene of a double murder on 30 October 1974, when Roger Levesque and Raymond Laurin were shot down by armed gunmen. This double killing was to culminate in even greater bloodshed at the Gargantua.

Soon after midnight on 21 January 1975, a fire was reported at the club. The fire service was called out and before the blaze was brought under control, the building was gutted. When firefighters were checking the scene they discovered a padlocked refrigerated storeroom which had a jukebox pushed hard up against the door. Removing this obstacle and breaking down the door, investigators found the bodies of thirteen people, four later identified as employees, the others presumed to be customers. One man, Rejean Fortin, the manager of the club, had been shot, while the other twelve had died of asphyxiation. Fire experts were able to confirm that gasoline or some other type of accelerant had been sprayed around the club before it was set alight.

The death toll was the worst Montreal had seen in a single incident since September 1972, when thirty-seven people died and fifty-three were injured when three would-be customers threw Molotov cocktails into the Bluebird Cafe after being refused entry. Two men, James O'Brien and Jean-Marc Boutin were jailed for life after pleading guilty to murder, and Giles Eccles received a similar term after pleading guilty to manslaughter.

In the case of the Gargantua fire, police named Richard Blass as their prime suspect and a coroner's warrant for his arrest was issued. Blass, who had escaped from prison a week before the shootings while serving a sentence for armed robbery, was popularly known as 'The Cat' and was considered to be one of Canada's most dangerous criminals.

Detectives believed Blass had wanted to silence two people at the club who knew of his involvement in major crimes, and that the others were killed simply to eliminate all witnesses.

A major manhunt was launched and Richard Blass was traced to a mountain-top cottage near Val David. During a twenty-man police raid on 24 January, he was shot twenty-five times by two police sergeants with 9mm sub-machine guns, who later claimed that when they broke into the cottage Blass had a revolver in his hand and therefore they had to shoot to kill.

At a subsequent inquest on the Gargantua victims, witnesses accused Blass and one of his associates of being responsible for the killings, though there was never enough evidence to bring the second man to trial.

GIBSON, Monk, and **POWELL, Felix** In September 1905, a white family comprising J. F. Conditt, his wife and their five children moved on to a small farm in the predominantly black district of Edna, Texas. Conditt appeared to alienate the locals not only by moving into the area, but by refusing to allow them to continue to use a water supply on his farm.

On 28 September, Monk Gibson and a friend, Felix Powell, were employed by Conditt to do some work around the farm during the rice harvest. Powell made sexual advances to Conditt's eldest daughter, twelve-year-old Mildred, and was not unnaturally rebuffed. Not long after, both Gibson and Powell returned to the farm where they raped Mildred and killed Mrs Lora Conditt and four of the children, Mildred, Herschell, aged ten, Jesse (six) and little Joseph (three), with an axe and a knife. For some reason they spared the ten-month-old baby Lloyd.

At around noon on the same day, Gibson reported to neighbours that the Conditt family had been killed by two black men. The sheriff was called and started by questioning Gibson himself, who was evasive in his replies and unable to explain bloodstains found on his hands and clothes. Gibson and Powell were arrested and taken to the local jail, but because a lynch mob was forming, it was decided to move them. While the prisoners were being transferred Gibson escaped, and the Texas Rangers, accompanied by bloodhounds, started a manhunt. Gibson surrendered to the authorities on 5 October, and on 9 October Powell was indicted by the Jackson County grand jury for murder, and Gibson for being an accessory.

Felix Powell and Monk Gibson were tried separately. Powell was tried first, convicted, sentenced to death and hanged on 2 April 1907. Gibson's attorney asked for a change of venue in view of the unlikelihood of being able to find an impartial jury in Jackson County. Eventually, Gibson's trial was held in San Antonio where evidence was given that as a child he had attempted to hang a young girl. The hearing resulted in a mistrial, apparently because the judge had difficulty in apportioning guilt between

Gibson and Powell. A second trial was held, with another change of venue, this time to DeWitt County, and on this occasion the jury returned a verdict of guilty and Gibson, like his partner, was sentenced to hang.

The Texas Court of Appeal confirmed the sentence and conviction on 22 April 1908. Among the grounds of appeal was Gibson's claim that he was only sixteen at the time of the murders, and as a result he was not eligible for the death penalty under Texas law. The court stated that since he was born in September 1888, it made him just over seventeen at the time, and in any event this issue had previously been raised at the trial and the jury had still decided on a capital sentence.

Gibson was publicly hanged at Cuero in DeWitt County, watched by a gathering of around 2,500 people including 500 who had travelled from Edna by a special train. Gibson, aged nineteen at the time of his execution, maintained his innocence to the end.

GILL, Colin   On 22 April 1986, Colin Gill, his wife and their four children were found shot to death in their home at Redruth. Gill, who ran a private detective agency after serving twelve years in the Devon and Cornwall Police was believed to have gone berserk and shot his family before killing himself. A shotgun was found in the house and used cartridge cases were found in the rooms where the victims were lying.

An inquest at Redruth on 20 August heard that thirty-eight-year-old Mrs Linda Gill had been having an affair with a young man of twenty-one. She had returned home from a rendezvous with her lover to find her husband waiting for her. The police reconstruction of the killings was that Gill had shot his wife and then gone upstairs and shot seventeen-year-old Stephen and fourteen-year-old Robert, Mrs Gill's sons by her first marriage, and then killed their own two children David, aged nine, and two-year-old Dorian. After this Gill had returned downstairs, fired two more shots into his wife's body, and after waiting around for an hour put the barrel of the shotgun into his own mouth and pulled the trigger. A pathologist's report described all six victims as having 'horrific head wounds' resulting from shots at point-blank range.

Evidence was presented to the coroner that Colin and Linda Gill had recently been discussing separation and that on the day before the killings Gill had seemed very troubled and had been drinking heavily. The coroner returned a verdict that Mrs Gill and her sons had been unlawfully killed and that Colin Gill took his own life.

GONZALES, Francisco P.   Beset by financial and marital problems, twenty-seven-year-old Gonzales, a warehouse worker in Reno, Nevada, determined on a spectacular suicide in which he would not go alone. He had regularly threatened to kill himself to his friends and family, but without disclosing his final plan. On the evening of 6 May 1964, Gonzales purchased a Smith & Wesson revolver and the following morning went to Reno airport. On his arrival he first bought $100,000 worth of life insurance and then a ticket on Pacific Air Lines flight 773 to San Francisco.

Once the plane was airborne Gonzales produced the gun and forced his way into the cockpit where he shot the pilot, fifty-two-year-old Ernest Clark, and the first officer, Ray Andress, in the back. A nearby airport picked up a final stark message over the radio: 'Skipper's shot. We've been shot. Trying to help.' Another plane in the area at the time reported seeing a black cloud of smoke which looked like an oil or gasoline fire.

The plane crashed into a hill near San Ramon, California. All forty-four passengers and crew aboard died.

GONZALEZ, Julio   The Happy Land social club was a Mecca for the Hispanic community of the East Tremont district of New York's Bronx. Occupying the second floor of a rickety, rundown building at 1959 Southern Boulevard, the Happy Land was the proverbial 'accident waiting to happen'. The construction of the second storey had been carried out without official permission, and the owners of the club had been repeatedly warned over violations of fire regulations – not least that there was no emergency exit.

On Sunday 25 March 1990, thirty-seven-year-old Julio Gonzalez, a refugee from Cuba, dropped into the Happy Land for a few drinks with friends. On the way out he got into an exchange of angry words with a former girlfriend named Lydia Feliciano, resulting in Gonzalez being manhandled out of the club by one of the bouncers. Enraged with Lydia and humiliated by being publicly thrown out of the club, Gonzalez walked down the block and bought a dollar's worth of petrol. He returned to the Happy Land, soaked the entrance with gasoline and set fire to it. Only five people survived the resulting holocaust; ironically, one of them was Lydia Feliciano, the target of Gonzalez' crazed arson attack.

When the trial of Julio Gonzalez opened in the Bronx County Courthouse on 8 July 1991, there was never the suggestion that anybody other than Gonzalez was responsible for setting the terrible fire; in fact, he had admitted as much in three separate statements. The heated debate that took place during the six-week hearing centred on Gonzalez' culpability for the crime, because he had pleaded not guilty on grounds of 'lack of criminal responsibility because of mental disorder or defect'. In other words, a plea of insanity.

By the end of the first week, one might have been forgiven for thinking that the long-awaited trial of one of America's worst mass killers had not yet begun. Even the judge was constrained to confide to the jury: 'This is not the stuff from which television dramas are made.' Indeed it was only the flamboyant Judge Roberts' frequent jokes that kept the court even half-full. The only time the courtroom was crowded to capacity was when the fortunate Lydia Feliciano took the witness stand. Although she was there as a prosecution witness to testify that on the night of the fire, during their row, Gonzalez had told her: 'You'll see. Tomorrow you're not going to work here any more. I told you and I swear to it,' Ms Feliciano was rated by many as only marginally less guilty than the defendant himself. The reason for this was that it was alleged that as soon as she became aware of the fire, instead of raising the alarm she called herself a cab and disappeared into the night. It is only fair to add that according to her own recollection, Lydia Feliciano shouted 'Fire' before she left.

Then the series of psychiatric specialists appearing for the defence presented their opinions as to Julio Gonzalez' sanity, and it soon became clear that the matter pivoted on alleged brain damage suffered by Gonzalez during childhood, in a fall from a bicycle, aggravated by the severe beatings he claimed he was given when he was imprisoned for deserting from the Cuban army. The prosecution then exercised its right to refute the defence's medical evidence, and Dr Jose Valciukis entertained the court with allegations that according to Gonzalez' own words, he and a fellow-employee had once planned to burn down the factory where they worked after a disagreement with their boss. Then a Dr Berger laid the foundation of any prosecution's refutation of a diminished responsibility plea – the fact that the arson attack was *premeditated*. He reminded the jury of the fact that Gonzalez had been specific in asking the garage for just one dollar's worth of petrol, because it was all the money he had on him; and when the pump attendant was reluctant to sell him such a small amount, Gonzalez invented a car which had just run out of gas. Dr Berger also pointed out that if Gonzalez was being instructed by 'voices', as he claimed to be, then they were very sensible voices, because by his own admission Julio Gonzalez had waited outside the Happy Land until a trickle of patrons who were leaving had got out of sight.

It was on the afternoon of Monday 19 August 1991 that the foreman of the jury, after three days of deliberation, rose to deliver their unanimous verdicts – guilty on all 176 counts. Eighty-seven counts of second-degree murder (one for each victim) resulting from depraved indifference to the lives of other people; eighty-seven counts of felony murder, where death results from the commission of another felony (in this case arson); one count of first-degree arson, which involved causing serious injury or death; and one count of assault, which was the injury sustained by the club's disc jockey who survived the fire. At a separate hearing on 19 September, Julio Gonzalez was given the maximum sentence possible under state law, twenty-five years to life.

GRAHAM, Eric Stanley George   Graham, known locally as 'Stan' Graham, was a farmer at Koiterangi on New Zealand's South Island. He was a cantankerous man forever quarrelling with his neighbours over unfounded suspicions that they were poisoning his cattle and generally attempting to do him down.

On the morning of 8 October 1941, a farmer named Anker Madsen was threatened by Graham with a rifle as he cycled past his farm. Madsen reported this incident to the local policeman, Constable Best who, knowing Graham's reputation as a crack shot of unreliable temperament, realized the potential danger. The constable went out to the farm where he found Stan Graham, still waving the gun around, still raging about his spiteful neighbours. Best thought it wise to leave and drove over to Hokitika police station where it was decided that he and Sergeant Cooper, both armed, together with Constables Jordan and Tulloch would see Graham and attempt to calm him down. By the time they got back to Koiterangi, Graham appeared quite rational, so the officers then went to pay a visit to the neighbours. However, when they returned to Graham's farm they found a changed man; standing now in the doorway of his house, a rifle trained on the four men as they walked towards him. Sergeant Cooper tried to grab the gun and Graham fired, wounding the sergeant in the arm. Constables Tulloch and Jordan rushed in and Graham fired again, hitting both men with, it was believed, a single shot. Constable Best begged Graham to put his rifle down, and was shot in the hand for his trouble. Jordan groaned and as Best went to his assistance, Graham fired again and the constable fell to the ground shot in the back. Sergeant Cooper ran outside and was shot again by Graham, and a third time as Cooper collapsed. Within seconds, three of the four policemen were dead and the fourth fatally wounded.

When Constable Best asked Graham to get a doctor, the now severely disturbed farmer agreed so long as Best made a statement that it was he who had gone to the farm looking for trouble. Graham's wife, who had been in the house the whole time the shooting was going on, wrote at her husband's dictation 'I. E. M. Best intended to murder Stan Graham' and Best added a shaky signature with his left hand. Mrs Graham then went for help, which arrived in the person of a neighbour named Ridley; Ridley, with more courage than good sense, attempted to intervene, and Graham fired once again, seriously wounding him. Stan Graham then filled a haversack with food and ammunition and took to the hills up beyond the farm.

Guards were stationed around the farm. At around 7.45 p.m. Graham appeared; when challenged, he shot and fatally wounded one of the officers, Gregory Hutchinson, before being driven off by the fire of the other guards. Nearby, other police officers were shot at by Graham, who killed a man named Max Coulson as he ran for cover. Amuri King, another neighbour who had joined the siege, fired back and had the impression he had hit the gunman.

The next day, as soon as it was light, groups were organized to search the hills for Stan Graham, but by nightfall he had not been sighted, and for a second night guards were stationed around the Graham farm. The next sighting of the fugitive was at Kokatahi, three miles away, where Graham exchanged fire with guards but managed to escape. On the Saturday, Constable Best died of his wounds in hospital. On the following morning, police on guard near Koiterangi encountered Graham again and managed to get a couple of shots at him before he escaped. However, this time bloodstains were found on the ground suggesting he had been hit. On Monday another sighting, another exchange of shots; then nothing for almost a fortnight. It was not until 20 October that Stan Graham was spotted creeping along a river valley. This time he did not see his pursuers, and as Graham got closer a police constable shot him and he fell to the ground, groaning 'Don't shoot again. I'm done.' Graham was taken to Westland Hospital, severely wounded, and died during the night. His final death toll was eight, Mr Ridley dying later from his wounds.

GRAHAM, John Gilbert   At 7.03 p.m. on 1 November 1955, United Airlines flight 629 en route from Denver, Colorado, to Portland, Oregon, exploded over Longmont just eleven minutes into its journey, killing all forty-four passengers and crew.

Crash investigators sifting through the wreckage discovered the puzzling fact that only tiny fragments could be found of the luggage of one of the passengers, Mrs Daisy King. The airport insurance officer later reported that a $62,500 insurance policy had been taken out on Mrs King's life just before she boarded the plane. What was more interesting was that the beneficiary was her son Jack Graham, who had already been the subject of an investigation into alleged fraudulent insurance claims. As a consequence Graham was questioned and so was his wife, who indiscreetly volunteered the fact that Jack had put 'a present of a set of drills' into his mother's luggage. After making a half-hearted attempt at behaving like a broken-hearted son, Graham finally signed a confession that it had been a dynamite bomb which he had hidden in his mother's suitcase.

At his trial in April 1956, John Gilbert Graham presented an appearance of stubborn indifference to his fate as the evidence was painstakingly built into a solid wall around him. On 5 May 1956 the jury confirmed his guilt.

Jack Graham was executed at Colorado State Penitentiary on Friday 11 January 1957. Before he entered the gas chamber he was asked by a reporter whether he had any last words; Jack had: 'I'd like you to sit on my lap as they close the door in there.'

GRAY, David   Thirteen people died on 13 November 1990, shot by a crazed gunman in the small New Zealand village of Aramoana, seventeen miles from Dunedin in the South Island. The carnage was reminiscent of the Hungerford Massacre (see page 285).

The killings began when thirty-three-year-old David Gray set fire to a neighbour's house after a dispute. As firefighters tried to put out the blaze, Gray started shooting, driving them off and at the same time wounding two children living in the house. A local policeman who had gone to the same school as Gray tried to talk him into giving himself up and was shot dead for his trouble. Gray then turned his attention on passers-by, firing indiscriminately at local people. Among those fatally wounded were several children, Rewa Ariki Bryson and Jasmine Holden, both eleven years old, and two six-year-olds, Leo Wilson and Dion Percy, as well as Dion's parents Vanessa and Ross Percy. When he ran out of live targets, Gray loosed off a volley at the police helicopter hovering overhead, before taking refuge in his hill-top house.

The police decided to wait until daybreak before moving in, and then launched a tear-gas assault on his home. This forced Gray to make a break into the nearby hills where he was finally cornered and shot dead by armed officers. During a twenty-three-hour period David Gray had killed around one-fifth of the population of Aramoana.

GREENSBORO KILLINGS It is reasonable to expect that a mass killing in full public view, leaving five dead and four seriously injured, filmed by television reporters and where a number of the armed perpetrators were arrested leaving the scene, would amount to a watertight case for prosecution in the courts. Yet just such a scenario at Greensboro, North Carolina, on 3 November 1979, resulted in two trials and the complete acquittal of those concerned.

The cause of the bloodbath was anti-Ku Klux Klan agitation organized by the Communist Workers Party (CWP). For some years the CWP had been campaigning against the Klan and other Nazi right-wing sympathizers in North Carolina. On 3 November, the Party was leading a demonstration at a Greensboro housing project known as Morningside Homes.

At 11.21 a.m., as the demonstrators were preparing for

their march, a line of cars and trucks approached. As they neared the CWP parade, the motorists and their passengers started firing on the demonstrators, and people began to fall to the ground. A group of thugs from the invading party charged into the demonstrators wielding axes and striking out indiscriminately. Inside three minutes, bodies were strewn all over the street, some dead, others badly injured. As the attackers were leaving, police arrived and took twelve men into custody. A final assessment was that four people were dead, and a fifth died later in hospital; four others were seriously injured.

Initially, the twelve men detained were charged on four counts of murder and one of conspiracy to murder. Two more were subsequently arrested on similar charges. In early 1980, the prosecutors dropped the conspiracy charge and presented indictments of first-degree murder (five counts) and one count of felony riot to the Guilford County grand jury. True bills were returned against David Matthews, Coleman B. Pridmore, Jerry P. Smith, Wayne Wood, Lawrence Morgan, Roy C. Toney, Junior McBride, Harold D. Flowers, Billy Joe Franklin and Terry W. Hartsoe, all Klan members, and Jack Fowler, a Nazi sympathizer.

When the case came to trial, the prosecution elected to proceed first against Fowler, Smith, Pridmore and Morgan, as the four defendants most clearly identifiable on the media video of the killings. The defence pressed for Matthews and Wood to be included in this trial which, with more time-wasting, the judge eventually allowed. It took five weeks to select twelve jurors and four alternates, and the trial began on 4 August 1980. It was not until three months later that the jury was sent out to consider its verdict; they returned on 17 November, acquitting all six defendants on all counts. The charges against the untried defendants were dropped.

In April 1982, nine of the right-wing supremacists involved in the Greensboro killings were indicted on Federal charges of conspiracy to violate the civil rights of persons because of their race or religion or because they were participating in an activity. The trial began on 9 January

1984. The jury retired on 12 April and returned three days later with a clutch of not guilty verdicts.

The only crumb of comfort that may be drawn from an otherwise grossly unsatisfactory series of trials is that later, civil actions brought by dependants of those who died in the killings, and the injured, resulted in awards being made against the City of Greensboro and several of the defendants and those arrested but untried.

GUAY, Albert The scene being played out at Quebec airport on that afternoon of 9 September 1949 was a mirror of scenes being enacted in airport departure lounges the world over. Albert Guay was saying an affectionate farewell to his wife Rita as she boarded the Canadian Pacific Airlines Dakota on its scheduled flight to Baie Comeau; with them was Guay's five-year-old daughter. They gave a final goodbye wave, turned and left the building. Here the similarity with any other 'bon voyage' scenario ended.

The aircraft had been in flight for little more than five minutes before a huge explosion blew it out of the sky over dense woodland near Sault-au-Cochon, killing every one of the twenty-three passengers and crew. It happened so soon after take-off that most of the relatives of passengers were still in the airport surroundings and rushed back to receive any news of loved ones; they included Albert Guay, apparently so beside himself with grief that a family took pity on him and drove him and his daughter to a hotel.

The crash investigation team at the site were examining the luggage area of the shattered hulk when they found a patch where burned and melted metal indicated exposure to intense heat. This was clearly the most likely seat of the explosion, and subsequent chemical analysis revealed evidence of dynamite. In major disasters such as this every single piece of information, every tangible clue must be gathered and examined and correlated with every other clue, every other piece of information. Which is how investigators got to hear of Marie Pitre. A check of the baggage list detailed the item: 'Crate: containing religious statuary'. The puzzle was that, although the crate was definitely signed on board, and fragments of the container were found, there were no statues or pieces of statues anywhere amid the wreckage.

With the sort of luck such inquiries need, the police managed to trace a taxi-driver who remembered taking a woman and the crate in question from home to the airport. A visit to the address turned up the information that the woman in question, Marie Pitre, was in hospital receiving treatment for a self-administered overdose of barbiturates. Her first words to detectives were: 'He made me do it.' 'He' turned out to be Albert Guay, Madame Pitre's former boyfriend. There was more; Guay had also persuaded her to steal some dynamite for him and had commissioned her wheelchair-bound brother Genereux Ruest to cobble together a timing device capable of detonating it. Despite the fact that Marie Pitre had been thrown over for the younger, more vivacious Marie-Ange Robitaille, and that Marie-Ange had been moved into her apartment, Guay still exerted sufficient fear or affection for her to ferry the home-made bomb to the airport and check it in as freight. Meanwhile, Guay had insured his wife for $10,000.

When Albert Guay was put on trial in March 1950 the background to this strange tale proved almost as bizarre as its conclusion. Guay, it seems, was one of those men for whom one woman is never enough. Apart from minor walk-on players, the first mistress of significance was Marie Pitre, a waitress, who Guay set up in her own apartment. In 1946 Albert Guay was, not unusually, in a nightclub when he fell for the cigarette-girl Marie-Ange Robitaille. Guay's wife had been more than a little peeved at this development, not least because her rival was just sixteen years old. So she went to spill the beans to Marie-Ange's father, who liked it even less – and threw his daughter out of the house. At this point Albert Guay decided to keep all his eggs in one basket, and moved Marie-Ange in with Marie Pitre. Not a situation at which Madame Pitre was entirely amused; so she moved out. Then Marie-Ange became disillusioned and packed *her* bags. It was clear the only way Guay could keep her was manacled by a wedding ring. But he was already married . . .

It was at this stage that Albert tried to recruit his old friend Lucien Carreau to dispose of Rita by lacing her cherry brandy with poison; wisely, Carreau refused to have anything to do with such a mad-cap plot – especially for a measly $100. And that is when Albert Guay hit on the exploding plane idea. The court heard how, in the aftermath of the bombing, Guay tried to bribe Lucien Carreau, this time with $500, not to disclose his earlier offer. He also put the fear of hell into Marie Pitre by describing in gory detail what it would be like when she swung from a noose as an accomplice – which is what had nudged her into attempting suicide. In a nutshell, Albert Guay came over to the jury as being exactly what he was, a callous, brutal and greedy man who would not stop short of destroying the lives of two dozen people just to rid himself of the inconvenience of an unwanted spouse. They found him guilty, of course, and in January 1952 he was hanged. And when, at their own trials, Marie Pitre and her brother Genereux were proved to have been more than willing collaborators, they too kept an appointment with the hangman – whether Guay had given Marie an accurate description we will never know.

GUILDFORD PUB BOMBINGS On Saturday 5 October 1974, IRA terrorists planted bombs in two Guildford public houses. The first bomb, in the Horse and Groom, exploded at around 8.50 p.m., blowing the entire front of the pub into the street. Two young women soldiers, two young Scots soldiers and a civilian were killed; fifty-seven other people sustained injuries, many of them serious. Shortly before 9.30 p.m., a second bomb went off, this time in a nearby pub, the Seven Stars in Swan Lane. This second explosion occurred after the premature closure of their regular Saturday disco-dance following the earlier blast at the Horse and Groom, and mercifully no more than five people were injured.

On the following day a massive police operation was set up to catch the bombers. Security and intelligence organizations were contacted to establish what information was available on terrorists active on the British mainland, forensic examination of debris from the explosions was organized and teams were set up to trace all the customers using the two pubs on the night of the blasts. Forensic officers had meanwhile established the location where the bomb had been placed in the Horse and Groom and the police issued a description of a 'courting couple' who had been in that alcove.

On 28 November, police arrested an Irishman named Paul Hill in Southampton. On the following day Hill made statements in which he admitted involvement in the Guildford bombings and he was charged with murder. Another man, Gerard Conlon, was arrested in Belfast on 30 November, made his own confession on 2 December and was charged with murder on 4 December. Subsequent police raids at Kilburn and Harlesden in London led to the arrests of Patrick Armstrong and an Englishwoman named Carole Richardson. The Harlesden arrests included Anne Maguire and others who became known as the 'Maguire Seven'. On 7 December, Armstrong, Richardson, Anne Maguire and three other men were charged with the murder of the Guildford victims. The charges against Anne Maguire and the three other men were dropped; it was later that the Maguire Seven were charged with being in possession of explosives.

The trial of Hill, Conlon, Armstrong and Carole Richardson for the Guildford murders opened at the Old Bailey on 16 September 1975. Hill and Armstrong also faced two murder charges arising from another bombing at the King's Arms, Woolwich, on 7 November the previous year. In addition, all four accused faced charges of conspiracy to cause explosions. The prosecution case relied mainly on confession evidence which defence attorneys alleged had been obtained by force and intimidation. The trial closed on 22 October 1975, with the conviction of the Guildford Four on all charges. Mr Justice Donaldson in passing life sentences on the three men, recommended that Conlon should serve at least thirty years, Armstrong thirty-five years and that Hill should only be released on the grounds of age or infirmity. It was also disclosed that Paul Hill had in the interim been convicted of complicity in the murder of a man in Northern Ireland for which he had been given a life sentence. Carole Richardson was ordered to be detained during the Queen's pleasure.

In March 1976, the so-called Maguire Seven were convicted on charges of being in possession of explosives, and received sentences ranging from four to fourteen years. The appeals of both the Maguire Seven and the Guildford Four were dismissed by the Court of Appeal in July and October 1977 respectively.

As in the case of the Birmingham Six (see page 38), public doubts immediately began to be expressed about the safety of the convictions. In February 1977, the trial of four terrorists for their part in the Balcombe Street siege and many other offences ended at the Old Bailey. During this trial statements were made alleging the innocence of the Guildford Four, and these were later confirmed in interviews given by the Balcombe Street defendants to the Guildford defence team. Both the Guildford and Maguire cases were debated in the House of Lords, following which the scenario mirrored that of the Birmingham case, with television playing a major role. In 1984 and 1986 respectively, two programmes, 'Aunty Annie's Bomb Factory' and 'The Guildford Time Bomb', were transmitted in the ITV series 'First Tuesday'. Considerable doubts were now being openly expressed about the veracity of the police evidence at the original trial, but in January 1987 the Home Secretary declined his right to refer the case back to the Court of Appeal.

Public pressure mounted, with support coming from such luminaries as Lords Devlin and Scarman and Cardinal Hume the Archbishop of Westminster; and on 16 January 1989, the Home Secretary announced he was now prepared to refer the case to the Court of Appeal. Prior to the hearing it was revealed that irregularities had been found in statements and police reports indicating that documents had been altered. At a hearing on 19 October the Crown conceded defeat and declared they would not be opposing the appeal; it only remained for the Lord Chief Justice, Lord Lane, to quash the convictions of the Guildford Four. Subsequently, the convictions against the Maguire Seven were also quashed.

In the wake of what was clearly a most unsatisfactory state of affairs, an inquiry was set up under former High Court Judge Sir John May to examine the two cases. An internal examination of the police actions was also carried out by officers of the Avon and Somerset constabulary. Following this latter inquiry charges of conspiring to pervert the course of justice were brought against three former officers who had been involved in the original police investigation; these charges resulted in the adjournment of Sir John's inquiry. The trial of the three ex-policemen was heard at the Old Bailey and ended on 19 May 1993 with not guilty verdicts being returned in each case. At the same time, it was alleged in court that the three former officers had fabricated the confession of one of the Guildford Four, Patrick Armstrong. In the officers' defence it was argued that Armstrong was guilty and his confession was therefore true. None of the three defendants gave evidence on their own behalf, and following the verdicts Armstrong, Conlon and Hill all declared themselves outraged at the way this trial had been conducted, claiming that it was a retrial of the Guildford Four rather than a hearing involving policemen alleged to have fabricated evidence.

H

HAGGART, Robert Lee   Family guests calling for supper at the Post farmhouse near Farwell, Michigan, around 6.30 p.m. on Tuesday 16 February 1982, were surprised to find the place in darkness. The visitors cautiously entered the kitchen and switched on the light; they were horrified to see, lying in pools of blood, the bodies of forty-two-year-old Mrs Vaudrey Post and her twenty-three-year-old daughter Garnetta Haggart. They rushed from the building and drove to the next farmhouse to call the sheriff.

When they arrived, the sheriff's officers proceeded to search the house and the area around it; that was how they found the body of Mrs Post's husband, George, in the basement. In a pick-up truck in front of the farm building, were the bodies of another daughter, twenty-nine-year-old Helen Gaffney, three of her children, ten-year-old Angela, Tom, aged eight, and Amy, seven. Lying among the bodies, amazingly unscathed, was Helen Gaffney's youngest child, a one-year-old girl, who had apparently been protected from harm by her mother's body. The pick-up had been riddled by what appeared to be a fusillade from a shotgun. A preliminary medical examination showed that six of the victims had died from shotgun wounds and one of the children had been killed with a hand-gun. It was subsequently discovered that Mrs Post's car was missing from the farm, but because there was no indication that anything else had been taken, robbery did not seem to be one of the options when it came to motive.

Detectives questioned other members of the Post family

and many volunteered the suspicion that Garnetta Haggart's estranged husband, Robert Lee Haggart might be responsible. On the following day, Garnetta Post had been due in court to sue for divorce from her husband. Haggart was also wanted by the police to answer a charge of fraud and had a previous conviction for a sexual offence. The sheriff decided to issue a warrant for Haggart, who was thought to be driving Mrs Post's missing car.

On Thursday 18 February a man in Haletown, Tennessee, read a newspaper article about the Post murders, and was amazed to see the suspect named as Robert Lee Haggart; he was amazed because he happened to be sharing an apartment with Haggart. The man took his story to the authorities, telling them that Haggart was currently in Alabama, outside the authority's jurisdiction. However, he agreed to contact Haggart and arrange to meet him on the Tennessee side of the border, so that he could be arrested. When he was later confronted by police officers, Haggart surrendered without offering any resistance, though he had in his possession a loaded .38 pistol. In his Haletown apartment, detectives found bloodstained clothing. Haggart waived extradition and was returned to Michigan, where he was charged with seven counts of murder.

Haggart came up for trial on 8 September 1982. The prosecution case included expert evidence that the bloodstaining on the clothing found in Haletown matched the blood groups of two of the victims found in the pick-up and was of a different group to Haggart's. The bullet which killed one of the children was demonstrated by ballistics experts to have been fired from the pistol found in Haggart's possession when he was arrested. After a trial lasting a month, the jury found Haggart guilty of six counts of first-degree murder, one count of second-degree murder, one of attempted murder and eight of possessing a firearm during a felony.

On 22 October Robert Lee Haggart was sentenced to life terms on each of the seven murder charges, thirty to fifty years for attempted murder and two years on the firearms charges.

HALL, Leo On the morning of 31 March 1934, Tom Sanders left his home in Erland Point, Washington State, on his way to work. As he passed the next-door cottage, home of the Fleider family, Sanders was puzzled by the noise of their three dogs howling and barking from the rear of the house. Probably a bit more inquisitive than he should have been, Tom Sanders wandered around the back of the house and found the three poodles locked in a car. He opened the car door and let the dogs out, and then peered through one of the cottage windows and saw, to his horror, two bodies slumped on the floor. Sanders ran home and called the police who arrived fifteen minutes later (don't forget, it is 1934). Officers broke into the cottage and found not two bodies but six, and signs that something approaching a battle had taken place in the kitchen.

In this room lay the bodies of Magnus Jordan and Peggy Chenevert; in a bedroom those of Fred Balcolm and Mrs Fleider. In the living room Eugene Chenevert and Frank Fleider lay dead in pools of their own blood. Autopsies carried out on the victims established that there had been three murder weapons. Magnus Jordan and Peggy Chenevert had been shot; Anna Fleider and Fred Balcolm had had their throats cut; and Eugene Chenevert and Frank Fleider had been battered to death with a hammer – the bloodstained hammer was lying beside Eugene Chenevert's body. The house had been ransacked and jewellery belonging to Anna Fleider was missing. Samples of blood taken from around the house provided one major clue – blood found in the bathroom belonged to a different group to that of any of the victims, which indicated that the killer or one of the killers had been injured during the slaughter.

Various leads were pursued without success until the owners of a local bar reported to the police that on the morning following the murders a girl who worked for them arrived home soaked to the skin and in 'pretty bad shape'. The girl's name was Peggy Paulos and she said she had been picked up by a sailor who had played rough and in the resulting struggle she had lost the heel from one of her shoes. Detectives were not slow in linking this with a heel found close to the Fleider house. Miss Paulos was questioned and satisfied the police that whatever else she had been up to she was not involved in murder. The only other clue was a vague report that a man giving the name of Leo had been seen on the Erland Point ferry with an injury to his head; he told anybody who cared to ask that he had been in a bar-room brawl.

The investigation got absolutely nowhere for around eighteen months, then an ex-convict named Larry Paulos facing a stretch in prison for robbery told the police his wife (yes, Peggy) had been having nightmares and mumbling about 'Fleider' and 'murder'. Larry Paulos also revealed that his wife was involved with an underworld figure named Leo Hall. Now they were getting somewhere; now there were some names, some faces. Officers from the murder team showed witnesses who had seen the injured man on the ferry pictures of Leo Hall, and they identified him. A warrant was issued for the arrest of Hall and he was picked up in Portland, Oregon. Peggy Paulos was also arrested and during questioning described how Hall had taken her to the Fleider house intent on robbery. She had helped him tie and gag the victims and had been present while Hall killed them, one by one. They were jointly charged with murder.

Leo Hall and Peggy Paulos came up for trial in December 1935. Peggy pleaded that she had only gone to the Fleider house under duress, and the jury, heaven knows why, must have accepted this defence for they found her not guilty. Leo Hall was a different matter; he was found guilty, sentenced to death, and was hanged at Walla Walla State Penitentiary.

HAMILTON, Thomas The killings of children and their teacher at the Scottish town of Dunblane on 13 March 1996, are considered by many to be one of the worst instances of mass murder of all time. Many other cases have involved a greater number of victims, but the singling out of small children as targets was rightly considered to be a monstrous evil.

Thomas Hamilton, the perpetrator, had long been regarded as a strange man in Dunblane and had been nicknamed 'Mr Creepy' by some in the town. A loner, he had failed in his efforts to establish himself in youth work, both in the Scouts and Boys Club movements. His activities in both these ventures had led to complaints from parents of boys placed in his care. A closet paedophile, his care of young boys during activities was at times brutal and showed a great desire of his need to dominate his charges. He would always insist that they changed clothes in his presence and took photographs of the boys in their swimming costumes, which he always demanded must be black. Following these complaints, he was the subject of a police inquiry but no further action was taken. Nevertheless, his activities in youth work were at an end.

This fostered a bitter feeling of resentment on the part of Hamilton who considered he had been the victim of prejudice. He contacted the local council, badgered his Member of Parliament and a short while before the killings even wrote to the Queen. He joined the local shooting club and was known to practice his marksmanship on every possible occasion. When he applied for a permit to own firearms he was once more intereviewed by the police but again, no action was taken and he was free to acquire guns and ammunition.

On the fateful day, he drove to the Dunblane Primary School, stopping outside to cut what he thought were the school telephone lines, but which were actually those of nearby houses, and entered the gymnasium armed with two semi-automatic pistols, two revolvers and 700 rounds of ammunition. A class of five- and six-year-olds were assembled and Hamilton immediately started shooting, firing what was later established as twenty-nine shots from the doorway. Then unbelievably, coldbloodedly walked among the fallen children firing further shots into the dead, dying and wounded. Momentarily, he left the gynmasium to fire randomly at anyone he saw before returning and killing himself with a bullet to the head. A total of sixteen children and a teacher were dead and seventeen were wounded.

The element of planning which he put into the massacre and the lack of any psychiatric problems in his background would seemingly rule out any question of insanity and it can only be concluded that he was motivated by revenge against the parents of the children and was, as stated by locals, just truly evil.

HARRIS, Frank   On Friday 20 December 1963, a farmer was at his home in Poinsett County, Arkansas; like most folks at that time of the year, he was preparing for Christmas. For no special reason he looked out of the farmhouse window and saw an orange glow in the sky over in the direction of a neighbour's farm. The farmer thought no more about it until suddenly two small children rushed into his kitchen. He recognized them as nine-year-old Ronald Dever and his sister Mary, aged six. They appeared to be in a state of shock and their hands and clothes were burned. He calmed them down and asked them what had happened. Ronald said, 'Our house burned up and our mummy and daddy burned up too.' Mary Dever said, 'A bad man killed our daddy and then he burned up everybody in the house.'

The farmer decided to take the children to the local sheriff's office, whereupon a couple of deputies were sent out to the Dever farm. By the time they arrived the house had burned to the ground and Leonard Dever, his wife and four other children aged between four and eight and one-year-old Janet were all dead.

Slowly and patiently, the authorities started to question Ronald and Mary Dever. They said they heard a noise from downstairs while they were in bed, and had got up to see what was happening. A stranger was in the living room with their parents and he demanded whisky and threatened Leonard Dever with a gun. Dever had taken a gun from a drawer and hit the stranger, who then shot their father. The man ordered their mother to pass him her husband's wallet, and when she had done so shot her as well. The stranger then got a can of paraffin from the kitchen and poured it around the room before lighting a match and setting it ablaze. Ronald and Mary had run out of the house, straight into the stranger who picked them up and threw them both back into the fire. However, the plucky children managed to escape through another door and ran for help.

A team of police searchers combing the area found a car dumped in a gravel pit not far from the blackened ruins of the farmhouse. In the car, which was registered to a Frank Harris of Jonesboro, was half a can of paraffin and stains which might have been human blood. Police officers paid a visit to Harris's home, where they found him burning clothes, which he claimed were oil-stained from working on his car. What was more, it was noticed that Harris had a gash on his cheek. He was arrested and confronted with the surviving Dever children who were so terrified that they shrank away from him. Autopsies on the dead had by now proved that the adults had not died in the fire but had been shot. Harris persisted in his denial of the murders, but was at a loss to explain how his wallet contained documents belonging to Leonard Dever, or why tests on his hands showed that he had fired a gun in the previous thirty hours.

Frank Harris was charged with the murders of the Dever family, though when he came up for trial in March 1964 he was indicted only for the murder of Leonard Dever. The evidence of the surviving Dever children created a profound impression on the court, and when the time came for the defence to put its case, Harris's attorney announced he would not be calling any evidence, but would simply contend that the state had failed to prove its case. The jury clearly thought otherwise, because they found Frank Harris guilty, but were unable to agree on a suitable sentence. At the judge's insistence the jury retired once again, and eventually fixed the penalty as life imprisonment.

HARRIS, Joseph M. On the evening of Thursday 10 October 1991, Joseph M. Harris sat at the table in his tiny Paterson, New Jersey, apartment and stared at the blank sheet of paper in front of him. He was not worried about getting ready for the night-shift because he did not have one to go to any more – the Post Office had seen to that when they sacked him from his position as an overnight mail sorter back in April 1990. For eighteen months Harris had plotted his revenge, particularly on that bitch Carol Ott who got him fired! But he didn't just want blood, he wanted the whole world to know about his hatred; he wanted them to know *why*.

In the end it took two pages to get the venom out of his system; then he left the note where it would be seen and put on his vengeance uniform. Dressed in a bullet-proof jacket, black military fatigues, black combat boots and a black Ninja-style hood, and armed with a 9mm Uzi handgun, a .22-calibre machine gun, a samurai sword and an assortment of grenades and home-made bombs, Joe Harris was ready for the killing to start. Before he left, there was just one refinement to attend to – he rigged the front door of the apartment with a lethal booby-trap bomb.

First stop was the nearby suburb of Wayne, where he hacked supervisor Carol Ott to death in her own home with the vicious oriental sword; then, as he watched television in a different room, Carol's fiancé Cornelius Kasten was shot through the head. Now Harris made his way through the night to Ridgewood Post Office where he instantly shot dead letter sorters Donald McNaught and Joseph Vander Paauw. Then he waited.

At shortly after 2.00 a.m. truck-driver Marcello Collado pulled into the loading-bay on his regular mail-bag delivery, just like he did every morning. But today there was something strange about the place – the doors were locked for a start, and the building seemed to be in darkness. As Collado made his way down to the basement entrance, he came face to face with a masked gunman, and nearly face to face with a bullet as well. As the gunman raised his deadly weapon for a second shot, Marcello Collado made the sprint of his life, and did not stop running till he hit the local police station half a mile away. Within minutes of hearing his story, Sergeant Robert Kay and police officer Peter Tuchol were themselves carefully inching down the basement ramp of the Ridgewood Post Office, but were soon forced to retreat for their lives as Joseph M. Harris began to lob home-made bombs out of the door. Around 3.15 a.m. a crack squad of SWAT officers took up positions around the building while negotiators tried to reach Harris over the office telephone. When they were unable to make contact by six o'clock armed officers entered the building by a side door and shortly before seven re-emerged with Harris in custody.

Later, stunned colleagues expressed little surprise that Harris had gone berserk, describing him as 'a walking time bomb' who was always prone to threatening violence to anybody who crossed him. Harris had joined the US Postal Service as a sorting clerk in 1981, and in 1984 he was officially reprimanded for intimidating his fellow-workers. In 1990 Carol Ott, who had been Harris's supervisor on the night-shift, asked him to undergo the usual 'fitness for duty' evaluation; he refused. There was a row, Harris threatened to attack the supervisor and was dismissed; much to the relief and satisfaction, it seems, of everybody.

Born in Trenton, the state capital of New Jersey in 1950, Joseph Harris had served with the US Navy between 1974 and 1977, and was engaged on the repair of electrical equipment; it was around this time that he developed a fascination with explosives and firearms, and began a practical study of the martial arts.

It took almost five years to bring Harris to court on these charges as it was decided to try him first on another separate murder charge – he was convicted on this charge and given the death penalty. At his trial for the Post Office murders, he was found guilty on four counts of first degree murder. A separate jury was empanelled for the penalty phase and they returned the rather bizarre decision that he should die for the murder of Carol Ott's fiancé, Cornelius Kasten, and receive life imprisonment on the other three counts. Nevertheless, the death penalty was passed and he thus received his second capital sentence.

HARVEY, Julian   In November 1961, Arthur Duperrault, a wealthy Wisconsin optician, chartered the ketch *Bluebelle* for a cruise from the Florida Keys to the Bahamas. Accompanying Duperrault were his wife Mary and their three children: Brian (fourteen), Terry Jo (eleven) and Renee (seven). The ketch was crewed by Julian Harvey, a former air force officer and well-known local yachtsman, and his wife Mary.

The vessel left Fort Lauderdale on 8 November 1961 and was sighted cruising past the islands on its way out to sea. On 13 November, the crew aboard the oil tanker *Gulflion* en route for Puerto Rico saw a man waving from a dinghy which was drifting towards them. The tanker slowed down as it neared the dinghy, and crew members could hear the man shouting, 'Help. I have a dead baby on board.' The tanker picked up the man and the dead body of a small child.

On board, the man identified himself as Julian Harvey, skipper of the ketch *Bluebelle*, which he said had gone down after being hit by a sudden squall which had caused the mainmast to snap. Following this disaster, a fire had broken out and Harvey could not get to the passengers or his wife and was forced to take to the dinghy. While he was in the dinghy the dead body of the child had floated by and he had pulled her in; she was the Duperraults' youngest daughter, Renee. The tanker put in to the nearest port, which was Nassau, where Harvey was questioned by the authorities, and although there were some who expressed doubt, Harvey's story was accepted, and he was allowed to return to Miami. The whole affair would almost certainly have been recorded as yet another tragic maritime accident, were it not for a curious occurrence on 16 November.

The Greek freighter *Captain Theo* was bound for Houston, Texas, when they picked up a small girl floating on a balsawood raft. The girl, although suffering from starvation and extreme exposure, was able to identify herself as Terry Jo Duperrault. A helicopter was sent from Miami to pick the girl up and she was rushed to hospital in a critical condition. After intensive treatment, however, she improved steadily and was taken off the danger list; though, in view of her still weak state, she was not subjected to any questioning. The authorities naturally informed Julian Harvey of Terry Jo's rescue and that her condition was improving. Harvey's response was to exclaim: 'Oh my God', though he added hastily: 'Isn't that wonderful.' He then asked to be excused because he was tired and returned to his motel. The following morning Julian Harvey was found dead with his wrist and throat slashed. A razor blade lay nearby with a note reading: 'I got too tired and nervous. I couldn't stand it any longer.'

When she had recovered from her ordeal, Terry Jo Duperrault told her story. She had been woken from her sleep on the ketch by the sound of her brother Brian screaming. Deciding to investigate she had got up, and had come upon the bodies of her mother and brother in the main cabin. Up on deck she had bumped into Harvey who had struck her and forced her below. The next thing she knew the boat seemed to be sinking and Harvey was diving off and swimming to the dinghy. She had run to the life raft, cut it free and floated on it away from the sinking vessel.

Given such clear evidence of foul play, an investigation was mounted into Julian Harvey's recent activities which led to the discovery that he had taken out a double indemnity insurance on his wife's life. Whether this was the motive for the multiple murder we will never know. But it should go on record that just before his suicide, Harvey had told a friend that his only crime had been abandoning the boat to save himself and not looking after those in his charge when it ran into difficulties.

HEBARD, Harry 'Butch'   When 'Butch' Hebard's parents divorced, it seemed natural for him to stay with his mother, and this arrangement proved mutually satisfactory until the boy was nine years old. Then his father married for a third time and applied to the court for custody of his son. The former Mrs Hebard did not oppose the order, so Butch joined his father and stepmother in Wisconsin Rapids. There are some people, however, who just cannot stay married for very long; Butch's father was like that. In no time at all his latest relationship faltered and, after just a year, young Hebard found himself living alone with his father. But if Jack Hebard was not a very successful husband, then at least it was not for want of trying. In 1957, Hebard married for the fourth time, to a widow named Joyce Rudell, who had twin daughters and a son of her own.

The family moved to Green Bay, Wisconsin, and at first all appeared to be going well, everything considered. In 1963, though, at the age of seventeen Butch Hebard began to have trouble with his schoolwork and he and his stepmother began to quarrel. On 18 February 1963, Butch skipped school after telling a friend he planned to run away. When he arrived home, his stepmother told him he would not be allowed to eat with the family that night. Later, the young man explained that he felt so frustrated with his family that he took a .22-calibre pistol and a rifle from his father's gun collection and killed them. First he shot his father in the head as he lay sleeping on the couch, then he rushed into the kitchen, where he shot and killed the eleven-year-old twins Janice and Joyce and his fifteen-year-old stepbrother John. When his stepmother came into the kitchen carrying groceries, Butch shot her dead too.

After the bloodbath, Hebard changed his clothes, left the house and went to a friend's home where he persuaded the family to let him stay for the night. The following morning neighbours noticed there were none of the usual signs of activity at the Hebard home and called the police. As well as the bodies of Butch's family, police searching the house found a list made out by the teenager of his preparations for running away, including the name of his friend and the address where, within the hour, Butch Hebard was arrested.

On 20 February, Hebard was charged with first-degree murder, but with only four counts; a cautious District Attorney held one charge back so that in the event of Butch being cleared, he could be tried again on the fifth.

On 25 February, the trial judge ordered a routine psychiatric examination, and on 13 March Butch Hebard was certified insane and ordered to be confined to a state mental hospital. The psychiatrists diagnosed him as suffering from schizophrenia rendering him unfit to plead, and therefore incompetent to stand trial.

However, in 1967 Hebard was re-examined and declared sane and fit to stand trial. He was subsequently convicted of the murders and jailed for life.

HEDIN, Tore On the night of 27 November 1951, fire broke out in an old mill and its neighbouring house at Tjornarp, Sweden; the buildings were occupied by the miller, Folke Nilsson. Firefighters were unable to save either building, and when it came to a search of the smouldering rubble, they found Nilsson's charred remains. The local constable, Tore Hedin, had been called out to the blaze and reported to his superior officer that he had seen a stranger near the scene of the fire. A post-mortem examination of Nilsson established the fact that he had been killed before the fire had been lit. A broken-open cash box was also found in the ruins and it soon came out that a local farmer had paid Nilsson almost fifteen hundred kroner the day before his death; robbery, then, seemed the most likely motive.

Constable Hedin was a good, loyal policeman, and he found himself attached to the murder squad investigating the killing and arson in the capacity of liaison officer, which involved quite a lot of extra work. His mother and his girlfriend, Ulla Ostberg, noticed that Hedin seemed to be under great strain but put it down to the additional duties. On 20 August 1952, Ulla arrived for work at the old people's home in Hurva where she was a nurse, with her face covered in bandages. When her colleagues expressed concern, she explained that on the previous evening Hedin had sadistically beaten her up.

On 22 August, the murder squad was notified that Hedin's parents had been burned to death in a fire at their home in Kvarlov. The blaze had been very intense, and one of the firefighters who had been at both incidents said it reminded him of the blaze at Tjornarp, where the miller had died. Tore Hedin was nowhere to be found. Not long after the Kvarlov inferno, a report came in of another severe fire at the old people's home in Hurva. Several patients were feared dead, and two members of staff were known to have perished – the matron, Agnes Lunden, and a nurse, Ulla Ostberg. A post-mortem examination established the fact that the victims had not died in the fire but had been killed beforehand with an axe. Post-mortem examinations on Per Hedin and his wife Hilda confirmed that they too had been killed by blows from an axe before their house was burned down.

A warrant was issued for the arrest of Tore Hedin. In a matter of days, searchers found his car concealed on the shore of Lake Bosarpasjon, about fifty miles from Hurva. In the vehicle was a detailed statement written by Hedin, confessing to the murders of miller Nilsson, his parents, Agnes Lunden and his girlfriend Ulla Ostberg. The note was signed 'Tore Hedin, Murderer'. Police divers carrying out a search of the lake eventually found Tore Hedin's body roped to two stone blocks.

HENDRICKS, David Around his home town of Bloomington, Illinois, David Hendricks was widely regarded as a devoutly religious man, a pillar of his local church, a good husband and a loving father to his three children. Even in business he was altruistic, as he made his living designing aids for people suffering from back problems and had patented a successful back brace.

In November 1983, Hendricks left for a business trip to Wisconsin to market his invention. On the eighth of the month, relatives became worried when Susan Hendricks failed to keep a date for dinner and this was emphasized when her husband phoned from Wisconsin saying he was unable to get an answer from their home. The police were called and went to the house which appeared to have been ransacked. In the bedrooms they found thirty-year-old Susan Hendricks and her three children battered and stabbed to death; an axe and a butcher's knife left lying on a bed were presumed to be the murder weapons.

Post-mortem examinations showed that Mrs Hendricks had died from a blow to the left side of the head and her eldest daughter, nine-year-old Rebekah, had suffered a fractured skull, both wounds apparently inflicted with an axe. Of the two younger children, seven-year-old Grace had died from knife wounds to the neck, and five-year-old Benjamin from a fractured skull and a slashed throat. Official doubts as to the theory that the murders had been committed during the course of a burglary were aroused when it was discovered that many items of value had not been taken.

Hendricks was contacted in Wisconsin and immediately returned to Bloomington. He told police he had left home at around midnight after kissing his wife and children good-bye. Earlier in the evening, around seven o'clock he said, he had taken the children to a pizza restaurant for a meal. Hendricks appeared to be in a state of total shock.

Speaking to reporters Hendricks said he believed his family were now with God in heaven and that he hoped the person responsible for the murders would be caught but spared the death penalty in order that his soul could be saved. He also told the press that some things in the house had been stolen. As Hendricks had not been allowed into the house on his return this fuelled police suspicions that it was, in fact, a fake burglary; the focus of attention on David Hendricks intensified. It was established that, supposedly in furtherance of his work on disabled people's aids, he had hired young women as models to try out his products. Interviews with the women confirmed that he had frequently persuaded them to strip off in order that he could draw diagrams on their bodies. In many cases this had led to him fondling their breasts and making open sexual advances. One of the models said Hendricks admitted to having had several affairs and saw nothing wrong with this, though he later denied ever making this statement. Enquiries in Wisconsin revealed that he had not made any appointments or contacts regarding his back brace.

In an attempt to establish the time sequence of events on the night of the killings, the contents of the children's stomachs were sent for forensic analysis; the results proved that the children had died within two hours of eating, and so *before* the time that David Hendricks claimed to have left the house to make his business trip to Wisconsin.

On 5 December 1983, Hendricks was arrested and charged with the murder of his family; on 29 November 1984, he was found guilty, and on 12 January of the following year was sentenced to life imprisonment without the possibility of parole.

HENNARD, George   In a country not unused to killings on a large scale, the enormity of George Hennard's apparently senseless rampage left the nation stunned. With a victim count of twenty-two dead and eighteen wounded, it was America's worst mass shooting to date (the record had previously been held by James Oliver Huberty).

At around 12.40 p.m. on Wednesday 16 October 1991, thirty-five-year-old Hennard drove his pick-up truck through the main entrance to the car park of Luby's cafeteria, one of a chain of busy eateries situated on the Interstate 190 at Killeen, in Bell County, Texas. Hennard suddenly pushed his foot down on the accelerator and catapulted the pick-up through the plate-glass front window, showering diners with glass and debris and trapping one man underneath the truck. As the vehicle came to a halt, Hennard swung himself out of the driver's seat yelling: 'This is what Bell County has done to me!' As the terrified man trapped under the truck managed to pull himself free, Hennard raised his right arm; gripped tightly in his hand was the grey metallic bulk of a Glock-17 semi-automatic pistol. The first bullet tore through the fleeing man's skull, after which Hennard turned his attention to the cowering group of diners. With a crazed fury, the gunman began methodically to cut them down with rapid fire, always on the move, always shooting, and when one clip was exhausted, Hennard had plenty more in his pockets. With Hennard choosing his victims apparently randomly and shooting at point-blank range, there is no telling how long the massacre would have continued if armed police had not arrived on the scene. During the early panic one customer had hurled himself through a large unbroken side window, suffering serious cuts to himself but allowing others to escape and raise the alarm.

Now Hennard's attentions transferred to duelling with the police marksmen who were gradually closing in. It was a police bullet that finally stopped George Hennard, and bleeding from a wound he fled into the corridor behind the eating area; with a last gesture of defiance he pumped a bullet through his own left eye and deep into his deranged brain. The killing spree had lasted just ten minutes; amid the blood and wreckage lay twenty-two dead and eighteen wounded. As helicopters and military and civilian ambulances were ferrying the wounded to local hospitals, a refrigerated lorry was commandeered for use as an *ad hoc* morgue to keep the bodies of the dead out of the searing Texan heat.

Meanwhile, another team of police officers and detectives had sealed off the elegant mansion which George Hennard had shared with his mother at Belton, just ten miles from the carnage at Killeen.

The town of Belton, Bell County, is on the periphery of the huge US army base at Fort Hood. Hennard's father, also called George, had been a surgeon with the army, and like many other sons and daughters of military personnel, George junior had been uprooted frequently during his father's numerous postings. He managed to get through school with neither academic nor sporting distinction, but his spell with the navy seems to have been mutually satisfactory. In the early part of 1979 George Hennard enlisted in the merchant marine. Sadly, by this time he had picked up a drug problem – nothing too serious, just a fondness for smoking marijuana, and in another person it might have remained just a pleasing recreation. But Hennard was a loner by nature, and the effect of the drug was to remove him even further from reality, drive him even further into his own isolation. All of which did not make George Hennard an ideal candidate for life aboard ship, and after one particularly vicious brawl he was dismissed from the merchant marine and lost his seaman's licence.

During Hennard's absences at sea his father had served at

the Fort Hood base and bought himself a luxury home in nearby Belton. By the time George found himself land-locked, George senior and his wife had separated and George took up residence with his mother. In Belton he began to acquire a reputation for unbalanced behaviour; he was sullen and abusive to the neighbours, and for no obvious reason would stand screaming and shouting on the front lawn. Then he developed a one-sided passion for two sisters and bombarded them with irrational and rather frightening letters. Although these missives were passed on to the police there was not a lot that George could be charged with. However, it is quite clear that by now some real or imagined grudge had buried itself deep in his mind.

Throughout this time, George Hennard had been trying, with increasing desperation to gain back his seaman's ticket; his chances could not have been helped by his rapidly growing dependence upon drink and drugs. At the begin-ning of 1991, the US Coast Guard tribunal finally and officially refused to give George his licence back. Days later he bought a gun, the Austrian-made Glock-17 which, come the autumn, would rob twenty-two people of their lives.

Quite what triggered the final rampage we are unlikely ever to know; still less what was going on in George Hennard's head as he stood like the angel of death amid the wreckage of Luby's cafeteria. Some people have said it was because he hated women, and it is true that the majority of his victims were women (fourteen). Perhaps it is because he knew he would never be able to go back to sea again, the only place he was really happy. Was the massacre at Luby's the elaborate and ghastly suicide note of a man who had nothing to live for? Whatever the reason, nobody could ignore George Hennard now. As *Daily Mirror* correspon-dent Michael McDonough reported from Killeen: 'Sud-denly, the nobody from nowhere was the maniac behind the worst gun massacre in American history.'

HICKS, Albert E. (aka William Johnson)   On 16 March 1860, the sloop *E. A. Johnson* left New York, with a crew comprising Captain Burr, two boys, Oliver and Smith

Watts, and a man calling himself William Johnson. On the morning of 21 March, the vessel was found drifting deserted and towed back to New York. Blood was spattered over much of the deck, and the state of the cabin indicated foul play; however, no trace of any bodies was found. The next day two men, who had heard of the mystery, informed police that a man they knew as 'Johnson', and who had been one of the ship's crew, had arrived home not only safely, but with a lot of money.

Johnson was traced to Providence, Rhode Island, where he was positively identified as a member of the missing crew. In his possession was a watch which had once belonged to Captain Burr, and a photograph, known to have been given to Oliver Watts by a lady-friend.

William Johnson was charged with the murder of Captain Burr and was arraigned for trial before the United States Circuit Court in May 1860. After a retirement of only seven minutes, the jury found him guilty and he was sentenced to death.

While awaiting execution in the Tombs Prison, New York, Johnson made the following confession:

My true name is Albert Hicks. At about 10 p.m. on the second night at sea, Captain Burr and one of the Watts boys were asleep in the cabin, while I was steering and the other Watts boy was on the lookout at the bow. Suddenly, the devil took possession of me and I determined to murder the remainder of the crew and steal everything on board worth while. Procuring an axe, I crept up behind the boy on deck and I struck him one blow, dashing out his brains. The noise attracted his brother, who came on deck and I also struck him one blow, knocking him senseless. I then proceeded to the cabin, but the captain made a desperate struggle for his life until I felled him with a blow from the axe, which killed him. I then returned to the deck, where I observed that the second boy I struck was not dead but had recovered consciousness and was struggling to his feet. I picked him up with the intention of throwing him overboard. I got his body over the side of the boat but with a death grip, he clung to the taffrail. Reaching for my axe I cut his hands off and he fell into the water and sank immediately. After throwing the other bodies over-board I rifled the captain's money bags and taking all other valuables I could, I headed the sloop for the shore. When I got in close, I used the small boat to effect a landing.

Hicks was hanged at Bedloe's Island at 10.45 on the morning of Friday 13 July 1860 in front of a crowd of some 10,000 people.

HIRASAWA, Sadamichi   Shortly before the Shiinimaki branch of the Tokyo Imperial Bank closed on the afternoon of 26 January 1948, a representative of the Welfare Department named Dr Jiro Yamaguchi walked in and asked to speak with the manager. The bank was by now empty of customers and the chief cashier was locking the main doors. Meanwhile, Dr Yamaguchi was explaining to Mr Yoshida that the American occupation forces under General MacArthur (this is just after the Second World War), were worried about the spread of a dysentery epidemic and in collaboration with the Welfare Department were providing preventive medicine for all employees. The manager lined up his fourteen clerks, each with their tea-cup, as the doctor passed along pouring a little liquid from a bottle into the cups. Then, as one man, the clerks lifted their cups to their lips and drank. Many spluttered, some began coughing; Dr Yamaguchi responded by pouring another tot of medicine and encouraging the bank-clerks to drink up. They did, and with varying physical expressions of agony fell to the floor; twelve died, three, including Mr Yoshida the manager, were saved by emergency hospital treatment. Meanwhile, Dr Yamaguchi had helped himself to what money was lying about: around $400, not a lot for a dozen deaths.

Of course Dr Yamaguchi was not really from the Welfare Department, in fact he was not even Dr Yamaguchi; and the preventive medicine was potassium cyanide. What's more, Inspector Ohori of Tokyo's police department, who was detailed to look into the case, found to his utter amazement that the same 'doctor' had pulled the same stunt less than four months previously at the Ebara branch of the Yasuda Bank. Thankfully on that occasion the assassin had made an error in the poison mixture and the eighteen bank-clerks had just been taken very ill, forcing 'Dr Shigeru Matsui from the Welfare Department' to flee empty-handed.

So who *was* doctor death? Inspector Ohori started at the obvious place – at the beginning, with the information that he already had. Officers were set to the task of checking the medical registers first for a Dr Jiro Yamaguchi – there wasn't one; then for Dr Shigeru Matsui – and there was. Now it happens that among Japanese professionals and businessmen it is a polite custom to exchange business cards. As 'Dr Matsui' had with the Yasuda bank manager; except that it was not Dr Matsui. However, the good doctor was able to focus the police investigation. In March of the previous year he had attended a medical conference and, according to tradition had exchanged business cards with the other ninety-six delegates. Better still, Dr Matsui had kept all the cards he had been given in return for his own. It was a long shot, but their best one yet, and detectives set about putting faces to the names on the business cards. One of them was called Sadamichi Hirasawa, a professional artist and head of a national arts association, and he fitted the description of the bogus Welfare Department officer in both cases – a mole on his left cheek and a scar beneath his chin being among the identifying features. Employees of the banks later picked Hirasawa out as the man who had poisoned them; and if motive were needed it could be proved that the suspect went from trying to borrow money before the robbery to putting money in to the bank after it.

Although Hirasawa confessed to mass killing while he was in police custody, by the time he came to trial he had withdrawn his statement, now claiming innocence. Although he was found guilty by the court and sentenced to death, Sadamichi Hirasawa had his sentence commuted to life imprisonment. For Hirasawa (as for many of Japan's lifers), the sentence meant just that, and, still protesting his innocence, he died in prison in 1987 at the age of ninety-five. It should be added that Hirasawa had considerable support for his claim that he was suffering a miscarriage of justice, and in 1992 – forty-four years after his conviction – Sadamichi Hirasawa's attorneys were filing their nineteenth request for a posthumous retrial in order to clear his name. The main thrust of their appeal is that new evidence has come to light that the poison used on all the victims was not potassium cyanide, which Hirasawa had at his home, but acetone cyanohydrin. According to defence lawyers, this substance was made by a laboratory of Japan's Imperial Army and only available to military personnel.

HOFFMAN, Victor Ernest   A multiple murder committed without any reason or explanation occurred in the small farming community of Shell Lake, Saskatchewan, on the morning of 15 August 1967. Wildrew Lang drove over to his neighbour James Peterson's smallholding to help with some work, but when he arrived at the granary on the Peterson farm, there was no sign of his friend, so Lang made his way to the farmhouse. He opened the door, peered into the kitchen and was appalled to see the body of his neighbour lying on the floor – very still.

But James Peterson was not the only casualty. When Corporal Richards of the Royal Canadian Mounted Police arrived in response to Wildrew Lang's anxious phone call, he found the body of eleven-year-old Dorothy Peterson in the living room. In the children's bedroom were the bodies of Pearl (nine), Jean (seventeen), Mary (thirteen), William (five) and Colin (two). Sandwiched between the corpses of Pearl and Jean, Richards found four-year-old Phyllis Peterson, still alive. Outside the house lay the bodies of Mrs Peterson and her one-year-old son Larry. All nine victims had been shot in the head. The only clues were a single footprint on the kitchen floor, made by a boot with the marking 'Made in Taiwan' on the sole, and the fact that the bullets which had robbed the Petersons of their lives had been fired from a .22-calibre rifle.

Three days after the murders, the RCMP received an anonymous telephone message suggesting they check on a local man, twenty-one-year-old Victor Ernest Hoffman. Hoffman had been in trouble with the police before, and lately had been acting very strangely; not least he had been observed firing a rifle in the air claiming he was shooting at the devil. His behaviour had been so erratic that his parents had been obliged to commit him to a mental hospital, but he had been released on 26 July 1967.

The police wisely take notice even of anonymous tip-offs, and in this instance they were well rewarded. Hoffman was questioned and admitted the killings. Tests on his rifle and boots confirmed that Hoffman's gun had fired all the fatal shots and that his boots had made the impression on the Petersons' kitchen floor.

While awaiting trial, Hoffman was examined by psychiatrists and as a result was formally certified not guilty by reason of insanity and ordered to be confined in a mental institution.

HONA, Henare In 1933 a nineteen-year-old Maori named Henara Hona was working on a sheep station in the Rangitoto district of New Zealand. As he was good at his job and popular with all the locals, things might have continued on an upward path for the lad; that is, if he had not the following year fallen in love with a young Maori girl from a different tribe. In October 1934, Henare went through the time-honoured ritual of approaching the girl's parents to discuss marriage. Poor Henare; so concerned were those good parents about tribal differences that they decided to send their daughter away.

Greatly distressed, Henare Hona tried to obtain a rifle for the purpose, he said, of 'shooting bandits'. When he succeeded in getting hold of a gun on Tuesday 9 October 1934, he took off into the bush followed by a party from the sheep station who feared he would be looking for revenge. They tracked Henare Hona through the bush towards the sheep station run by Mr and Mrs Davenport and their two sons Albert and Edward. By this time it was getting dark, forcing the party to return home, from where they called the police; the police then telephoned the Davenport station. Mr Davenport told a confused tale about a Maori who had said his son Edward had been attacked, how or why we do not know, but it had been enough to send Davenport's elder son Albert rushing off to the rescue; neither son had yet returned.

There was no reply at all to a later phone call, so three constables were despatched on the thirty-mile drive to the Davenports' sheep station. On the way they saw a man's hat lying in a pool of blood by the roadside. Stopping to investigate, they stumbled upon Edward Davenport lying close by in a ditch with severe head injuries. After arranging for Davenport to be taken to hospital the officers continued on to the farm, where they found the house in flames. When the fire died down the charred remains of two bodies, later identified as the Davenports, were discovered in the rubble. That same day the body of Albert Davenport was found, shot through the head, on an access road about four miles away. A few days later Edward Davenport died in hospital as a result of his wounds.

Though a nationwide manhunt was launched for Henare Hona, no sightings of him were reported until 20 October when news came from Morrinsville, some sixty miles away, about a young Maori calling himself Laurie King who had obtained work at a nearby farm. The local policeman, Constable Heaps, drove to the farm to question King, and noticed that the youth standing in front of him had some missing teeth and the tip missing from a little finger – the identifying features of the wanted man. Realizing Heaps had identified him, King suddenly pulled out a revolver and fired, hitting the constable in one arm and in the temple; he was rushed to hospital for emergency surgery, but died the next day.

Police reinforcements were called in, and a party of ninety armed officers set out to hunt for Henare, who was reported to be near Kiwitahi. As the police arrived the fugitive leapt from the ditch in which he had been hiding and shot himself in the head. Still alive, Henare Hona was taken to hospital but, like the last victim of his madness, he died shortly after arrival.

HUBERTY, James Oliver James Huberty had always been angry looking. Greatly affected by the break-up of his parents' marriage, he also suffered a debilitating series of childhood ailments which appeared to make him feel aggrieved. Nevertheless, he married, had two children and he and his wife worked very hard to maintain their family. Ominously, his only passion in life was collecting guns and over the years he amassed a veritable arsenal.

In 1984, the family were living in San Ysidro, where he was unable to find regular employment, being reduced to working as a security guard. By July, he had been dimissed from even this poor employment and was suffering from severe depression. He telephoned a mental health clinic but was told they would not be able to see him until the following week.

The following day, Wednesday 18 July, he loaded his car with guns and ammunition and told his wife he was going hunting – some later reports said that his words were 'I'm going hunting humans'. He drove to McDonalds Restaurant on West San Ysidro Boulevard in San Diego. Entering the restaurant, he called out, 'I've killed thousands and now I'm going to killed thousands more' before opening fire. People dropped from their seats, dead, dying and wounded. He walked through the bodies shouting 'Come buy your burgers with ketchup on.' After the initial killings, he began to shoot wildly at the restaurant fittings. His next targets were people on the street outside or cars driving by on the nearby freeway. By now, he appeared to be quite calm, stopping at times to take soft drinks and tune the radio in to reports of the killings.

Police moved in and surrounded the building but he kept them at bay for over an hour. Finally, he made a mistake while firing at a police detail – exposing himself at a window he was shot through the head by a police sharp shooter. He left a total of twenty-one dead and twenty wounded.

HUGHES, William Thomas During the latter months of 1976, William Hughes was being held in custody at Leicester Prison on remand from Chesterfield on charges of rape and causing grievous bodily harm. He had been making regular appearances before the magistrates, escorted by two prison officers in a hired car with a driver. On 12 January 1977, the usual procedure was followed in that he was collected from his cell, handcuffed to an officer and together they travelled in the back seat of the car with the other officer in front with the driver. On the M1, Hughes asked if they could stop so that he could go to the lavatory and his request was granted at one of the service areas. After he had relieved himself, Hughes was again handcuffed and the journey proceeded. Suddenly the officer in the front felt a blow on the back of the neck and realized he had been stabbed. Hughes ordered him at knife point to get in the back and forced his escort to release him from the handcuffs. He gave the driver instructions on where to drive and when they came to a field ordered the three men to leave the car and walk across the field; Hughes then made his escape in the car.

Hughes drove towards his hometown of Chesterfield; on the outskirts, at Eastmoor, he broke into Pottery Cottage, the home of an elderly couple named Minton. Also staying at the cottage were their daughter and son-in-law and an adopted granddaughter, aged ten. Hughes tied the family up and sat tight. The alarm was not raised until two and a half days later, when the daughter was allowed to go to a neighbour and ask for help to tow the Mintons' car from the icy drive. Although it is believed that Hughes was listening while this was being arranged, the terrified woman still managed to whisper to the neighbour: 'The man from the moors has got my husband tied up.' Upon hearing this, the neighbour said he would get his own car but instead drove to a nearby farm and called the police.

Hughes, realizing the alarm had been given, drove off in the family car taking the daughter as a hostage. They were chased by police and intercepted at Tideswell Moor by officers in an unmarked car. Hughes held an axe to his hostage's throat and forced the police to give him their car. Other police vehicles carrying armed officers joined the chase to Rainow, Cheshire, where Hughes crashed the car. A witness said later, 'The woman was still in the car, and the police said the man had an axe and a knife. The woman, who apparently had a knife at her throat, screamed "Please help me. Get me out of here." Three policemen crept up on Hughes from behind and pounced. They fired seven or eight shots into the car at point-blank range and the man slumped down bleeding from head wounds.'

In the meantime police had gone to Pottery Cottage, where in the house they found the bodies of seventy-four-year-old Arthur Minton, his son-in-law, aged forty, and the little girl. Outside lying in the snow was the body of seventy-year-old Mrs Amy Minton. All of the victims had suffered terrible injuries from stabbing and throat wounds.

HUTCHINSON, Arthur On 23 October 1983 Mr Ivor Woolfe married Miss Suzanne Laitner at their local synagogue. A grand reception, with a guest list of 200, was held that afternoon in a marquee on the lawn of the Laitner family home, in Dore, Sheffield; after nightfall, a further, uninvited and most unwelcome guest paid a visit to the Laitner home.

Forty-three-year-old Arthur Hutchinson was at the time on the run after escaping from prison in Selby, North Yorkshire, where he was awaiting trial. Described as 'arrogant, self-centred, manipulative, and with an excessive interest in sexual abuse, alcohol, violence and the use of weapons', Hutchinson, the invader of the Laitners' home, was looking for a victim; he was looking for somebody to rape.

But instead of a sleeping girl in an upstairs bedroom, Hutchinson encountered Suzanne's twenty-eight-year-old brother Richard who, after a spirited attempt to defend himself, was stabbed to death. When solicitor Basil Laitner rushed upstairs to investigate the disturbance in his son's room he, too, was knifed to death. Downstairs Hutchinson attacked Basil's wife Avril in a ferocious assault, plunging a knife into her body no fewer than twenty-six times. Back upstairs now, the blood-crazed Hutchinson burst through the last unopened door, where he found the youngest daughter, Nichola. He raped the girl at knifepoint in her bed, then dragged her out, through her father's blood, bragging about the killings as they went, into the marquee where she was handcuffed and raped a second time. 'You have got to enjoy it or I will kill you,' was his perverse threat. As dawn approached Hutchinson led Nichola back to her bedroom, where he raped her again before leaving her tied hand and foot with two of her brother's ties.

Over the next thirteen days, while nine police forces combined resources in the manhunt, Hutchinson boasted in tape recordings and letters of being 'the Fox', but consistently denied the murders. When he was finally picked up by Detective Superintendent Terry Stuart – from a boarding house where he was registered in the name of 'A. Fox' – Hutchinson denied ever having been at the Laitner house. When faced with overwhelming forensic evidence, though, he claimed that Nichola Laitner had invited him back for sex after having previously met him in a Sheffield pub.

Arthur Hutchinson made a further wild and distressing fabrication in court, accusing Mr Michael Barron, a journalist covering the case for the *Sunday Mirror*, of committing the atrocity of which he himself stood accused. The court, though, was having none of it, and the jury found Hutchinson guilty on three charges of murder, one of rape, and a further charge of aggravated burglary. He received three life sentences, with a recommendation that he serve a minimum of eighteen years' imprisonment. The trial judge, Mr Justice McNeill, ruled that while there was no indication of mental illness, Hutchinson had a severe psychological disorder which was unlikely to respond to treatment.

According to a senior detective working on the case, it was Hutchinson's sexual arrogance which led to his downfall: after repeatedly forcing Miss Laitner to submit to intercourse he genuinely believed she would be under his spell, and that her 'affection' for him would deter her from betraying him to the police. If this were not the case, it is hard to understand why Hutchinson would have left alive a girl who had seen his face, and heard his admission of guilt.

I

ICE-CREAM WARS It was a little after midnight on Monday 16 April 1984, when the fire brigade was called out to a council block in Backend Street, Ruchazie, Glasgow. The top-floor flat, where the Doyle family lived, was ablaze. They found fifty-two-year-old Lilian Doyle perched on a window ledge, ready to jump; she was eventually persuaded to come down by ladder. Mrs Doyle's son Stephen had already jumped, and amazingly had survived the fifty-foot drop on to concrete, albeit with back and leg injuries.

The cause of the fire was not difficult to find, in fact it was as simple as it was deadly: petrol had been poured through the letterbox and ignited. In all, six members of the Doyle family perished in the inferno, including Lilian's husband, daughter, three sons and grandson. But who was the arsonist? Thirty-one-year-old Thomas Campbell – or 'TC' as he liked to be known – stood at the head of the list of suspects. Campbell's target, if he were guilty, had been eighteen-year-old Andrew Doyle.

Doyle, called 'Fat Boy', had worked as a 'minder', a heavy, for the Marchetti brothers. His remit was to protect the Marchettis' ice-cream vans as they plied their lucrative trade around Glasgow's streets and housing estates. More specifically, they needed protection from the rival firm of Fifti Ices, which was beginning to muscle in on the Marchetti territory. Vans had been smashed up with pickaxe handles, a manager threatened over the phone, and worse was to come. On 29 February 1984, a masked man had stepped out of a Volvo car and blasted two holes in Andy Doyle's windscreen with a shotgun; the following week he was beaten up.

On 3 September 1984, seven men stood before Lord Kincraig in the Glasgow High Court. They were charged variously with murder, attempted murder, attempted robbery, fire-raising, assault and malicious damage. Between all the lies, the contradictions, accusations and retracted statements aired in court, a seemingly coherent picture at last began to emerge.

TC was a villain with a reputation for feckless violence, who had spent half his adult life in jail. During a ten-year stretch in Barlinnie he had devised a scheme for ruining the Marchetti brothers and capturing their trade. On release he drew George Reid into the conspiracy as a 'money man', who financed Campbell and led the legitimate £250,000 negotiations for Fifti Ices. Vans were purchased; the money started rolling in. In the autumn of 1982 the campaign to warn off Marchetti vans began, and TC was delighted to find a little intimidation went a very long way. Only Doyle, the Fat Boy himself, proved obstinate, and so Tommy Campbell set his henchman Thomas 'Tamby' Gray on to him. It was Gray who had ambushed Doyle's van and shot at him through the windscreen. But TC, along with a petty thief named Joseph Steele, was the one who had driven to Backend Street and laid the trail of petrol; TC who sat in his car and watched the blaze, not lifting a finger to help the innocent family who were to perish.

And it was TC who received a sentence of life imprisonment, with a recommendation that he serve not less than twenty years. For his part, Joseph Steele was sent down for life, and Tamby Gray was given fourteen years. Other less significant foot soldiers in the ice-cream wars received various lesser sentences on minor charges.

But was that 'coherent picture' the true one? It is important to ask because nine years later the accused are still protesting their innocence. Would Thomas Campbell really have kept the baseball bat, three pickaxe handles, six woollen masks and a map with Backend Street circled, lying about the house where the police claim to have found them? Would he have told them: 'The fire at Fat Boy's was a frightener which went wrong'? Would Joseph Steele have said: 'I'm nae the one who lit the match', when arson had not been mentioned in the charge against him? Would William Love, the driver of the Volvo, have confessed to the police and grassed his confederates quite so readily? Or was the case, as Donald Macaulay QC put it, that 'There is something rotten at the core of this investigation. The police officers . . . have completely abused the public trust placed in them – and fabricated evidence.'?

The case continues both in the courts and with outside agitation. Joe Steele escaped from prison and super-glued himself to the railings of Buckingham Palace to draw attention to the case. Appeals have been heard but to date the convictions stand. At the time of writing, a date for a further appeal, following a referral by the Scottish Criminal Cases Review Commission is awaited.

INGENITO, Ernest   Ernie was born in 1924 into a poor rural Pennsylvanian family, and did not benefit overly much from an early education, save that kind of *ad hoc* training absorbed through running with the local street gangs. At fifteen the boy was arrested during the course of a burglary – not his first crime, just the first he was caught at – and put away in the Pennsylvania State Reformatory. In 1941 Ernie's much-loved mother died, and with her passing the last restraint on his criminous career was severed. Like so many of his kind Ingenito drifted into the US Army having failed to appreciate that it necessarily ran on discipline; after a brief and undistin-guished service he was sentenced to two years in the stockade for assaulting an officer before being dishonour-ably discharged.

In 1947 Ernest Ingenito married Theresa Mazzoli and went to live with the Mazzoli family in Gloucester County where, over the course of the next few years, he fathered two sons. The domestic arrangements were not ideal; for a start Theresa's mother, Pearl, took against Ernie, and had a tendency to nag him. And Mike Mazzoli did not seem to understand his son-in-law's attraction to drink and other women. It was this that finally led Mazzoli to throw Ernie out on his ear and forbid him from ever seeing the children again. On 17 November 1950, Ernie Ingenito was told by his lawyer that he would only get access to his sons through a court order. It was the final straw. Ernie returned to the lodging-house where he had taken a room and selected a .32 carbine and two pistols from his collection of guns. Then he went visiting.

When he knocked on the front door of the Mazzoli house he came face to face with Mike Mazzoli, who told him in plain language to push off. They were the last words Mazzoli uttered as his son-in-law gunned him down. Next on the hit-list was Theresa, though mercifully she later recovered from her wounds in hospital. When the shooting had started, Pearl Mazzoli fled to her parents' home nearby, but nothing was going to stop Ernie now – he was going to track down every last damn member of the Mazzoli family. After shooting Pearl, he rampaged through the house slaughtering Pearl's mother, Teresa Pioppi, her sister-in-law Marion, brother Gino and Gino's nine-year-old daughter, and finally brother John. Ernie had just one more murderous trip to make – out to Mineola where Michael Mazzoli's parents lived; there he massacred Frank and Hilda Mazzoli. It was all over; it was midnight, and Ernie Ingenito had wreaked his insane revenge. He had also, not surprisingly, attracted the attention of the police.

Before armed officers took him into custody, Ernie made a half-hearted attempt to take his own life, but he was patched up in time for his trial in January 1951. He was indicted on a sample charge of murdering Mrs Pearl Mazzoli and sentenced to life imprisonment, and as Ernie was clearly daft as a brush this sentence was ordered to be served in the New Jersey State Hospital for the Insane at Trenton. It was, to be sure, a rather more benign punishment than the one suggested by Ernie's wife from her hospital bed: 'I wish they would hang Ernie', she said. But just to keep everyone happy, Ernest Ingenito was eventually put on trial again in 1956. This time he faced a further four counts of murder, was convicted, and was handed down a life sentence on each charge.

IQBAL, Shaied   Five young girls and three adults died when fire swept through their house in Osborne Road, Huddersfield, West Yorkshire on 12 May 2002. The victims were Nafeesa Aziz (35), her five young daughters, Tayyaba Batool (13), Rabiah Batool (10), Abeeqa Nawaz (6) and Najeeba Nawaz (6 months), Nafeesa Aziz's brother, Mohammed Ateeq-ur-Rahman (18), also died in the fire, and their mother Zaib-u-Nisa (54) died in hospital from serious injuries sustained from jumping from an upstairs window. Investigations by forensic specialists soon established that arson was the cause of the fire. Petrol had been poured through the letterbox and petrol bombs thrown through windows into the house.

An informer contacted police to say that he had heard twenty-six-year-old Iqbal, the known leader of an Asian gang in the town, talking to Nazar Hussein (24), Shakiel Shazac (23) and another man in a McDonalds and boasting how successful they had been in bombing the house. He had said 'They should not have messed about with me in the first place. They got what they deserved'. Iqbal had added that this was revenge on Ateeq-ur-Rahman, who had interfered with relationships which he and the fourth man had been having with other women.

Iqbal, Hussein and Shazad were all detained and charged with eight counts of murder and conspiracy to commit arson. The fourth man escaped and is still being sought by the police.

After a protracted trial at Leeds Crown Court, Iqbal was found guilty on all eight counts of murder and conspiracy to commit arson. After further retirements, the jury found Hussein and Shazad guilty of eight counts of manslaughter and conspiracy.

On 30 July 2003, the judge sentenced Iqbal to life imprisonment on each of the murder charges together with a fourteen-year term to run concurrently for conspiracy. He told Iqbal that his recommendation to the Home Secretary as to the minimum term he would serve would 'reflect the ruthlessness with which you orchestrated and executed the design'. Hussein and Shazad were each given eighteen-year sentences for manslaughter with fourteen-year concurrent terms for conspiracy.

ISAACS, Carl, *et al.* In 1973 the Alday family lived in a trailer home on their 500-acre farm in Seminole County, Georgia. Jerry Alday supported his wife Mary by growing corn and peanuts.

On the morning of 14 May, Jerry Alday's brother arrived on a visit and found five male members of his family dead in the bedrooms. All had been shot – sixty-two-year-old Ned Alday, his sons, Jerry (34), Jimmy (25) and Chester (nicknamed Shugie) (30), and their uncle Aubrey, aged fifty-eight. In a forest some distance away lay the body of Jerry's twenty-nine-year-old wife Mary. She had been stripped, beaten, raped and sodomized.

A hue and cry was raised for the killers who were thought to be escaped convicts from a Maryland work camp. State troopers with bloodhounds hunted the fugitives into the hills of West Virginia and eventually ran four of the exhausted escapees down. They were identified as Carl Isaacs and his stepbrother Wayne Coleman, escapees from the prison camp, fifteen-year-old Billy Isaacs, Carl's brother – who had decided to join them – and a black man named George Dungee, who had walked out of the minimum security camp with Isaacs and Coleman.

During the interrogation the men admitted their part in the killings, and a plea bargain arrangement was made with Billy Isaacs whereby in exchange for a plea of guilty to lesser charges and a promise to testify against the others he would receive two twenty-year sentences to be served consecutively.

Carl Isaacs was tried first, and brother Billy, in his testimony, accused him of all the murders and the sexual assaults on Mary Alday. After a retirement of just over an hour the jury found Carl Isaacs guilty on all counts. An even shorter retirement – thirty-eight minutes – was all they needed to return with a sentence of death in the electric chair.

The separate trials of George Dungee and Wayne Coleman followed a similar course ending with verdicts of guilty and sentences of death in the electric chair.

Following the customary appeals, the Georgia Supreme Court quashed the convictions and ordered new trials. At the retrials, Billy Isaacs once again gave evidence, Carl was once again found guilty on all counts, and once again sentenced to death. Wayne Coleman and George Dungee were also once again found guilty, but on this occasion the jury at a penalty hearing gave them a reduced sentence of six life terms each.

On 30 November 1989, the Georgia Supreme Court upheld the conviction and sentence on Carl Isaacs. After almost twenty-nine years on Death Row, he was finally executed by lethal injection on 6 May 2002.

William Andrews (*top*) and
Dale Selby Pierre who were
responsible for the notorious
'Hi-Fi Killings'. (*Popperfoto*)

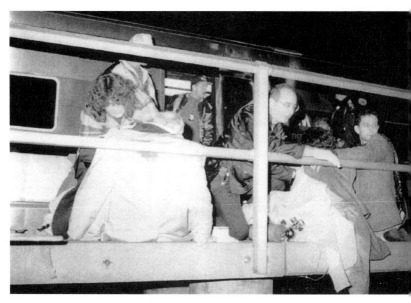

Long Island Railroad passengers are comforted after Colin Ferguson's three-minute killing spree left five people dead and eighteen wounded. (*Popperfoto/Reuter*)

Colin Ferguson arrives in court wearing a bullet-proof vest. (*Popperfoto*)

Sheila 'Bambi' Caffell with her sons, Nicholas and Daniel, and her adoptive mother, June, at White House Farm where they were shot dead in August 1985. (*Syndication International*)

'Grieving' Jeremy Bamber is comforted by his girlfriend, Julie Mugford, at the funeral of the family he murdered. (*Syndication International*)

Wade John Frankum (*Popperfoto/Reuter*)

Police officers stand near the body of Wade Frankum on the floor of a Sydney car park. (*Popperfoto/Reuter*)

Ernest Ingenito after his arrest, handcuffed and guarded by a State Trooper.

The body of Marion Pioppi, the 28-year-old aunt of Theresa Ingenito.

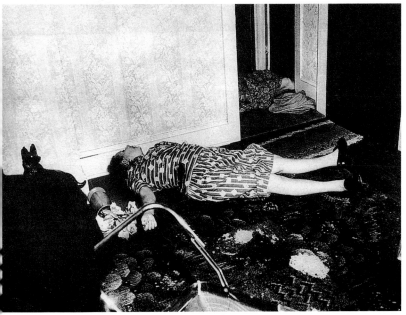

Thomas Hamilton, nicknamed 'Mr Creepy' by some in the Scottish town of Dunblane, where he gunned down sixteen children and their teacher. (*Syndication International*)

Dunblane Primary School where the shooting took place on 13 March 1996. (*Syndication International*)

Marc Lepine. In December 1989 his deep hatred of women led him to open fire into a crowd of women students at the University of Montreal. (*Popperfoto*)

A Montreal Police SWAT team runs into a University of Montreal building. (*Popperfoto*)

Brenda Spencer. She went on a shooting spree at Cleveland Elementary School because 'I just don't like Mondays . . . I did it because it's a way to cheer the day up'.
(*Popperfoto/Reuter*)

Mrs Florence Ransom, the 'attractive redhead' who was found guilty of the murders of Mrs Dorothy Fisher and her daughter, and their maid, Charlotte Saunders.
(*Popperfoto*)

J

JAIN, Rattan Bai   On Saturday 1 May 1954, three teenage girls, Satyabala, Raj Rani and Kanta were rushed to a New Delhi hospital by ambulance after collapsing at their homes with severe convulsions. In spite of the most strenuous efforts by hospital staff, eighteen-year-old Kanta died the following morning. A well-known toxicologist was called in to examine the possibility that the girls could have been suffering from some venomous snake-bite. A common link between the three young women was established when it came to light that they all worked at the Nari Kiwan Karyalaya fertility clinic run by a couple called Milkhi Ram Jain and his wife Rattan Bai. Mrs Jain was without doubt the dominant partner, and she had made such a success of the business that they now employed a manager to run it.

An examining magistrate was appointed to investigate the death of Kanta and the illness of the other two girls, who were still on the critical list. The magistrate visited Mrs Jain who assured him there was no possible way the girls could have taken anything harmful at the clinic; it was more likely, she thought, that they had eaten something at a picnic they had been planning. Mrs Jain appeared, as always, very self-possessed – almost cold, the magistrate thought. The police and magistrate left the clinic after obtaining the manager's name and address, and returned to the hospital to be informed that Raj Rani's condition was worsening; she died the following afternoon.

The next person to be interviewed was the fertility clinic's manager, Jagannath, who was adamant there was no poison at the clinic; and what was more, he knew of no picnic. Asked if they had eaten anything out of the usual, Jagannath suggested: 'It might have been the peras.' Peras are a sugary sweet popular with young girls, and indeed, the nurse present just before Raj Rani died reported that the girl had been mumbling something about peras before she died. The last of the three girls, Satyabala, died the same evening after telling nurses that Mrs Jain had given her peras. Analysis of the stomach contents of the three girls established that they had all received a lethal dose of white arsenic.

The police applied for a warrant to arrest Mrs Jain and her husband but when they arrived at the house the couple had fled. They were detained at Jakhai, about a hundred miles away, and returned to New Delhi for questioning. Milkhi Ram Jain denied any involvement but confided that his wife was insanely jealous of the young and pretty girls they employed. Mrs Jain admitted giving sweets to the dead girls, but accused the manager, Jagannath, of coating them with arsenic. Jagannath naturally denied this, and all three suspects were kept in custody while enquiries continued. The police had a lucky break when they talked to a pedlar of herbs who remembered selling Mrs Jain arsenic, which she said she needed to kill vermin. In view of this evidence the police released the two men and charged Mrs Jain with murder.

The trial opened on 6 July 1954, before Mr Y. L. Taneja the Additional Sessions Judge, and four assessors. Rattan Bai Jain was convicted of murder and sentenced to death.

Mrs Jain's appeal was dismissed by the High Court of the Punjab on 3 September and her application for leave to appeal to the Supreme Court of India was rejected. A petition for mercy to the President of India also failed, and Rattan Bai Jain was hanged in New Delhi on Monday 3 January 1955, the first woman to be hanged in the Indian capital. She was also the first woman to be executed on the sub-continent since independence in 1947.

JOHNSON, Patricia In the early hours of the morning of 11 October 1986, firefighters were called to a house in Johnson Road, Trail Creek, Indiana, which was blazing fiercely. Neighbours had been woken to see an orange flame swirling out of the thick smoke which surrounded the house. In spite of the firefighters' efforts they were unable to do more than contain the flames and stop the fire spreading; the home of Roland and Betty Kirby was swiftly reduced to blackened rubble and ashes.

The fire team recovered four bodies from the charred building and these were latter identified as the Kirbys and two visitors, Terry Ward and Eugene Johnson. Fire investigators at first thought that the blaze had been caused by an electrical short and this was the conclusion of their preliminary report. However, further forensic examination of the lower floor revealed evidence that an inflammable substance had been spread around the house. A fire expert brought in to supplement the local team confirmed that the fire had been the result of arson.

Enquiries were begun into the backgrounds of the victims and an informant reported that the night before the fire the four people who died had been in a bar in Michigan City where an argument had broken out between Eugene Johnson and his wife Patricia who objected to him being out with Terry Ward. The informant said that Patricia Johnson, who had been married for twenty-two years, had said 'I'm going to get that son-of-a-bitch' or something like that. The informant added that Patricia Johnson had been in the company of a man named Roger Griffin.

It was decided to question both Johnson and Griffin. Roger Griffin was prepared to admit to detectives that he had borrowed a car and driven Patricia Johnson to the murder scene. Patricia Johnson was questioned and eventually confessed that she had started the fire that killed the four people. On 17 October, they were both charged with four counts of first-degree murder.

Prior to the trial, plea-bargain arrangements were made with Roger Griffin, that he would be allowed to plead guilty to four charges of assisting a criminal. Such arrangements, however, can only be made with the approval of the court; in this case the plea-bargain was overturned. Negotiations to allow Patricia Johnson to plead guilty to murder with the possibility that sentences would be concurrent rather than consecutive were discontinued.

Patricia Johnson's trial opened in September 1987, when despite defence objections that her confession had been obtained illegally, a videotape was played to the court in which she described how she spread paint thinner around the Kirby home and set it alight. She said she had nothing against the Kirbys but wanted to punish her husband and his girlfriend Terry Ward. After deliberating for only ninety minutes the jury found Patricia Johnson guilty on all four counts of murder.

On 9 October 1987, she was sentenced to forty years on each murder count with the terms for counts one and two to be served concurrently with those for counts three and four which meant she was faced with a total of forty years' imprisonment before release. On 11 December, Roger Griffin was sentenced to ten years in jail on the four counts of assisting a criminal.

JONES, Reverend Jim   James Warren Jones was born in 1931 in Lynn, Indiana. His father was an alcoholic Klansman with a taste for religion, his mother was a self-declared mystic; it was little wonder that Jim turned out weird. For instance, he used to hold funeral services for dead animals, usually not long after a neighbour had lost a pet.

Jim Jones was also a precocious preacher of the fire-and-brimstone type so popular in the Midwest Bible-belt where he grew up. After dropping out of Indiana University and soon after getting married Jim and his wife went touring door-to-door for the Methodist Mission; though in the end he became just a tad too peculiar for the conservative tastes of the church fathers, and he was asked to leave. Which was fine by Jim – he just bought his own church in the broken-down black district of Indianapolis, and took his mission among the flock that nobody else wanted messing up their pews. Jim did so well at it that he was appointed by the mayor on to the City Human Rights Commission. The so-called People's Temple was making its mark. Later they were to amalgamate with the Disciples of Christ, and Jones was ordained a minister. Two years later Jim Jones transported busloads of his congregation across to California where he bought another church, another haven for the oddballs, the disadvantaged and the impoverished ethnic minorities. In 1975 Jones' influence among black voters was recognized when the mayor of San Francisco elected him on to the city housing authority.

The People's Temple could now lay claim to more than 20,000 followers, and power was beginning to control Jim Jones the way he once controlled power. He began to lay extravagant claims to healing powers, and started to refer to himself as God; he introduced an unhealthy sexual element into his meetings and was enjoying intercourse with a large proportion of his congregation. But something more sinister than all this Bible-thumping mumbo-jumbo was afoot. The People's Temple had a hidden agenda. In 1976 Jones began elaborating on the use of mass suicide as an expression of political dissidence – 'revolutionary suicide' he called it. At a New Year's Day meeting, Jones decided to put the loyalty of his followers to the test – he wanted them all to drink poison, or so he said. For those who were hesitant, the Reverend Jones staged a little charade acted out by members of his 'elite guard', his 'inner circle': a plant in the congregation would refuse to drink the liquid and make as if to run away, then one of Jim's guards would 'shoot' him. It proved very effective, and everybody ended up taking a swig of this quite innocuous drink. But Jim Jones had proved his point.

Some years earlier, Jones had entertained the idea of building his own Utopia, and had bought a lease on 27,000 acres of rain forest in Guyana. The foundation of what was modestly to be called Jonestown was going ahead apace. An advance guard of the faithful had upped and left to prepare for the expected exodus, and in all about a thousand disciples had invested their worldly goods in this distant Utopia. What they hadn't realized is that this Utopia was a dictatorship, with Rev. Jones as supremo and a handful of heavily armed sycophants as minor lieutenants. The reality was that life was extremely miserable; work was hard and thankless, sex was reserved for Jones and a few cronies, and any perceived misdemeanours – such as nodding off during one of the Reverend's interminable rambling sermons were punished with public beatings and torture. With such power Jones himself was becoming more than a little unbalanced, he was on his way to becoming a card-carrying psychopath. One report stated that electrodes were attached to children who failed to smile at the mention of the Leader's name. Anybody who was foolish enough to try to get out of town had first to get past the ring of armed guards stationed around the perimeter.

But this kind of behaviour cannot be kept secret for ever, and news began to filter out to the civilized world. In 1977 the San Francisco *Examiner* began to print decidedly un-flattering reports of the state of affairs in Jonestown, and the discomfort generated by such news encouraged California congressman Leo Ryan to put together a formidable fact-finding team consisting of eight journalists and a number of parents of cult members. On 14 November 1978 they flew to Jonestown.

There was, on the face of it, a warm enough welcome for the party in Utopia – or there was until a reporter made the mistake of pressing Jim Jones on the purpose of the heavily armed guards; Jones had to be restrained from attacking him. Amid an increasingly hostile atmosphere of menace the fact-finding mission beat a hasty retreat back to their waiting aircraft. They got just as far as the landing strip when they were overtaken by a truck-load of gun-toting cultists from Jonestown. In the massacre that followed three of the departing journalists, one defecting cult member and congressman Ryan were shot dead.

Meanwhile, back in Jonestown, the faithful were being mobilized for Big Jim's 'revolutionary suicide'. While some prepared large vats of purple Kool-Aid drink laced with cyanide, mothers were feeding it to their babies; children and adults drank the lethal liquid from paper cups. Those who showed a lack of enthusiasm to join in the 'political dissent' were encouraged to do the right thing by armed guards; then the guards drank. Within five minutes more than 900 men, women and children lay dead where they fell. Jim Jones, his mission accomplished, put a gun to his head and pulled the trigger.

JONES, William What was described by local newspapers of the time as the 'most terrible crime ever committed in Sunderland' came to light on Sunday 22 May 1910.

A man walking along a street in the Millfield district heard groaning and a cry for help coming from the back yard of one of the small cottages lining the road. On investigation he found a figure lying on the ground with blood pouring from a wound in his throat. The injured man pointed feverishly towards the cottage behind him, pleading by his gesture for the stranger to go inside. With what trepidation we cannot guess, but our good samaritan cautiously walked into the house, where he was horrified to find a young woman lying on a bed, her head savagely battered. Beside her was a baby girl, and in another bed close by were three other children all of whom had their throats cut.

When a doctor had certified life extinct the police moved in to try to make sense of the apparently motiveless carnage. The dead woman turned out to be twenty-eight-year-old Susannah Jones, her four children were James, aged eight, Polly, seven, Susannah, five, and year-old-baby Alice. The man lying in his own blood outside the house was thirty-three-year-old William Jones, husband and father of the victims. Jones was rushed to hospital, where after emergency surgery he recovered.

The local newspapers, always hungry for tragedy, had already nicknamed the cottage the 'House of Horrors' and published graphic descriptions of the wounds suffered by the victims. It was also reported that the words 'Revenge is sweet' had been scrawled on the wall of the bedroom where the bodies were found.

When Jones had recovered sufficiently to answer police

questions he claimed that his wife had been unfaithful, though enquiries among the family's friends suggested that there was no basis whatever for this obsession. Quite the contrary, Susannah Jones was considered by all who knew her to be an exemplary wife and mother; indeed, since Jones had lost his job some time before, Susannah had been reduced to begging for money to feed and clothe the children. What neighbours had heard on the night of the killings was Jones violently berating his wife not for her infidelity, but for not having begged enough money that day. Just one other snippet of information gleaned by the police was that Jones's immediate neighbours had heard him shout out during the night: 'It's the comet.'

William Jones was eventually charged with five counts of murder and in due course was committed for trial. He stood in the dock at Durham Assizes on 25 June 1910 still bandaged from his self-inflicted throat wound. When invited to plead he at first replied 'Guilty', but following representations from his defence counsel this plea was withdrawn and one of not guilty substituted. To nobody's surprise, Jones's defence was one of insanity, and expert psychiatric witnesses were brought before the jury to testify that Jones's aberration could have arisen as a result of 'privation and poverty'. It was a concept that the jury clearly sympathized with, for they returned a verdict of guilty but insane, and William Jones was ordered to be detained during His Majesty's pleasure.

JOYCE, Myles, *et al.* In the early hours of the morning of 18 August 1882, John Joyce, his wife Bridget, his mother Margaret, his daughter Margaret and sons Michael and Patrick were attacked in their home at Maamtrasna in the West of Ireland. Joyce, his wife, mother and daughter were already dead when villagers entered the house on the following morning. The two boys were still alive although seriously injured, and Michael died not long afterwards in hospital. Two of the victims had been shot and four had been savagely beaten with blunt instruments and horribly disfigured. It was estimated by police and medical experts that the massacre had been completed in less than five minutes.

Before dying, young Michael Joyce had been able to give detectives descriptions of the murderers. A nearby farmer also recalled seeing a party of men, all known to him, heading along the road to Maamtrasna on the night of the murders. Within a week, this information led to thirteen arrests. In the end ten men were charged with murder: Anthony Philbin, Thomas Casey, Myles Joyce, Martin Joyce, Paudeen Joyce and his son Thomas Joyce, Patrick, John and Michael Casey and Patrick Joyce. Four of the men were cousins of the victims from a branch of the family with whom they had been feuding for some time. On 29 October a true bill was returned against all the prisoners and the case was ordered for trial at the Commission Court in Dublin.

On Wednesday 1 November, all ten men stood before Mr Justice Barry and pleaded not guilty. The hearing was adjourned until 13 November, when it was announced that the defendants would be tried separately, and the first case to be heard was that against Patrick Joyce. Meanwhile, Anthony Philbin had elected to turn Queen's Evidence and testify against the others. Another of the men, Thomas Casey, hearing of Philbin's action, also agreed to become what was known as an 'approver'. At the end of the trial, after a retirement of just eight minutes, the jury returned a verdict of guilty and Patrick Joyce was sentenced to death. The Crown formally entered a *nolle prosequi* to the charges entered against Philbin and Thomas Casey and these were withdrawn. Following Patrick Joyce into the dock was Patrick Casey, and a similar case followed resulting in a verdict of guilty after only twelve minutes' deliberation; Casey was also sentenced to death. The third trial, that of Myles Joyce commenced on Friday 17 November and concluded the following day, the jury returning after a record six minutes with another verdict of guilty on the capital charge.

On Monday 20 November, the trial of Michael Casey opened, though by the following day, Casey and the four remaining defendants, Paudeen Joyce and his son Thomas, Martin Joyce and John James Casey, had decided to change their pleas to guilty. As in the other cases all five were sentenced to death.

It was (indeed it still is) an unwritten understanding that defendants who plead guilty and thus save court time, effort and expense, will be treated more leniently; so it was that the three Joyces and two Caseys had their sentences commuted to penal servitude for life.

Of the three remaining men, both Patrick Joyce and Patrick Casey made statements insisting that Myles Joyce was innocent of any part in the murders. Not that it made any difference; on Friday 15 December 1882, Patrick Joyce, Myles Joyce and Patrick Casey were hanged in Galway Prison by executioner William Marwood. It was not one of his more skilful executions, and Myles Joyce (almost certainly an innocent man) died from slow strangulation.

K

KANG MIN-CHIU and **ZIN MO**   Twenty-one people, including four South Korean cabinet ministers, died and forty-eight others were injured when a bomb exploded in the Martyrs Mausoleum in Rangoon, Burma, on 9 October 1983. The occasion was an official visit by a South Korean presidential delegation, and the blast occurred just minutes before the arrival of the president himself, Chun Doo Hwan, who was due to lay a wreath on behalf of the visitors. A large section of the mausoleum's roof collapsed, burying the waiting audience under rubble and debris. Eye-witnesses reported seeing bloodstained victims staggering from the building.

Investigations into the terror attack concentrated on North Koreans resident in Burma, and in the course of inquiries it was discovered that three army officers from that country had recently entered Burma illegally. Police were informed that the officers were hiding out in the home of a local North Korean, where the attack had been planned. The house was raided and one of the men, Captain Sin Ki-Choi, was shot dead while attempting to escape. The other two, Major Kang Min-Chiu and Major Zin Mo were placed under arrest. During his interrogation, Kang gave full details of the plot, explaining that they had been ordered by a North Korean general to assassinate President Chun. On 8 October, they had planted three remote-controlled bombs in the roof of the mausoleum. Major Zin Mo had detonated the explosives when he thought the visiting dignitaries had arrived but mercifully President Chun had been delayed and escaped the blast.

On 5 December, the two army officers appeared before a court in Rangoon. Kang pleaded guilty but Zin Mo refused to speak at all when the charges were read. The hearing was adjourned for prosecution and defence attorneys to prepare final arguments in writing. On Friday 9 December, Kang and Zin Mo were convicted and sentenced to death by hanging.

Zin Mo was hanged in Rangoon Central Prison on 6 April 1985. The death sentence on Kang Min-Chiu was commuted to life imprisonment on account of his 'assistance' to the prosecution.

KEHOE, Andrew   In 1927 the local authorities at Bath, Michigan, decided to build a new schoolhouse, the funds for the project to be raised by a special tax on local property owners. Among those affected by the levy was Andrew Kehoe, a farmer, though he had been largely unsuccessful in his efforts to wring a living out of the land. Kehoe was nevertheless called on to contribute $300 towards the schoolhouse, and after paying up he found himself unable to keep up the mortgage and faced the loss of his home and his farm. Andrew Kehoe was not a happy man and swore revenge against the school board whom he accused of squandering local residents' hard-earned money.

On the morning of 18 May 1927, the newly erected schoolhouse was devastated by a huge explosion. The second floor collapsed into matchwood and rubble and crashed down on to the first floor. Thirty-seven children and one teacher lost their lives in the explosion and forty-three were seriously injured. At the time of the blast, Andrew Kehoe was sitting in his car outside the school and watched as local people, led by the head teacher, struggled to rescue injured children from the wreckage. Kehoe called the head teacher over to his car and when he stood beside it Kehoe detonated the final bomb; it was in the car, and killed himself and the head of the school. Piecing together the fragments of information available, it was later established that Andrew Kehoe had been seen around the school on several nights before the explosion, and it had to be assumed that on those occasions he had been planting dynamite in the building.

KIM HYON-HUI and **KIM SUNG-IL**   Korean Airlines flight 858 from Baghdad to Seoul carrying 115 passengers and crew aboard disappeared over the Andaman Sea near the coast of Burma on 29 November 1987. Sabotage was suspected when fragments of the aircraft were found floating in the water. Enquiries concentrated on a couple claiming to be Japanese, who had left the plane at Abu Dhabi and then taken another flight to Bahrain where they had been detained for allegedly having false identity papers. The couple, an elderly man travelling as Shinichi Yachiya, and a young girl, Mayumi Hachiya, at first refused to answer any questions, and when pressed to do so, swallowed capsules later found to contain cyanide. The man died instantly, but the girl recovered in hospital.

The Korean authorities applied for the girl's extradition to Seoul and on 15 December she was flown to South Korea with her mouth heavily bandaged to prevent a second suicide attempt. On arrival in the capital, she was subjected to intensive interrogation as investigators attempted to establish a North Korean connection.

An extraordinary development in the case, at least by Western judicial standards, was the appearance of the girl on South Korean television on 15 January 1988. By now she had been identified as Kim Hyon-Hui, a North Korean intelligence officer, and in front of cameras she confessed that she and her accomplice, Kim Sung-Il, who had killed himself in Bahrain, had been ordered by Kim Jung-Il, the heir of North Korean dictator Kim Il-Sung, to blow up the aircraft in order to deter other nations from attending the Seoul Olympics. Kim Hyon-Hui admitted that they had planted a bomb in the toilet behind the plane's flight deck. Very emotional and constantly fighting back tears, Kim said she deserved to die a hundred deaths for her crime, which had been without meaning. The appearance of this very attractive girl on television seemingly totally contrite caused a sensation throughout South Korea. A public debate followed as to whether Kim Hyon-Hui should be put on trial or freed as a reward for her contrition. Nor could it be ignored what a powerful propaganda weapon Kim might be against North Korea, and if tried and convicted she could be pardoned, rehabilitated and presented as an anti-communist convert.

Eventually it was decided she should be put on trial and the hearing opened in Seoul Central District Court on 7 March 1989. The process was constantly disrupted by distraught relatives of victims of the bombing who began screaming and wailing whenever Kim spoke in answer to the prosecutor's questions. On the second day of the trial, as Kim was demonstrating to the court how she set the timer on a replica of the bomb, she was hit by a shoe thrown from the public gallery. The trial ended on 25 April, when Chief Judge Chung Sang-Hak gave judgement finding Kim Hyon-Hui guilty and sentencing her to death by hanging. Government sources, however, made it clear that the sentence would be commuted because it was felt that Kim had been duped by North Korea into carrying out the attack, and because she had cooperated fully with the authorities in Seoul.

On 27 March 1990, the Supreme Court upheld the conviction and sentence but Justice Ministry officials insisted Kim would be granted a special amnesty and pardon.

In April 1992, it was reported that Kim Hyon-Hui had written her autobiography, *Now I Want To Be a Woman*, and the book had sold over 1.8 million copies in South Korea and Japan. She embarked on a heavy schedule of public appearances and one report observed cynically that she was no doubt repenting all the way to the bank.

KIM JAE-KYU *et al.* The South Korean news agency reported that President Park Chung Hee and five of his bodyguards had been shot dead on Friday 26 October 1979, at a dinner in Seoul with Kim Jae-Kyu, head of the Korean Central Intelligence Agency. Considerable confusion was caused by initial reports that the shootings were 'accidental' even though Kim had been arrested.

Shortly afterwards, Kim Jae-Kyu was taken by police to the scene of the shootings for a re-enactment of the events. Watched by invited journalists, Kim demonstrated how he had excused himself from the room, collected a revolver from an ante-chamber, returned and shot first the president's chief bodyguard and then Park himself. The scene was exactly as it had been on 26 October, with dishes on the table and bloodstains visible throughout the room. Six men who had been in another room also described the killing of the remaining members of the presidential bodyguard.

Subsequently, Kim was charged with the murder of President Park and six others; chief secretary Kim Kae Won, protocol chief Park Sun Ho, army colonel Park Jung Joo and KCIA guards Lee Ki Ju, Yu Sung Ok and Kim Tae Won were charged with assisting in the assassination of the president and with the murders of the bodyguards. An eighth defendant, KCIA employee Yu Suk Sul, was charged with destroying evidence of the assassination. They were remanded for trial by a military court.

A two-week trial was held before a five-man military tribunal in Seoul. The prosecution contended that Kim had intended to replace the president as head of state. Kim testified that he had assassinated the president to protect democracy and political freedom in South Korea. He said he had no regrets and urged the tribunal to take into consideration that the other men were acting under his orders. At the final session of the court on Thursday 20 December 1979, all the defendants were found guilty. Kim and the six men convicted of actual participation in the killings were sentenced to death. The eighth man, Yu Suk Sul, was given three years' imprisonment for destroying evidence.

On 26 December, the military commander confirmed the court's findings, and a military appeals court dismissed appeals by six of the men. Colonel Park Jung Joo, as a serving army officer, had no right of appeal and he was executed by firing squad in Seoul on 6 March 1980. The death sentence on chief secretary Kim Kae Won was commuted to life imprisonment by the Army Command

Council who confirmed the sentence of Kim Jae-Kyu and the other five accomplices; they were hanged on 24 March 1980.

KING, Alvin Lee King, a forty-eight-year-old former school-teacher, drove from his home to the First Baptist Church in Dangerfield, Texas, on the morning of Sunday 22 June 1980, carrying an arsenal of weapons including an M1 carbine, an automatic rifle, two revolvers and 240 rounds of ammunition. Bursting into the church, he shouted 'This is war' and opened fire with the carbine. With the first shots, Gina Linam, aged seven, and seventy-eight-year-old Thelma Robinson fell dead and Mrs Gene Gandy, aged forty-nine, was fatally wounded and died later the same day.

Another member of the congregation, Christopher Hall, grappled with King and succeeded in knocking the rifles out of King's hands and dislodging his spectacles. No doubt the loss of King's glasses was responsible for saving Chris Hall's life; at least as he fled after the struggle he was not hit by shots from the gunman's revolver. James McDaniel and Kenneth Truitt were the next people to try to tackle King. First, McDaniel managed to pull King to the ground but in the struggle was shot dead; then Truitt charged at King while he was on the floor, but was also killed by revolver fire. Ten other members of the Dangerfield First Baptists' congregation received gun-shot wounds of greater or lesser severity. Leaving behind one of his revolvers Alvin King ran from the church, dropping another of the guns as he did so; once outside he made an ineffectual attempt to shoot himself in the head.

The day after the shootings, King had been due to face trial on a charge of incest involving his nineteen-year-old daughter; he had also been a suspect in the stabbing to death of a local minister who had persuaded the daughter to contact police regarding the incest allegation.

On 11 July, Alvin King was charged with five counts of first-degree murder and ten of assault with intent to kill. On 28 July a jury found him to be of unsound mind and he was sent to a state hospital for the criminally insane until he was judged to be 'rehabilitated'. On 24 November 1981, he was certified fit for trial. On 19 January 1982, a week before the date fixed for his trial, Alvin King hanged himself in Dangerfield town jail using strips torn from a towel.

KINNAISTER, Charles, *et al.* Former convicts Charles Kinnaister, William Hawkins, James Perry, Edward Foley, James Cates, John Russell and John Johnson had been transported from England to Australia, and after serving their sentences had stayed on as stockmen and shepherds to the settlers of New South Wales. On 10 June 1838, they came upon a small tribe of around thirty aboriginals going about their business in the bush area outside Liverpool Plains; the bandits tied the natives together with a rope and dragged them off further into the bush where, at a suitably isolated spot they dismounted from their horses and proceeded to slash the unfortunate men, women and children to death. When the slaughter was complete they piled all the bodies together and set them on fire in an effort to conceal their grisly crime. It was not to be, for nobody could ignore the significance of the sinister birds of prey which began to hover over the site of the killings; subsequently enough bones were discovered to reveal the enormity of the massacre. Kinnaister and his band had already been reported in the area around the time of the mass slaughter, and they were detained, their own admissions adding to the circumstantial evidence found at the scene of the crime.

On 15 November 1838, Charles Kinnaister and his murderous gang appeared for their trial before the Chief Justice, Sir James Dowling, on a sample charge of murdering an aboriginal man called Daddy whose remains had been positively identified. In their defence they claimed they had simply been protecting settlers' property from the natives who, they insisted, were spearing and killing cattle. The prejudice against the aborigines in the area was well known, and nobody could have advanced a more successful defence; despite the strength of the evidence, the jury found the prisoners not guilty.

However, other, separate, indictments remained against

the men, and in December they were again put on trial for murder. On this occasion, the whole gang was found guilty and sentenced to death. Despite strenuous efforts to obtain reprieves, the governor, Sir George Gipps decided that the law should take its course and on 15 December 1838 they were all hanged.

KNIGHT, Virgil   Only a week after being divorced and losing a custody battle for his three children, twenty-six-year-old. Virgil Knight went on a murder rampage which went down in Oklahoma City history as the 'Christmas tree massacre'.

On 14 December 1987, Knight went first to the home of his former sister-in-law Carrie and shot her and her boyfriend Allen Lockhart dead. He then went to his former home, where he shot his ex-wife Deeta and two of their children, six-year-old Curtis and two-year-old Kevin. The only survivors were his daughter Shelly, aged four, who suffered a severe head wound, and Deeta Knight's twin brothers, eighteen-year-old James and Christopher Dolan, who escaped from the house after being fired at by Knight. Finally Knight turned the gun on himself and was found lying dead beside the family Christmas tree, the bodies of his wife and children around him.

Virgil Knight's mother said later that he had been very depressed after the divorce and the custody battle, but she had not realized that this would turn a quiet loving family man into a killer.

L

LAMMERS, James One January night in 1951, people living in a caravan camp in Troy, Kansas, were awakened by a blazing fire. Going outside they saw that the caravan occupied by the Lammers family was a mass of flames. In less than twenty minutes the caravan was a total ruin despite the best efforts of the local fire department. The sheriff was called, and by the light of a torch it was just possible for him to make out the charred remains of three small children lying in their beds and another body, that of an adult, on a larger bed. When the ruins had cooled down, the corpses were brought out and on the following morning post-mortem examinations were performed. Reports on the children indicated that they had died as a result of the fire, there being characteristic sooty deposits in the lungs associated with smoke inhalation. The autopsy proved that the adult body was that of a woman – presumed to be the children's mother, Mrs Geneva Lammers. In her case there was no trace of soot or carbon monoxide gas in the lungs, so she must have died before the fire started. Fire officers examining the burned out caravan found that petrol and oil had been poured around it. The sheriff had already made enquiries at the camp regarding James Lammers, the owner of the caravan, and was told he had left town the previous evening to look for work. Now a broadcast was made appealing for Lammers to contact the police.

A witness reported that there had recently been a fight between Lammers and another man, apparently over Geneva Lammers. The man was detained and readily admitted that he was in love with Geneva but denied he had any involvement in the fire at Troy. Rather inconveniently, he also admitted that he had been near the caravan on the night before the fire in order to talk to James Lammers – he added quickly that he had changed his mind at the last minute and gone home. Pending further enquiries the man was detained.

A further search of the caravan area revealed a blood-stained torch hidden in some bushes. At that moment, who should drive up in a truck but the missing James Lammers. He had, so he said, only just heard of the tragedy because he had been away in Topeka. Lammers confirmed that he had been in a fight over Geneva, but added that he completely trusted his wife. A search of his truck revealed a receipt for petrol.

The next morning the sheriff ordered the release of James Lammers' sparring partner and had Lammers himself brought in for questioning. The sheriff told his suspect that enquiries showed that he had bought seventeen and a half gallons of petrol in Kansas City. If he had driven from there to Topeka as he said, he could not possibly have used the amount of fuel he had. In addition, the observant lawman noticed that the hair on Lammers' right hand had been burned off. Having ordered a check on all the barber shops in Topeka as the result of an inspired guess, the sheriff was rewarded with reports of one barber who remembered a man coming in to have his hair cut to disguise the fact that it was singed. Hearing that the hairdresser had identified him, Lammers confessed that he had strangled his wife and set fire to the caravan. He claimed he had killed Geneva Lammers because she was expecting another baby and the children got on his nerves.

Lammers was charged with four counts of first-degree murder and at his trial was found guilty and sentenced to death; he was hanged on the gallows at Kansas State Prison on 5 January 1952.

LA MON HOUSE BOMBING The bombing of the La Mon House Restaurant at Castlereagh Hills, near Belfast, was a classic example of the IRA's use of incendiary devices.

Called blast incendiaries by the army, they consist of a small quantity of explosive with a very short timing fuse fastened to a can of petrol. The device would be hung with a butcher's meat-hook from the wire-mesh security grill, which used to protect many buildings in the Province.

On 17 February 1978, police received a telephone warning about a bomb at the La Mon House only minutes before the explosion, which occurred as they arrived. The blast caused a fireball sixty feet high and forty feet wide which turned the building into a blazing inferno within seconds. The restaurant was packed with diners, including many attending a motorcycle club dinner-dance. Panic-stricken guests, children looking incongruous in bright fancy dress, rushed for the doors and leapt from the windows. People staggered from the blaze with their clothes on fire, many suffering severe burns. The fire brigade, when it arrived at the scene of the blast, was able to do little to bring the blaze under control. Twelve died and thirty were injured.

On 28 September, Edward Manning Brophy, an unemployed shot firer aged thirty-nine, was charged with the murder of the twelve victims and with being a member of the Provisional IRA. He was subsequently charged with causing eleven other explosions.

After a forty-five-day trial at Belfast Crown Court which ended on 1 April 1980, Mr Justice Kelly acquitted Brophy of the murder and explosives charges because it was impossible to be sure that confessions allegedly made by Brophy at the Royal Ulster Constabulary holding centre at Castlereagh had not been induced by 'torture, inhuman and degrading treatment'. In his evidence Brophy claimed that detectives had ill-treated him and concocted confessions between themselves. The judge said the evidence of three doctors showed that some kind of ill-treatment had been suffered, and while he accepted Brophy may well have fabricated the allegations, in law he needed to be sure; and he was not sure. Mr Justice Kelly convicted Brophy on the charge of being a member of the Provisional IRA on evidence he gave during the trial as to the validity of his confessions and Brophy was jailed for five years.

Edward Brophy appealed to the Northern Ireland Court of Appeal, which finally quashed the conviction on the grounds that his admissions were in a 'trial within a trial', and could not be used in the full hearing. In June 1981, the Crown appealed this decision to the House of Lords but they unanimously upheld the Court of Appeal ruling.

While the case against Brophy was continuing police arrested another man, twenty-three-year-old Robert Murphy, and charged him with twelve counts of murder in the La Mon case and with causing four other explosions in Belfast. He appeared for trial at Belfast Crown Court in September 1981 before Lord Justice Gibson. On 28 September, the fifteenth day of the trial, Murphy, a self-confessed IRA member, changed his plea to guilty to manslaughter of the La Mon victims and admitted the other charges. Murphy was sentenced to life imprisonment for manslaughter with a concurrent term of fourteen years on the other charges.

On 7 November 1991, Brophy was shot and seriously wounded by a masked gunman in a store near Belfast city centre. It was thought that responsibility for the shooting lay with the loyalist Ulster Freedom Fighters.

LAYTON, Philip Eric It was the night of 8 March 1982, when neighbours alarmed by the sound of what could only be gunfire, called the police to the Tweed Heads, Sydney, home of twenty-seven-year-old Mrs Margaret Ann Ross and her four children.

When the police broke into the house they found the bodies of the four children, Petrina aged seven, Natalie (six), Clinton (five) and Vicki, just fourteen months; they had been shot through the head while lying in bed. The corpses of twenty-six-year-old Craig Alexander Ross, his wife Margaret Ann, and a man named Philip Layton were discovered in another room. A .22-calibre rifle lay on the floor beside Layton's body.

Neighbours told police that Layton had been having an affair with Mrs Ross, who was separated from her husband and had been living in the flat with her children for around seven months. It also came to the notice of the investigation team that Mrs Ross had complained to friends that Layton had threatened to 'shoot them all' – and this, from a man who had already been charged with assaulting Craig Ross and slashing his car tyres, needed to be taken seriously.

Police later ruled out any possibility that Layton was the notorious 'Balaclava' rapist believed to be responsible for ten rapes and the murder of Jeffrey Parkinson in the Queensland and NSW border area between December 1979 and December 1980.

LEE, John D. Murder has regularly bedevilled the activities of the Mormon Church in the United States, and notable contemporary cases include the activities of Ervil Lebaron and his followers, and those of Mark Hofmann. Among earlier killings were the assassination of Joseph Smith and the religious massacre known as 'Mountain Meadows'.

In September 1857, a wagon-train was transporting some 140 men, women and children westwards through Utah. On the 7th of the month, at a place called Mountain Meadows, the caravan was attacked by what at first sight appeared to be Indians. After an initial skirmish in which twenty of the immigrants were killed, the fighting was interrupted by the arrival of Bishop John D. Lee of the Mormon Church with a large group of men. Lee, who was also the Indian agent for the area, offered to escort the wagon-train safely to Cedar City, the only condition being that the settlers lay down their weapons. Greatly relieved, and happy to accept this offer, they disarmed; whereupon Lee and his party together with the original attackers proceeded to massacre most of the party, leaving only seventeen young children – too young to give evidence – alive.

When rumours of the slaughter began to spread, Brigham Young the Mormon leader took no action, and it was eighteen years before the federal authorities were able to come up with sufficient evidence to put John Lee on trial. At Lee's first trial, the jury was unable to agree on a verdict – largely due to the presence among its number of four members of the Church of Latter Day Saints. At the second trial in September 1876, Lee was found guilty of first-degree murder. Judge Boreham, in passing sentence of death, told Lee that under Utah state law he had the choice of being shot, hanged or beheaded. Lee replied calmly: 'I prefer to be shot.' On 23 March 1877, John D. Lee was taken back to Mountain Meadows, where he was seated on the edge of a prepared coffin. A five-man firing squad levelled their rifles, aimed, and sent a barrage of gunfire into Lee's body, the impact tipping his lifeless corpse into the waiting coffin.

LEPINE, Marc   By the age of twenty-five French-Canadian Marc Lepine had developed a deep and bitter hatred of women; or, more accurately, he was peeved because *they* did not like *him*. And, to be truthful, the cause was not difficult to identify – Lepine had a fanatical obsession with war and violence, and it showed; though he had a number of girlfriends none of them hung around for very long, and even female neighbours avoided his company. Perhaps it was the skull in the window that gave the game away, or the ceaseless sound of battle that vibrated from the room in which he watched non-stop a collection of war films. The result of Marc Lepine's feelings of rejection was that, like most mass and many serial killers, he found a convenient scapegoat – feminists, or rather any woman who dared to think and speak for herself, especially when the word was goodbye. It is difficult to know how long Lepine would have been able to contain the growing anger and frustration had one of his girlfriends not become pregnant. This suited Marc Lepine quite well. It meant, for a start, that the mother was less likely to leave him, and it would also provide him with another human being to bully. Things turned decidedly sour when Lepine's girlfriend insisted on her right to have the pregnancy terminated – this was militant feminism if ever he heard it; for Marc Lepine it was the final straw.

On a day in December 1989, Lepine burst into a classroom at the University of Montreal with an automatic gun in his hand – just as he imagined it felt in the films that had helped turn his fragile mind. First, he ordered the male students to one side of the room and the women to the other; then, shouting a few barely coherent curses against feminists, Lepine opened fire into the crowd of terrified women students. He claimed fourteen lives before turning the gun on himself.

In the wake of the massacre, two further revealing pieces of information were added to the Marc Lepine story. It turned out that earlier in the same year, 1989, he had been rejected for a place at the University of Montreal's engineering faculty. There had also been an earlier rejection: the Canadian Armed Forces which he so admired turned him down as a recruit – they thought he was mentally unstable.

LIST, John Emil The List family had lived in Westfield, New Jersey all their married life. In 1971, the household consisted of List himself, aged fifty-six, a well-respected local accountant and devout churchgoer, his wife, Helen Morris Taylor List, their three children, Patricia Marie, aged sixteen, John Frederick, fifteen, and Frederick Michael, thirteen, and List's eighty-five-year-old mother Alma.

By early December 1991, the Lists' neighbours were becoming concerned that they had seen no sign of the family for some weeks, and the lights in the three-storey Victorian house had been on all the time. On several occasions, neighbours had been on the verge of contacting the police but had been restrained, as is not uncommon in middle-class districts, by not wanting to appear nosey. Finally, on 7 December, Patricia List's drama coach became so concerned at her non-attendance at classes that he resolved to visit her home.

While the drama coach and his assistant were looking round the outside of the house, a neighbour called the police thinking they might be burglars. Which is how the police eventually came to be climbing in through an open side window of the List family home. In the kitchen and surrounding area there were dark stains on the walls and the house seemed very cold with a dank smell in the air. What officers later described as 'church-like music' appeared to be coming from the main downstairs room which the Lists always affectionately called the 'ballroom'. As they walked into the room, the policemen saw what at first glance looked like clothes stacked in the middle of the floor; on closer inspection the piles of laundry turned out to be four bodies lying side by side. Trails of blood marked the floor where the corpses had been dragged into the room. The victims were Helen List and her three children, and over the face of each a piece of towelling had been laid.

Following the sound of the eerie music, officers moved up the stairs where they were assailed by the sickly smell of decomposing flesh. In an upstairs kitchen they found the body of Alma List; she had been killed with a bullet which entered her head above the left eye, and her face had been draped with a towel.

Examination of the bodies downstairs revealed that they too had died from gunshot wounds. The body of young John List displayed several bullet wounds and it was safe to assume that he had received these in a life or death struggle with the killer. A search through the official records established that John List senior had applied for a gun permit in the previous October. A closer examination of the scene of the murders by a special team turned up some quite extraordinary notes, apparently written by List, sometimes addressed 'To the finder' and indicating where certain personal documents could be found. One of these notes was addressed to his employer and set out details relating to his business arrangements and prospects for winning new clients. Other written messages were for members of List's family, expressing his regret at what had happened, but stating that he was unable to give his wife and children and his aged mother the financial support they deserved and he could not bear the thought of the family being reliant on welfare payments. The final letter was to the pastor at his local church, in which John List claimed that, although it looked bloody, he had taken special care to ensure nobody suffered by shooting them in the back of the head. He added that John junior put up a struggle but probably did not suffer for very long. List concluded on the pious note: 'I got down on my knees and prayed after each one.'

Not unnaturally, the murders created a national sensation, and no effort was spared in the hunt for the fugitive John List. The search, however, proved unsuccessful until eighteen years after the killings, when the case was featured on the TV show 'America's Most Wanted'. The show featured a clay model of List, and although it was based on photographs taken in 1971, the sculptor Frank Bender had allowed for the ageing process and produced a bust showing how List could look in 1989. The List item with the bust was televised on Sunday 21 May 1989, and a number of people watching the show in Aurora, Colorado, remarked to each other how much the bust looked like Robert P. Clark, formerly a local accountant, who had recently moved to Midlothian, Virginia, with his wife. In spite of misgivings, one of Clark's friends in Aurora contacted the TV station who routinely passed the information on to the police, along with details of other calls received.

Following exhaustive enquiries, the man calling himself Robert P. Clark was arrested on 1 June 1989. At first he strenuously denied he was John List, but a check on his fingerprints proved otherwise, and by the time an extradition hearing had been set for 29 June, Clark waived his right and was returned to New Jersey. When he appeared before the court in Elizabeth charged with the five murders, List was still insisting his name was Clark; but in February 1990, the defence attorney announced that his client had admitted he was John E. List. At his trial List acknowledged that he had killed his family but said he felt he had no alternative. His lawyers fought hard to obtain a verdict of not guilty because of a mental defect but the jury found him guilty on all five counts of first degree murder. On 1 May 1990, he was sentenced to five consecutive life sentences.

LOCK AH TAM   In the early hours of 2 December 1925, PC Drysdale took an emergency call which had been passed to the police station through the Birkenhead exchange. The caller gave his name as Lock Ah Tam and his message was simple: 'Send your folks please. I have killed my wife and child. My house is 122 Price Street.'

In the luxurious room behind Tam's shop in Price Street officers found his Welsh-born wife, Catherine, and youngest daughter, Cecilia, both dead from gunshot wounds; the eldest daughter, Doris, aged twenty, was mortally wounded. Tam himself seemed quite calm and collected at that stage, but at the police station he became so wild that at first the superintendent refused to charge him.

They knew Lock Ah Tam; knew him well, as a highly respected and influential member of the local Chinese community. Since he had arrived in England from Canton in 1895, as a ship's steward, Tam had risen to a position as European representative of the stevedores' organization Jack Ah Tai; he was president of the Kock Mai Tong, a secret Chinese Republican organization; and head of the Chinese Republican Secret Service in Europe and South America. He was a personal friend not only of the great revolutionary leader Sun Yat Sen, but also to many of the poor and needy Chinese in Birkenhead and Liverpool, to whom he distributed charity and hospitality.

A commercial disaster in 1924 had affected Lock Ah Tam most cruelly: his whole personality seemed to change, and he would suddenly fly into fits of uncontrollable temper, smashing crockery and foaming at the mouth. He also began to drink heavily. Even so, the party Tam gave for his son's coming of age on 1 December 1925, was to all appearances a happy occasion; happy, that is, until the departure of the last guest. Then Tam snapped, he began to shout and rave at his wife, then he went upstairs, loaded a revolver, and grabbed a shotgun. It was this weapon that he turned on his wife and daughter Cecilia, shooting both at close range. He found Doris hiding behind a door, and shot her twice with the pistol. Only his son, Lock Ling, who ran for help, survived the massacre.

A subscription was raised among his friends for Tam's defence, sufficient to secure the services of Edward Marshall Hall, one of the most eminent barristers of his day. The defence Marshall Hall put forward at Chester

Assizes in February 1926 was one of temporary insanity. Dr Ernest Reeve, an expert on mental diseases, gave his opinion that the prisoner had been in a state of 'unconscious automatism' resulting from epilepsy, and induced by alcohol. This is something quite distinct from what is commonly known as an epileptic 'fit'. Lock Ah Tam would have been in a condition rather like a sleep-walker, apparently knowing what he was doing, but with no subsequent recollection. The prosecution, however, was unwilling to concede more than that such an explanation was 'speculative'.

Marshall Hall's closing speech for the defence was among his most inspired and impassioned: 'You cannot believe,' he told the jury, 'that this sudden revolution in a man's mind, which converted him from a loving father to a murderer, was not the result of his reason being dethroned.' Sadly for Tam, the days when epileptic automatism would be covered by a plea of diminished responsibility were several decades away, and the fact that he had called the police immediately after the killings 'proved' that Tam knew that what he had done was 'wrong', thus depriving him of protection under the M'Naghten Rules for proving insanity.

After a retirement of only twelve minutes, the jury found Lock Ah Tam guilty of murder. It was said by an observer that in a courtroom full of Tam's sobbing friends, before a judge so moved that he could hardly speak the words of the death sentence, only Tam remained apparently calm – an inscrutable peace that stayed with him until the drop opened beneath his feet, and the rope tightened around his neck.

LORTIE, Denis Murder in a seat of government is rare but not unknown. The assassination of Prime Minister Spencer Perceval by John Bellingham in the House of Commons in London in 1811, and the assault on the White House in Washington by Puerto Rican nationalists in 1950 are cases in point. The attack in the Quebec National Assembly on 8 May 1984 resulted in mass murder.

A man dressed in army fatigues and heavily armed

arrived at the legislature building and first sprayed the outside with bullets before entering and opening fire indiscriminately in the Chamber. Three officials, Georges Boyer, Camille Lepage and Roger Lefrançois were shot dead and thirteen other people wounded. The man later identified as a Canadian soldier named Denis Lortie, was shouting 'Where are the Assembly members? I want to kill them all.' During his four-and-a-half-hour rampage, Lortie had sat in the Speaker's chair while shooting at everything that moved. He told one of those he wounded, 'I am sorry I had to shoot you but that's life.'

Lortie was finally secured by police as a result of the courage shown by the Assembly's sergeant-at-arms, René Jalbert, who engaged him in conversation and finally persuaded him to surrender. It was subsequently learned that Denis Lortie had left an audio cassette message at a local radio station in which he made clear his disapproval of the government and his intention to destroy it.

Lortie was eventually charged with three counts of first-degree murder and nine of attempted murder. His trial opened in Quebec City on 6 January 1985, when he pleaded not guilty to the first-degree murder charges; the other charges were not proceeded with at this hearing. Witnesses testified that Lortie had screamed out: 'I'm going to rid the province of this government' while spraying the Chamber with machine-gun fire. The court watched videotape recordings taken by the Assembly's remote-controlled cameras which showed Lortie waving his gun around firing wildly. Lortie's lawyers advanced a defence that at the time of the shootings he was suffering paranoid delusions about the government; in other words, an insanity plea. However, in his summing-up, Superior Court Judge Ivan Mignault warned the jury that although they could *consider* the diagnoses of the psychiatric witnesses their evidence should be treated as hearsay. On 13 February, Lortie was found guilty as charged and sentenced to life imprisonment with no possibility of parole for 25 years.

Denis Lortie appealed against conviction, and in September 1986 the Quebec Court of Appeal ordered a new trial on the grounds that the original trial judge had been in error when he ruled on the psychiatrists' evidence.

At his second trial, in January 1987, Lortie – with the agreement of the state prosecutor – pleaded guilty to three reduced charges of second-degree murder and nine counts of attempted murder. After a lengthy hearing during which Lortie testified in his own defence, and the court heard long-winded and sometimes complex psychiatric evidence, the judge, Mr Justice Jacques Ducros, refused to accept the guilty pleas because he felt Lortie had a possible defence against the charges; he consequently ordered a new trial before another judge.

The third hearing opened on 24 March 1987 before Mr Justice Gaston Desjardins who, two days later, reversed the previous decision and *did* accept Lortie's plea of guilty to the three counts of second-degree murder and nine of attempted murder. On 11 May he was sentenced to life imprisonment with eligibility for parole after ten years which was to include the three years already spent in custody prior to sentencing. An appeal against this sentence was dismissed by the Superior Court of Canada on 9 November 1990.

LOS ANGELES TIMES **BOMBING** The atrocious bombing of the *Los Angeles Times* building had its origins in the deeply antagonistic views of its owner, General Harrison Gray Otis, on the newly emerging strength and influence of the American trade union movement, and his regular use of the newspaper's columns to broadcast opposition to organized labour.

On 1 October 1910, the *Times* headquarters was devastated by a single explosion. One wall of the building blew out and two floors crashed downwards into the basement carrying printing machines and workers with them. The gas main and heating plant were fractured causing a fire which was further fuelled by burning printing ink spilling from the damaged ink store, turning the broken shell of the building into a blazing inferno. In the aftermath it was learned that twenty members of the *LA Times* staff had died and the same number had received injuries which would maim them for life.

Shocked city fathers summoned William J. Burns of the celebrated Burns Detective Agency to lead the investigation when it was discovered that three more bombs had been planted in different parts of the city on the same day, including one at the home of General Harrison G. Otis. These devices had failed to detonate, and William Burns was able to trace the source of the dynamite and to identify James B. McNamara, his brother John J. McNamara who was a trade union secretary, and Ortie McManigal as its purchasers. After a nationwide hunt, the McNamara brothers and McManigal were arrested in Detroit in April 1911. Timing devices, similar in construction to those used in the Los Angeles bombs, were found in their possession. Burns finally persuaded Ortie McManigal to make a confession implicating the McNamaras and two other men, David Caplan and Matthew A. Schmidt; the McNamara brothers and McManigal were extradited to Los Angeles on 26 April.

Labour organizations sprang to the defence of the prisoners, staging national demonstrations and parades announcing that they had been framed. The American Federation of Labour engaged America's legendary defence lawyer and champion of the oppressed, Clarence Darrow.

Burns, meanwhile, continued to gather evidence in support of the brothers' guilt and by the time they came to trial, Darrow was convinced they would be convicted. Faced with the choice of fighting a hopeless case as a defence of the union movement which would end with the defendants becoming martyrs for the cause, or pleading them guilty in the hope of avoiding a capital sentence, Darrow chose the second option. James McNamara was jailed for life; John McNamara received fifteen years' imprisonment for an earlier bombing, on charges brought in the absence of any direct evidence linking him to the *Times* bombing. McManigal as a state witness was freed. Caplan and Schmidt were arrested in 1915 and given life imprisonment.

It was Clarence Darrow's last case in defence of the trade

union movement and his final appearance in a California court. Following the trial of the McNamara brothers, Darrow found himself in the embarrassing position of being indicted for allegedly attempting to suborn a juror; although after a long trial he was acquitted, it would not be the last time that 'America's defender' would have his credibility questioned by those elements who were opposed to his predisposition to champion the 'unpopular' causes of the poor and the left-wing.

LOWENFIELD, Leslie O. It was 30 August 1982, and Leslie Lowenfield had just bought himself a .22-calibre rifle; now Leslie and his gun were in a taxi heading towards Robinson Avenue, Marrero, Louisiana, where he would exact a bloody revenge on his former girlfriend and her family. Lowenfield paid the cabbie off before reaching Robinson, and walked up the street making a mental note of the eight men sitting playing cards in the front garden of a nearby house. Around five-thirty in the evening he burst through the door and opened fire. His one-time girlfriend, twenty-seven-year-old deputy sheriff Sheila Thomas fell to the ground with gunshot wounds in the head and arm; her four-year-old stepdaughter Shantel was shot in the head, and Shantel's father, Carl Osborne, died from a bullet which entered his right ear and lodged in his brain. Sheila's mother, Mrs Myrtle Griffin was shot twice, once through the heart and once in the lungs. The noise of the shooting aroused Mrs Griffin's husband Owen, who had been outside with the card school, and he rushed into the house scattering cards and loose change as he ran; Owen Griffin got no further than the front porch before he was cut down with a bullet in his face. Lowenfield did not wait around to see who else his massacre had attracted.

Of the five victims only little Shantel Osborne was alive when the police arrived, and she died shortly afterwards in hospital. Investigations managed to turn up the taxi driver who had brought Lowenfield to Robinson Avenue, and who remembered that the man was carrying what looked like a brand-new .22 rifle. A subsequent search of the house revealed the weapon hidden under Sheila Thomas's bed – a bizarre touch was that her name had been written several times on the gun's stock. Also in Sheila's bedroom searchers found a notebook containing a number of obscene death threats. Detectives learned later that Sheila had once had a boyfriend, a native of Guyana, called Leslie Lowenfield; they also learned that Lowenfield had repeatedly uttered threats against the family.

A warrant was issued for the immediate apprehension of Leslie Lowenfield, and on 5 October 1982 he was picked up in Brooklyn by FBI agents who recognized him from the description on the wanted notices. While he was in custody awaiting extradition to New Orleans, Lowenfield wrote several letters claiming that he had not intended to shoot the child Shantel; it had only happened because her father had been using her as a human shield when he opened fire.

Leslie O. Lowenfield came up for trial in May 1984, when he pleaded an alibi, insisting that he was in Jacksonville, Florida, at the time of the killings. It was an alibi which was effectively shattered when a prosecution witness testified that she had received a telephone call from Lowenfield that same day – from Alabama. On 14 May Leslie Lowenfield was found guilty of the first-degree murders of Sheila Thomas, Carl Osborne and Myrtle Griffin, and the voluntary manslaughter of Shantel Osborne and Owen Griffin; a fortnight later he was sentenced to death.

Following an unsuccessful series of appeals, Lowenfield went to the electric chair on 13 April 1988.

LUNDGREN, Jeffrey, *et al.*   Standing in the centre of the small town of Kirtland, Ohio is the vaguely sinister gothic revival edifice known as the Temple; it was erected in 1836 in celebration of the recent founding of Joseph Smith's Church of Jesus Christ of Latter-Day Saints. By 1986 it was an established centrepiece of the local Mormon community. That was the year in which Jeffrey Lundgren, his wife Alice and their four children arrived in Kirtland where Lundgren was to be the official Temple guide. It was a job at which he proved an unqualified disaster – so much so that in the following year he was dismissed. It was not an entirely promising start for a man who, within a short time, would be proclaiming himself a prophet of God. Nevertheless, Lundgren the prophet, or 'Father' as he insisted on being addressed, began to attract a steady stream of converts from the Kirtland Temple, and in no time he had turned his modest rented farm into a religious community. Among the dozen or so families attached to the commune, though not living on the farm, were Dennis and Cheryl Avery and their daughters Trina, Rebecca and Karen.

Around the beginning of 1988, Jeffrey Lundgren began to receive visions and hear voices. There was, he informed his spellbound congregation, about to be a great earthquake; however, divine salvation would be enjoyed by those faithful who, on 3 May (Lundgren's birthday) accompanied the Father to Kirtland Temple and expelled the 'infidels'. It was no coincidence that Lundgren had recently been excommunicated from the Church. Such a crack-pot scheme could not have remained a secret for long, and before the Day of Judgement dawned the local police paid a visit to Lundgren and made it clear that the commune's every move was being closely monitored. Doom did not crack on 3 May, nor did the earth quake, and Jeffrey Lundgren did not sack the Temple at Kirtland. Instead he turned his farm into an armed fortress and his followers into a highly trained paramilitary force. They also began to drink quite a lot. Just prior to Jeffrey's birthday on 3 May 1989, he became privy to another revelation, the long and short of which was that in order for the group to be cleansed in preparation for what Lundgren described as 'a journey into the wilderness in search of the Golden Sword', lives must be sacrificed.

On the morning of 17 April 1989, Dennis Avery and his family packed their few belongings and set off for the farm from where the Great Journey would begin. What they could not have guessed was that as they were joyfully looking forward to paradise, Lundgren, his family and a few close cronies were adding last-minute details to plans for the Averys' murder. That night, after the communal supper, Dennis Avery and his family were lured one by one to the old barn where they were shot through the head and thrown into a ready-dug pit. Then the murderous messiah ordered the pit filled in with rocks and rubble before, on the night of 18 April, the commune left for the 'wilderness'.

It was not until January 1990 that the Avery family's corpses were unearthed, and on the 5th of the month one batch of zealots were arrested and two days later the remainder, including the Lundgren family, were also taken into custody and indicted on an assortment of murder and conspiracy charges. Lundgren himself faced five counts of aggravated murder and five of kidnapping, and on 31 August 1990 the jury at the Lake County Common Pleas Court returned guilty verdicts on all charges. Two days earlier the same court had convicted Lundgren's nineteen-year-old son Damon on counts of multiple murder and kidnapping and he was sentenced to four consecutive twenty-year terms plus assorted ten- to twenty-five-year stretches. Mrs Alice Lundgren had already been sentenced to five consecutive life terms for murder and was transferred to the Maryville Women's Prison.

At his sentencing hearing on 21 September, forty-year-old Jeffrey Lundgren showed no sign of emotion as Judge Martin O. Parks sentenced him to death. Jeff's defence that he had simply been acting on instructions from God clearly did not enter either the jury's or His Honour's calculations. The execution was scheduled for 17 April 1991, but mandatory appeals inevitably delayed the process; besides, the state of Ohio has not executed anybody since 1963 – Lundgren will just join the other hundred or so other prisoners on Death Row.

M

M62 BOMBING Judith Theresa Ward was born and brought up in the town of Stockport, Cheshire, by an English mother and an Irish father. In her early youth Judith developed a love of horses, and after leaving school she took a job as a groom working in Dundalk in the Irish Republic. There she settled easily into rural life and was exposed to the dream of a united Ireland and tales of the fight against Erin's old enemy England. Four years later Judith Ward returned to Stockport where, ironically, she joined the WRAC; unwisely, she made little secret of her Irish nationalist sympathies. In October 1971 Judith went absent without leave and returned to Ireland, but in late 1973 she was back in England enthusiastically endorsing the Irish cause in both London and Birmingham. The following year she started work as a groom with Chipperfield's Circus at Belle Vue, Manchester, and subsequently toured with the circus.

On 3 February 1974 a coach left Manchester on its scheduled run, and by the time it reached the M62 there were fifty-six passengers aboard including several soldiers. Just after midnight, as it was cruising down the motorway at a steady speed of fifty miles an hour, the vehicle exploded. According to the driver, who survived the explosion: 'There was a great blast and the windscreen just came at me.' Forensic explosives experts later identified the cause of that blast as a bomb planted in the luggage compartment at the rear of the coach. Twelve people, including two children, died in the explosion, another fourteen were seriously hurt and the coach was wrecked.

Later that same month Judith Ward left the circus and travelled to Liverpool with the intention of returning to Ireland; she was arrested while sleeping in a shop doorway. Questioned by the police, Judith once again felt obliged to reveal her nationalist sympathies, and for good measure gleefully confessed not only to the M62 coach bombing, but also to causing two other explosions, one at London's Euston railway station, the other at Latimer in Buckinghamshire. In her first statement, Judith claimed that she had actually planted the bomb on the coach, but she later withdrew the admission, insisting that she had only carried the bomb to Manchester.

At her trial at Wakefield Crown Court in October 1974, the prosecution case rested on Judith Ward's confessions and also swabbing tests which, it was said, proved she had handled explosives. Although she had by this stage withdrawn her confessions, Judith was nevertheless found guilty on all charges and given twelve life sentences with concurrent thirty-year sentences for the London and Buckinghamshire bombings.

In 1992, following a strenuous campaign on her behalf and the quashing of the convictions of the Birmingham Six (see page 38) where similar confession and forensic evidence had been discredited, the Home Secretary referred Judith Ward's case back to the Court of Appeal. On 11 May 1992 the Court of Appeal quashed her conviction following a Crown decision to withdraw the forensic evidence. In the Court's judgement all three grounds for appeal were allowable – unreliable confessions, discredited scientific claims and the non-disclosure of vital evidence by the prosecution to the defence. Suffering from their customary inability to issue a direct apology, the judges said they 'greatly regretted' what had happened – that is, that an innocent woman had been incarcerated for almost twenty years. However, the understandable public alarm generated by the wrongful convictions in the cases of the Birmingham, Guildford and M62 bombings should not be allowed to overshadow the fact that these were very real terrorist outrages as cowardly in their destruction of innocent lives as they were horrendous.

McCABE, Henry   At eight-thirty on the morning of Wednesday 31 March 1926, the Gardai barracks at Malahide, just north of Dublin, was visited by young Harry McCabe, son of the gardener at La Mancha, a large house on the outskirts of the village. The boy, so he told officers, had been sent by his father to tell them that La Mancha was on fire.

When the police arrived at the scene they found smoke pouring from the house which by that time was blazing furiously. With the local fire brigade on their way, the advance team from the Gardai broke into the building in case any of the occupants had been trapped and overcome by smoke; they hardly expected the sight that met their eyes. In one room the body of one of the servants, James Clarke, was found with a large wound on the side of his head. In other rooms lay the bodies of La Mancha's owners, Joseph and Peter McDonnell, their sisters Annie and Alice McDonnell and the other servant, Mary McGowan. The corpses were pulled from the burning house and laid temporarily on the lawn. As for La Mancha, it too died that morning, for despite the best efforts of the firefighters all that remained in the wake of the inferno was its smoke-blackened skeleton.

When the fire investigators were able to examine the ruins it became obvious that the blaze had not originated in one place, but that several separate fires had been set in different parts of the house; there was also a strong smell of petrol. All of which pointed to the inevitable conclusion that a murderous arsonist was on the loose. As he was the only member of the La Mancha estate to survive the fire, the Gardai concentrated their attention on the gardener Henry McCabe. Officers at the scene of the incident recalled how, when helpers and firefighters were searching the hulk of La Mancha, McCabe just stood around passing comments about how easily 'intruders' could have broken into the house, and during questioning he produced a bunch of keys which he claimed to have found in Peter McDonnell's bedroom; the keys opened the main safe in the house, which was now empty. When McCabe's house was searched, six pairs of trousers that were not his own and a pair of bloodstained boots were the final pieces of evidence which convinced the Gardai, on 11 April, to charge him with the six murders and arson.

The trial opened on 8 November 1926 before Mr Justice John O'Byrne, and lasted six days. In accordance with legal precedent, the trial proceeded on one charge only – the murder of Peter McDonnell – though evidence was allowed on each of the other fatalities. The three men had died of fractured skulls resulting from blows delivered from behind with a heavy blunt instrument. No cause of death could be proved in the cases of the three women owing to the extensive fire damage to their bodies. All six corpses were found to contain traces of arsenic, though it must be said that no evidence was offered connecting McCabe with the poison.

The result of a fifty-minute deliberation by the jury was that Henry McCabe was predictably found guilty as charged and sentenced to death. Following an unsuccessful appeal he was executed on 9 December 1926.

McCALLUM, Frederick Moses   Father Andre Darsche, a Roman Catholic missionary stationed in Buffalo Narrows, Saskatchewan, was woken from his sleep at about 3.20 a.m. on 30 January 1969 by a telephone call from Frederick McCallum, a nineteen-year-old labourer who told the priest in a vague and hesitant way that he wanted him to 'see something'. Even the good Father Andre was not at his most tolerant at such an hour of the morning and he made it quite clear that he was going nowhere unless his caller told him the full story. McCallum was finally obliged to confide that he had killed somebody and wanted the priest to administer the last rites.

Father Andre, a good citizen as well as a good priest, immediately called the police to report the conversation, adding that, according to McCallum, he was at the

Pederson home, a two-roomed house in the Buffalo Narrows community. When they arrived at the Pedersons' place, officers found the dead bodies of thirty-two-year-old Thomas Pederson, his wife Bernadette and their children Grace Ann, aged eight, Robert Thomas, five, Richard Daniel, four, and two-year-old Rhoda Beatrice. A house guest, Jean Baptiste Herman, was also dead, and a sixth child, seven-year-old Frederick Donald was found alive but suffering from serious head injuries. All but Herman had been attacked in their beds, he was found lying on the living-room floor. In each case the victim had been struck with a single-bladed fire axe which was found in the house. As luck had it, the Pedersons' two elder daughters were away from home that night.

Thirty minutes after the discovery of the bodies, Frederick McCallum was detained by the police and charged with seven counts of non-capital murder. He appeared in court the following morning and was routinely remanded in custody for psychiatric assessment. At a later hearing McCallum was sent for trial on two sample charges – the non-capital murders of Thomas Pederson and Jean Baptiste Herman.

McCallum appeared before the Saskatchewan Queen's Bench Court on 14 October 1969, and pleaded not guilty. The opening day of the trial was taken up by the necessary but tedious process of jury selection. In this case it was delayed by McCallum's attorney objecting to a jury panel which did not include any Indians or Metis – people of mixed Indian/white ancestry, which he claimed would rob his client of the right to be tried by 'a jury of his peers'; it was an objection neatly countered by Mr Justice Walter Tucker who suggested that it would be even more 'outrageous' to question potential jurors about their racial origins.

When the trial eventually got under way, Father Andre Darsche described for the benefit of the jury the telephone conversations he had had with McCallum on the night of the massacre, and this evidence was supported by McCallum's aunt, from whose home the calls were made. Given the nature of his client's crime, McCallum's attorney was successful in presenting a defence of insanity, a plea which found favour with the jury; on 21 October they found Frederick McCallum not guilty by reason of insanity. McCallum was ordered to be detained in a correctional institution during the pleasure of the lieutenant-governor.

In January 1970 a psychiatric report on McCallum indicated that he was no longer mentally ill, and the Saskatchewan cabinet decided that as he no longer required treatment in a psychiatric facility he should be transferred to a maximum security penitentiary.

McCULLOCH, Thomas Neil, and **MONE, Robert Francis** Both Mone and McCulloch had been judged psychologically unfit to plead at their respective trials – Mone to a charge of murder, McCulloch to one of attempted murder – and had been detained at Carstairs State Mental Hospital under the Mental Health Scotland Act (1960). Robert Mone had been in detention since his appearance at Dundee High Court on 23 January 1968 on a charge of murdering a school teacher, Mrs Nanette Hanson, and sexually assaulting two schoolgirls while terrorizing a Dundee school the previous November. McCulloch had shot and wounded two people in a Glasgow hotel in May 1970, and had been committed to Carstairs from Glasgow High Court on 20 July 1970.

While in Carstairs, Mone and McCulloch struck up a friendship, the practical result of which was an escape plan. Over the next few years they polished their plan, and McCulloch set about collecting a small armoury of homemade and stolen weapons; by the time they were ready, Mone and McCulloch had even cobbled together a long rope ladder and a couple of disguises. On 30 November 1976, they made their move. In the late afternoon both men were in the charge of Nursing Officer Neil MacLellan. Unfortunately for his future, another prisoner named Ian Simpson (declared unfit to plead to a double murder charge in 1962) had insisted on joining them so that he could talk to Officer MacLellan. As MacLellan and Simpson chatted in a small office, Mone and McCulloch burst in and sprayed a strong caustic paint stripper into both men's faces, McCulloch following up with savage slashes with a home-made knife, and Mone stabbing Simpson with a garden fork. After a brief diversion to cut the main telephone lines, McCulloch returned to inflict even more appalling injuries on his victims, from which they would both die. Using Officer MacLellan's set of keys the two prisoners unlocked the doors and slipped outside; everything was going according to their plan. At the perimeter they scaled the walls with the rope ladder and dropped to the other side and freedom.

At around 6.45 that evening the bodies of Ian Simpson and Neil MacLellan were found, but it was at least half an hour before an outside alarm was raised. At the same time, Robert Mone and Thomas McCulloch were putting the second stage of their plan into operation. Mone lay stretched out on the road as if he had been involved in an accident, while McCulloch, looking authentic in his nurse's cap, flagged down an approaching car. This is the point at which fate began to smile less benevolently on our escapees, for although the driver of the car stopped and got out, so did the two-man crew of a passing police panda car.

As Constables George Taylor and John Gillies approached, Mone and McCulloch attacked them so savagely that PC Taylor later died of his injuries. Mone and McCulloch made good headway in the stolen police car until about ten miles beyond Carnwath when McCulloch, behind the wheel, hit a stretch of icy road and lost control of the car which skidded and crashed. Two men passing in a van stopped to offer help and for their troubles were badly beaten and thrown into the back of the van before their attackers drove off in it at a reckless speed. Near Roberton the van became bogged down, forcing Mone and McCulloch to abandon it and proceed on foot to a nearby farm where they forced the owner to give them the keys of his car.

But the police were now hot on their tail, past Dumfries and over the border at Gretna where the chase was taken up by the Cumbrian force. The getaway car was eventually rammed by a police vehicle near Carlisle, and after a brief struggle Robert Mone and Thomas McCulloch were taken into custody.

Both men appeared in the dock at the Edinburgh High Court on 28 February 1977. McCulloch admitted three charges of murder and three of attempted murder; Mone pleaded guilty to the murder of PC Taylor, but not guilty to the murders of Ian Simpson and Neil MacLellan. For the sake of convenience, the prosecution accepted these latter negative pleas and Lord Dunpark proceeded immediately to sentencing. In handing down terms of life imprisonment, the judge added: 'I will recommend that you are not to be released from prison unless and until the authorities are satisfied, if ever, that you have ceased to be a danger to the public.'

MacDONALD, Jeffrey R.   In the early hours of 17 February 1970, an emergency telephone call was received by the authorities at Fayetteville, North Carolina, the site of the US army base at Fort Bragg. The caller, who identified himself as Captain Jeffrey MacDonald, a doctor in the Green Berets said: 'I've been stabbed.' A squad of military policemen was despatched to MacDonald's quarters, where they found him lying on the floor with some minor stab wounds and what appeared to be a blow to the head. Beside MacDonald lay the half-naked body of his pregnant wife Colette, who had been bludgeoned and stabbed to death. 'Pig' had been scrawled in bloody letters on the headboard of their bed. In another bedroom lay the bodies of the MacDonalds' two daughters, six-year-old Kimberley and two-year-old Kristen; both children had been stabbed to death.

MacDonald told the investigators that they had been attacked by three men and a woman. In the semi-darkness he saw the intruders stabbing his wife before he too was stabbed and knocked unconscious. He thought the attackers must have been on drugs as the woman kept screaming 'Kill the pigs', a scenario chillingly reminiscent of the 'Sharon Tate murders' carried out by Charlie Manson's drug-crazed 'family' (see page 236).

The military police became suspicious of MacDonald when they received reports that the couple were having marital difficulties and Colette MacDonald had been making allegations of infidelity against her husband. Nor had it gone unnoticed that compared with those suffered by the dead victims, MacDonald's wounds were merely superficial. On 6 April Jeffrey MacDonald was officially informed by the army that he was a suspect, and on 1 May he was formally charged with the murders of his wife and children. A preliminary hearing was set up at which it was ruled that the case as presented by the investigators did not justify either a court-martial or trial proceedings. MacDonald was freed and asked for an immediate discharge from the service; it was granted and MacDonald went into private practice in California.

Throughout the military proceedings, Jeffrey MacDonald had received the untiring support of his parents-in-law, Mr and Mrs Alfred Kassab, but following his discharge the Kassabs reviewed all the evidence again and gradually became convinced of MacDonald's guilt, eventually pressing for a fresh investigation into the killing of their daughter and grandchildren. The result was a grand jury hearing at Raleigh, North Carolina, at which MacDonald was summoned to give evidence. In January 1975 Jeffrey MacDonald was arrested and charged with the murders of his wife and children.

On account of the several petitions made by his defence team to have the charges dismissed, MacDonald did not stand his trial until July 1979. A great deal of court time was expended on hearing the forensic evidence centring on the bloodstains found both on MacDonald himself and around the house. MacDonald's attorneys retained the original defence that the murders were committed by drug-crazed hippies who had invaded the house.

On Wednesday 29 August 1979, after deliberating for six and a half hours the jury returned a verdict of guilty of first-degree murder in the case of Kristen MacDonald and guilty of second-degree murder in the cases of Colette and Kimberley. Jeffrey R. MacDonald was sentenced to three life terms.

MacDonald appealed against his conviction, and after a hearing at the Circuit Court of Appeals the conviction was overturned and MacDonald released. In March 1982, the Supreme Court reinstated the conviction and MacDonald was returned to prison. Subsequent appeals have been rejected.

Jeffrey MacDonald still has many supporters who believe passionately in his innocence, and even suggest that the case is an American equivalent of the notorious Dreyfus affair. These supporters have also been responsible for the publication of a periodic *MacDonald Newsletter* to publicize their belief in his innocence.

McILVANE, Thomas   After serving with the US Marines (from which he was dishonourably discharged after deliberately driving a tank over a car), thirty-one-year-old McIlvane joined the ranks of the US Postal Service as a postman attached to the regional office at Royal Oak, Michigan. A prickly character by nature, McIlvane was popular neither with his supervisors, nor, it appears, the customers along his delivery route with whom he frequently argued and occasionally fought. This latter problem had already led to one suspension from duty, and in 1990, after a series of disagreements with managers, Tom McIlvane was dismissed. The fact is that McIlvane was not the only employee at the office who was having problems with his supervisors, and the postal workers' union supported his appeal against dismissal. The court of arbitration finally ruled against McIlvane on 8 November 1991.

On 15 November Tom McIlvane walked through the unlocked employees' entrance at the Royal Oak depot and into the sorting room where he opened fire with a sawn-off Ruger semi-automatic carbine. As the employees dived for cover, some even making a jump for safety from the second-storey windows, McIlvane singled out the supervisors, shooting three dead; in the brief six-minute shooting spree a further six victims fell wounded. McIlvane then turned the rifle on himself and put a single shot through his own head. Thomas McIlvane was still alive when he arrived at the

William Beaumont Hospital at Royal Oak, but died early the following day.

McIlvane was very much the stereotypical mass killer. Like the majority he was either serving, ex-, or quasi-military and had a passion for guns. He was also deeply involved in the macho world of martial arts (he was a black-belt kick boxer). Almost a psychological profile for a spree killer. Which must also have occurred to the office of the United States Postmaster General which, on the day after the Royal Oak shootings, announced a systematic check of all personnel records in order to identify staff who had a history of violent or threatening behaviour. In addition, a telephone hot-line was to be established to coordinate information from employees who have been threatened in the course of their work. Ironically, as the announcement was being made, the William Beaumont Hospital released a bulletin stating that one of the six victims wounded at Royal Oak – a female supervisor – had died of her injuries.

McKINLIE, Peter, *et al.* Captain Glass, the son of a minister of the Church of Scotland, had distinguished himself both as a ship's surgeon and latterly as the master of a privateer, those heavily armoured vessels manned by government-licensed pirates to plunder foreign ships on the seven seas. Late in 1765, after a long series of adventures, Glass determined to return home with his wife and twelve-year-old daughter, and to this end secured passage on a ship which was chartered to carry treasure taken by privateers back to England.

What the ship's owners, or indeed the master, could not know was that all the while it was being provisioned for the voyage a plot was being hatched by members of the crew to murder everybody on board except each other and snatch the treasure. The conspirators numbered the bosun Peter McKinlie, George Gridley the ship's cook, and two other men named Richard St Quentin and Andrew Zekerman.

After three abortive attempts to seize control of the ship, this mutinous quartet made a final desperate bid on 13 November when the vessel reached the mouth of the Bristol

Channel. At around midnight the master was attacked and killed; hearing the commotion, two other seamen came up on the quarter-deck and were swiftly murdered and their bodies thrown overboard. The swash-buckling Captain Glass meanwhile had laid hand to his sword and engaged the conspirators in spirited combat, though by sheer strength of numbers they overpowered and slew him with his own sword before throwing his bloody corpse over the side. As to Mrs Glass and her innocent daughter, despite their pleading for life, they were simply tossed into the sea. These black-hearted villains then set sail for the Irish coast. On 3 December the vessel lay at the mouth of the river Ross, where they loaded the longboat with their spoils and, after scuttling the ship, rowed for shore, leaving two apprentice boys on board to drown. One of the lads swam out to the longboat but was struck by Zekerman with such force that the unhappy boy sank straight below the waves.

These murderous mariners landed on Ireland's shore and in the town of Ross sold off some of their ill-gotten booty before travelling on in the direction of Dublin. Meantime the wreck of the privateer had washed up off Fishertown where suspicion had already been aroused by the behaviour of McKinlie and his crew as they passed noisily through, and a message was sent ahead to Dublin to have them detained and questioned. McKinlie and Zekerman were arrested together and interrogated until they confessed and obligingly implicated Gridley and St Quentin. Those two buccaneers had already left Dublin for Cork where they meant to seek passage on a craft bound for England; instead they were arrested at an inn on the Cork road and with a little persuasion made their own confessions.

On 19 December 1765 McKinlie, Gridley, St Quentin and Zekerman were strung up and their bodies later hung in chains as a grim reminder to all who passed through the fair city of Dublin of the wages of sin.

McVEIGH, Timothy   On 19 April 1995, in what was until the advent of September 11, the worst terrorist act on American soil, the Alfred P. Murragh Federal Building in Oklahoma City was destroyed by an explosive-laden truck which had been parked outside. A total of 168 people died in the blast, including nineteen children, and many hundreds were injured.

Excellent forensic work by the FBI on the remnants of the truck, led them to identify the type of vehicle and the agency from which it had been hired. Identikit pictures of the hirer soon identified him as Timothy McVeigh, a decorated ex-soldier turned anti-government activist. On hearing of his arrest, an old army comrade of McVeigh's, Terry Nichols, turned himself in to his local law officers admitting he had been involved. McVeigh admitted the bombing, describing how he had driven the truck to the building and then detonated it but refused to talk in more detail about the outrage other than to say it was necessary to inflict pain and suffering when attempting to control the power of the State.

McVeigh went on trial in a Federal Court on 24 April 1997 and remained completely detached throughout the proceedings. On 2 June, after twenty-three hours deliberation, the jury returned with verdicts of guilty on all charges (including eight specimen counts of murder). The penalty phase followed and on Friday 13 June, the same jury returned with the death sentence for Timothy McVeigh.

Having refused all his rights to appeal, McVeigh was executed by lethal injection on 11 June 2001 – the first Federal prisoner to be executed for thirty-eight years.

Terry Nichols was tried separately on similar charges but was found guilty on reduced counts of manslaughter and sentenced to life imprisonment without parole.

MADRID MASSACRE   On the evening of 24 January 1977, three men entered a building at 55 Atocha Street in central Madrid. One remained on guard in the doorway, while the other two went into the hallway where they shot the porter dead. The pair then went up to the third floor and burst into a room where eight lawyers, all left-wing sympathizers, were gathered. The lawyers had just finished a meeting with Communist trade union officials. It was just over a year after the death of Franco, and unions were still illegal. On entering the room, the two men produced machine guns and opened fire at point-blank range, leaving four of the lawyers dead and four seriously wounded. The assassins then rejoined their accomplice guarding the doorway and fled. Responsibility for the shootings was later claimed by a right-wing terrorist organization calling itself the 'Triple A'.

Widespread police enquiries resulted in three men being taken into custody and charged with four counts of murder and four of attempted murder. For some inexplicable reason one of the men was given leave from prison and not surprisingly fled the country. The remaining two, Jose Fernandez Cerra, aged thirty-three, and Carlos Garcia Julia, twenty-five, were left to face trial along with three others charged as accomplices.

The trial opened in Madrid's Palace of Justice on Monday 18 February 1980. Cerra and Julia openly admitted they were responsible for the shootings, claiming they were 'fighting for liberty and against Communism'. Their defence lawyers argued that they had a right to amnesty under a recent Spanish law, but the prosecution countered with a claim that their crimes were unpardonable and outside such legislation; which also happened to be the view of the judges. On 4 March 1980, all five defendants were found guilty. Cerra and Julia were given prison sentences totalling 193 years each; sentences were to run concurrently, and the judges ruled they should serve no less than thirty years. The accomplices each received concurrent prison sentences.

MAK, Kwan Fai, *et al.* In the early 1980s a series of burglaries and robberies of Chinese restaurants in Seattle escalated into murder, first with the shooting of a local resident, seventy-one-year-old Franklin E. Leach, in October 1981, and then the killing of two Chinese beanshoot growers, Lau King Chung and her daughter Chan Lai Kuen Lau, in July 1982. But this was not the end; in 1983, the crime wave culminated in the worst mass murder in the seaport's history.

On 19 February 1983 a man knocked on the door of the Wah Mee (Beautiful Place) gambling club. After an uneasy wait during which scuffling could be heard from inside, the door opened and a man staggered out and fell to the ground. The police were called and the wounded man said that he and many others inside the club had been shot and robbed. After securing an ambulance to take the wounded man to hospital, police officers tackled the door of the club; it would have been easier to crack a bank. The automatic doors had slammed shut, and eventually the fire-brigade were obliged to use crowbars and a great deal of brute strength to force an entry through three steel doors.

Inside, the police found thirteen victims, all bound, all shot through the head, lying in pools of blood. Of the two still alive, one was rushed to hospital but died later of his wounds. This left just one survivor, and he was unable to speak because a bullet had entered his skull, miraculously missed the brain, and exited through his mouth.

A subsequent police report stated that the victims had been shot 'methodically', and ballistics tests indicated that at least two different guns had been used. A total of thirty-two spent shell casings were recovered at the scene. The victims, all Chinese, were gradually identified; one man worked at the club as a janitor and the rest were assumed to be patrons, including one woman and her husband who owned a local restaurant.

The sole survivor of the massacre was Wai Chin, and when police interviewed him he was still unable to speak; however, by a judicious use of nods and shakes of the head, and a bit of sign language, he was able to tell officers that he knew the man who shot him, and that three men were involved and he recognized two of them. Detectives showed Wai Chin a photograph of Benjamin Ng, their chief suspect for the murders of the beanshoot growers. Chin identified Ng, and another villain, Kwan Fai (known as 'Willie') Mak.

As a result of this information a squad of officers raided the house on Beacon Hill where Benjamin Ng was known to be hanging out with his girlfriend. In the search following

Ng's arrest, $9,013 in cash was found along with a .38-calibre revolver and ammunition, and an M1 rifle. Willie Mak's home was also raided and two rifles, two shotguns, four handguns and about $5,000 in cash were seized. Willie Mak was taken into custody later. The third man in the Wah Mee assassination team was identified as Wai-Chiu ('Tony') Ng (though no relation to Benjamin other than brother-in-crime). Tony had gone to ground and would not emerge for some time.

Benjamin Ng and Willie Mak came up for trial in the summer of 1983, when the judge upheld a defence application for two separate trials on the grounds that each man's defence would necessarily be detrimental to the other; in other words, they were going to blame each other. Benjamin Ng's trial was scheduled first, and opened on 16 August 1983. His attorney admitted that Ng had taken part in the robbery, but insisted he had not done any shooting. Nevertheless, on 24 August he was found guilty of aggravated first-degree murder, and at a subsequent penalty hearing was sentenced to life imprisonment without possibility of parole.

Mak stood his trial a month later, and in evidence claimed that he had left the club before the shooting even started. The jury simply did not believe him, and at the penalty hearing another jury voted for the death penalty. Willie Mak is still waiting patiently on Washington State's Death Row. The only execution in the state since 1963 was that of Westley Alan Dodd who was hanged on 5 January 1993 following his conviction for the murders of three little boys.

Tony Ng was eventually picked up in Calgary, Alberta, almost two years after the Wah Mee killings, and extradited to Seattle. He claimed that he was an unwilling participant in the murders and that Willie Mak had threatened his life. And a jury believed him. Not that it mattered in practice, because Ng was sentenced to seven life terms anyway, on multiple counts of robbery.

MANSON, Charles, *et al.*   Just after midnight on Saturday 9 August 1969, four shadowy figures were skulking about the grounds of the secluded mansion at 10050 Cielo Drive in Beverly Hills: 'Tex' Watson, Patricia 'Katie' Krenwinkel, 'Sadie' Atkins and Linda Kasabian, members of Charlie Manson's notorious Family, about to commit the crime that was to send shock-waves throughout the state of California. 10050 Cielo was occupied that night by actress Sharon Tate (her husband, the film director Roman Polanski, was away on business), who was heavily pregnant, and four friends. In an orgy of overkill, the Family left five victims literally butchered. Voytek Frykowski alone was stabbed more than fifty times, slashed, shot and so savagely bludgeoned with the butt of a gun that the weapon shattered. On the front door to the house the word 'Pig' was painted in blood; not one of the murderous gang had the slightest idea whom they had killed – they were just random victims.

Only one person back at Family headquarters was not pleased – Charlie Manson. When news of the bloodbath came through on television it apparently offended Charlie's sensibilities that it had been such a messy job. He decided to show everybody how it should be done.

On 11 August, just two days after the Tate murders, after they had motivated themselves with drugs, Manson led a group of his disciples on a second murder spree. At shortly after 1.00 a.m. the Family invaded the Silver Lake home of businessman Leno LaBianca and his wife Rosemary; like the Cielo Drive victims, the choice was entirely random. After stabbing and slashing the LaBiancas to death, Manson and his gang inscribed the mottoes 'Death to the Pigs', 'Rise', and 'Helter Skelter' in blood on the walls. In a final act of gratuitous violence, the word 'War' was carved into Leno LaBianca's abdomen.

Following these utterly mindless killings, the Family went to ground. Shortly afterwards Susan 'Sadie' Atkins was arrested on a prostitution charge and while she was in custody admitted her part in the Tate murders to a cellmate. The information filtered back to the prison authorities, and on 1 December 1969 the Family was rounded up and charges of murder were laid against the principal members. All those tried received sentences of life imprisonment or death – including Manson. However, in view of the state of California's suspension of the death penalty, the capital sentences were subsequently reduced to life imprisonment.

Although no further charges were brought, there is reason to believe that many other murders could be laid to the account of Charles Manson's Family, including several of their own members. Vincent Bugliosi, prosecutor in the Tate/LaBianca trial, in his book *Helter Skelter* does not dismiss Manson's own claim to have committed thirty-five murders – indeed, he now feels that it may have been an uncharacteristic understatement.

Charles Manson has been eligible for parole for many years now. Serving his time in San Quentin, he applies for release at every opportunity, hoping to use what he believes are his uncanny powers of psychological persuasion to convince the parole board that he is sane and safe. He fails with equal regularity, and it is unlikely that the person once described as the most dangerous man in America will ever be released.

MATUSCHKA, Sylvestre   Although murder aboard railway trains is no unique event, the curious career of the self-styled 'train wrecker' Sylvestre Matuschka must rank as the most bizarre crime of its type in the history of European multicide.

Matuschka was born in the village of Casantaver in what was then the Austro-Hungarian Empire. After serving as a lieutenant during the First World War, he returned to Budapest where he married Irene Der and in time fathered a daughter. A shrewd and unscrupulous businessman, Matuschka became involved in any number of more or less honest endeavours from exploiting the post-war black market to managing a delicatessen. Following a trial in 1927 the result of which was his acquittal on a charge of fraud, Sylvestre Matuschka seemed to lose all common sense, sold off his business interests in Budapest and decamped to Vienna. In 1931 he took up the new occupation of train wrecker. On New Year's Day he tried unsuccessfully to derail the Vienna-Passau express near Ansbach. In August of the following year he succeeded in overturning several coaches of the Vienna-Berlin express at Jueterberg which then fell down a steep embankment injuring seventy-five passengers.

On 12 September 1932 Sylvestre Matuschka pulled off the big one – an explosion on board the Hungarian Railways Budapest-Vienna express train as it was crossing the viaduct at Bia-Torbagy. The wreck cost twenty-two people their life. Amid the confusion which followed, Matuschka daubed himself with a victim's blood and lay down among the injured waiting to be 'rescued'. Later he had the audacity to try to sue the railway company over bogus injuries, but it was not, as it turned out, a very wise move, because the investigation team discovered that Matuschka had never even been aboard the fatal train. Furthermore, a routine search of his home turned up a heavily marked railway map revealing plans of destruction in Amsterdam, Paris, Marseilles and Ventimiglia.

Sylvestre Matuschka's first trial opened on 15 June 1932, and in support of a rambling defence of insanity he referred to a long ago incident in which a country fair hypnotist supposedly implanted the idea of crashes in his mind. The prosecution psychiatrist, on the other hand, presented a lucid argument that Matuschka killed simply out of sexual sadism. The effect was that the jury was so bewildered that it became impossible to reach a verdict. At a second hearing it was clear that Matuschka had perfected his pretence of insanity and throughout the trial alternated between crying and moaning and falling to his knees in prayer; asked his occupation, he replied: 'Train wrecker, and before that businessman.' Then Matuschka told the court about Leo – the spirit whose voice ordered him to kill. Inventive it might have been, convincing it clearly was not, because the new jury convicted him of murder and the new judge sentenced him to death.

The finale to this extraordinary case is shrouded in doubt. Some reports claim that Matuschka was executed by hanging in Vienna on 20 November 1934. Others that his sentence was commuted and the train wrecker spent the remainder of his days in prison 'dreaming of disasters which might have been'. However, the inimitable crime historian Jay Robert Nash presents us with this supremely ironic conclusion: 'His sentence was commuted to life imprisonment and he was reportedly released during the Second World War by the Russians, who employed him as an explosives expert.'

MITCHELL, Brian   Trust Feed is a small black community on the outskirts of Greytown in the Natal Midlands; thirty-four-year-old Brian Mitchell was in charge of the local police station. During the tense and often violent times before and during the transition to a new constitution, it was part of the job of officers such as Mitchell to keep an eye on gatherings of politically active groups that could undermine security and stability. One of these groups was the United Democratic Front, sympathetic to the then banned African National Congress. Under cover of dark on the night of 2 December 1988, Lieutenant Brian Mitchell led a group of four black African special policemen in an attack on a house in Trust Feed. It was Mitchell's belief, and there is no reason to doubt the truth of that conviction, that the house was occupied by UDF activists. From outside, Mitchell fired two shots in the direction of the house and then sent his specials in, guns blazing. A total of eleven people lost their lives, seven of them women, two of them children aged four and nine.

The massacre itself was bad enough – but it was not even the right house. The building stormed by Mitchell's officers was occupied by supporters of Inkatha, who were gathering for a family funeral; one of the victims was the dead man's sixty-eight-year-old widow. Even so the situation might have been dragged back from the brink of total disaster, had Lieutenant Mitchell confessed his error and offered to resign. As it was, he took the opposite option – he tried the cover-up approach, first ordering his specials to set fire to the death-house and then sending the officers away on extended leave. Unfortunately, when matters did, inevitably, come to light, the higher police authorities set to investigate the case proved obstructive and uncooperative. In the end it was only the persistent Captain Frank Dutton who, despite threats to his own life, courageously exposed the whole ugly story, and brought Brian Mitchell to court. It did nothing to calm disquiet over the police inquiry system and the police in general, when it was announced during the investigation that Mitchell had been promoted to captain.

Captain Mitchell appeared before Mr Justice Andrew Wilson at the Supreme Court in Pietermaritzburg in the spring of 1992. There was little doubt that Mitchell would be convicted; what was always in doubt was whether, against expectation, the judge would exercise the full right of punishment. He did; Captain Brian Mitchell became the first white policeman to be sentenced to death for a quasi-political crime. In fact, he received eleven death sentences. More surprising still, given the popular conception of judges as the epitome of white double-standards in the country, was Mr Justice Wilson's undisguised distaste for the manner in which the police had handled the investigation and his call for a public inquiry into the cover-up. It was a brave stand, and without doubt a genuine one; but the fact is, Mitchell's capital sentence will never be carried out, and as for the inquiry, all that law and order minister Hernus Kriel would offer was a departmental inquiry. When the four special policemen involved in the Trust Feed shooting appeared before him, Judge Wilson took a more lenient view; bearing in mind that they were acting under orders given by a superior officer, he sentenced them to fifteen years' imprisonment.

MONE, Robert senior   On 4 January 1979, officers of the Dundee police force engaged in the search for missing seventy-eight-year-old Agnes Waugh forced an entry into an old people's flat in the Hilltown district of the city. The ground-floor flat occupied by seventy-year-old Mrs Jane Simpson formed part of a block of twenty-four single apartments built as a sheltered housing estate under the supervision of health and social workers. In the flat police found not only the dead bodies of Mrs Simpson and her friend Agnes Waugh, but also that of newly married Mrs Catherine Millar, a twenty-nine-year-old who had been missing since 29 December, just a week after her wedding. Post-mortem examinations later established that all of the victims had died on 29 December and all had been strangled.

Following a major investigation, fifty-four-year-old Robert Mone, a nephew of the late Miss Waugh, was arrested and charged with three murders and indecent assault. Mone's trial opened at Dundee High Court on 28 May 1979, when evidence was heard from Mrs Millar's widower that she had telephoned him on the day she disappeared to say she was on her way home. When she failed to arrive, Millar called at her friend Mrs Simpson's flat three times but could get no reply. Forensic examination had shown that a green jade ring belonging to Mone bore traces of blood, and a mark on Agnes Waugh's face had been caused by it. The court also heard that Mone had earlier attacked another elderly woman and told her and a friend that he had murder on his mind.

The trial closed on 4 June with the jury returning a guilty verdict. Only then was it disclosed that Robert Mone had boasted to friends that he intended to commit murder so that he could join his son, Robert Mone junior in prison where he was serving a life sentence for murder (see page 226). It was Mone's bizarre ambition to become a more notorious killer than his son. Whether anybody could rival the wickedness of Mone junior is debatable, but his father did achieve one of his aspirations at least, he was sentenced to the mandatory life imprisonment with a recommendation that he serve a minimum of fifteen years.

Mone never had the opportunity to outdo his son, though, because on 13 January 1983 it was reported that he had been slashed to death during a brawl at Craiginches Jail, Aberdeen. After enquiries fellow-inmate Anthony Currie was charged with Mone's murder. Currie stood his trial at the High Court of Justiciary, Aberdeen, on 12

May 1983, and he pleaded not guilty, claiming that he had acted in self-defence when Mone attacked him. On 17 May the jury returned a verdict of culpable homicide and the judge, Lord Allanbridge, jailed him for eight years to run from May 1985, the date his present sentence ended.

MONGE, Luis Jose Monge, a salesman of Denver, Colorado, and his wife Dolores had always wanted a large family. By early 1963, they had more than achieved their ambition by producing ten children, ranging between the ages of eighteen years and eleven months; the eleventh child was due later that same year. Not surprisingly, Luis Monge was considered by most to be the perfect family man. However, the façade of loyal husband and loving father concealed a terrible secret – for several years Monge had indulged in sex games with his daughter Janet, now thirteen years old. His wife had found out about the incestuous liaison and quite understandably had demanded that he should stop; for his part, Monge had promised to control himself. Unfortunately, in Luis Monge's case the flesh proved as weak as his resolve, and the 'problem' returned. This time Dolores, with support from the family priest, made it quite clear to her husband that, if he should so much as lay a finger on Janet again, he would be reported to the authorities.

On the night of Friday 28 June 1963, Luis Monge found himself irresistibly drawn to Janet's bedroom, where she slept with her sister Anna. Believing Anna to be sleeping, Monge climbed into Janet's bed and began fondling her in his very unfatherly manner. As he did so, Anna woke, saw what was going on, and threatened to tell her mother. If she did, then Luis Monge, the 'perfect father', would soon be exposed to the world as a child abuser.

As Monge later told the police, he panicked and decided he would kill his family and then himself. First, he took hold of a poker and hit his wife four or five times over the head with it. When she was dead he cleaned up the body and then got out his stiletto-bladed knife and plunged it into eleven-month-old Tina; when she cried out, he covered her mouth until she suffocated. Monge then almost ritually cleaned the baby's body and laid it in bed beside her mother. Next it was four-year-old Thomas's turn; he was choked before being placed by his dead sister. The last victim was Monge's favourite son, six-year-old Freddie, whom he struck twice with the poker afterwards covering his mouth until he stopped breathing. The cleansing ceremony followed, and the body was laid in bed with the others. In his statement to the police, Monge said that at that point he could not go on, and thought of killing himself in the car with exhaust fumes. Instead, he called his brother on the telephone and then the police, saying: 'I've just killed my wife and three of my kids. You'd better come over before I kill somebody else.'

When Luis Jose Monge appeared in court, he stood accused only of the murder of his wife; no immediate charges were made in connection with the deaths of the children. Although he pleaded guilty, Monge was routinely transferred to the Colorado State Hospital for a psychiatric assessment, and following two examinations was declared sane and fit to plead. On 23 October 1963, Monge again entered a formal plea of guilty to the court and signed a statement admitting responsibility for the murder of his wife.

Before the penalty hearing, the judge arranged for Monge to have a reunion with his remaining children, where he was completely reconciled with the family who, with remarkable compassion, told him they forgave him everything.

The penalty hearing began on 23 November, by which time Monge had already instructed his lawyers that he did not intend to fight for his life. Obligingly, the jury returned a recommendation for the death penalty, but before a judge could formally pass the death sentence, on 18 December Monge changed his mind and instructed his attorney to lodge an appeal. On 1 November 1965 the Colorado Supreme Court rejected his appeal. In January 1966, the state governor issued a stay of execution to all condemned prisoners in advance of the referendum which was to be held on the whole issue of capital punishment. After a hard-fought campaign on the issue, Colorado voters elected to retain the death penalty by a margin of two to one.

In early 1967 Luis Monge decided on another appeal and took on a new lawyer. The attorney did put in the appeal, but he also proposed an alternative motion that, if Monge was to be executed, then it should take place outside Denver City Hall and be televised. This was clearly an attempt to demonstrate capital punishment as being degrading and repugnant, but the scheme misfired badly and received such heavy publicity that Monge was obliged to abandon the whole appeal in order to protect his family from the pressure of media attention.

Luis Jose Monge duly went to the gas chamber in Colorado State Penitentiary at 8.00 p.m. on Friday 2 June 1967 – the last man to suffer the death penalty in America until the execution of Gary Gilmore in Utah on 17 January 1977 heralded the return of capital punishment to the United States.

MOONEY/BILLINGS CASE This case is widely accepted as being one of the worst miscarriages of justice in American legal history, and the investigation was heavily prejudiced by attitudes against the pro-labour activities of Thomas J. (Tom) Mooney. As a leading member of the Industrial Workers of the World, Mooney had for many years espoused the cause of international Socialism and he had been heavily engaged in fighting on behalf of the McNamara brothers over the *Los Angeles Times* bombing case (see page 215). Warren K. Billings was Mooney's protégé in many of these activities, and because he had picked up a conviction for possessing explosives in 1913, he was an easy target for those investigating the so-called 'Preparedness Day bombing'. In the same year, 1913, Mooney had been acquitted of plotting a further explosion.

In 1916 Mooney, his wife Rena and Billings were in San Francisco attempting to organize the streetcar employees. At the same time, local business interests were planning a Preparedness Day Parade on 22 July as a patriotic demonstration of America's readiness to enter the First World War on the side of the Allies. By 1.30 p.m. that day, the streets had been cleared of traffic for the parade. Thousands of people lined Market Street for the procession which was to consist purely of flag-waving citizens. As the parade moved off from Steuart Street into Market Street, there was a deafening explosion and a cloud of smoke hung over the area. When it cleared, the bodies of men and women could be seen strewn everywhere, and the whole scene seemed to be drenched in blood. Emergency services were obliged to perform amputations in the street in an effort to save lives; the final toll was ten dead and forty injured, many permanently maimed.

The district attorney leading the investigation immediately settled on Mooney and Billings as his prime suspects, not least because Tom Mooney had spoken out publicly against America's participation in the war. Never slow to boost their circulation by scare stories, the press launched an inflammatory campaign against what it called Socialist anarchist bomb fiends. Within forty-eight hours Billings was arrested together with three other radicals. Mooney had left San Francisco unaware of the campaign, but when he heard that Billings had been arrested, telephoned the chief of police offering to return and face his accusers. At a grand jury hearing, witnesses testified that they had seen Tom Mooney in Market Street prior to the explosion, and that he had been carrying a suitcase; the implication being that it contained the bomb. As a result of the hearing, indictments for murder were returned against Mooney, his wife Rena, Warren Billings, Israel Weinberg and Edward D. Nolan.

Billings was the first to be tried, in September 1916; he was found guilty as charged and sentenced to life imprisonment. The trial of Tom Mooney opened on 3 January 1917. A surprise witness was a man named Frank Oxman, who claimed he had seen Mooney, Billings and Weinberg place a satchel containing the bomb against a saloon wall. The witnesses who had spoken out before the grand jury also confirmed that they had seen Mooney in the area. The jury went into retirement on 9 February and returned with a verdict of guilty, following which Tom Mooney was sentenced to death by Judge Griffin.

Rena Mooney's trial began in May and continued until July 1917, when she was acquitted. Weinberg was found not guilty after his trial in October and November 1917, and the charges against Nolan were eventually dropped.

Subsequently, Frank Oxman was shown to have committed perjury – it was proved that on 22 July, the day he swore he saw the bomb planted he had been in another town entirely. In September 1917, Oxman was put on trial for subornation of perjury but was inexplicably acquitted. Another witness who had placed Mooney on Market Street later admitted he had lied in order to obtain the reward money which had been offered for the capture of the bombers. Already considerable discomfort was being felt about the conduct of the investigation and the trial, and in the end no less an official than President Woodrow Wilson called on California's governor to intervene on behalf of Mooney, with the result that his sentence was commuted to life imprisonment.

Thomas J. Mooney remained in prison until January 1939 when Culbert Olson, newly elected governor of California, granted him an unconditional pardon. Billings was freed in October of the same year.

MOORE, James Allen On the evening of Monday 3 February 1992, Constable Moore was taken into custody by his fellow officers in Comber cemetery, County Down, after being reported firing shots over the grave of his close friend and fellow policeman Norman Spratt who had been buried earlier in the day. Constable Spratt had been shot dead a few days previously and his wife was now in police detention charged with his murder.

Twenty-four-year-old James Moore had served as a member of the Royal Ulster Constabulary for five years, with an unblemished record and a Queen's commendation for bravery; but on this day a combination of grief and anger had resulted in a bout of heavy drinking. Moore was questioned at the police station and his service revolver was confiscated, but he was released at around 3.30 in the morning. Later that day he was interviewed again by a senior officer, and told that arrangements had been made for him to see the police medical officer after midday.

James Moore did not keep his appointment; instead, at about 1.15 p.m. he drove to the Falls Road, Belfast, and parked his car near the offices of Sinn Fein, the political wing of the IRA. He told the doorman he was a journalist with an appointment, and while this was being checked, Moore produced a shotgun and shot and killed the doorman; he then fired indiscriminately at a group of people, killing twenty-two-year-old Michael O'Dwyer and forty-one-year-old Patrick McBride. A third man was seriously wounded and a woman received minor facial injuries. Moore fled from the the offices to his waiting car and drove away at high speed. Half-an-hour later he telephoned the police station at Newton-abbey, confessed to the killings and told the duty officer where they could find him in the Moira area near Lough Neagh, some dozen or so miles away. Fifteen minutes later, he called in again to announce that he was at Ballinderry.

A police search team found Moore's red BMW parked in a quarry near Lough Neagh, with his body lying nearby; the shotgun, which he had apparently turned on himself, was by his side. It was reported later that James Allen Moore was 'demented' with grief over the death of Constable Spratt, and a senior RUC officer added: 'Obviously he was out of his mind. He had seen too much bloodshed and butchery perpetrated by the IRA.'

MOR, Eitan On 8 September 1992 twenty-five-year-old Eitan Mor, a security guard with a history of mental instability, broke into a psychiatric health clinic in the Qiryat Ha Yovel district of Jerusalem armed with a Uzi sub-machine gun and shot and killed four women members of staff before fleeing on foot.

He later tried to hijack a car, but failed. Then Mor was seen hugging and kissing an elderly man before climbing to the roof of a block of apartments and opening fire on people in the street below, wounding two passers-by. Police attempts to talk the gunman down met with a renewed burst of gunfire, which this time was returned by police marksmen who shot and wounded Mor; he died later in hospital.

In the wake of the spree, police issued a statement to the effect that Eitan Mor was enraged at being turned down when he applied for a lorry driver's licence.

A more important concern, perhaps, than whether a mentally unbalanced man should be given a driving licence, is whether a person known to be so seriously disturbed should be accepted for work as a security guard and given access to firearms.

MOUNTBATTEN BOMBING   Earl Mountbatten of Burma, Second World War Allied Supreme Commander in South-east Asia, last Viceroy of India, member of the royal family and survivor of many heroic sea battles during the war, had for many years been accustomed to take his holidays at Classiebawn Castle, near Mullaghmore Bay, Co. Sligo in the Irish Republic. During his visits the Garda Siochna habitually maintained a very high security presence, to the extent of sending officers to accompany the Mountbatten party when they went on fishing or sailing trips. In later years, and at Lord Mountbatten's request, this more intimate security was relaxed, and the Garda instead maintained a constant vigil from the shore while he was sailing. Security in the area around the castle was increased at the time of Lord Mountbatten's stays, and during his 1979 visit, on Monday 27 August, the Garda had detained two men in a yellow car acting suspiciously at Lisheen, Co. Roscommon.

At Mullaghmore Bay that morning of the 27th Lord Mountbatten and some of his guests, including his son-in-law and daughter Lord and Lady Brabourne, their twin sons, fifteen-year-old Nicholas and Timothy Knatchbull and the dowager Lady Brabourne were preparing for a trip in the boat *Shadow V* to check lobster pots. At the harbour the party was joined by fifteen-year-old Paul Maxwell who often helped out on the Mountbatten boat. At around

11.40 a.m. they set off across the harbour. A member of the Garda keeping watch from the shore said later: "At exactly 11.45 a.m., when the boat was still a short distance from the pots, there was a loud explosion; there was a loud bang and a huge cloud of smoke. The boat completely disintegrated.'

When police and coastal rescue craft rushed to the scene of the disaster they found Lord Mountbatten, Nicholas Knatchbull and Paul Maxwell dead in the water; Lord and Lady Brabourne and their mother were rescued badly injured and rushed to hospital where, on the following day, the dowager Lady Brabourne died. Timothy Knatchbull escaped with only minor injuries.

Within a very short time the Provisional IRA had claimed responsibility for the bombing of Lord Mountbatten's boat. It was not the only act of Republican terrorism that day; at 4 p.m. an IRA terror group detonated a landmine at Warrenpoint, Co. Down, which killed eighteen British soldiers.

The Garda immediately launched a major investigation, beginning by questioning known Republican sympathizers. Officers established that the two men detained earlier in the day at Lisheen had been seen in their yellow car in the Mullaghmore Bay area. They were identified as Thomas McMahon and Francis McGirl. Forensic tests on the suspects' hands and clothes and on the car revealed traces of explosives; they also showed flakes of paint identical to that used on *Shadow V*. McMahon and McGirl were charged with the murder of Lord Mountbatten.

The trial of the two men was held at the Special Criminal Court in Dublin in November, with Mr Justice Liam Hamilton presiding. Although the evidence was entirely circumstantial, the judge rejected a claim that the men had no case to answer. McGirl was subsequently acquitted because the judge felt that the evidence seeking to show he had been near the Mountbatten boat was inconclusive. McMahon, however, was found guilty and sentenced to life imprisonment. In the following January both men made separate court appearances, charged with being members of the IRA. They both denied the charge on oath and were acquitted; McGirl was discharged and McMahon returned to prison to continue serving his sentence.

In May 1993 it was reported that Thomas McMahon had been moved from a maximum security prison to an ordinary jail in preparation for his release that summer. It was said he had earned remission because of good behaviour. Among the many who felt aggrieved by this apparent leniency towards a brutal and callous multiple killer was Ulster Unionist MP David Trimble, who insisted: 'Life should mean life and nothing else.'

N

NELSON, Dale Merle   West Creston, British Columbia. A nowhere kind of place, bushland and forest, a scattered community of loggers and labourers. Dale Nelson was pretty typical of these, eking out a precarious living by irregular work for local logging companies. Little wonder, perhaps, that his usual mood was introverted, seasoned with bouts of surliness. But at the end of the day he would go home to the meagre pleasure of his wife and three young children, in the wooden shack they shared out on the dirt road.

At least that is what happened most of the time. Once in a while, though, Dale Nelson needed to get away from all that, to go on a spree, waste some money, drink recklessly. Which is what he was doing on 4 September 1970, his final 'lost weekend'. From noon until midnight Nelson sustained a boozing session which would have seen many lesser men under the table; after which, what could be more natural than to get in his car and drive home?

But home was the one place Dale Nelson did not go that night. His first stop was the house of Maureen McKay, a distant relative who lived alone with her four-year-old daughter. Finding the lights on and guests visiting, Nelson resisted knocking on the door, driving instead a couple of hundred yards down the road to the home of another relative, Shirley Wasyk, and her three daughters, aged seven, eight and twelve.

This time he did knock; he knocked, entered, and battered Shirley Wasyk to death. Then he strangled the youngest daughter, before ripping her body open from chest to groin, thrusting his face into the gaping wound and eating undigested food from her stomach. On the eight-year-old he inflicted oral sex; only the eldest Wasyk girl was not touched.

The night was still young. Dale Nelson was back in his car, speeding over the rough tracks which criss-crossed West Creston, heading out into the wasteland. The last outpost of human activity was the farm worked by a man named Phipps. He was not someone Dale Nelson had had dealings with, not a relative, in fact he was probably the nearest to a stranger that you could find in such a tight-knit community. Nevertheless, with no provocation, Nelson set about the Phipps family with rifle, knife and club; all six of them, husband, wife, children aged from eighteen months up to ten years, all done to death.

Another girl, another atrocity. The eight-year-old-Phipps girl he abducted, and drove out to the wastes where he subjected her to buggery. And then, most outrageously of all, Nelson returned to the Wasyk household where his earlier butchery had been discovered, the alarm raised, and the house left temporarily unguarded while a manhunt was set in progress. Creeping inside, Nelson snatched up the body of the youngest murdered girl, headed back to the wasteland, and dismembered her corpse.

For what comfort it was to anybody; the court was informed by expert psychiatric witnesses that Nelson's crimes were motivated by the desire to 'possess' the girls, and that the murders were 'incidental'. If he was capable of driving, it was argued, then he was presumably capable of forming the intent to murder, so there was no recourse to a manslaughter charge. And while the defence not unreasonably proposed a plea of insanity, it was evident that Nelson knew quite well what he was doing and knew that it was wrong. Even so, Dale Nelson was lucky. Under the terms of the recently amended Canadian Criminal Code the West Creston murders were not categorized as capital offences; instead Nelson was sent down for life.

NELSON, Simon Peter Nelson was a forty-six-year-old executive with an employment agency in Rockford, Illinois. At the time the world sat up and took notice of him, Simon Nelson was having marriage problems with his wife Ann, a thirty-seven-year-old skating instructor and the mother of his six children. She had, in fact, left him and gone to Milwaukee. On Friday 6 January 1978, Nelson followed his wife to the motel where she was staying and beat her up. The police were called and Nelson was arrested on a charge of aggravated battery. As he was being interviewed by the police Nelson suddenly confessed to murdering his children back in Rockford. The reason, according to his rather emotional statement, was to 'get even' with his wife who was threatening to divorce him.

The police at Rockford were alerted and officers dispatched to the Nelson home where they forced an entry and discovered that Simon Nelson was telling no lies. In their beds lay the dead bodies of twelve-year-old Jennifer, ten-year-old Simon, Andrew, aged nine, Matthew, eight, Roseann, five, and David, just three years old. They had all been killed as they slept – bludgeoned with a rubber-headed mallet and then stabbed repeatedly with a hunting knife. The family's pet dog had also been butchered, mutilated almost beyond recognition.

Simon Nelson agreed to return voluntarily to Rockford where he was charged with six counts of first-degree murder. He offered no defence to the charge, and during the arraignment just sat in court sobbing. At his trial in May 1978, Nelson was convicted on all counts and sentenced to life imprisonment.

NGUYEN, Vu Linh, and **PHAN, Van Thinh** A Chinese gambling club in the basement of the Oriental Provision Store in Gerrard Street, Soho, the heart of London's China-town, burst into flames on Saturday 17 July 1982. The whole building was gutted by the fire and seven of the gambling patrons died from the burns they received. Witnesses later gave statements claiming they had seen Chinese men running away from the building just prior to the explosion when the shop front went up in flames. It was of more than passing interest to detectives that the police had been called to the club just two hours previously after a fight had broken out.

An inquest opened into the seven deaths on 23 July, and police investigators presented evidence that the blaze had been started deliberately with some as yet unidentified form of incendiary device, though not necessarily a fire bomb. Meanwhile, rumours were circulating around Soho that the owners of the club owed protection money to one of the Triad gangs and, because they had decided to stand up to the racketeers, the club had been bombed.

The police continued to follow several lines of enquiry, and on 30 July they arrested a Vietnamese man. On 1 August twenty-three-year-old Vu Linh Nguyen appeared before the magistrates charged with the murder of the seven Chinese victims and with arson. A fellow Vietnamese national, Van Thinh Phan, aged twenty-one, was also arrested and charged with the same offences. Following the customary remand appearances both men were committed for trial at the Old Bailey.

The trial opened on 7 June 1983, and a silence fell over the court as the sole survivor of the fire described how a fight had developed at the club between some Vietnamese customers and the staff; this led to the Vietnamese being evicted. As they left the men were heard threatening to return and kill the club's owners. About two hours later a group of Vietnamese had burst into the club carrying sticks as weapons and poured petrol on one of the gaming tables, setting it alight before running away.

On 15 June Nguyen and Phan were found guilty on both the murder and arson charges. Mr Justice Farquharson stressed that they had condemned the victims to a horrible death, and jailed both men for life, adding that in his extensive legal experience it was the most dreadful case he had ever heard.

O

OBERST, Owen On the evening of 20 April 1928 the farmhouse owned by William F. Oberst, which nestled at the foot of the Flint Hills of Kansas near the town of Florence, was devastated by a fire which claimed the lives of seven of the eight members of the family. The victims were forty-three-year-old Oberst himself, his wife and five of their children – Dorothy, Ralph, Hugh, Edith and Herbert, ranging in age from six to sixteen. The only survivor was seventeen-year-old Owen who was away from the farm at the time of the conflagration.

As neighbours stood looking on in horror at the charred remains of the farmhouse, Owen Oberst drove up in the family car, stopped in the lane leading to the house and, his face drained of all colour, walked through the silent crowd to the ruin that was until so recently his home. When he had regained his composure sufficiently, Owen explained that he had taken the car earlier and driven to Florence, leaving his family sitting together in the kitchen; and it was in the kitchen that their charred remains were found.

The investigation into the tragedy posed a number of puzzles to Florence's sheriff; one above all – how, he wondered, could seven people be trapped in a small kitchen which had two exit doors and two large windows? Owen Oberst was questioned repeatedly about his movements on the night of the fire and his story was that he had left the farm before six o'clock. It had been estimated that the fire had broken out just before seven. However, a witness claimed to have seen Oberst leaving the farm around seven, and nobody in town had seen him before eight o'clock. During the painstaking search for clues among the blackened debris of the farmhouse, a .22-calibre automatic pistol was found in the stove, and parts of a repeating rifle lay about the kitchen; both weapons showed signs of recent firing.

On the morning of 5 May, Owen Oberst was formally charged with seven counts of first-degree murder, following which he made a statement saying: 'I just got mad at them and shot them. I had asked father for the car and he told me I couldn't have it, and so that night I got ready and killed him. When he opened the door I shot him, dragged him inside the kitchen and set the house on fire. I just shut my eyes and pulled the trigger. I fired seven shots with the rifle – killed them about six o'clock. No one ever suggested it to me; I just got mad with my father. I figured it out when I was going home that afternoon . . .'

Oberst later retracted his confession and entered a plea of not guilty; then at trial he changed his plea back to guilty and was sentenced to life imprisonment.

OHMURA, Ichiro During a night in early December 1950, in Kyoto, a wood-constructed house owned by Masaaki Suki, an executive with a Japanese film company, burst into flames and, in spite of the efforts of the fire brigade, quickly burned to the ground. When fire fighters began their systematic search of the still-smouldering rubble, they discovered first a child's body, thought by neighbours to be the remains of the Sukis' four-year-old son Shintaro. Next, they found the body of Mrs Kyoko Suki, and later Mrs Suki's younger sister Noriko, who had been a guest in the house; all three members of the family appeared to have been battered about the head. Finally the remains of the servant were found, though the body was too badly burned to determine cause of death. The major mystery as far as the police were concerned was that the bodies appeared to have been dressed in day clothes, while the fire occurred at a time when everybody should have been sleeping. While the investigation was proceeding, Masaaki

Suki arrived back at the smoking remains of his home, announcing that he had just returned from a business trip to Tokyo. For obvious reasons the police lost no time in checking Suki's story, but it was equally quickly confirmed that the grief-stricken man was telling the truth.

Detectives, now entirely convinced that the four victims had been murdered and that arson had been used in an attempt to hide the crime, ordered a detailed forensic examination of the scene of the fire. Among the first results was evidence that someone had opened some tins and eaten the food inside, leaving the cans scattered about. The remains of two bloodstained towels were found, and a carpet known to have belonged in the servant's room was wrapped around the body of Noriko. The searching and sieving of the ashes revealed no trace of Mr Suki's expensive camera, Swiss watch or gold cuff-links, nor of his wife's jewellery. Descriptions of the missing items were circulated to jewellers and pawnbrokers.

Almost immediately a Kyoto pawnbroker contacted the police with information that on 11 December a man named Ichiro Ohmura had pawned a camera matching the description of that stolen from the Sukis. A warrant was issued for the apprehension of Ohmura, and his description was circulated nationwide. Eventually he was traced to Shirahama, staying at the hotel where he had spent his honeymoon; this time he had registered under an assumed name.

Ichiro Ohmura was arrested and returned to Kyoto where he made a full confession. He said he had broken into the Suki house during the day and had been surprised by the servant whom he struck down with an axe. The noise attracted Noriko, whom he also dispatched. It was while Ohmura was ransacking the house that Kyoko Suki arrived home and he took the axe to her too. As for little Shintaro, the killer claimed he did not have the heart to strike him with the axe, but instead beat him unconscious with his fist. Ohmura then left the house and made his way to the railway station to deposit the bag containing his booty at the left-luggage. Back at the house he discovered that Shintaro and

Noriko were still alive but unconscious, but before trying to cover his tracks by torching the Sukis' home, Ohmura first went around the house wiping off fingerprints; ironically, the one set of prints he forgot to wipe clean were on the handle of the bloodstained axe.

In due course, Ichiro Ohmura was put on trial, convicted, sentenced to death . . . and executed.

OKAMOTO, Kozo In the early 1970s, Western security forces became aware of a sinister alliance between the Japanese terrorist faction the Red Army Brigade and Middle Eastern groups such as the Palestine Liberation Organization (PLO) and the Popular Front for the Liberation of Palestine (PFLP) to cooperate on terrorist activities. It was known that a band of Red Army members had travelled to the Lebanon for special training with the PLO. This was at a time when their lack of popular support among Japanese youth due to increasing use of extreme violence was resulting in a serious curtailment of Red Army activity on the home front. It was thought that this new spirit of 'internationalism' might expand those terror activities.

The Red Army's first independent assault in the Middle East began on 30 May 1972, when three young Japanese boarded an Air France flight at Rome bound for Tel Aviv. They passed through personal screening at the airport, but their baggage was put aboard the plane unchecked. On arrival at Lod Airport, Tel Aviv, the three men walked through customs and simply reclaimed their baggage. Then, without warning, they opened the suitcases taking out hand-grenades and machine guns, hurling the deadly grenades into the densely crowded baggage hall and firing indiscriminately at point-blank range into the knots of fleeing passengers.

As the panic-stricken crowd attempted to escape the mayhem, one of the Japanese accidentally blew himself up with a hand-grenade; another, who had been firing at aircraft on the runway, was shot dead by security guards. The third man ran on to the runway, shooting at anybody in his line of fire, and was eventually overpowered by airport mechanics. Twenty-eight people died in the attack and seventy-two were injured.

The PFLP claimed responsibility for the massacre, describing it as: 'A brave attack launched by one of our special groups in our occupied land'.

The surviving terrorist at first gave the police a false name but, following close cooperation with the Japanese force, he was identified as Kozo Okamoto. The Tokyo police were also able to confirm that he and his dead companions were members of the Japanese Red Army Brigade. At his trial, Okamoto admitted acting in partnership with the Palestinians, and he was sentenced to life imprisonment. Despite demands that Okamoto should be executed, Israel stuck to its principle that the death penalty is only invoked for those convicted of war crimes (such as Adolf Eichmann).

The Japanese Red Army reappeared in the news in February 1993, with the conclusion of the trial of two of its members, Hiroko Nagata and Hiroshi Sakaguchi. They were sentenced to death in Japan for the murders of twelve of their comrades whom they had accused of betraying the movement. They were also convicted of murdering two policemen and a photographer at the time of their arrest.

ORGERON, Paul Harold In September 1959 a forty-seven-year-old demented ex-convict named Paul Orgeron paid a visit to the Edgar Allan Poe Elementary School at Houston, Texas, accompanied by his seven-year-old son Dusty. Although he claimed he wanted to enrol his son in the second grade, Orgeron was unable to produce the child's health certificate or to give the school authorities a home address. Told that it was a usual condition of enrolment, Orgeron scowled and said he would return later in the day with the necessary documentation.

Paul Orgeron did return, with his son, but this time carrying a suitcase which he announced to the school secretary contained a large bomb which was triggered to go off if the case fell to the ground. Courageously, but rather stupidly, one of the teachers tried to overpower Orgeron, forcing him to lose his grip on the suitcase which dropped to the floor and exploded. The blast killed Orgeron himself, his son, two teachers and two other young children; nineteen others were injured.

No specific reason was ever established for the suicidal attack, though a psychiatric review carried out during one of his many terms of imprisonment had described Paul Orgeron as being obsessive and nurturing fantasies of power.

ORSINI, Felice, *et al.* On the evening of 14 January 1858, Emperor Napoleon III and the Empress Eugénie arrived at the Paris Opera House for a special performance in their honour. As the three carriages transporting the Emperor's party arrived, three explosions, one after the other, rocked the area around the front of the theatre. The third blast was directly under the Emperor's carriage and, had it not been for the precaution taken in building it with an iron lining, the occupants would certainly have perished. As it was, Napoleon escaped unhurt and the Empress Eugénie suffered a slight graze on her face. Not nearly so lucky were the crowds of spectators gathered in the street, among whom the force of the explosions created absolute carnage; in the aftermath it was reported that two people had been killed instantly, six more died later in hospital and 158 were injured, many of them seriously. Having been assured that everything possible was being done for the victims, the Emperor and Empress behaved in true Imperial fashion, leading their party into the Opera House for the performance.

Much to their embarrassment, it was later revealed that the police had been warned in advance of the assassination attempt. An Italian nationalist named Felice Orsini, who was then living in exile in London, had been heard blaming Napoleon for failing to live up to his promises for the independence of Italy. Senior officers had also been told that Orsini had been recruiting men to join him in a plot to assassinate the Emperor. In fact, one of Orsini's associates, Giuseppe Andrea Pieri, had been arrested close to the Opera House just before the attack. Pieri told detectives who interrogated him where he had been living, and it was at this address that officers arrested a man who claimed to be Thomas Allsop but later admitted his real name was Felice Orsini. Two other men were detained at the same time, and were subsequently identified as Antonio Gomez and Carlo di Rudio. Gomez and di Rudio made full confessions to their involvement in the bomb attack, and Orsini made a statement which was more of a political justification than a confession. A fifth man, Dr Simon Francis Bernard, was arrested in England at the request of the French authorities on a holding charge of conspiracy to murder.

The trial of Orsini, Pieri, di Rudio and Gomez, not as might have been expected on charges of murder but on what was apparently regarded as more serious – attempting to assassinate the Emperor and Empress – took place at the Assize Court of the Seine on 25 and 26 February. Gomez and di Rudio confirmed their confessions, but Pieri denied any involvement in the explosions. Orsini's counsel, the celebrated advocate Jules Favre, presented his client's justification that he had only acted as any Italian patriot would.

The jury took just two and a half hours to reach their verdict; they rejected the charge of attempted assassination of the Empress in all cases, and found extenuating circumstances in the case of Antonio Gomez. Orsini, Pieri and di Rudio were condemned to death and Gomez was sentenced to life imprisonment.

On 11 March, appeals against the capital sentences were dismissed, though on the following day the death sentence on di Rudio was commuted to penal servitude for life. On Saturday 13 March Orsini and Pieri, dressed in the veil and shirt customarily worn by parricides, were guillotined in the Place de la Rocquette.

The trial of the mysterious Dr Bernard opened on 12 April 1858 at the Old Bailey in London. He stood facing the capital charge of the murder of a member of the Paris Civil Guard, who had been killed in the bomb attack. After a six-day hearing, and despite the judge making it quite clear that he thought the case had been proved, the jury found Bernard not guilty and he was discharged.

OWEN, John The tiny Buckinghamshire village of Denham was thrown into a state of shock when, in May 1870, the blacksmith Emmanuel Marshall and his family were savagely butchered in their own home.

On Saturday evening, 21 May 1870, Taverner, the village constable, saw what he described as 'a rough-looking man' heading towards Denham from the direction of Uxbridge. Suspicious by profession, the policeman stopped and questioned the man, but short of good reason could not detain him. The following morning a neighbour passing the smithy saw a man leaving the adjoining cottage where the Marshall family had their home. She waved a cheery good morning and asked after the Marshalls; 'gone away on holiday', the man told her. And so matters rested until the following day, when a child sent on an errand to the Marshall home to deliver a bridal dress for the blacksmith's sister, could get no reply to her knocking. Looking through the window of the cottage the girl saw to her horror the bodies of what looked like two or three children lying in the fire-grate covered with ashes and soot.

The vigilant Constable Taverner was raised, and he broke in to the cottage to find the bodies of two children clasped in the arms of their grandmother. In the back kitchen the bodies of two more children and that of Mrs Marshall were discovered. All six victims appeared to have had their heads beaten in with a heavy weapon. At first it was thought that Marshall might have had a brainstorm and slaughtered his family, but when Taverner searched the smithy he found the battered body of the blacksmith.

The constable immediately issued a description of the man he had seen earlier on the Uxbridge road, and word came back that he was staying in a public house at Reading, where, after a struggle, he was arrested. The man was wearing Emmanuel Marshall's clothes and boots, and had in his possession the smith's pistol. He identified himself as John Owen, though for no honest reason he sometimes called himself Jones. Owen had recently been released from prison and had returned to Denham to avenge a grudge against the blacksmith who once refused to pay for some shoddy work that he had carried out.

At his trial at Buckinghamshire Assizes John Owen, alias Jones, was convicted and sentenced to death. He maintained a stolid indifference, replying 'Than'ee Sir' to the judge after sentence.

Owen was hanged at Aylesbury Prison on 8 August 1870. His final words before being dispatched by executioner William Calcraft were: 'My friends, I am about to suffer for the death of – let's see – Emmanuel Marshall; but my friends, I am innocent.'

P

PACKER, Alferd In March 1874, Alferd Packer dragged himself through the door of the Los Pinos Agency in Utah, exhausted and begging for food. He had, he said, been one of a party of gold prospectors who had set out from Salt Lake City the previous autumn. When the weather closed in on them ten men had returned to civilization, leaving Packer to lead the expedition on to the source of the Rio Grande, but not before a further four declined his invitation to join them. Two would die in blizzards on the return journey. What happened next varied in Packer's account according to who he was talking to, and how much he had had to drink. Anyway, foul play was suspected, and Alferd Packer was arrested on suspicion; a suspicion which was much exacerbated when two Indians rushed into the Agency carrying strips of what they claimed was 'human meat'.

Packer's story was that the party was starving in the mountains and living on roots. He had returned from a forage for food to find that a member of the team named Israel Swan had been bludgeoned to death, and the others had begun carving up his body to eat. The whole party apparently indulged in this cannibal feast, and Swan's money was divided equally among them. When the flesh ran out a man named Miller fell victim to the same abuse; then it was Humphrey, and then Noon. Packer and Bell, the last survivors, called a necessary truce, but when a frenzied Bell attacked Packer he, too, was routinely dispatched. The strips of flesh picked up by the Indians were the remains of the packed lunch made of Bell's flesh which had sustained Packer on his trek back to civalization.

The following morning found Packer leading another expedition into the mountains – only this time he was a vital part of a murder investigation. Although he claimed to have forgotten the scene of the crimes, the five corpses were found soon enough, and it was immediately apparent that Alferd Packer had been rather economical with the truth. Four of the victims had been shot in the back of the head; Miller was the odd man out, having been done in with the butt end of a rifle. The ribs of all the corpses were exposed, where the flesh of the breast had been flayed for consumption. Packer had made his home in a nearby cabin while he sat out the worst of the weather, leaving the bodies outside in Mother Nature's cold store.

Before he could be brought to trial, Packer succeeded in escaping and it was a further nine years before he was brought to justice, following his arrest at Cheyenne, Wyoming, on 29 January 1883. A death sentence was reduced at retrial to forty years in jail, and a pardon was granted after Packer had served eighteen years; he died near Denver in 1907. The comparative leniency of the sentence seems to suggest that the court believed that cannibalism was practised only as a last resort, and in preference to the whole party perishing from cold and starvation.

PAN AM FLIGHT 103 The destruction by terrorists of Flight 103 over the town of Lockerbie in Scotland on 21 December 1988 resulted in the deaths of 259 passengers and crew and eleven residents of the town. The original flight departed Frankfurt for Heathrow where passengers and baggage were transferred to a 747 for direct flight to New York.

The 747 left Heathrow twenty-five minutes late – had it departed on time the explosion would have occurred over the Atlantic, which may have been the bomber's plan. The aircraft entered Scottish air space at approximately 6.45 p.m. and was routinely logged by the local Air Traffic Control Centre and its flight plan agreed. At around

6.56 p.m., it disappeared from the ATC radar screen and parts of the aircraft plummeted down on Lockerbie and the surrounding area. Lockerbie, a small market town of some 2,700 inhabitants, was devastated. The southern district looked more like a war zone, dominated by a 20–30 foot wide crater. Houses were demolished by burning sections of the plane and corpses were strewn over a wide area.

It was later disclosed that American diplomats had been warned earlier in the month that a bomb would be planted aboard a Frankfurt to New York flight. On Wednesday 28 December, the Chief Constable of Dumfries and Galloway announced that investigators were satisfied that the disaster had been caused by a bomb and that there would now be 'a mammoth criminal investigation of international dimensions'.

Expert reconstruction of parts of the aircraft and the luggage established that the bomb had been concealed in a radio cassette player in baggage probably loaded at Frankfurt. An official inquiry conducted by Sheriff John Mowat QC, concluded that stricter baggage checks at both Frankfurt and Heathrow might well have prevented the disaster.

On Thursday 15 November 1991 the US Attorney General and Scotland's Lord Advocate jointly announced that arrest warrants had been signed for Adelbaset Ali Mohmed Megrahi and Al Amin Khalifa Fhimah, two Libyan intelligence officers, on charges of conspiracy, murder and contravention of the 1982 Aviation Security Act. The men have consistently denied their guilt, and despite international pressure the Libyan political and military leader Colonel Gadaffi has so far refused to hand the men over for trial in either the United States or Scotland.

The controversy over security at Frankfurt airport resurfaced in February 1993, when a lone hijacker smuggled a pistol on board a Lufthansa airbus carrying 104 passengers and crew. The hijacker beat the supposedly improved security system at Frankfurt, but on this occasion there was no damage or loss of life as, having forced the pilot to fly to New York, the gunman surrendered to the authorities.

Eventually agreement was reached with Libya in April

1999, that the two men would be surrendered into Scottish custody for trial by three judges without a jury. The trial to be in a neutral country. It was decided that the court would be sited at Camp Zeist in the Netherlands, which for the duration of the proceedings would be designated Scottish territory.

The trial opened in April 2000, and occupied eighty-five sittings over a period of almost nine months. Judgement was given on 31 January 2001, when Megrahi was found guilty and sentenced to life imprisonment with a recommendation he should be detained for twenty years. Ffimah was found not guilty and allowed to return to Libya.

Megrahis' appeal was dismissed on 14 March 2002 and he is currently serving his sentence in a special wing of Barlinnie Prison, Glasgow.

In August, 2003, Libya finally accepted responsibility for the bombing and pledged to pay $2.7 billion, (£1.7) billion in compensation to the families of the 270 dead.

PHILLIPS, Morgan   One March night in the year 1779, the inhabitants of Narbeth in the county of Pembroke awoke to see smoke and flames rising from one of the farmhouses that lay on the outskirts of the hamlet. In no time at all, it seemed, the house was virtually razed to the ground, and there was no sign of its occupants. Searching the smouldering ruins neighbours found the body of farmer Thomas, but the remains were so badly burned that it was impossible to say how he died. The body of Thomas's niece was lying across a half-burned bedstead, one thigh broken and an arm missing. In the ruins of another room the charred body of one of the farm labourers lay with a gaping wound in the back of his head; and finally, the corpse of the servant-woman was discovered somewhat less severely burned than the others but displaying several deep wounds to the back of the head. Given the obvious facts, it seemed clear that the occupants of the farm had been murdered and the perpetrators had fired the building in an effort to conceal their crime. But who were those perpetrators?

A local man named John Morris, who had already collected an impressive record for assorted offences, was the immediate suspect, and he was detained. However, before he could be questioned, Morris threw himself to his death down a mine-shaft despite the best efforts of the constables to restrain him. Suspicion next fell on Morgan Phillips, and following some robust questioning he admitted that, in company with the late John Morris, he had carried out the murders at the Thomas household in order to rob the farmer; they had then set fire to the farmhouse.

Phillips came up for trial at Haverfordwest, was found guilty and sentenced to death; he kept his appointment with the hangman on 5 April 1779.

PORTEOUS, Captain John Captain Porteous had been in command of the Edinburgh City Guard for some ten years when, during the course of an execution on 14 April 1736, there occurred an event which led first to the captain's indictment for murder and then to his lynching by a mob.

Porteous, widely regarded as a coarse, brutish man, and his City Guard, many of whom were no better, were ordered by the Lord Provost to keep order at the execution of one Andrew Wilson, a smuggler who had turned his talents unsuccessfully to robbery. Wilson, on account of his rather colourful exploits, was held in particular affection among the city's low-life, and a massive and sympathetic crowd turned out to watch him die. Porteous managed to show at one and the same time his total inability to read the mood of the crowd and his innate sadism when he began the proceedings by crushing Wilson's hands in the iron cuffs before setting off on the journey to the scaffold which had been erected in the Grass-market.

Arriving at that place, the execution took its grim course without interruption from the crowd, who remained uncharacteristically and ominously restrained. Then, as the hangman climbed the gallows to cut Wilson's body down, the mob burst into a loud and spontaneous jeering and stones were thrown which drove the hangman from his task and hit several of the City Guard. The Guard made ready their rifles, firing a barrage of shot into the screaming rabble, and it was said later that Captain Porteous fired the first shot and killed Charles Husband, though this was never precisely established. In any event, six people in the crowd were shot dead and many others were wounded.

Porteous was arrested, charged with murder and appeared for trial at the Edinburgh High Court of Justiciary on 19 July; on the following day he was found guilty and sentenced to death. On 26 August, the sentence on Captain Porteous was respited for a period of six weeks on the order of Queen Caroline.

This was not calculated to appease local feelings, and a plot was set afoot in which a mob would capture the Edinburgh Tolbooth where Porteous was being held, and ensure that the judge's original sentence was carried out. On the morning of 7 September, an angry crowd gathered in the city centre, attacked the Tolbooth, overpowered the guards and seized the despised Porteous. He was unceremoniously dragged to the Grassmarket and strung up from a dyer's pole.

Although two men were later arrested as accessories to the murder of Captain Porteous they were both acquitted.

POUGH, James Edward   In mid-1996, Pough, a poorly paid labourer living in Jacksonville, Florida, was angry and in the depths of despair. In January his wife had left him and two months later had obtained a court order forbidding him from contacting her. Now a finance company had repossessed his Pontiac car as he was unable to keep up the payments from his wages. To compound his anger, the company, General Motors Acceptance Corporation was now pressing him for $6,394 outstanding on his loan, in spite of the fact that he had surrendered the car voluntarily.

On 18 June 1996, he called his work saying that he would not be in that day as he had some important things to do. Armed with a revolver, Pough then went to the finance company offices. On entering the office, he immediately shot dead two people waiting at the service counter. He then forced his way into the back office and started firing at the staff. As the staff attempted to run for safety, he followed them firing, shooting several of them many times over. Seemingly, when he was satisfied he had killed as many as possible, he put a bullet through his own head. Seven women and one man were dead and five other severely wounded.

A later investigation into the case established he had shot and killed two pedestrians on the evening before the massacre bringing his total of victims to ten. It was thought this may have been practice for his main target, the finance company.

PULAU SENANG MURDERS By the 1960s the government of Singapore was faced with an escalation of crime originating from the numerous secret societies operating in the republic. To combat this menace, special powers were introduced for the arrest and detention without trial of suspected gangsters. However, in conjunction with this somewhat draconian measure, the government embarked on a scheme aimed at rehabilitating the detainees and attempting to break their loyalty to the societies. The plan was to create a prison without bars on an islet off the main island and to introduce a programme of hard work and discipline for those confined there. The site eventually chosen was Pulau Senang, and the man picked to supervise the operation was Prison Officer Daniel Stanley Dutton, a firm believer in the maxim that the best weapon with which to combat evil was hard labour.

Dutton arrived on Pulau Senang for the first time in June 1960, with fifty prisoners who were immediately set to work clearing the undergrowth and creating a settlement with at least the rudimentary trappings of civalization. From these modest beginnings Pulau Senang went from strength to strength, and many of the detainees were eventually released back into society, with a very low re-offending rate. By 1963 the population had increased to around four hundred, with Dutton, three assistants and an unarmed staff of forty overseeing them.

On the morning of 12 July 1963, Dutton called the

Director of Prisons on the radio alerting him to a rumour circulating around the islet that trouble was brewing, and that certain elements were 'out to get him'. Dutton had taken the precaution of confining the ringleaders; the situation, he said, seemed to be under control. Nevertheless the Director ignored Dutton's reassurances and insisted on mobilizing a squad of police officers to take charge of security. A further call was broadcast by Prison Officer Dutton at around 1.12 p.m., now asking for urgent assistance to quell widespread rioting that had broken out in the settlement. By the time reinforcements arrived the prison buildings were aflame and Dutton and his assistants had been massacred; though the detainees surrendered meekly enough to the heavily armed police riot squad.

Subsequent investigations established that the riot had begun when the detainees stopped work for lunch. The rioters had attacked and overpowered the warders and then advanced on the administrative building. Dutton was trapped in his office. The rioters broke in through the roof, poured petrol over him and threw in blazing torches. When he rushed out of the door, his clothing in flames, they cut the officer down with axes and stood round cheering as his body burned. Two of Dutton's assistants were also slaughtered and the third received severe injuries from which he later died. The only explanation for the disaster was that the chief of the leading secret society on Pulau Senang had decided to destroy the penal settlement to demonstrate that his power was greater than that of the government.

On 26 August 1963, seventy-one detainees were charged with three counts of murder, one of attempted murder and rioting. Following a prolonged hearing before a magistrate, sixty-four were committed for trial. When the trial opened in the High Court on 18 November 1963 before Mr Justice Buttrose, fifty-nine prisoners stood in a specially constructed dock, the Public Prosecutor having taken the decision not to proceed against five of those originally committed. The hearing straggled into the following year, finally closing on 12 March 1964. All the defendants had pleaded not guilty, but the seven-man jury returned verdicts of guilty of murder against eighteen of them, found twenty-nine guilty of rioting and acquitted the remainder. The judge sentenced those convicted of rioting to terms of between two and three years' imprisonment; and passed the death sentence on those found guilty of murder.

The eighteen convicted of murder appealed unsuccessfully against their sentence in the Singapore Court of Appeal and the Judicial Committee of the Privy Council. A petition for their reprieve to the island's president was also rejected. On Friday 29 October 1965 they were hanged at Changi Jail in batches of three.

PULLIAM, Mark Fire broke out at the farm home of Mark Pulliam and his family near Chatsworth, Georgia, on 2 November 1942. Within minutes, and despite the efforts of neighbours who had rushed to the scene to help, the house collapsed in a mass of flames and sparks. As the roof fell in the neighbours' thoughts, every one, were for Mrs Pulliam and five of their eight children. Times being as hard as they were, the three eldest children had been sent out to work and were, thankfully, living away from home; Mark Pulliam was also away, following his trade of logging.

When the sheriff and the coroner arrived a search began for what was feared would be six corpses. And so it proved; one child's body was found lying near the kitchen door, two in the front room and one in the living room. On the charred remains of a bed there were two bodies, one a child and the other apparently Mrs Winnie Pulliam. The victims were removed to the Dalton undertaker and, as things stood, there was no reason to suspect the fire was any more than a tragic accident.

No sooner had the sheriff returned to Chatsworth and got his feet back under the desk than he received an agitated telephone call from the undertaker; he had been preparing the bodies for burial as best he could when he discovered a knife wound in Mrs Pulliam's abdomen which had severed an artery. The undeniable conclusion was that the unfortunate woman must have been dead when the fire started. The sheriff wasted no time before ordering autopsies on all the fire victims, and set in motion the administrative machinery required for a murder investigation.

Meanwhile, Mark Pulliam had been located and returned to Chatsworth to face the sheriff. Pulliam had been logging, so he said, and had last seen his family as he left for work. He expressed disbelief at his family being murdered – after all they were poor people, what possible motive could anyone have for killing them? However, just in case the sheriff had been sniffing around, Pulliam thought it wise to add that there had been trouble between himself and his wife in the past – over his failure to support them – but that had all been sorted out now.

The result of the autopsies carried out on Pulliam's family showed that the children had all been chloroformed before the house was set on fire; and arson experts had discovered traces of inflammable coal tar on charred floorboards in the ruins. The final link in the chain of evidence that tied Pulliam to the death of his family was found by agents checking on his movements in the days leading up to the fire. They learned that Pulliam had taken out a $2,800 life insurance on his wife and the five children who had died in the blaze, but noticeably not on the three children living away from home. The case was consolidating now, especially when it was revealed that Mark Pulliam had recently bought chloroform in order, so he claimed at the time, to calm two vicious mules before they were taken to be shod. The local blacksmith agreed that he had shod two mules for Pulliam, but they were docile enough beasts and there would have been no need for chloroform.

So, after a speedy and efficient investigation, Mark Pulliam was charged with the murder of his wife and children; on 13 February 1943 he was found guilty of first-degree murder and sentenced to life imprisonment.

PURDY, Patrick   On Tuesday 17 January 1989, the Cleveland Elementary School at Stockton, California, was turned into a slaughterhouse when Patrick Purdy, a twenty-six-year-old drifter, returned to his old school to wreak havoc.

Purdy had been brought up in Stockton where, as a child,

he had acquired a reputation for being a loner. Over the years he had accumulated a criminal record for drug offences, robbery and burglary, before eventually moving away to live with relatives in Sandy, Oregon. Then, without a word of explanation, Purdy upped and left Sandy on a one-way ticket back to Stockton; before departing, he bought an AK47 assault rifle over the counter of a local gun-store.

At 11.40 a.m. on 17 January, Patrick Purdy drove up to Cleveland Elementary in his battered Chevrolet station wagon, parked and strode through a gate carrying the machine gun and two handguns. He walked purposefully into the school building, entered a classroom and started shooting randomly at the children sitting at their desks. At almost the same time his car, which he had set fire to outside the school, blew up. Purdy then casually strolled outside, loosing off the AK47 in wide sweeps of automatic gunfire in all directions. Children in the playground dropped to the ground like flies. A teacher who survived the shooting said afterwards: 'He was not talking, he was not yelling, he was very straight-faced, it did not look like he was really angry.' After firing something like 130 shots from the AK47, Purdy took a handgun from his waistband, raised it to his head and pulled the trigger.

In little more than a minute and a half, Patrick Purdy had massacred five children aged between six and nine, all from Vietnamese and Cambodian refugee backgrounds; thirty-nine others had been injured, six of them seriously.

R

RANSOM, Florence   It had all begun on the afternoon of 9 July 1940; the location was the village of Matfield, seven miles or so from Tonbridge, in the county of Kent. The victims were Mrs Dorothy Fisher and her nineteen-year-old daughter, both of whom had been shot dead in the orchard adjoining their garden, and Charlotte Saunders, their maid, who lay dead where she had been shot, apparently running from the cottage. When police officers arrived at the scene they faced the dilemma of motive; because although the cottage seemed to have been ransacked, the intruder had made no attempt to steal the jewellery or cash which had been scattered about with other possessions. When she was killed, the maid was in the process of carrying a tray of crockery into the garden, and by piecing together and counting the number of cups, saucers and plates, it became clear to detectives that the Fishers were about to receive a guest to afternoon tea. This theory was given some confirmation when a search of the spot in the orchard where the women had been killed revealed a single white leather woman's glove. Of its companion there was no trace either inside or outside the cottage, and it seemed reasonable to assume that the assassin had been a woman and that she had dropped a glove. Routine questioning of neighbours turned up several sightings of a woman hanging around outside the cottage on the afternoon of the murders, and other witnesses reported seeing the same woman later on the road between Matfield and Tonbridge, where it was ascertained she took the 4.25 p.m. train to London. The woman was described as being an attractive redhead, who had been carrying a long, narrow object wrapped in paper – quite probably the shotgun with which the victims had been killed.

It was while they were tracing Mrs Fisher's family that police came face to face with the mysterious redhead. At the time she was calling herself 'Mrs Julia Fisher', and was living as the wife of Lawrence Fisher, estranged husband of the late Dorothy Fisher. The woman's real name was Florence Ransom, and she and Fisher were working a farm at Piddington, in Oxfordshire. Further enquiries revealed an even more tangled set of relationships; Mr Fisher was, it seems, still on excellent terms with his wife and was a frequent visitor to the cottage at Matfield; Dorothy Fisher had a new lover in her life and he was known to Lawrence. However, what Lawrence Fisher was in the dark about was the fact that the man he had taken on as cowman was in reality Florence Ransom's brother; and their live-in housekeeper was her mother. It did not go unremarked either, that the cowman had been teaching Florence to use a shotgun.

Several witnesses from Matfield identified Florence Ransom as the woman who had been hanging about the Fisher cottage, and within a short time senior officers were confident enough of the strength of their case to charge her with murder. The trial at the Old Bailey was brief, and Florence denied everything. However, some of the most damaging evidence was provided by her own family when both the cowman brother and housekeeper mother testified that Florence had been away from home on the day of the murder and that she had borrowed the cowman's gun that same day. Although she was convicted and sentenced to death, Florence Ransom was later certified insane and committed to Broadmoor.

REYNOLDS, Vernon It was the last day of the year 1991 when Vernon Reynolds stabbed to death his estranged wife and then allegedly committed suicide by deliberately ramming his car into another vehicle killing its three innocent occupants.

The incident took place at the North Wales coastal resort of Llandudno, where forty-three-year-old Reynolds and his wife Denise owned and ran the Clovelly House guesthouse. In the early part of December the couple separated and Vernon left the family home, though there were reports that he regularly pestered his wife for a reconciliation. On New Year's Eve Denise was holding a party for her family at Clovelly House when, at a little after 11.00 p.m., Reynolds burst into the house and in front of the horrified gaze of their three children lashed out at his wife with a kitchen knife. As Denise ran from the room and into the garden a crazed Reynolds chased after, hacking at her until she fell to the ground dead. Her elderly father was also seriously wounded as he tried to protect Denise, and her sister Pauline fled to summon help from a neighbouring house where she too was stabbed almost to death on the doorstep.

Injuring several other members of the party during his escape, Vernon Reynolds climbed into his metallic green Marina and sped away from town south on the A470. At the time a police patrol was dispatched to intercept him, Reynolds had reached Tal-y-Cafn where he was in a head-on collision with a Mini containing three young men on their way to a party. Robert Jones, Arwyn Roberts and Brynley Roberts all died instantly; Reynolds was still barely alive as rescue teams arrived, but died before he could be cut from the wreckage. Although they were unprepared to rule out the possibility of an accident, the police were seriously considering a scenario in which Vernon Reynolds, who was after all an experienced cab driver, had caused the crash deliberately while in a distressed state of mind for the purpose of taking his own life.

ROBERTS, Harry, et al. On Friday 12 August 1966, Police Constable Geoffrey Fox, Detective Sergeant Christopher Head and Detective Constable David Wombwell were on the nine-to-five shift in 'Q' car

Foxtrot Eleven, an unmarked police vehicle. They had spent the morning chauffeuring Detective Inspector Coote to Marylebone magistrates court, had just eaten a modest lunch at the Beaumont Arms and were now travelling along Braybrook Street, East Acton, a road that runs around the perimeter of Wormwood Scrubs prison. In front of them, the officers noticed a battered blue Standard Vanguard Estate car. For some indefinable reason, perhaps a combination of its disreputable appearance and its proximity to the prison, they decided to stop the vehicle and check on the driver.

Inside the blue car were three small-time crooks: John Witney, Harry Roberts and John Duddy. Witney, the owner and driver of the car, was a thirty-six-year-old unemployed lorry driver with a number of previous convictions for petty theft. About a year earlier Witney had teamed up with Harry Roberts and together they had done a number of jobs, stealing lead and other metals. Roberts, aged thirty, had a similarly long criminal record, but was a much harder man, having done his National Service in Malaya, which taught him guerrilla warfare and jungle survival techniques; he had recently served a four-year stretch and had resolved that he would do almost anything to avoid getting caught again. John Duddy was a heavy drinker who had a history of petty theft, but had always avoided violence. He had joined the other two more recently and they had begun to carry out a series of small robberies on betting shops and rent collectors. For this purpose they had decided to get 'tooled up' with firearms to use as 'frighteners'. Between the two front seats of the estate car was a canvas hold-all containing three guns.

It was about 3.15 when the police car overtook the Vanguard Estate and flagged it down. Sergeant Head and DC Wombwell got out of their car and walked back to the driver's window of the estate. Head asked to see the Road Fund Licence and Witney replied that he was awaiting his MOT Certificate. This was followed by a request for Witney's driving licence and insurance certificate, the details of which Wombwell wrote down in his notebook.

Sergeant Head then moved round to inspect the rear of the car and Witney said: 'Can't you give me a break. I've just been pinched for this a fortnight ago.' As DC Wombwell inclined his head towards the driver's window to reply, Roberts drew a gun and shot him in the left eye. Wombwell fell to the ground and Roberts and Duddy clambered out of the car in pursuit of Sergeant Head. Head ran backwards towards the 'Q' car and Roberts fired a shot which missed. The sergeant was trying to crouch behind the bonnet as Roberts shot him in the back. Meanwhile, Duddy had run up to the police car and fired three shots through the window at PC Fox, one of the bullets hitting him in the left temple and killing him instantly. This released the brake pedal of the 'Q' car which horrifyingly ran over the body of the dying Sergeant Head, trapping him against the rear wheels. The two criminals then turned and ran to their car, which Witney reversed down the road in panic, and, turning, sped away past a surprised young couple driving in the opposite direction. Thinking this might be a prison escape they took the number of the van – PGT 726 – and drove on, to be faced with the scene of bloody devastation.

By nine o'clock that evening the number of the estate car had been traced to John Witney and the police had organized a raid on his house, taking him into custody. Witney's first story was that he had sold the car that very lunchtime to a man in a pub for £15. That evening a description of the car was broadcast over television and radio, resulting in a sighting in Tinworth Road, south London. The car still contained three .38 cartridges and Duddy's .38 pistol on the back seat. On the Sunday, Witney was formally charged with the three murders, and made a confession naming Roberts and Duddy as the main villains.

Meanwhile, Roberts and Duddy had met up on the Saturday morning and, after burying the remaining guns on Hampstead Heath, decided to separate and make a run for it. Duddy made for Glasgow, his home town, and was arrested several days later in a Carlton tenement. Roberts thought his best chance of survival was to lie low for a while using the techniques in which the army had so thoughtfully trained him. Although the police received over six thousand sightings of Roberts in response to the massive manhunt, he was still at large when it was decided to put Witney and Duddy on trial at the end of November. Then in the middle of November a gypsy farm labourer named John Cunningham came across a man living rough in a tent in Thorley Woods, Bishop's Stortford. By the time the information reached the police the camp had been deserted, but fingerprints left behind matched those of Harry Roberts. With the whole area sealed off by the police and systematically searched, it was only a matter of time before Roberts was run to ground in a disused aircraft hangar.

The trial eventually opened at the Old Bailey on 6 December with Mr Justice Glyn-Jones presiding. Witney and Duddy pleaded not guilty to all the charges and Roberts pleaded guilty to the murder of DC Wombwell and DS Head, but not guilty to the killing of PC Fox. All three were found guilty on all counts and sentenced to life imprisonment with the recommendation that they should each serve a minimum of thirty years. John Duddy died in Parkhurst Prison in February 1981.

ROTTMAN, Arthur   In 1914 with the war raging in Europe anti-German sentiments were being expressed by ordinary citizens as far away as New Zealand, though there, at least, little official government action was taken to prevent German nationals from working in the country as long as it was in occupations that had no bearing on national security.

Twenty-one-year-old Arthur Rottman was one of those sons of the Fatherland, and at the time was working on a farm at Ruahine and was well thought of by his employers, Joseph and Lucy McCann, and by their neighbours. On Boxing Day 1914, Rottman went drinking with friends and became rather the worse for it. He had already expressed his liking for his employer, but was not so keen on the wife, because – he claimed – she bullied her husband and drank too much. He also told his drinking companions that he did not want to return to the farm that day as he was likely to be reprimanded for being absent at milking time. The following day Rottman delivered the milk to the factory in the usual way and seemed to be fairly normal apart from suffering from a hangover. The day afterwards he delivered the milk very early which was unusual, and the quantity was short which he explained by saying McCann had spilt some. On his way back to the farm Rottman was stopped by the local constable and told of a new regulation which required aliens to apply for permission if they wished to leave their present place of residence; Rottman replied he had no intention of leaving. Nevertheless, not long after this encounter Arthur Rottman was seen boarding a train for Wellington.

The next day, 29 December, there was no milk delivery at all from the McCann farm, so the manager decided to see if anything was wrong. When he arrived at the farm he could see no signs of life anywhere; and in the cowshed he stumbled upon the dead body of Joseph McCann, with his head split open. In the house were the bodies of Lucy McCann and her baby son, both with similar head wounds. Police later found a bloodstained sheet in Rottman's room and two axes, both bloodstained, were lying on the ground between the house and the cowshed.

A hue and cry was put out for the missing Rottman and the first sightings of him came from the Wellington suburbs. A man working on the Karori Rock lighthouse reported seeing Rottman heading towards Makara. A police party was sent out and arrested Rottman near Te Karama. Told he was being arrested for the murder of the McCann family, Rottman replied: 'I am guilty. I know I'm done. God punish the man who brought me or drink to this country.' He was returned to Mangaweka to attend the inquest at which a verdict of wilful murder was brought in against him.

Arthur Rottman was tried at Wanganui before Mr Justice Chapman. Police evidence was heard that he had said in a statement that he accidentally hit McCann with an axe, following which he got drunk and simply could not remember anything more. His counsel asked for a verdict of not guilty by reason of insanity, because at the time Rottman had been gripped by an alcohol-induced frenzy. On 13 February, the jury found Rottman guilty on all three charges of murder and Mr Justice Chapman passed sentence of death.

Before his execution at the Terrace Gaol, Wellington, on 8 March 1915, Rottman made a final statement in which he blamed drink for his crime and the war for his fate.

ROUCOULT FAMILY CASE   In one of the worst incidents of mass murder in recent French criminal history, a whole family was massacred at their home in Wallers, and their bodies transported across the French-Belgian border to be dumped in the Harchies woods at Beloeil, on the autoroute between Tournai and Mons.

The victims were twenty-nine-year-old Frederic Roucoult, his wife Anne-Marie and their three-year-old daughter, plus two nephews, Jonathan Fiorantino and David Faehr, aged nine and fourteen. All except Jonathan had been shot just once through the forehead or in one eye; he had been shot four times, and forensic experts trying to reconstruct the murders believe that he may have been killed trying to escape. Time of death was calculated to be some time during the night of Monday 5 August 1991. The bodies had been trussed up with electrical flex shortly after death, and then tied in plastic garbage sacks and driven over the border where they were discovered by a jogger the following morning. Although the Tournai public prosecutor, Monsieur Guy Poncelet, was reported as saying: 'We are working closely with the French police, but we have not so far established a motive', he added, 'I can tell you that it was not a simple matter of robbery, it is more complex than that.'

The case remains unsolved, though reports were received that Belgian police believe the murders may be linked to a dispute over the purchase of a second-hand sports car. One of the prime suspects has to be the unnamed man, unemployed and in his late twenties, from whom Monsieur Roucoult bought the car. He has not so far been traced.

RUPPERT, James Easter Sunday 30 March 1975; this was the date on which one of the worst cases of familicide in American history took place. Charity Ruppert, a sixty-five-year-old grandmother, had planned a family gathering, and invited her elder son Leonard, his wife Alma and their eight children to join her and her other son James, who was unmarried and lived with her in Hamilton, Ohio, for a special Easter dinner.

Leonard Ruppert and his family arrived early and spent some time playing games in the garden. Forty-one-year-old James Ruppert, who had recently lost his job and had been very depressed, had been out drinking the night before and was still sleeping it off. He got up around four in the afternoon and came down from the bedroom armed with an arsenal of three pistols and a rifle. As the rest of the family came back into the house, James drew a gun and started firing. Leonard Ruppert was the first to drop, then his wife. Charity Ruppert made an attempt to stop her son, but she was the next to be shot down. The children, Leonard (seventeen), Michael (sixteen), Thomas (fifteen), Carol (thirteen), David (eleven), Teresa (nine) and John (four), all fell in a fusillade of shots. Ruppert fired a total of thirty-one shots, hitting most of the victims in the head. Three hours later he called the police with the laconic phone message: 'There's been a shooting here.'

James Ruppert was arrested and charged the same day with eleven counts of aggravated homicide. He refused to talk to the police and made it clear that he was going to plead a defence of not guilty by reason of insanity.

When his trial opened in June, the prosecution alleged that Ruppert had planned the killings of his family for the purpose of inheriting the family money, property and life insurance valued at over $300,000. He had been prepared to be sent to a mental hospital, because he was convinced he would eventually be declared sane and would then be able to inherit the family estate. In his defence, Ruppert's attorney told the court that his client had suffered from an unreasoning obsession that his family and the authorities were conspiring to persecute him. Ruppert was described as a 'gun freak' and the state prosecutor pointed out that, a month before the shootings, he had been enquiring about getting a silencer for his guns. The case was heard by three judges who, at the end of the trial, declared him guilty on all eleven counts of murder and sentenced him to life imprisonment.

On appeal James Ruppert was granted a new trial on legal grounds. At the retrial, he was found guilty of murdering his mother and brother but not guilty by reason of insanity of the other nine deaths. The sentence remained the same, and Ruppert was returned to prison to serve his life sentence.

RYAN, Michael On Wednesday 19 August 1987, the historic market town of Hungerford, Berkshire, was turned into a blood-bath with sixteen people shot to death and another fourteen injured, eight of them seriously. The butchery ended only when the gunman, twenty-seven-year-old Michael Ryan, was cornered in a school and turned the gun on himself.

The first victim was Susan Godfrey, who was picnicking with her two children in Savernake Forest, a few miles from the town and across the boundary in Wiltshire. Ryan, dressed in combat gear and flak jacket, forced Mrs Godfrey into the forest at gunpoint, where he shot her thirteen times. Then he drove to the Golden Arrow filling station on the A4 at Froxfield, where at 12.40 p.m. he filled up his silver Vauxhall Astra, and a five-litre petrol can. Replacing the can in the car boot, Ryan lifted out a Kalashnikov AK47 semi-automatic rifle, crouched slightly, raised the butt to his right shoulder, took aim at the cashier and fired. The shot went wide; Kakaub Dean dropped to the floor and made the first of the many calls which the emergency services were to receive that afternoon.

Ryan's next port of call was Hungerford, where the

madness escalated; running and jogging, Ryan began firing indiscriminately into the crowded market-day streets. Roland and Sheila Mason were shot while preparing to go shopping; Ken Clements as he was walking with his family. Douglas Wainwright was cut down while out house-hunting, and Abdur Khan when simply mowing his lawn. Anyone, and anything that moved. Fourteen-year-old Lisa Mildenhall was playing in the garden when she saw Ryan. 'I looked straight at his face and he smiled at me. I fixed my eyes at his eyes and he then crouched down and aimed the rifle at me. I just froze. He fired the gun . . . It must have been about four shots.' Lisa survived after emergency surgery.

While Ryan was busily decimating the local community, Kakaub Dean's emergency call resulted in the despatch of two police cars, one of which was unlucky enough to get in the way of Ryan's Kalashnikov, leaving PC Roger Brereton dead in a hail of twenty-four bullets. The officer heroically managed to get out a distress call just before he died. That call was picked up by PC Jeremy Wood, who immediately called for a firearms team and a helicopter, set up a road block and evacuated picnicking families. By this time, Michael Ryan had rewarded his mother Dorothy's love and affection by gunning her down too, after which he set fire to the house.

The rampage continued, down Priory Avenue where Eric Vardy was shot in his delivery van; a salvo at the junction into Cold-harbour Lane killed Francis Butler and cabbie Marcus Barnard; through Bulpit Lane and into Priory Road, where Sandra Hill was killed in her Renault car. Mr and Mrs Gibb, drinking tea in their kitchen, were gunned down, Jack dying instantly and Myrtle later in hospital. Finally Ryan shot Ian Playle, driving his blue Sierra. Playle would die two days later.

By six o'clock in the afternoon Hungerford is in a state of siege. All telephone lines to the town have been shut down; all roads in and out of town are blocked. The police are moving in, and Michael Ryan, the focus of everybody's attention, is holed up at the John O'Gaunt secondary school. Specialist siege negotiators and marksmen surrounding the school try to persuade Ryan to surrender. The gunman appears chillingly lucid, almost reasonable, as he talks to the police. Then, quite unexpectedly: 'It's funny, I have killed all those people but I haven't the guts to blow my own brains out.' At just after 7.00 p.m. a muffled shot from inside the building breaks the uneasy silence. It was a further three hours before the police cautiously entered the school, the team of two officers covering each other as they dodged from room to room. In a back classroom they found Michael Ryan, sitting in a corner with a gun between his knees. He was dead.

So what do we know about this twenty-seven-year-old psychopath who was responsible for Britain's worst killing spree? He had been, by all accounts, an awkward kid, surly, shy and self-conscious. The only child of elderly parents, Michael had few friends, apparently none of them girls; in business, as in life, he was a failure. Ironically, the only living creatures that Michael Ryan seemed genuinely fond of were his mother, whom he was said to have beaten regularly and finally shot, and his dog – which also died in the massacre. Of the inanimate objects in his life, Ryan cherished his car; but above all, his guns. He kept these in a garden shed, where he treated them rather in the way better-balanced individuals might treat their pets. On the day of the massacre, Michael Ryan had selected from his private arsenal the AK47, an M1 US carbine, two pistols, and some grenades.

Ryan was obviously a very disturbed young man, suffering, according to Broadmoor's medical director Dr John Hamilton, from either schizophrenia or a psychopathic disorder. In the wake of what became known as the 'Hungerford Massacre', Ryan's uncle, Leslie, claimed the youth had been devastated by the death of his father: 'When he went, Michael seemed to go strange.' And Dr David Hill, a clinical psychologist with the mental health charity MIND, pointed out the very real danger which comes when somebody severely stressed or mentally ill has a gun. When they crack, he said, 'the amount of damage done is directly

related to the power of the weapons available . . . If there is
a gun in the house, it will be used.'

Michael Robert Alfred Henry Ryan was cremated at
Reading Crematorium on 3 September 1989. The single
wreath on his coffin bore the inscription: 'Our Saviour will
receive him fittingly.'

S

SAINT VALENTINE'S DAY MASSACRES It wasn't Chicago in the 1920s but New York in 1991; it wasn't about bootleg booze but about drugs. What they had in common was Saint Valentine's Day and a gun massacre.

It had been around midnight when neighbours in a low-rent housing block in the crime-ridden Hispanic district of New York's South Bronx heard banging on one of the apartment doors, banging fit to wake the dead; then the crack of gunshots followed by what sounded like two people running away. Nobody interfered, nobody went to find out what had happened, nobody called the cops; in that part of town – a centre for the cocaine and heroin trade – police informers too often ended up dead heroes, just another statistic among the city's annual average of two thousand murders. It wasn't until a resident walked past the apartment door next morning and saw the bodies that the alarm was raised.

When they reached the sixth-floor flat on Prospect Avenue and 152nd Street, officers found six bodies, all black Hispanics originally from the Dominican Republic; five were lying on the floor face down with a bullet in the back of the head, a sixth, a woman, had been shot in the face. One of the victims, a seventeen-year-old drug dealer named Edwin Santiago was probably the main target in a drugs-related assassination; the others who died were Santiago's disabled mother, his sister and her boyfriend, and two teenaged friends who had also lived on the block.

The original Saint Valentine's Day Massacre took place in 1929, in Chicago.

Among Big Al Capone's few effective rivals during those profitable days of Prohibition bootlegging was the audaciously successful George 'Bugs' Moran. Certainly the Moran gang's hijacking of the Big Man's liquor shipments, their blowing up of his speakeasies, and the sniping at his lieutenants were costing Capone plenty of dollars; what was worse, his pride was hurting. So Capone laid the plans for a vicious and most ingenious revenge. On 13 February 1929, Moran received a telephone call from one of his own bootleg suppliers: a haul of whisky was waiting to be delivered to Bugsy's warehouse. Arrangements were made for ten-thirty on the following morning, 14 February, Saint Valentine's Day. While seven of Moran's gang were waiting in the warehouse a police car screamed to a stop outside and out jumped two uniformed cops and three plainclothes men. They relieved the gangsters of their weapons, lined them up against a wall, and straffed back and forth with their machine guns – stomach, chest, head. The seven dropped into a lake of their own blood. So, with a squad of men masquerading as policemen, Capone had the last laugh. Or did he? Miraculously, George Moran was late for that ten-thirty appointment with death, arriving only after the real police had got to the scene of the butchery. In fact, Bugs Moran outlived his rival by many years, succumbing in the end not to an assassin's bullet, but to lung cancer.

SARTIN, Robert Monkseaton, Tyne and Wear, Sunday 30 April 1989: a quiet town on a quiet day. Twenty-two-year-old Robert Sartin rose leisurely, brushed back his pony-tail, dressed in his favourite black, and completed his uniform with a combat knife strapped to his thigh and a pair of sunglasses. After loading his father's shotgun into his Escort the young man drove sedately into town. He parked in Pykerley Road and set off on foot, the 12-bore under his arm. Moments later, at around midday, Judith Rhodes received the first blast from the gun through the windscreen of her car. With admirable presence of mind she braked and ducked under the dashboard, taking some of the second shot in her left hand. Robert Sartin reloaded, fired an insolent round in the air, and strolled back down the street. The shooting spree had begun.

The next victim was Lorraine Noble, standing talking to her neighbour William Roberts at his garden gate. She took the full blast of the shot and collapsed to the ground, seriously injured. Robert Wilson, hearing the noise, stepped out of his front door and was hit in the face and left side of his body by the next volley. A pot-shot at Kathleen Lynch, looking out of her window, went wide, but Brian Thomas was less fortunate. Cycling down the street at that most inopportune of moments he was flung from his bike by two shots, but managed to drag himself, agonizingly, to the safety of a nearby house.

From the other end of the road another target approaches. A car, which has to swerve to avoid Brian Thomas's abandoned bicycle, takes a hail of gunfire which seriously injures the driver, Robert Burgeon, his wife Jean and their daughter Nicola. Further up the road another car receives a blast through the windscreen and veers uncontrollably into a wall, injuring Ernest Carter; at almost the same moment, Jean Miller is shot in the stomach as she weeds her front garden.

Vera Miller wants to know what is going on. 'It's me,' Sartin matter-of-factly informs her. 'I am killing people. I am going to kill you.' But the random nature of his compulsion saves her when he lowers the gun and walks away.

Along Windsor Road Kenneth Mackintosh is delivering leaflets for his local church, and looks up to see the menacing figure of Sartin bearing down on him, shotgun at the ready. A blast from both barrels sends Mackintosh reeling; his plea for mercy is met with: 'No, it is your day to die.' Two more shots at point-blank range kill the father of two instantly.

Robert Sartin was arrested that evening, as he sat in a car park, gazing out to sea. He had killed one man, and injured fourteen others.

The trial opened exactly one year later, on Monday 30 April 1990, at Newcastle-upon-Tyne. Sartin's schizophrenia, his conviction that his mind was controlled by another, was described by Mr David Robson QC. An obsession with the macabre, with Satanism, with the Moors Murderers; a 'pilgrimage' to the scene of Michael Ryan's Hungerford Massacre (see page 285); all this was revealed to the court. But what really drove Sartin was the voice of Michael. Michael Myers, the fictional teenage psychopath who hacks his family to pieces in the film *Halloween*. Sartin saw Michael, heard him, drew pictures of him . . . was possessed by him.

There was only one suitable verdict, and the jury chose it: unfit to plead. It is doubtful that Robert Sartin will ever be considered psychologically fit enough to stand trial.

SAVILLE, William William Saville became romantically attached to a young woman named Ann Ward who, in the course of time, fell pregnant by him; following promises of financial reward by her family, Saville undertook to marry her. They were wed at Sneinton in Nottinghamshire in 1835, and immediately moved to Radford with their own baby and another illegitimate child, a reminder of one of Ann's earlier indiscretions. Despite a brief and rather bitter separation shortly after the wedding, the couple seemed to patch up their differences and celebrated by having another child.

In January 1844 William Saville deserted his wife and their three children, Harriet, Mary and Thomas. Posing now as a single man, he went into lodgings at New Radford where he met another young woman and asked her to marry him and emigrate to America. And things might have gone more smoothly had his new amour not learned of the existence of Saville's wife, and had Saville's wife not got hold of his new address and decided to pay a visit. Thus were William Saville's plans to marry bigamously and start afresh in the New World thwarted.

On the morning of 21 May 1844, apparently quite by chance, Saville met his wife and at his suggestion she and the children took a stroll in his company along Colwick Lane, near the Colwick Woods. Along the way they turned into a field where, as quick as a flash, Saville pulled out a razor and slit the throats of his entire family. Celebrating a job well done, Saville returned to his lodgings later that afternoon and sat down to a hearty meal.

The bodies were not discovered until three days later and, as Ann Saville was found with a razor in her hand, it was tempting to believe that in some fit of anguish she had killed her children and then herself; or it might have been, were it not known all over town that William was courting another woman.

In his twenty-ninth year, therefore, William Saville appeared for his trial at the Nottingham Assize on 27 July 1844 before Lord Denman. The process was brief, and evidence that while awaiting trial Saville had made a confession to a fellow prisoner secured a speedy conviction, and he was sentenced to death.

While awaiting execution, Saville made a final, thoroughly preposterous statement to the prison chaplain that he had witnessed his wife kill their infant son and had then seen the two girls lying dead in the grass. He had struggled with his wife for possession of the razor, but in the fight that followed her throat had been cut. Even that most kind and generous-hearted of chaplains could find little in this to believe. And so on Thursday 7 August 1844, William Saville was led from the prison to the scaffold erected outside Nottingham County Hall; at three minutes past eight o'clock the trap opened and he plunged to his death.

As was customary, an immense concourse had gathered for the spectacle, and as soon as the trap fell a great surge of people moved forward for a closer look at the swinging man, as the pressure of the crowd grew and panic spread, people were crushed and trampled underfoot, there being no exits from the street leading to the scaffold. Twelve people died in the crush and more than one hundred received serious injuries.

The location of the murders, in Colwick Woods, is still known as Saville's Spinney.

SCHLAEPFER, Brian   A telephone rang at the Auckland, New Zealand, police station at around 7.40 on the morning of Tuesday 19 May 1992, and it was routinely answered by Constable Jeff Stuck; it was a telephone call he will never forget. At first there was briefly the hysterical voice of a woman pleading for help, followed by screams, shots, and the sound of the telephone being dropped on the floor; and then an eerie silence. For five minutes Constable Stuck patiently talked into the telephone's mouthpiece, trying to get attention, listening intently for some clue as to what the hell was going on out there. After what seemed like an hour Jeff Stuck was rewarded with a small, scared voice coming quietly down the line; over the next three hours, nine-year-old Linda Schlaepfer would give a running narrative of one of the country's most bloody cases of familicide, detailing the gradual massacre of her own family by her own beloved grandfather.

Constable Stuck asked: 'Linda, what's happening out there, love?'

'My grandad's shot my brother.'

'Shot your brother?'

'Yes, and he's coming to shoot me.'

'He's going to shoot you now?'

'Yes, he's looking for me.'

'Is your mum there; can your mum come to the phone?'

'No.'

Mrs Schlaepfer most certainly could not come to the telephone; as Linda told the officer: 'Mummy's dead. My brother's been shot and he's groaning and twitching.' In fact, quite a few more of the family were also lying dead in various corners of the farm; only Linda survived and managed to direct the police to where she was hiding.

The Schlaepfer family had arrived as immigrants from Switzerland almost a century before, settling into the small farming community around Paerata, about nine miles to the south of Auckland. Over three industrious generations the Schlaepfer farm had spread to three hundred acres, and most of the family lived in properties built on the farm, notionally at least in the charge of the sixty-four-year-old patriarch Brian Schlaepfer. The family enjoyed the respect and affection of their neighbours, and Brian especially had made his mark on local life, founding the gliding club, and donating a camping ground to the Scouts and Guides, with whom he served as a scoutmaster.

But within the family circle a bitter feud was smouldering. Hazel Schlaepfer, resentful of the slow, old-fashioned ways of her father-in-law, plotted to usurp his position as head of the family, and had already persuaded some of the menfolk to take over control of the farm. The bitterness of this imminent defeat had begun to eat away at the old man's soul, and aggravated by a long-term heart condition the family pressure was already unbalancing the fragile state of his mind. It was around dawn on that morning of 19 May that Brian Schlaepfer's reason finally snapped, and in a blind and desperate rage against all mankind he first hacked his own wife to death with a knife, then burst into the bedroom of his second son, thirty-three-year-old Karl, and shot him dead. Now he was like a hunter stalking his own family: next to fall was eleven-year-old Aaron, but an attempt to grab little Linda was foiled by the intervention of her mother who received the full blast of his gun. Now Schlaepfer stumbled out of the house and on to where his other sons, Darrell and Peter were working on the farm. Meanwhile, Linda was talking to Jeff Stuck, telling him where she was . . .

When the police arrived at the farm, backed up by marksmen from the special New Zealand Armed Offenders Squad, they carried out a cautious search of the buildings. At just after 3 p.m. they found Brian Schlaepfer lying dead on open ground, a self-inflicted shotgun wound to his head; in his pocket police found a suicide note. In the end, Brian Schlaepfer received earthly forgiveness at least – for when Jocelyn, Karl, Hazel, Aaron, Darrell and Peter Schlaepfer were buried in the tiny local churchyard, Brian, by request of the surviving members of the family, was buried beside them. Looking on, too numb even to weep, was the bewildered nine-year-old who had just escaped from hell.

SCHWARZ, Bernhard Schwarz was a twenty-two-year-old plumber from Nuertingen, near Stuttgart, and a regular client at the Starlight Discotheque at Frickenhausen. He spent the evening of Saturday 11 October 1986 at the disco, and engaged in heavy drinking into the early hours of Sunday morning. As he left the building to go to the car park Schwarz was detained by the police and breathalysed. They found him well over the legal limit, and as a precaution confiscated his driving licence and car keys, informing him he could collect them from the police station the following day on condition he had sobered up. To say that Bernhard Schwarz was angry would be to underestimate his reaction; Schwarz was enraged. He made his way home, picked up a spare set of car keys and returned to the discotheque where he drove off in his vehicle, still seething with rage and apparently determined to kill as many people as possible before dying in his beloved white Volkswagen.

Schwarz sped away driving on the wrong side of the road, then turning on to the autobahn in the direction of Wendlingen where he deliberately ran down Harald Mueller. The accident investigators calculated that Schwarz had been travelling at seventy miles per hour, sufficient for the impact to throw Mueller thirty-eight feet across the road.

By now, traffic police in the area had begun to receive calls from motorists who had been threatened by the white Volkswagen. On another section of the autobahn, for example, a car driven by Friedrich Braunmueller was making its way to Frankfurt airport. The passengers were the driver's fiancée, Rosemarie Reichert, his brother Wolfgang and Claudia Schneider, Wolfgang's fiancée, and they were on their way to catch a plane for a Caribbean holiday. Braunmueller and his happy party were totally unaware that rushing towards them down the wrong carriageway was the crazed Schwarz. He had already attempted to ram two other motorists on his way, but they had managed to take avoiding action when they saw his headlights coming towards them. Realizing this potential impediment to his plans, Schwarz had turned his lights off before crashing head-on into the holidaymakers' Audi 80. Rosemarie

Reichert died instantly on impact and so did Wolfgang Braunmueller and Claudia Schneider in the back seat. Friedrich Braunmueller survived with several broken ribs, probably saved by his safety belt. Bernhard Schwarz received only minor injuries.

When he was questioned by the police, Schwarz admitted killing Mueller and the Audi passengers, adding that his choice of victims was entirely random; finally, he insisted that the whole episode should be blamed on the Frickenhausen police. Schwarz was tested for drink and drugs and the police surgeon's report stated that even though he had been under the influence of drink earlier, there was no evidence that this was the case at the time of the motorway mayhem; a psychiatric examination resulted in him being declared fit to stand trial.

In court, Schwarz again confessed to the killings and restated his belief that it was all the fault of the Frickenhausen police; on 9 October 1987, he was sentenced to life imprisonment.

SEEGRIST, Sylvia   This is an unusual case of a gun-toting female spree killer and regrettably an example of an unbalanced person who's potential for violence seemingly went unnoticed.

On 30 October, 1985, Sylvia Seegrist, dressed in battle fatigues and carrying a rifle, walked into a shopping mall in Springfield, Pennsylvania and immediately began firing at the passing shoppers. Her first victim was a two-year-old boy, shot down at point-blank range. She then continued to advance into the mall, firing wildly as she went. Within minutes, three people were dead had seven wounded. More would have fallen to her gun and not a courageous shopper tackled her and wrestled the rifle from her.

When she appeared in court, she told the judge, 'Hurry up man. You know I'm guilty. Kill me now.' At her trial, on three charges of murder, seven of attempted murder and aggravated assault, she was found to be criminally insane and committed to a secure hospital.

In a civil action, the victims and relatives of the dead brought a case against the shopping mall owners for failing to provide a safe environment for their shoppers. Evidence was led that on several occasions before the shooting, she had visited the mall, making gestures and acting in a threatening manner. She had visited the McDonald's restaurant in San Ysidro, California, where **James Huberty** had killed twenty-one people. At the restaurant, she had intimated she would like to do the same thing in Springfield and pointed her finger like a gun while saying 'rat-tat-tat'. Lawyers for the mall owners contended that it was not practical for them to apply to have Sylvia Seegrist committed to a hospital and that even if she had been detained, she would not have been held very long. In addition, they claimed the only way to have prevented the shooting would have meant turning the mall into an armed camp. Nevertheless, in February 1990, the jury returned a verdict for the plaintiffs and awarded undisclosed damages.

SEGEE, Robert Dale In July 1944 the famous Ringling Brothers circus arrived with its brass bands, elephants, liberty horses, clowns and tumblers in the small town of Hartford, Connecticut. The big top mushroomed as if by magic, watched by an entranced audience of children of all ages. And when the huge tent had been erected the seating was installed in readiness for the first show scheduled for 6 July. By early afternoon queues were forming, and soon the crowds of children, parents and grandparents were settling into their seats in anticipation of the spectacle to come.

At around 2.30, after the orchestra had blasted out the overture and the eyes of the audience were straining upwards to catch every daring and dangerous movement of the trapeze act, a sinister figure huddled in the shadows was starting a fire against the canvas wall of the big top. The heavy material might have proved difficult to ignite, but in compliance with local regulations it had been coated with paraffin wax to ensure it was waterproof. A few moments later there was a shrill cry of 'Fire! Fire!', and the audience, circus hands and performers watched with amazement as they saw a flame flickering upwards near the main entrance. At first there was little concern, it seemed to be a small enough fire, and surely somebody was attending to it . . . Suddenly there was a strong gust of wind, a fury that set the big top billowing and flapping, and fanned the fire into a sudden burst, igniting the wax coating and sending strips of blazing canvas snaking down on the shrieking audience. Now the crowd was on its feet, scurrying blindly for the steel runway which served as the exist; on the runway the panicking mass of desperate bodies jammed themselves to a standstill, a crowd so dense it was impossible to move, impossible now even to breathe. Flaming debris continued to rain down, setting alight hair and clothing . . .

Within five minutes of the fire being lit 169 people were dead, either as a direct result of the inferno or by crush asphyxia in the attempt to escape it. More than 250 more were ferried to hospital for emergency treatment, many of them suffering from serious injuries.

Although the police suspected arson there were no early indications of a likely suspect, and the investigation was not helped by the fact that many of the circus hands were casual employees who moved around the country never staying too long with any one circus. It was not until six years later, when detectives were running a cross-check on all suspected cases of arson in which any of the circus hands employed on the fateful day at Hartford appeared, that they came up with a name – Robert Dale Segee, called 'Little Bob'. Enquiries indicated that Segee was a morose individual who nursed a growing hatred of people he thought were, in his own phrase, 'treating him as no account'. In June 1950 he was traced to Ohio and taken in for questioning. Segee admitted he was responsible for the circus fire and that he had also started a few more. And just for good measure Little Bob laid claim to an impressive list of other homicides – a young girl in 1938, a nightwatchman who had tried to stop him lighting a fire in Portland, Maine, in 1943, and two young boys, one in Portland and one in Japan while he had been serving with the army. Segee claimed that for years he had been haunted by nightmares in which he was told he must start fires.

Although there was little enough evidence on which to indict Robert Segee on any of the crimes to which he was prepared to admit, he was eventually charged with ten counts of arson. Certified fit to stand trial, Segee pleaded guilty and on 4 November 1950 was sentenced to two separate terms of two to twenty years' imprisonment.

SHEARING, David William On 6 August 1982, two families met up at the Wells Gray Provincial Park campsite near Clearwater, British Columbia. George Bentley and his wife Edith had been eagerly looking forward to meeting their daughter, Jacqueline Johnson, her husband Richard and, most of all, their grandchildren, eleven-year-old Karen and thirteen-year-old Janet. The Johnsons arrived by car and the Bentleys in their 1981 red and silver Ford camper van, with a boat and outboard motor strapped to the roof.

They were never seen alive again, and a widespread search of the wilderness area failed to uncover any clue until 13 September, when the Johnsons' car was found burned out some way outside the park area; inside the vehicle were the charred remains of Mr and Mrs Bentley and the four Johnsons, though their bodies were so badly burned that they could only be identified from dental records. Subsequent post-mortem examination established that several of the victims had been shot before the car was set ablaze.

At this stage in the investigation the Bentleys' camper was still missing, and when the police were informed that two French-speaking men had been seen driving a similar vehicle in the area, they initiated a country-wide search. Police officers staged a televised reconstruction, and even had a team of men drive a similar camper across Canada in an attempt to find witnesses. However, it was not until October 1983 that any trace was found of the camper. Two forestry workers reported finding the vehicle, burned-out like the Johnsons', in a ravine about twenty miles from where the victims had been found. This effectively narrowed the investigation to the Wells Gray Park area and police commenced house-to-house enquiries in Clearwater. In the course of these interviews, officers were told by a resident that a man he knew, David William Shearing, had spoken to him about a vehicle he owned with a bullet hole in the door. This information was highly significant because the police had never disclosed the fact that a bullet hole had been found in the door of the Bentleys' camper.

Twenty-five-year-old Shearing was detained for questioning, and while he was in custody made a full confession. He described how he had reconnoitred the campsite the night before the killings, returning with his rifle and shooting each of his victims in the head. Shearing explained he had pushed the bodies of the adults into the back of the car and hid the corpses of the two young girls in the boot; then had driven the car to remote road, walked back to the campsite to collect the camper, and driven it to where he had left the car, which he then drove deeper into the woods. The following day Shearing doused it with petrol and set it on fire. A few days later, he returned to where he had hidden the camper, had a few beers and set that on fire too. Shearing said he really had no idea why he killed the two families; he added: 'I feel really bad about it and nothing else.'

David Shearing appeared in court at Kamloops, British Columbia, on 21 November 1983, charged with six counts of second-degree murder. He later waived a preliminary hearing and was committed for trial. At the Supreme Court at Kamloops on 16 April 1984, Shearing pleaded guilty to all six counts of second-degree murder and the following day he was sentenced to life imprisonment without the possibility of parole for twenty-five years. Describing the murders as 'the cold-blooded and senseless execution of six defenceless and innocent victims', Supreme Court Justice Harry McKay said that in spite of Shearing's actions there was no suggestion that he suffered from any kind of mental illness. It was believed to be the first time in Canadian legal history that a life sentence without parole for twenty-five years had been given on a second-degree murder conviction.

After the hearing, the prosecution insisted that Shearing was not charged with first-degree murder because it could not be proved that the killings were 'planned and deliberate'. In view of his own admission that he had spied on the victims the night before the slaughter this may be considered debatable, and presumably the judge had this doubt firmly in his mind when he imposed the same sentence that would have been mandatory in the case of a first-degree murder conviction.

SHERRILL, Patrick Henry The worst of the recent 'post-office massacres' – indeed, one of America's worst mass murders of all time – took place on 20 August 1986, at Edmond, Oklahoma. Patrick 'Sandy' Sherrill, a forty-four-year-old part-time postal worker attached to the main post office in this suburb of Oklahoma County, had been warned the day before his killing spree that he was facing dismissal for unsatisfactory work. It was not the first time Sherrill had been in trouble, and reports from the postal authorities claimed that he had already been under suspension once in the year since he joined as a postman in 1985.

Sherrill was always prepared to tell anybody with an inclination to listen that he was a Vietnam veteran, which was quite untrue. However, he was a member of the Oklahoma National Guard, and a considerable marksman with their competition team. In this position of trust, Pat Sherrill was able to withdraw guns from the ONG arsenal for the purpose of entering shooting competitions, and on 5 April 1986 he borrowed a .45-calibre automatic pistol. On 10 August he borrowed another, identical, weapon and three hundred rounds of ammunition.

On the hot Wednesday morning of 20 August, Patrick Sherrill, wearing his regulation postman's uniform, drove to work as usual, taking with him the two .45s plus his own .22-calibre handgun and the ammunition. He walked towards the post office, stopping just once to shoot dead a fellow-worker who was crossing the car park, before passing through the employees' entrance into the single-storey building. After locking several doors in order to maximize his kill, Sherrill began, in the words of the police, 'shooting people as though they were sitting ducks'. Although FBI marksmen were deployed around the building after an employee escaped and raised the alarm, Sherrill refused to speak to the specially trained siege negotiators.

When the police eventually stormed the building they found the bodies of fourteen men and women, and seven other badly wounded victims. Patrick Sherrill lay dead where he had put a single bullet through his own head, his arsenal of guns and ammunition beside him.

It is alarming to recognize how closely Patrick Sherrill fitted the stereotype of a mass killer. He was, typically, a loner with no known family – in fact, it was some days before he could be cremated because nobody could be found to claim the body. Although he was described as a happy, pleasant person, Sherrill was only really content when he was involved in the military activities of the National Guard, where he developed his passion for guns; it is significant that although he had never seen active service, he claimed to have fought in Vietnam. It is impossible to know why Patrick Sherrill stopped shooting when he did – he still had plenty of ammunition, and the .22 was found unfired. He did, however, end his own life with his own gun, as the majority of mass killers do.

SIMANTS, Erwin Charles Herbert On 19 October 1975 an emergency call was received by the authorities in Sutherland, Nebraska, reporting that there had been a shooting at Henry Kellie's home. A nurse was despatched immediately and when he arrived he found blood and bodies everywhere.

In the living room lay the bodies of fifty-seven-year-old Mrs Marie Kellie, her grandchildren Deanne, aged six and Daniel, aged five, and her son David Kellie. In one of the bedrooms were the corpses of sixty-six-year-old Henry Kellie and another granddaughter, Florence, aged ten. The nurse found that there were still signs of life in David Kellie and arranged for an ambulance to rush him to hospital for emergency treatment, but he died a few minutes later.

All the victims had been shot, some repeatedly. The telephone operator who had taken the emergency call told the police that she was sure the voice was familiar, but could not recall where she had heard it before. The first break came the following day, when a next-door neighbour of the Kellies telephoned the sheriff and told him she suspected that a relative who had been staying with her, Erwin Simants, had been responsible for the killings. Police officers went immediately to the house, where Simants gave himself up without offering any resistance.

Erwin Simants admitted to the detectives that he was responsible for the shootings, but when pressed as to whether there had been a sexual motive he became vague in his replies. A young nephew said Simants had left the house and walked next door to the Kellie home on the night of the murders, armed with a .22-calibre rifle. Both the nephew and Simants' mother said that he had confessed the murders to them. Erwin Simants was charged with six counts of first-degree murder to which, in the cases of the female victims, charges of first-degree sexual assault were added.

When Simants came before the court for trial his attorneys led with a defence of mental incompetence at the time of the killings. On 17 January 1976, the jury rejected this plea and returned a verdict of guilty of first-degree murder. On 29 January Simants was sentenced to death on each of the six counts of murder.

Erwin Simants appealed against his conviction, and the Nebraska Supreme Court ruled that he should be granted a new trial on the grounds that there had been complaints that the sequestered jury had been in contact with the local sheriff.

The retrial ended on 17 October 1979 with the jury returning a verdict of 'not guilty by reason of insanity', a verdict which was roundly criticized by the presiding judge. Under Nebraskan law, this meant that Simants became the responsibility of the Mental Health Board which, in theory, could release him at any time if it was decided he was not a menace to others. However, at a meeting of the Board on 26

October 1979 it was accepted that Erwin Simants was both mentally ill *and* dangerous and he was committed to a regional mental health centre for an indefinite period.

SIMECECK, James   A quadruple murder that took place near Ellsworth, Wisconsin, in 1942 arose out of the lust of a twenty-five-year-old farmer for one of his neighbours. In January of that year the home of the Petan family burst into flames. A neighbour passing by had time to drag three bodies from the inferno before the roof fell in. None of the victims had died in the fire – Mrs Verna Petan, aged twenty-eight, had been raped, stabbed and shot; six-year-old Neil and three-year-old Sylvia had died from having their throats slashed. The badly burned body of the eldest child, ten-year-old George, was later recovered from the smouldering ruins.

The first suspect in the case was a tramp who admitted to the sheriff's officers that he had been near the Petan home around the time of the murder; he also admitted a previous conviction for rape, but emphatically denied he was capable of killing a young mother and her children. He was quickly eliminated from the enquiry when a local doctor informed the police that just before the murders he had given the tramp a lift in his car past the Petan house. But the doctor had another, more vital piece of information. As they were passing, he had noticed an old car parked in the driveway of the Petan smallholding.

The following day a woman came forward to say she had seen a neighbour, James Simececk, driving towards the Petan home that afternoon. Simececk was questioned and claimed that he often called in to see Verna Petan to see if she wanted anything fetching from town as she did not have a car. He freely admitted he was at the house on the afternoon of the killings, 'but Verna said she was pretty well stocked up and would wait until my next visit'. The neighbour who had recovered the bodies from the blazing house was questioned again and he remembered seeing a box of groceries on a chair in the kitchen, which looked as though someone had not had time to put away.

Simececk's house was searched and bloodstained clothing was found; and a .32 revolver which, when test-fired, proved to be the weapon which had fired the bullet recovered from Verna Petan's body. Hairs caught in her wedding ring matched samples taken from Simececk. When presented with this evidence, Simececk confessed, admitting: 'I'd an urge to make love to her but when she started screaming, I shot her and stabbed her.' He also confessed to killing the children when they ran into the house after hearing their mother screaming.

James Simececk was charged with four counts of murder and, at his trial in March 1942, was found guilty on all counts and sentenced to four terms of life imprisonment.

SIMMONS, Ronald Gene Simmons, a former Air Force Master Sergeant, dominated his wife and seven children. The family's original home had been in Cloudcroft, New Mexico, until 1981; until school officials filed charges against Simmons of incest with his sixteen-year-old daughter Sheila, who it later transpired was pregnant by her father. Wisely, perhaps, the family moved to Russellville, Arkansas.

Just before Christmas 1987, Ronald Simmons made a conscious decision to kill all the members of his family. On the morning of 22 December he first bludgeoned and shot his son Gene and his long-suffering wife Rebecca; then he strangled his three-year-old daughter Barbara. After having a beer, Simmons dumped the bodies in the cesspit he had made his children dig. Now Simmons sat back and awaited the return of his other children. When they arrived off the bus he said he had presents for them but wanted to give them one at a time. First to receive her 'gift' was eldest daughter, seventeen-year-old Loretta, who Simmons strangled and held under the water in the rain barrel. The three other children, Eddy, Marianne and Becky were despatched in a similarly callous manner.

Around midday on 26 December, the remaining members of the family arrived for their planned Christmas visit; it was to be their last Christmas. The first to die was

Simmons' son Billy and daughter-in-law Renata, both shot dead; then his grandson Trae was strangled and drowned; then daughter Sheila and her husband Dennis McNulty were shot. Ronald Simmons' child by his own daughter, christened Sylvia Gail, was strangled, and finally grandson Michael. Simmons laid the bodies of his whole family in neat rows in the lounge. All the corpses were covered with coats except that of Sheila, who was laid in state covered by Mrs Simmons' best tablecloth. The bodies of the two grandsons were wrapped in plastic sheeting and left in abandoned cars at the end of the lane. After popping out for a drink in a local bar Simmons returned to the house and, apparently oblivious of the corpses lined up around him, spent the next two nights and the Sunday drinking beer and watching television.

On the Monday morning Ronald Simmons drove into Russellville and at a law office shot dead a young woman named Kathy Kendrick, who for some reason he blamed for many of his problems. Next stop on his murderous tour was an oil company office where Simmons shot dead a man named J. D. Chaffin and wounded the owner. He then drove on to a store where he shot and wounded two more people. Now on to another office where he shot and wounded a woman. And that was the end of the killing spree. Simmons simply sat in the office and chatted to one of the secretaries while waiting for the police. When they arrived he handed over his gun and surrendered without any resistance.

Simmons was charged with a total of sixteen counts of murder and sent for psychiatric examination. Found fit to stand trial he was first tried for the two killings and four attempted killings in Russellville. He refused to take any part in his defence and was speedily and predictably found guilty. Before sentence was passed, Simmons read a prepared statement requesting that no action should be taken to lodge an appeal on his behalf. He was sentenced to death for murder, and to 147 years in jail on the other counts. Appeals were nevertheless filed by anti-capital punishment groups (as is their practice), but Simmons countered by obtaining a court ruling that he was competent to waive appeal.

For good measure it was decided to put him on trial for the killing of his family, and the hearing opened on 6 February 1989 in Clarksville. During the trial, Simmons distinguished himself by scuffling with the prosecuting attorney, striking him on the jaw before being overpowered by court guards. It seems that this charade was played out in order to persuade the jury to return a guilty verdict and another capital sentence; which they obligingly did.

Ronald Simmons continued to refuse the opportunity to appeal and because of this action he was isolated from the other prisoners on Death Row. As they saw it, he was weakening their position, and they had threatened to kill him themselves. They did not need to bother, as on 31 May Arkansas governor (later President) Bill Clinton signed Simmons' execution warrant, and on 25 June 1990 he died, as he had chosen to do, by lethal injection.

SIMPSON, Charles   On Friday 21 April 1972, twenty-five-year-old Charlie Simpson, a farmhand from Holden, was driven into Harrisonville, Missouri, by a friend. With his shoulder-length black hair and a waist-length army fatigue jacket Simpson cut a bizarre figure as he jumped from the car and sprinted across Independence Street into Pearl Street. As he ran he spotted two young officers from the local police force, Donald Marler and Francis Wirt, approaching him. Without any hesitation, Simpson pulled an M1 semi-automatic carbine from under his jacket, dropped into a crouch position and opened fire on the policemen. The officers never had a chance to return fire, they dropped to the sidewalk, both badly wounded. Simpson ran over to where they were lying and stood over them lining up his gun for more shots. Marler managed to scream: 'Don't shoot me. God. Oh God', before Simpson fired two further bursts into both men. Marler was hit twice in the chest, the abdomen and through each hand and Wirt twice in the abdomen and three times in one arm. Horrified passers-by threw themselves to the ground and cars in the street crashed into one another. Charlie Simpson ran into a nearby bank building and indiscriminately fired another burst of shots into a wall. Two book-keepers were wounded by ricochets. Then he fled from the bank, down the street in the direction of the local sheriff's office. On the way Orville T. Allen, the manager of a dry-cleaning store, was getting out of his car on the other side of the street; Simpson fired a burst from his carbine and Allen fell into the gutter riddled with bullets.

From inside his office sheriff Bill Gough heard sounds, but did not immediately associate them with gunfire; so he went outside to see what the noise was about and caught one of Simpson's wild shots in his right shoulder before managing to duck back into his office and take cover.

Simpson made no further move towards the sheriff, but simply turned on his heels and walked back towards the main square where he stopped, put the barrel of the M1 into his mouth and blew the back of his head off.

SLAVIN, Patrick, *et al.* Robert McKenzie had emigrated from his native Scotland in the second quarter of the last century to settle in New Brunswick, a province of eastern Canada. From modest beginnings as a tailor, McKenzie expanded into real estate and finally into money-lending. With his wife and four children this prosperous businessman lived comfortably in a large house at Mispeck, outside Saint John. On Sunday 25 October 1857 a visitor found the McKenzies' isolated home burned to the ground and no sign of the family. A subsequent search of the burned-out shell of the house solved the riddle of the disappearance of the McKenzies – the charred bodies of a woman and four children were found among the blackened rubble and ashes, while in a smaller building which had also been razed the trunk of a man was discovered, his head and arms missing. The remains were identified as those of Robert McKenzie, his wife and their children. By way of a clue to the motive for this horrible crime, an empty money chest was also found in the ruins.

Enquiries in the immediate neighbourhood established that the younger children of an itinerant labourer, Patrick

Slavin, had been seen outside their home playing with large amounts of money. Police officers visited the house and spoke to Mrs Slavin, who professed no knowledge of the murders, but did say that a man named Hugh Breen had been staying in the house for some time. One of the Slavin children added that he had heard his father and Breen discussing the murders at the same time as they seemed to have come into money.

Warrants were issued for the apprehension of Patrick Slavin, another son thought to be with him, and Hugh Breen; they were detained while holing up in some nearby woods. Charged with the murders of the McKenzie family, Slavin and Breen pleaded guilty at their trial in November, while Patrick Slavin junior entered a plea of not guilty. It transpired during his trial that Hugh Breen had been the instigator of the crime, though Slavin the elder had been responsible for most of the actual bloodshed; boy Slavin went along as look-out. After a three-day hearing, all three defendants were sentenced to the gallows, though young Slavin's sentence carried a recommendation to mercy and was commuted to one of life imprisonment. Hugh Breen hanged himself in his cell five days before his appointment with the hangman. Patrick Slavin senior was strung up at Saint John on 11 December 1857.

Patrick Slavin junior escaped from Saint John penitentiary after serving fourteen years. He was later taken into custody in the United States, but being outside the terms of the extradition treaty between the US and Canada he retained an uneasy freedom.

SMITH, Robert Benjamin Eighteen-year-old Smith was a popular high school major in Mesa, Arizona. Son of a retired army officer, Robert was known for his twin interests in Napoleon and the Wild West outlaw Jesse James. What was not so well known was his unhealthy fascination with the Chicago mass murderer Richard Speck (see page 313). It was this preoccupation that led him to contemplate a little murder and mayhem of his own.

On 12 November 1966, Bob Smith left his home armed with a revolver his father had given him and a knife, and walked into town. He entered a beauty salon, fired a single shot in the air and ordered the five women and two children in the salon to lie on the floor in a pattern looking like wheel spokes. Then he shot them all in the back of the head. The victims were Glenda Carter, Carol Farmer, Joyce Sellers, Mary Olsen and Mrs Sellers' three-year-old daughter Debra. One other woman was seriously injured and Mrs Sellers' baby Tamara Lynn miraculously escaped injury while being held in her mother's arms as she was shot.

When the police arrived at the scene of the carnage, they found Smith waiting outside the salon. He offered no resistance to arrest, and with a satisfied smile announced: 'I've just killed all the women in there.' Asked why he had done it, Smith said only: 'I wanted to get known – to get myself a name.'

Robert Smith was charged with five counts of murder and two of attempted murder. At his trial he was convicted on all counts, and on 24 October 1967 was sentenced to life imprisonment. It is a pity Bob Smith did not choose Napoleon as a role model rather than Richard Speck.

SOVEREIGN, Henry In the year 1828 Henry Sovereign faced trial at London, Ontario, for what in those distant days was a capital offence: he had shot a horse. The unhappy man was rightly convicted and then sentenced to death. The severity of the sentence aroused considerable sympathy for Sovereign's case, and served to crystallize many existing pockets of public resistance to the much despised British criminal code. The result was that, prudently, the judge, Mr Justice James Buchanan Morley, recommended clemency and Sovereign was released to return to his wife and family.

Some years later, on a bitter January day in 1832, Henry Sovereign appeared, dishevelled, banging at the door of a relative, bleeding from wounds to his arm and chest. The story he told was that his house had been broken into and he and his family had been attacked by two men. He had escaped and ran to get help for his wife and children. Wasting no more time, the relative armed himself and, with another neighbour, accompanied Sovereign back to his home. On the threshold of the building Sovereign suddenly stopped and said: 'I am afraid they have murdered my family.' He was not wrong, for in and around the house lay the bloody and battered bodies of his wife Polly and seven of their children. The youngest child, two-year-old Anna, was found alive, crying loudly but unhurt. It was God's mercy that three of the eleven Sovereign children were away from home that night, or the carnage might have been the greater.

It was the sad task of the local constable to investigate this awful crime, and accompanied by an increasingly agitated Henry Sovereign, he set out on the search for clues. Soon the officer found the bloodstained blade of a knife lying in the snow, and not far away was the handle. According to Sovereign this weapon had belonged to one of his children. Now it is a fact that years of working as a policeman will often sharpen a man's instincts; call it intuition, call it experience, but the solution to many a case has relied on that extra ingredient. And so it was now. Acting on impulse, the constable took Sovereign aside and requested that he should empty his pockets – and that is how a bloodstained jack-knife was found.

In August of that same year, 1832, Henry Sovereign pleaded not guilty to murder at his trial. It was an irony not missed by the court that this was the second time he had been arraigned before Mr Justice James Buchanan Morley; this time he could expect no similar leniency, no such compassion. As well as the evidence of the knives and a bloodstained maul belonging to Sovereign, hairs found grasped in Polly Sovereign's clenched hand were a perfect match for her husband's. As for the prisoner's own wounds, medical opinion was that they were of a very minor nature and most likely to have been self-inflicted.

Sovereign persisted in his story of being attacked by two strangers, but nobody believed him, and he was convicted and sentenced to death. As might have been expected, the judge made it quite clear that he would not be recommending clemency for a second time. Henry Sovereign was hanged in London on 13 August 1832; his body, according to common practice was afterwards given for medical dissection.

SPECK, Richard Franklin At twenty-four years of age, Richard Speck was a drifter, a seaman who went from job to job, town to town, drink to drink, and illicit drug to illicit drug. Wednesday 13 July 1966 was a pretty typical day in his life; typical indeed of the sort of man who boasted a tattoo reading 'Born to Raise Hell'. He was in Chicago now, starting the day with a drink, playing some pool, taking some barbiturates. After a walk by Lake Michigan – Chicago was enjoying a heatwave at the time – Speck was back in the bar. At around 6.00 p.m. he wandered off with some sailors who had a bottle of an unspecified liquid. Whatever it was, he wanted some – tied off his arm, pumped the syringe.

It was some hours later, about ten o'clock, that Richard Speck called at the nurses' house at 2319 East 100th Street, in the suburb of Jeffrey Manor. 'I'm not going to hurt you,' he assured Corazón Amurao when she answered his knock. 'I need your money to go to New Orleans.' Nobody was going to argue – Speck had a gun in his hand.

The six nurses who were at home were ushered into the large bedroom at the back of the house. One by one Speck sent them to fetch their purses. The money was counted: less than $100. Another resident, Gloria Davey, returned at 11.30 and added $2 to the kitty. All seven women were then tied up with strips of linen cut from a sheet.

Twenty-year-old Pam Wilkening was the first of the captives to be led from the room. A deep sigh; then silence. Around midnight Suzanne Farris arrived home with her friend Mary Ann Jordan. The nurses heard Speck lead the two women into another room; there was a muffled noise, then silence fell again.

Merlita Gargullo, Valentina Pasion, Patricia Matusek: one by one, at intervals of twenty or twenty-five minutes, the women were untied and led away, making little or no sound. Gloria Davey was the last, after being raped on the bed. At least, Speck thought she was the last. But Corazón Amurao had wriggled under the bed, out of sight; had lain perfectly still when Speck returned to see if anyone was left; had stayed in her hiding place till six in the morning. Surely he would not return now.

She crept down the hall to her room. What she discovered there broke her silence at last. She smashed the window, crawled out on to the ledge, and screamed uncontrollably.

Patrolman Daniel Kelly was first on the scene. Gloria Davey was in the sitting room, naked and strangled. Patricia Matusek in the bathroom, strangled; three women in one bedroom, strangled, two of them also stabbed in the neck; Mary Ann Jordan and Suzanne Farris in the second bedroom, both stabbed before being strangled; finally Pamela Wilkening, stabbed in the breast and strangled with a strip of sheet.

Speck had left sufficient clues – his fingerprints, clothing, Corazón's description – for the police to pick his name easily enough from their records. But their man was on the move. Not that he expected to be hunted, because Richard Speck had no memory in his drug-rotted mind of his crime. In fact, he was so astonished to hear his name broadcast on the radio as being 'wanted by the police' that he reacted characteristically, getting drunk then slashing his wrist with the broken bottle. Detectives picked him up at Cook County Hospital.

On Thursday 13 April 1967 Richard Speck was found guilty of murder with a recommendation that he suffer sentence of death. This date was fixed for September, but later that same year a moratorium on executions was declared, and Speck's sentence was commuted to a ponderous 400 to 1,200 years – the longest ever given in the United States at that time.

Richard Speck never even made the 400, he died of a massive heart attack in his cell at Joliet Prison on 5 December 1991.

SPENCER, Brenda There are many motives for murder, almost as many as there are murderers to commit them; but there can be few more fatuous excuses for taking two lives than that offered by Brenda Spencer. On Monday morning, 29 January 1979, sixteen-year-old high-school student Brenda Spencer took up her position outside the Cleveland Elementary School and waited for the principal to open the gate. As he did so, and as the children were milling around, Brenda opened fire with a .22 semi-automatic rifle. The twenty-minute shooting spree left principal Burton Wragg and the school caretaker dead and nine children between the ages of six and twelve wounded. Then Brenda ran back home to wait for the police.

Brenda Spencer lived with her divorced father and had always been a problem child. This was partly a reaction to her parents' separation and partly because she just was. Before her mid-teens she had been involved with drugs and petty theft, and was unhealthily addicted to violent films. For some years Brenda had owned a BB gun which she used to kill birds and break windows. Then at Christmas 1978, Brenda's father bought her a proper gun as a present – it was the gun she used to shoot up the Cleveland Elementary.

And now the outside of the house was swarming with heavily armed police and media reporters. At last Brenda was getting the attention she had craved for so long; she was famous. For two hours Brenda talked to negotiators and pressmen on the telephone. Why, they all wanted to know, did she do such a thing? Brenda explained: 'I just started shooting, that's it. I just did it for the fun of it. I just don't like Mondays . . . I did it because it's a way to cheer the day up. Nobody likes Mondays . . .'

Brenda Spencer was put on trial in Santa Ana, California, and convicted on two charges of murder for which she received two twenty-five to life terms, and one charge of assault with a deadly weapon for which she was sentenced to a concurrent forty-eight-year term.

STACK, James Following the death of his wife in 1865, Stack, a former soldier and well-known local bruiser, moved in with his mother-in-law Mrs Mary Finnigan to her cottage at Otahuhu, New Zealand. Also in residence were Mary Finnigan's three youngest sons: seventeen-year-old James, fourteen-year-old Benjamin and ten-year-old John.

On the first day of the Auckland Races, towards the end of September 1865, Mrs Finnigan and her three sons disappeared. Enquiries were instigated by Mary's eldest son, Alexander, who had been away serving with the army, but no trace could be found of his mother or his siblings. All James Stack could suggest, preposterous as it might sound, was that they had suddenly upped and left for the gold diggings at Hokitika.

There the matter rested, but persistent rumour, and perhaps a guilty conscience, resulted in James Stack taking to his heels. This would have been just a few days before Christmas. Now the local constable made a move. A thorough search of the cottage revealed nothing other than some partially burned clothing, so it was decided to dig up the ground around the house. It was by the side of the boundary fence that searchers found the body of James Finnigan; Benjamin's remains were uncovered in the same area, and Mary Finnigan's last resting place was beneath the vegetable garden. There was no trace of the body of John Finnigan. Medical examination proved that the three victims had died from massive fracturing of the skull; and in Benjamin's case his throat had been cut as well. A description of James Stack was sent out over New Zealand's newly installed telegraph system, and a reward of £20 was offered for his apprehension.

Meanwhile, an inquest into the Finnigan deaths ended in a verdict of wilful murder against Stack, and a further reward of £50 was offered for information leading to his arrest. On 27 December Stack was taken at Kaipara and returned to Auckland to be charged with murder. At his trial, James Stack was convicted and sentenced to death. Just before his execution he received a visit from Alexander Finnigan who implored him to reveal the burial place of his brother John; Stack, however, stubbornly continued to deny any part in the murders, and once more protested his innocence. It was not until some years later that the skeleton of ten-year-old John Finnigan was recovered, not far from the place where his mother and brothers had lain.

STEINHAUSER, Robert In February 2002, nineteen-year-old Steinhauser was expelled from the Johann Gutenberg Grammar School in Erfut, Germany, for forging medical certificates in order to skip lessons. This barred him from sitting the school leaving examination and thus progressing to university.

On the surface at least, Steinhauser did not fit the pattern of a potential killer – he had friends, played handball and was a dance music fan. However, as in so many of these cases he was a gun lover. He belonged to two local gun clubs (including one used by the local police) and this enabled him to get a permit allowing him to obtain guns and ammunition.

On 26 April, 2002, he returned to the school dressed in black, (possibly aping the **Columbine** killers, Eric Harris and Dylan Klebold), masked and armed with a pistol and a pump action shotgun. Systematically, over a period of around fifteen minutes, he killed thirteen teachers, two pupils, aged thirteen and fourteen, and a policeman. Ten others were injured. Surprisingly, he only used his pistol and not the more deadly shotgun.

The slaughter ended when a brave teacher, Rainer Liese, confronted Steinhauser, ripped off his mask and said 'It's you Robert'. Amazingly, he did not shoot Mr Liese, merely saying 'That's enough for today' before stepping back into a classroom, enabling the heroic teacher to shut the door and lock it. Almost immediately, there was a final shot and Steinhauser was found to have turned the gun on himself. Ironically, the massacre took place just hours before the German Parliament passed new laws tightening up the country's gun controls.

STONE, Michael Anthony On Sunday 6 March 1988, Sean Savage, Daniel McCann and Mairead Farrell, three members of an IRA active service unit were shot and killed by the SAS in Gibraltar. Their bodies were returned to Belfast, where the IRA set in motion a major propaganda exercise starting with the organization of a full paramilitary funeral prior to interment in the Republican plot at Miltown Cemetery.

The funeral was fixed for Wednesday 16 March, and thousands lined the streets of Miltown to wait for the passing of the cortège; in the cemetery a huge crowd had gathered to witness the burials. As groups of mourners, including Republican leaders Gerry Adams and Martin McGuinness assembled at the graveside, a man suddenly stood up from behind a tombstone and threw three grenades into the crowd around the open graves. In the panic, people dived for cover and the confusion was heightened when the man opened fire on the crowds with a revolver. The gunman was chased through the cemetery by some of the crowd, oblivious of the fact that another man with a rifle was giving him covering fire. An eye-witness said later: 'The gunman was very cool. He was even goading them to come and get him.' He threw more grenades and fired behind him at his pursuers, laughing out loud as he reloaded his gun. Eventually, one of the pursuers brought him down by throwing a traffic cone at him, whereupon the crowd gave him a ferocious beating before he was rescued by RUC officers who took him to hospital for treatment prior to detention and questioning.

By now volunteers were helping the emergency services to convey the dead and injured to hospital. Three men, Kevin Brady, aged thirty, Thomas McErlean, twenty years old, and John Murray, twenty-six, were dead and fifty-four others were injured. It was later announced that the gunman had been identified as thirty-six-year-old Michael Anthony Stone, a member of the Ulster Volunteer Force.

The theory that violence breeds violence was emphasized at the funeral of one of the cemetery victims, Kevin Brady, on 19 March, when two British soldiers in civilian clothing were savagely beaten and then shot dead when they inadvertently drove near the funeral procession.

On 22 March, Stone was charged with six murders –

those of Brady, McErlean and Murray at the Miltown Cemetery and also of Patrick Brady in 1984, Kevin McPolin in 1985 and Desmond Hackett in May 1987. When he was charged with the cemetery killings, Stone had replied: 'I alone carried out this military operation as a retaliatory strike against Provisional Sinn Fein and the IRA in response to the slaughter of innocents at La Mon (see page 204), Darkley, Brighton (see page 49) and Enniskillen. I am a dedicated freelance Loyalist paramilitary. No surrender.' In response to one of the other murder charges he commented: 'I read his file. He was a legitimate target.'

Stone's trial opened at Belfast Crown Court on 20 February 1989, when he pleaded not guilty to thirty-eight charges including the six murder counts. The prosecution case made use of television news film footage of the cemetery killings. Paradoxically, although pleading not guilty, Stone instructed his counsel not to cross-examine or to make any submissions on his behalf during the trial. On 3 March, Michael Stone was convicted on all charges and sentenced by Mr Justice Higgins to six life sentences with a recommendation that he serve a minimum of thirty years.

STRYDOM, Barend   Panic broke out on a street in central Pretoria during the afternoon of 15 November 1988, when a laughing white man, dressed in military camouflage fatigues suddenly began shooting with a semi-automatic pistol into crowds of black people. Passers-by ran for cover, some fleeing into the path of oncoming traffic. Eye-witnesses told later of seeing the street strewn with the bleeding bodies of the dead and injured. According to the hospital reports six people had lost their lives and seventeen were injured, many critically.

After a police chase through the streets a twenty-three-year-old man named Barend Strydom was arrested in possession of a 9mm pistol. Strydom turned out to be a former member of the South African police force who had been obliged to leave the service earlier in the year when an internal tribunal found him guilty of improper conduct; he had been disciplined after being found in possession of a photograph of himself holding a knife in one hand and the severed head of a black man in the other.

The authorities subsequently announced through South Africa's law and order minister that Strydom had admitted under interrogation that he was a member of the Afrikaner Resistance Movement (AWB), a powerful and violent group of white supremacists. He also claimed to be the leader of the White Wolves, a white guerrilla group which had been associated with earlier bomb attacks on churches.

Strydom appeared before a court on 17 November and was immediately remanded to a mental hospital for observation. Strydom himself had no doubts as to his own sanity, he told the court he was 'completely of sound mind at the present time and always have been so'. Despite his disposition to murder people, the psychiatrists agreed.

By the time Barend Strydom faced his trial at the Pretoria Supreme Court on 15 May 1989, another of those injured during his November outrage had died. Strydom was also charged with the earlier murder of a black woman at a squatter camp near Johannesburg. It was therefore with eight counts of murder and sixteen of attempted murder that he was charged; Strydom entered a not guilty plea to each indictment. During the presentation of the prosecution evidence, Strydom smiled and laughed a lot, seeming for all the world to be having the time of his life. In the witness box, he freely admitted the charges, including the earlier squatter camp murder which he explained had been committed in order to test his resolve to carry out the subsequent Pretoria shootings. Strydom concluded by threatening to kill again if he was set free: 'each black person', he insisted, 'threatens the continued existence of the whites'. He added that whites were the superior race, and demanded the establishment of an Afrikaner homeland.

On 25 May Mr Justice Harms convicted Strydom on all twenty-four charges and in passing the death sentence told him: 'You wanted to be the nation's hero but ended up being worse than any other terrorist. You must be removed from society for ever.'

In a gesture of white defiance, on the first anniversary of the Pretoria killings, the AWB held a meeting at the site of the mass murder to commemorate Strydom's actions. Brown-shirted AWB members shouted 'Sieg Heil' and called on Christ to accept him as a hero of the Afrikaner nation. A young white schoolteacher, Karen Rauchtenberg, who led the prayers at the meeting married Barend Strydom in Pretoria Central Prison on 24 November. Later she organized a petition calling for his freedom and it was a reflection of the support that had been generated for his cause that she collected 50,000 signatures. Following the African National Congress call for freedom for 3,000 supporters they considered to be political prisoners, right-wing elements demanded similar treatment for some seventy of their own supporters in prison for terrorist offences.

Consequently, on 17 April 1991, the South African Minister of Justice announced that Strydom's sentence would be commuted to life imprisonment. Sixteen other death sentences, including that on Robert McBride, an ANC member condemned for killing three women with a car bomb were reduced at the same time. The Minister of Justice did, however, take the opportunity to reassure a concerned public that Strydom and McBride would remain in prison for the rest of their lives 'unless special circumstances arise'.

It did not take long for those circumstance to arise, and on 28 September 1992, Barend Strydom and Robert McBride were among forty prisoners released under an agreement between the state president and the ANC. In a newspaper interview, Strydom claimed he felt no remorse, adding that he did not kill out of hatred for his victims, but out of love for his own people.

June 1993 added a tragic postscript to the case when it was reported that Strydom's murder count had risen to nine with the death in hospital of forty-eight-year-old Oupa Geelbooi Mabeena from complications arising from the bullet wound to his spine he had suffered four and a half years earlier.

STUELLGENS, Robert Wilhelm Tenants of an apartment block in Dusseldorf became concerned when, for two days, there was neither sight nor sound of their neighbours the Deck family: father, mother and two children. Finally, on Thursday 12 June 1980 they were so anxious that they decided to report it to the police.

Officers forced an entry to the flat and in the living room found the bodies of a young woman and a small boy. The woman, later identified as Margret Deck, was naked and her body was caked in dry blood. The boy was her two-year-old son Thomas, who was lying in his blood-soaked pyjamas on the other side of the room. In another room was the dead body of Christian Deck, aged six weeks. All three had been stabbed with a narrow-bladed knife, the woman repeatedly. There was no sign of the husband, twenty-eight-year-old Wilhelm Deck. Examination of the apartment by a scenes-of-crime team revealed that the killer had cleaned himself up in the bathroom, changed out of his blood-stained clothes, and left the soiled garments hanging in a closet. After his wash and brush up, the knifeman appears to have taken a snooze on the bed before letting himself out. A call was put out for the apprehension of Wilhelm Deck, the missing husband, and when the post-mortem report revealed that Margret Deck had been experiencing oral sex before she died, enquiries were set in motion to discover whether she had a lover.

It was a friend of Margret Deck's who provided the clue which broke the case. Margret had told her that a man living in another apartment in the same building was moving out and asked Margret if she wanted to buy any of his furniture or appliances. The two women had gone together to have a look, and although Margret saw nothing that took her eye, her friend bought a deep freezer; she also picked up the unnerving impression that the man was taking an unhealthy personal interest in Margret.

The man was identified as Robert Wilhelm Stuellgens, and detectives went to pay him a visit. As Herr Stuellgens did not appear to be at home, the police broke in and found the place wrecked; they also found a dead body in the living room; it was Wilhelm Deck, and he had been stabbed repeatedly with the same type of weapon that had destroyed his family.

Back at the station a check was run on Stuellgens and detectives learned that he had a previous conviction for rape and child molestation in 1973, for which he had been jailed for six years. It was now clear that Stuellgens had taken flight, but enquiries in his home town of Essen led to his arrest, still carrying the murder knife around in his pocket. Stuellgens was returned to Dusseldorf and charged with four counts of murder, whereupon he made a statement admitting the killings, explaining that the motive had been to have sex with Margret Deck.

At his trial Robert Wilhelm Stuellgens was found guilty as charged and sentenced to life imprisonment.

SWIFT RUNNER The sudden appearance of a Cree Indian named Katist-chen (translated as 'Swift Runner') at the Roman Catholic mission of St Albert near Edmonton, in March 1879, led to the discovery of a horrific tale of mass murder and cannibalism. Swift Runner claimed to be the sole survivor of a family hunting party consisting of his wife, mother, brother and six children, who had travelled deep into the north woods of the Sturgeon River area the previous winter. He said the hunting had been very poor and their food supply was soon exhausted. The youngest of the children had died, and Swift Runner's mother and brother left the camp in search of food; he never saw them again. One by one the other children died, and then his wife, grief-stricken by their loss, shot herself. Somehow the Cree had survived the winter, and when spring came he struggled back to the mission.

The priests were puzzled by Swift Runner's story, and not entirely convinced, because other Indians had reported *good* hunting in the Sturgeon River area, and for a man supposedly wracked with exposure and starvation, Swift Runner seemed to be in remarkably good physical shape. However, he was displaying obvious signs of an emotional disorder, and insisted that he was haunted by an evil spirit.

Just to be safe, the priests decided to report the matter to the Royal Canadian Mounted Police, who sent an officer over to the mission to question the Indian. His answers were so evasive and so inconclusive that it was decided to take Swift Runner back to the scene of the tragedy and investigate further.

Reluctantly he agreed, though on the journey he made two attempts to escape and tried to lead his escort on a false trail into the woods. When they finally arrived at the abandoned camp, the party discovered dozens of scattered bones, skulls and traces of flesh – but no complete bodies. Swift Runner had told the priests that the family had cut up and boiled their animal skin tent and chewed on the pieces; but the tepee was found hidden, and intact. And a kettle was found, the inside of which was coated with what later analysis revealed to be human fat.

The party returned to Fort Saskatchewan, where Swift Runner was charged with murder. The trial took place between 16 and 17 August 1879, and in evidence, Swift Runner admitted killing five of his children and his wife, but denied the other killings. He was found guilty and sentenced to death. While he was awaiting execution, Swift Runner made a full confession to the murder and cannibalization of his entire family. On 20 December 1879 he was hanged.

T

TAYLOR, John Merlin It was at 7.30 on the morning of Tuesday 10 August 1989 that the man described by his boss as 'a model employee, and as mellow and as nice as could be' went on a shooting rampage at the Orange Glen post office in Escondito, San Diego County. John Merlin Taylor, a fifty-two-year-old mail sorter only a few years away from retirement, arrived at work as he always did, and made his way to the picnic table in the loading-bay to join two colleagues for a cup of coffee and a cigarette before the shift started. Only this morning Taylor was carrying a .22-calibre semi-automatic pistol in his hand, and as he approached Richard Berni and Ronald Williams sitting at the table, he lifted the gun and shot them dead. Taylor then walked into the sorting office and fired another shot into a postman's arm. When office manager Bob Henley heard the shots he went to investigate and came face to face with John Taylor, who told him: 'I'm not going to shoot you', and loosed off more shots at random targets before turning the gun on himself.

Another eye-witness told police afterwards: 'He didn't have any emotion. He was stern-faced. He walked right by me towards the end of the building with the gun in his hand. He didn't say a word.' The man then saw Taylor raise the gun to his right temple and pull the trigger. John Taylor was rushed, still alive, to the Palomar Memorial Hospital and put on a life-support system, but was certified brain-dead later in the morning.

Police officers visiting Taylor's home in Begonia Street,

just a few blocks from the post office, were horrified to discover that before he had left on his killing spree at Orange Glen, John Taylor had first shot dead his wife Liz in her bed.

There was a sense of complete bewilderment over this totally uncharacteristic violence from a man who was well liked and well respected both by his friends and neighbours and by his colleagues at work. Paul de Risi, who escaped after being shot in the arm, told reporters: 'I just sat down outside and said to myself, "Why John Taylor? Why's he doing this?"' One bizarre feature of the case which may or may not have had some significance was that, just two days before the shooting, Taylor had been discussing Patrick Sherrill's post-office massacre (see page 302) with a fellow-sorter.

When investigators began to look deeper into John Taylor's past, facts emerged which indicated a rather less stable personality than that which he usually presented to the outside world. Principal among these was an incident which happened thirty years earlier, when Taylor was in his teens. One night his father came home drunk, as he frequently did, and started beating up his wife; the daughter, John's sister, tired of the constant threat of violence, picked up a gun and shot her father dead. There were also reports that John Taylor had, quite incorrectly, believed the postal authorities to have him under investigation for mail theft. Then the gossip began to spread about Taylor's first marriage which ended in divorce in 1977 because, according to his wife Mary, he was 'extraordinarily violent, frequently drinks to excess, has threatened [my] life on several occasions . . .' etc. However, it is only fair to add that during the divorce proceedings, Taylor's attorney strenuously denied these charges, and we have nobody's word but that of the former Mary Taylor that they were true. Relatives of John Taylor recalled in retrospect that he had been grumbling recently about the work at the post office, complaining that it was giving him back and shoulder pains. The fact is, of course, it could have been all, any or none of these factors which triggered John Taylor's moment of madness; as police Lieutenant Danny Starr told the *Los Angeles Times*: 'Unfortunately, the only person who could tell us is Taylor.'

THOMAS, Christopher Palm Sunday 1984 in Brooklyn, New York was all set to be more than just a calendar celebration for the Lopez, Perez and Bermudez families. The eleven children and three parents had recently taken possession of a new five-room apartment; at least it was new to them, and a great improvement on what two of the families had previously endured. It would also be of marked financial assistance to the previously sole tenant of the flat. The families were all related in one way or another and this, if nothing else, enabled them to live together in reasonable harmony.

At around 7 p.m. on that Sunday, Enrique Bermudez returned from his shift as a taxi driver and found the apartment looking more like an abattoir than a home. As he staggered from the building Bermudez cried out: 'Everybody in my house is dead.' Neighbours summoned the police, who arrived to find bodies everywhere and blood dripping from the walls and soaked deep into the floor. Seven of the victims lay dead in the living room, some still sitting in their chairs where they had been watching television. Other corposes were discovered in two of the bedrooms.

The dead were Bermudez' pregnant common-law wife Virginia Lopez, her sons, Eddie, aged seven, and Juan, four, and Bermudez' daughters: fourteen-year-old Betsy and ten-year-old Marilyn. The Perez family had also perished – Carmen and her young children Noel and Alberto, and Carmen's sisters Migdilia, fourteen years old, and Maria, aged ten. The only person left alive in the apartment was eleven-month-old Christina Perez, who was found crying on the living room floor, crawling in the pools of blood. Eight children and two adults were dead, shot by a combination of two guns, a .38 and a .22. Post-mortems later showed that the ten victims had fourteen bullet wounds, almost all of which had been inflicted at very close range, in some instances with the guns pressed close up against the victims' heads as they were fired.

Detectives, who knew their patch as well as the backs of their hands, instinctively suspected that the killings has arisen from a dispute over drug dealings. It also happened that Enrique Bermudez already had a conviction as a heroin pusher and at the time of the murders was on parole from his last sentence. The police interviewed Bermudez, who told them about a friend, Christopher Thomas who lived in the Bronx. According to Bermudez, Thomas had forced his way into the Brooklyn apartment a few days prior to the killings, searching for his wife. Thomas had a history of violent jealousy towards his partners and had been acquitted of the murder of a former girlfriend.

In the meantime, Christopher Thomas had been arrested for causing criminal damage at a day-centre where his children were being looked after. Released on bail, Thomas was swiftly rearrested and charged with attempted rape and sodomy on his mother; he was kept in custody first in the Bronx, and then transferred to Brooklyn for questioning over the Palm Sunday killings. By now two witnesses had come forward to testify that they had seen a man in and around the murder scene on the day of the crimes, and at a subsequent line-up they identified Thomas.

On 19 June, detectives announced that Christopher Thomas had been charged with ten counts of murder and speculated that the most likely motive was a mistaken belief that his wife was being unfaithful to him. At his subsequent trial, Thomas was found guilty on all counts and jailed for life.

THOMPSON, John The fire-bombings of two late-night drinking clubs in the Soho district of London in the early hours of 17 August 1980 were jointly responsible for the largest death toll in the history of English homicide.

The clubs were on the upper floors of a building in Denmark Place, and they burst into flames so rapidly that many of the people inside did not even have time to leave the tables at which they had been sitting. A total of thirty-seven people died and a further twenty-four were injured – some as a result of the fire and some through jumping from windows to escape the inferno. Subsequent police investigations were hampered not least by the fact that many of the clubs' patrons were South American immigrants, a high proportion of whom, it was suspected, had entered Britain illegally. Worse still, the police were unable even to identify many of the victims positively despite fingerprint checks and post-mortem examinations carried out by a team of pathologists led by Professor James Cameron. Three dentists were also attached to the medical team in an attempt to aid identification by checking teeth and dentures against the victims' dental records. Survivors who were interviewed thought that the fire had been started by a petrol bomb, adding that it was not possible to flee the building because of flames on the stairs. They had smelled petrol, there had been choking black smoke and molten plastic was dropping from burning ceiling fittings.

Murder squad detectives led by Detective Chief Superintendent Geoff Chambers carried out a painstaking examination of the gutted building, during the course of which they discovered a petrol can near the door of the club. Enquiries around the area established that a man carrying a petrol can had been seen walking in the direction of the building on the night of the fire. Furthermore, one of the injured victims said that before the blaze a customer in one of the clubs had complained about the service and claimed he had been overcharged. The man had left the club threatening: 'One day this bloody house will burn down.'

A photo-fit picture of the suspect was issued, and following a tip-off from a member of the public, a man was detained in another club close to the scene of the fire. On 27 August forty-two-year-old John Thompson, a 'general dealer', was charged with the murder of Archibald O'Donnell Campbell, one of the victims who had been identified.

John Thompson entered a plea of not guilty when his trial opened at the Old Bailey on 29 April 1981. The prosecution case pivoted on the allegation that Thompson had been seen outside the club with a petrol can and afterwards crouching near the door. Although he admitted being in possession of petrol, Thompson claimed he hid it near the club while he went off to steal a battery for his car. In a statement made in police custody, Thompson had said: 'I poured petrol on the door. I just struck a match on it and walked away'; however, he was now insisting that the statement was false – he said he was 'petrified' because a policeman threatened him. Thompson claimed: 'I was under the impression that if I didn't make the statement I would be kicked to hell.' He also stated that at the time he was 'coming down' after taking drugs and had 'the horrors'.

On 7 May 1981 John Thompson was found guilty of a single token charge of murder and sentenced to life imprisonment.

TOKYO SUBWAY GASSING Cults have become a frightening feature of the modern world. The havoc created by the **Reverend Jim Jones** and the Branch Davidians at Waco were eclipsed in Japan by the Aum Supreme Truth Cult. Headed by a charismatic, partially blind guru calling himself Shoka Asahara, it rapidly attracted a wide membership, particularly among the younger intelligentsia. Propagating a mixture of ancient Eastern beliefs, latterly with a prophecy that the end of the world was coming, it manipulated its disciples with a deadly cocktail of mind control and designer drugs. Those that rebelled were eliminated.

When in 1995, the prophecy of Armageddon showed no sign of happening, Asahara and his cohorts decided to give it a helping hand themselves. They arranged to obtain supplies of the deadly nerve gas sarin. On the morning of 20 March 1995, agents were despatched into the Tokyo subway armed with balloons containing sarin, which they were to release by piercing them with umbrellas.

The results were horrendous. Twelve people died and some 5,500 required hospital treatment and the city was brought to a standstill.

It did not take long for the police to establish that Supreme Truth were behind the outrage as they were already the subject of an ongoing investigation. Hundreds of cult members were arrested. Several other murders were uncovered – largely cult members who had opposed the leadership – and multiple trials were held in these cases.

The agents responsible for releasing the sarin on the subway and the chemist who made up the deadly concoction were convicted of multiple murder and sentenced to death. Life sentences were given to the cult members who drove the carriers to the subway.

At the time of writing, the trial of cult leader, Shoka Asahara, which started in 1996 continues. The prosecution had demanded the death penalty.

The cult remains active albeit under government surveillance. It has changed its name to Aleph, the first letter of the Hebrew alphabet, and insists it is just a benign religious group.

TRAN, John van Trung It was at the end of September 1987 that twenty-three-year-old John Tran was jilted by his fiancée Lieu Huynh, when she announced her engagement to another man. Now, on 10 October, Tran stood at the back door of the Huynh home in the Sydney suburb of Canley Vale. He paused for a moment and then entered the kitchen where he encountered Lieu's father, sixty-three-year-old Thuan Huynh, who was making himself a cup of tea. Before the old man could open his mouth, Tran shot him in the head and body; Huynh staggered into the back yard, collapsed and died.

Then Tran crept through the house stalking other members of the family and shooting them down where they stood: Mrs Huynh in her bedroom, and Lieu's twenty-nine-year-old sister Lan in the hallway. Brother Michael, aged eighteen, was shot dead in his bedroom, and twelve-year-old Steven was seriously wounded, but managed to escape from the house. Finally John Tran burst into Lieu's bedroom where he caught her trying to hide under a bunk; despite her pleading for her life, Tran shot her dead. Two other sisters, Hue and Phoung, aged twenty-one and twenty-two, were already hiding under another bunk in the room, and saw John Tran put the barrel of his M1 semi-automatic carbine to his head and pull the trigger. One of the girls jumped over his bleeding body to get out through the window and was conscious of Tran's dying eyes following her movements; her sister stayed put until he had stopped breathing.

Police revealed afterwards that Tran had left notes behind which suggested that the killing spree had not been the spontaneous gesture of a lovelorn young man, but had been ruthlessly and calculatedly planned.

TREMAMUNNO, Donato On 24 August 1962, Antonio Ragone and his friend Donato Tremamunno sat drinking wine together in the garden of Ragone's home at Torazzo, midway between Genoa and Turin. Although they were close friends they could not have had more different personalities: when they were younger, Ragone had stayed in Torazzo building up successful businesses in farming and manufacturing, while Donato Tremamunno had roamed the world, even including in his itinerary a spell in the French Foreign Legion. Tremamunno had recently returned to his home village newly married, and his old friend had given the couple the use of a cottage. However, Donato was encountering difficulties finding work and had called at Ragone's home that summer afternoon for a drink and to be cheered up. Then Donato suggested they go for a walk, leaving Antonio's wife and two daughters to clear up after their meal. A little while later Tremamunno returned to the house alone with the message that Ragone wanted his thirteen-year-old daughter Vita to join him in the pear orchard to pick up windfalls.

Vita cheerfully collected a basket and walked off by 'uncle' Donato's side. When they had not returned some time later, Mrs Ragone and her other daughter set off to the orchard in search of the rest of the family. The first thing they saw when they arrived was Vita's empty basket; next they found the dead body of Antonio, a bullet through his head. Shocked beyond words, they immediately summoned the police.

As Donato Tremamunno was presumably among the last people to see Ragone alive, the inquiry focused first on him, and officers visited his cottage where they expected to find Sebastiana Tremamunno nursing the baby boy she had given birth to since coming to Torazzo. However, when they arrived, the cottage was in darkness and there was no sign of life. Inside, detectives discovered the reason why – on a bed lay Sebastiana, who had been shot and had her throat slashed; in a cot at the side of the bed was the body of baby Emilio, who had also been shot through the head. Two cartridge cases were found on the floor of the room which had been fired from a 7.65 automatic pistol; the same calibre as the shell found beside Antonio Ragone's body. A thorough search of the Tremamunno cottage revealed a scribbled note in Donato's hand-writing, which included the words: 'I do not want to live any more. I shall welcome death with open arms.'

A widespread search of the area around Torazzo was undertaken and eventually the bodies of Vita Ragone and Donato Tremamunno were found. Vita had been stripped naked, savagely attacked and strangled. A post-mortem examination proved that they had died around the same time, and it was assumed that immediately after killing the girl, Tremamunno had put the barrel of his 7.65 automatic in his mouth and pulled the trigger.

TROPPMANN, Jean-Baptiste   Troppmann was a child of the social and economic upheaval of 1860s' France. Great fortune could be the reward of the ruthless and audacious adventurer; but for the weak and complacent, fate offered only an inevitable and rapid slide down the social ladder. Young Jean-Baptiste knew early on which way he wanted to go, and while still working in his father's factory he set up, secretly, a chemistry laboratory where he devoted his researches to the fascinating world of poisons, eventually mastering the distilling of prussic acid.

In 1869 Troppmann travelled on business for his father from his home town of Cernay in the province of Alsace to Roubaix. Here the morose youngster of wiry physique, sallow complexion and weak face was taken under the wing of Jean Kinck, a successful brushmaker who liked to boast a personal wealth of 100,000 francs. Jean-Baptiste was taken home to meet Monsieur Kinck's wife Hortense Juliette and their six children.

Troppmann's first taste of death occurred soon after, on the banks of a canal near the French frontier with Belgium, where he witnessed a knife fight, accosted the victor, and flung him into the canal to drown. Jean Kinck was fulsome in his praise of Jean-Baptiste's ability to look after himself, and it was clear that the young man had discovered something in himself, some greater strength which was, he thought, entirely to his satisfaction.

The wheels began to turn more quickly now, and a self-confident Troppmann sent his mentor Kinck off on a wild-goose chase to purchase a non-existent counterfeiting factory in Alsace. The two men travelled separately – to avert suspicion, Troppmann said – and met up on 25 August in the railway station at Bollwiller. Kinck's baggage contained banknotes and blank cheques; Troppmann's contained a bottle of prussic acid, and Monsieur Kinck was last seen alive on the Cernay Road, in Monsieur Troppmann's company.

A plan to extract 5,500 francs from Madame Kinck, using one of her husband's blank cheques, went badly awry when the Guebwiller Post Office refused to hand over to Troppmann a package of banknotes addressed to Kinck. And so Troppmann transferred his 'business' to Paris, where he sent out letters, purportedly dictated by Kinck, instructing the Kincks' eldest son to collect the package, and bring the family to Paris. Gustave Kinck eventually arrived in the capital on 7 September; the following day he was under a foot of earth at Pantin, near the Chemin Vert, his chest having been ripped apart by the vicious up-and-down jags of a knife.

Gustave, however, had not been despatched from this world before sending a telegram imploring his mother and siblings to come to Paris, bringing with them title deeds, household leases, ledgers, and all manner of other legal documents. And so the trap was sprung; and while the *famille* Kinck enter Paris, Jean-Baptiste Troppmann is in a hardware shop, buying a pick and a spade.

Together they later take a 'growler' to a deserted spot at Pantin, and Troppmann sets out with Mme Kinck and her infant daughter, along the Chemin Vert. Twenty minutes later he is back; alone. They are going to stay in the area, Troppmann announces. So the coachman is paid off and the three Kinck boys are led away, down the path along which their mother and sister will never return.

On the following morning a farm labourer walking across the fields came across something he did not like the look of. Somebody had been digging the ground over. Which is how the shallow grave came to be found, the bodies disinterred: young Mademoiselle Hortense, eviscerated with a knife; Alfred, stabbed and slashed in the back; Emile and Henri, strangled; Achille, butchered with a spade; finally Madame Hortense Juliette, stabbed fifty times.

The gendarmerie caught up with Troppmann at Le Havre, where he was trying to negotiate false papers for an escape to America. On 19 January 1870, before a huge and riotous audience, Jean-Baptiste Troppmann was executed by guillotine at the prison of La Roquette.

TYLENOL KILLINGS In the period of a mere forty-eight hours seven people died in Chicago after taking the painkiller Tylenol. The first victim died on 29 September 1982; she was schoolgirl Mary Kellerman. Waking in the early hours of the morning with influenza, Mary asked her father for something to make her feel better. Mr Kellerman fished a Tylenol capsule out of the bathroom medicine cabinet and his daughter swallowed it; almost immediately she collapsed and was dead inside two hours. Postal worker Adam Janus took Tylenol because of a pain in his chest, and suffered a similar death. With a cruel irony, Janus's brother Stanley and his wife Theresa came to comfort the bereaved family, took two Tylenol, and quickly joined Adam in the mortuary.

Mrs Mary Reiner had just left hospital with her three-day-old baby when she took Tylenol for a migraine, went into convulsions, followed by a coma and death. Later that same day, Mary McFarland developed a headache while working in a store; she took Tylenol as she always did in such cases, but this time she died. The final victim was thirty-five-year-old Paula Prince, who took two Tylenols after arriving home with a headache. Two days later worried friends found her body in the bathroom where it had fallen.

Police authorities and experts from the medical examiner's office established that the analgesic Tylenol had been taken by all the victims just before their untimely deaths, and an examination of the remaining capsules revealed that the Tylenol in the packs had been replaced by cyanide. The makers of Tylenol, McNeil Consumer Products, recalled every bottle sold in the state of Illinois and eight containers were found to have been tampered with, containing a total of seventy-five contaminated capsules.

Two weeks after the deaths, McNeil received a letter threatening that the killings would continue unless the company paid $1 million to a specified bank account. It was a fingerprint on the blackmail letter which led to the identification of James Lewis, who was wanted for fraud in Missouri, and had already been acquitted of the murder of seventy-eight-year-old Raymond West in 1978.

A nationwide hunt was set in motion for James Lewis, during which he wrote to several newspapers emphatically denying that he was the 'Tylenol killer'; shortly afterwards he was arrested in New York. Lewis admitted that he held the McNeil Company responsible for the death of his five-year-old daughter in 1974 after surgery, because following the operation she had been taking a McNeil-manufactured drug. However, he denied he was responsible for tampering with the capsules.

Despite the obvious connections, the police were unable to find any direct evidence of murder against James Lewis, and he was tried only on charges of attempted blackmail and fraud for which he received consecutive prison sentences of eight and ten years.

U

UNION STATION MASSACRE The killings at Union Station, Kansas City, on 17 June 1933 resulted from an attempt by gangsters to free from custody a notorious bank robber named Frank 'Jelly' Nash. Nash had earlier escaped from Leavenworth prison and immediately embarked on a fresh series of bank raids before being detained in Hot Springs, Arkansas. He had subsequently been brought by train to Kansas City from where he was to be transferred back to Leavenworth to continue his sentence. At least, that was the plan; but it was a plan which took no account of the level of corruption that was eating like a cancer at the heart of the Kansas City Police Department. As a result the itinerary of 'Jelly's' escort became well known to every petty crook and gangster in town.

The train carrying Nash arrived at Kansas City's Union Station on that Saturday morning in June and the prisoner, handcuffed and surrounded by seven law enforcement officers was taken to the parking lot and put into a waiting car. At that moment, three men armed with sub-machine guns suddenly appeared and in time-honoured fashion ordered the officers to raise their hands. For a few tense seconds there was no response, then one officer drew his revolver and fired two shots. Nash shouted, 'No, no' from the car but the leading gunman, later identified as Vern Miller yelled, 'Let them have it. Let the bastards have it.'

Hardly had the order left Miller's lips than his two cronies sprayed the car and the area around it with a hail of bullets. Police Chief Otto Reed, Detectives Frank Hermanson and W. J. Grooms were killed instantly; FBI

Special Agent Raymond Caffrey was fatally wounded. Other agents Reed Veterli, Joseph Lackey and Frank Smith received bullet wounds. The target of this brutal escape plan, Frank Nash, had ducked down in the car when the shooting began, at the same time shouting: 'Don't shoot me.' It made no difference, and he too was struck dead by the rain of gunfire which raked the car.

The assassins made their getaway in a waiting car and it was some time before their identity was known. Eventually the FBI announced that they were Vern Miller, a local bank robber, the notorious gangster 'Pretty Boy' Floyd and Adam Richetti. Underworld sources always insisted that the last two were not involved; indeed Floyd, when he was finally cornered and shot down by FBI agents maintained in his dying statement that he was innocent of the Union Station massacre.

Miller went on the run, going into hiding in Detroit where, on 29 November 1933, his body was found in a ditch, riddled with bullets and marked with dozens of cigarette burns inflicted before death. It was reasonably presumed that Vern Miller had fallen foul of rival crime bosses.

Adam Richetti was later arrested and charged with the murder of Detective Frank Hermanson. At his trial Richetti was identified by witnesses, including two of the wounded FBI agents; he was found guilty and sentenced to death. On 7 October 1938, Adam Richetti was executed in the gas chamber at Missouri State Penitentiary, the first person to die there.

UNRUH, Howard In the space of just twelve minutes, Howard Unruh shot dead thirteen people on the streets of Camden, New Jersey. He would certainly have claimed many more lives and provided a lot more work for the local medical services had he not run out of ammunition. 'I'd have killed a thousand,' he told a psychiatrist, 'if I'd had bullets enough.'

The shootings took place on 5 September 1949, but the problem had started years before that. A withdrawn, secretive man, Unruh just hated his neighbours. Of course, they were really no worse than anybody else's neighbours – it was Howard who had the problems. The folks in the next street wouldn't dream of persecuting him, Howard just thought they did, and had begun to keep a careful note in his diary of all these imagined grievances. At the same time he set about perfecting the marksmanship skills he had acquired on army service.

Unruh was twenty-eight years old at the time he made the headlines, and the predictable crack might not have appeared for some time if the security gate he had fitted to the house to keep the neighbours out had not been stolen. Perhaps Howard Unruh found the seclusion he so desired in the Trenton State Hospital for the Insane.

URICH, Henri On 28 June 1960, the commissioner of police in Morocco was surprised to see a notice in the newspaper obituary column announcing the death in Hannover of Liliane Winther, the twenty-two-year-old stepdaughter of a socially prominent local citizen, Dr Henri Urich. The commissioner was surprised because only two weeks previously Liliane had been full of life and enjoying herself at a party.

Shortly after this puzzling event, a woman contacted the police saying that she thought something may have happened to her neighbours, the Urich family, because their house appeared to be deserted. A search of the house was ordered and checks were run on Dr Urich's background. It turned out that Urich had been a high-ranking officer in the SS and at the end of the war he had made his way to Morocco via medical service with the French Foreign Legion. Rather more sinister was the information uncovered that the doctor had fallen passionately in love with his stepdaughter and had confided to friends that he could not live without her. His wife was, to all appearances, unaware of Urich's obsession. A further complication was that Liliane Winther had become involved with a young French mining engineer and Urich was doing his level best to prevent them meeting. Some of the neighbours had received postcards from the Urich family saying they were enjoying travelling in Spain and France – which was hardly consistent with Liliane's death in Hannover. The last postcard anyone had received announced that Liliane had been ill and was diagnosed as suffering from a brain tumour; regrettably an operation had failed to save her life.

Enquiries by the Hannover police failed to trace any record of such an operation or of the death of Liliane Winther. However, they did establish that a man answering Henri Urich's description had been seen in Germany driving a Mercedes car with Moroccan registration plates. Then one morning the police at Rou Beker received a call from one of Urich's neighbours – he had returned home, alone. Detectives were despatched to have a word with Henri Urich, and in answer to their questions the doctor insisted that he had taken his stepdaughter to a small private clinic for an operation which had proved unsuccessful. He offered details which he claimed could be verified, adding that his wife and their own daughter had remained in Germany with relatives to recover from the shock of their tragic loss. The Moroccan police relayed this information to their counterparts in Germany for confirmation, and in the meantime kept Urich under surveillance.

On 15 July, a report was received from the German authorities, the gist of which was that no verification could be found for any part of Henri Urich's story. Police officers returned to the villa, and when they failed to get an answer, forced an entry. Inside the house they found Henri Urich lying with a bullet through his skull, a revolver by his side. A thorough search of the house and grounds resulted in the recovery of three corpses from under the garage floor; they had all been shot through the head. To nobody's surprise, the victims were identified as Mrs Rose Urich and her two daughters Monique and Liliane. Evidence that Henri Urich had been responsible for the deaths of his family was provided by a houseboy who had worked for the Urichs, witnessed the murders and had been bought off by Dr Urich.

V

VAN HEERDEN, Cornelius Johannes Petrus Cornelius
Johannes Petrus van Heerden, a twenty-two-year-old railway worker, lived in the town of Bethlehem in the Orange
Free State. He had already collected a conviction for
stealing from his father, and in November 1931 he was
issued with a summons for negligent driving. Not a matter
calculated to turn a normal man's mind to thoughts of mass
murder, but van Heerden was not exactly normal. He had
problems enough already; for a start, the traffic summons
arrived on the day after he had been dismissed from his job
for repeated absenteeism. It was the final straw. Cornelius
van Heerden was going to take the quick route out of life –
and he was going to take a few people with him.

On Wednesday 25 November his family noticed that
Cornelius was acting strangely. The next day he bought fifty
rounds of ammunition for a small rifle and some cartridges
for a revolver. He told his friends: 'I want to shoot a kaffir
before I die, otherwise my soul will not rest.' Then he referred
to his forthcoming court appearance, saying: 'There is going
to be bloodshed before I appear in court.' At around midday
on that Thursday, van Heerden stopped Mr J. E. Darby,
who had been driving along the road between Bethlehem and
Reitz, and shot him in the head, killing him instantly. He
pushed Darby's body over on to the passenger seat and
drove back towards Bethlehem. On the way he saw a native
girl and shot and wounded her; he fired at a railway gang
working on the line, wounding two. Then he shot and killed
three other natives on the way in to Bethlehem. The next

victim was Commandant A. M. Prinsloo, a veteran of the Boer War and a well-respected local figure. Prinsloo was supervising tree planting on the outskirts of town when van Heerden drove up, shot him dead, and then wounded two natives who were assisting with the planting.

Finally, van Heerden drove on to Liebenberg's Vlei, a ford a few miles outside Bethlehem, where he stalled the car. Watched by a bridge construction party working nearby, van Heerden lifted his revolver, placed the barrel into his mouth, and shot the back of his head off.

If anybody wanted to know 'Why?', they were unlucky. The only explanation, if it can be called an explanation, was to be found in the note Cornelius van Heerden left behind for the police, which read: 'I just want you to know that though you now contemplate prosecuting me, you will probably have to prosecute my corpse. The weapons I will use are stolen and with them I am going to make a mess among the things [the natives], so you can go to Hell.'

VERONICA **MUTINEERS**   The S.S. *Brunswick*, a British tramp steamship, dropped anchor off the small island of Cajueira Tutoia, close to the northern coast of Brazil, on 28 December 1902. Her chief officer, William Watson, was surprised to see the lifeboat from a ship named the *Veronica* at the jetty, and even more surprised when the craft pulled out to the *Brunswick* and a motley crew of five came aboard. The five seamen introduced themselves as Gustav Rau, Otto Monsson and Harry Flohr, all German; Willem Smith, a Dutchman; and the black American cook, Moses Thomas. The tale they had to tell was that their ship, the 1,000 ton barque *Veronica*, out of St John's, New Brunswick, had been bound for Montevideo with a cargo of lumber. Two of the twelve-man crew had died in accidents, and then the cargo was discovered on fire. Rau, the second mate, had taken four men in one lifeboat, while the captain and remaining four crew members got away in the other. After five days with only water and eleven biscuits to sustain them, Rau's boat reached landfall at Cajueira.

The *Brunswick* sailed for Lisbon, where the five men were

to be handed over to the consul. During the voyage there was time to puzzle over the fate of the *Veronica* and it was not long before obvious discrepancies in the tale of the vessel's loss and the crew's escape became apparent: there was the newly caulked lifeboat, the journey without food, and the navigation without charts. Finally the cook, who had kept apart from the rest of his shipmates and was showing evident distress, confided to Captain George Brown a rather different history, later corroborated by Herr Flohr. As a result, the *Brunswick* sailed on to Liverpool, where three members of the Liverpool Police Force were waiting on the quay. On 29 January 1903, Rau, Monsson and Smith were charged with the wilful murder of Captain Shaw and six other members of the crew of the *Veronica*.

The trial of the '*Veronica* mutineers' opened at Liverpool Assizes on 12 May 1903, before Mr Justice Lawrance. The conspiracy to mutiny, the court was told, had been hatched between Rau, Monsson and Smith at the end of November, when the ship was lying in the Doldrums. Flohr had later been enlisted on pain of death. At midnight on Sunday 2 December, they made their first move. Paddy Durran, the fo'c'sle-head watch, was felled with three blows with a belaying-peg. Rau's next victim was First Officer MacLeod, killed with a single blow to the head and thrown overboard. The two aggressors Rau and Smith went aft next and shot and wounded the second mate, Abrahamson, and the Captain. Both officers retreated to their cabins, where they were locked in.

Julius Herrson was discovered by Monsson trying to climb out of a window and was clubbed on the head and thrown to the sharks. At this moment Paddy Durran recovered consciousness, and begged for water. 'I'll give you a good drink,' scowled Rau, and struck the sailor dead where he lay.

In the morning the two officers were summoned on deck. Abrahamson knew what was coming to him and, in a final desperate attempt to save his life, sprang overboard. After a fusillade of gunshots followed him, the second mate sank below the water. There remained just three non-mutineers: Bravo, Johanssen and Moses Thomas. An alibi was concocted and the men set to learn it, but Johanssen, proving an exasperatingly slow learner, was shot in the head by Smith to save wasting any more time. Bravo mishandled some sailing tackle and for his carelessness was ordered by Rau to be executed. Harry Flohr was elected executioner, but purposely shot to miss; Bravo, hit or not, went overboard. Moses Thomas alone was spared, a mercy the mutineers were to regret.

On 20 December the lifeboat was prepared, the ship and second lifeboat set afire, and the five men started out for land. As Rau and his murderous henchmen came in sight of Cajueira, charts, compasses, food and weapons were all jettisoned. If their story was ever to be believed, the crew would need to appear destitute.

In court the three accused, Rau, Monsson and Smith, offered the preposterous defence that Thomas had committed the entire crime single-handed. The case aroused considerable interest in the public mind, not least for the anachronism of brutal and treacherous piracy in the twentieth century; but also legally, for the complete absence of direct evidence. In the end, the Crown case relied solely on the testimony of the accomplice Harry Flohr, who had turned King's Evidence. On Thursday 14 May 1903, at 9.00 p.m., sentence was passed. The three mutineers were condemned to hang. In the case of Monsson the jury recommended mercy and his sentence was commuted to life imprisonment. The ringleaders, Rau and Smith, duly died on the gallows.

VITKOVIC, Frank　At 4.20 p.m. on Tuesday 8 December 1987, a man dressed in blue jeans and an army-style jacket drove a red station wagon into the side street beside Melbourne's Australian Telecom tower. There was nothing strange in that, except that the man was cradling a high-powered rifle as he ran five floors up a fire escape to the offices of a credit union company. Entering the offices, the gunman began by arguing with a male office worker; then, quite suddenly and without any warning, he raised the rifle and began firing indiscriminately around the room. Terrified office staff threw themselves in the direction of whatever shelter they could find, behind filing cabinets, under desks. One woman said later: 'He was screaming at everyone to lie flat on the ground.' The gunman then ran from floor to floor shooting wildly at anyone he saw. On one landing, he stopped as a lift opened and shot dead four people inside. A woman survivor in the lift told police: 'He shot down four of my friends right in front of me. He looked at me and I thought he was going to kill me, too. It was awful.' Awful indeed.

Eventually, on the tenth floor, the wild assassin was tackled and disarmed by the concerted efforts of a security officer and one of the male clerks. However, in a final desperate bid for self-destruction, the gunman hurled himself through a window but was saved from instant death on the street below by the quick-thinking security guard who grabbed his legs. With the strength of desperation the struggling killer kicked out and broke free, still shouting and cursing as he plummeted 130 feet to his death. An eye-witness said: 'He obviously wanted to die. Half of his body was dangling below the railing and somebody was trying to hold him by the ankles. Suddenly he hollered and fell to the ground.'

Eight office workers, including five women died at the hands of the gunman, who was identified as Frank Vitkovic, a twenty-two-year-old student. It had been the second mass killing in the city of Melbourne within a few months.

W

WAGNER, Franz Born into a humble German peasant family, Franz Wagner nevertheless made the most of his education, and with diligence and application finally qualified as a school teacher. The sad fact was that, despite his achievement, Wagner always retained a sense of inadequacy because of his modest origins – a problem which was not helped by what he regarded as his 'sexual sins'. Franz Wagner married in 1903 and fathered five children in quick succession, none of whom he particularly cherished, seeing them as a drain on his meagre income rather than an enrichment of his otherwise drab existence.

Most of Wagner's teaching career had been set in Muehlhausen and in time his deep sense of insecurity manifested itself in an irrational conviction that the men of the town were whispering behind his back. Franz Wagner's solution to the problem was to pack up his family and his few belongings and take himself off to a new teaching post in Radelstatten. Ten years later the situation had deteriorated again; Wagner's paranoia now led him to believe that the burghers of Muehlhausen were passing on rumours about him to the good folk of Radelstatten.

On the night of 4 September 1913, the inhabitants of Muehlhausen were prematurely awakened by a spate of fires breaking out around the town. Emerging bleary-eyed on to the street, householders encountered a man with his face covered by a black veil, and armed with two pistols. As they stood dumbstruck with horror the gunman shot dead eight men and a girl and wounded twelve others. Only when this madman's pistols ran out of ammunition was he overpowered and savagely beaten by the locals; he was identified by his brother-in-law as Franz Wagner, who later confessed that on the previous night he had killed his wife and five children in Radelstatten.

During the preceding week, Wagner had written a series of letters which he had not posted until the day of his final madness. In them he vowed to revenge himself on those citizens of Muehlhausen who had scorned and slandered him. Wagner had also intended to kill his brother and his brother's family, burn down their house and that in which he was born, and as a finale go to the royal palace of Ludwigsburg, overpower the guards, set fire to the castle and then kill himself.

Not surprisingly Franz Wagner was certified insane and committed to a mental institution, where he died in 1938.

WEAVER, Kevin Like the great majority of contemporary mass murderers, twenty-four-year-old Kevin Weaver was a gun fanatic; after his killing spree in 1987, police found an arsenal of shotguns and more than 500 rounds of ammunition in Weaver's car. Unlike the great majority of contemporary mass murderers, though, Kevin Weaver was English.

The killings started on the morning of 14 October 1987, when Weaver decided to bludgeon his sister Linda to death as she slept at the family home in the Redfield district of Bristol. Then he lay in wait for his fifty-five-year-old mother to return home from shopping and battered her to death too. Kevin Weaver's insane revenge against the world had begun. It would end later that afternoon; it would leave two more innocent people dead.

First Weaver turned the house into a rudimentary time-bomb by turning on the kitchen gas jets and leaving a pan of oil burning on the stove; then he loaded three of his collection of shotguns and several boxes of ammunition into the back of his late sister's car, donned an army flak jacket and drove across the city to Alexandra Workwear, the factory which employed his former fiancée, Alison

Woodman, as a computer operator. Alison had ended their relationship a couple of years earlier, and Weaver was still smarting over the rejection. He later told detectives that he had been planning to kill Alison for a long time: '. . . to punish her . . . but as soon as I saw her I changed my mind. I still like her.' And so she was spared. Not so her two colleagues in the computer department; as Weaver loosed off his pump-action shotgun at anybody in sight, John Peterson and David Pursall fell to the ground fatally wounded. Their assassin then climbed into his car and drove back across Bristol to the suburb of Whitchurch where the vehicle was stopped and Weaver was arrested by two unarmed policemen.

It was during his interview at the police station that detectives learned about Kevin Weaver's lethal time-bomb, and defused it by shooting out of the windows of the house to release the gas. Then they found the two bodies. Meanwhile, Weaver was going on to explain that he had only killed his mother and sister to save them from the distress and shame of his inevitable arrest for the murder of Alison Woodman. But the media had already uncovered a potentially more sinister piece of information. In March of the previous year Kevin Weaver had been found by the police asleep in his car outside Aberystwyth; also in the car were a shotgun and 225 cartridges, and the incident led to Weaver's firearms certificate being withdrawn and the weapon being confiscated. Following reports that he was a 'fit person' to possess firearms, Avon and Somerset police returned the shotgun; it was the weapon used to shoot John Peterson and David Pursall. Not surprisingly this revelation sparked off renewed demands from policemen and politicians that there should be far stricter firearms controls and safeguards; controls and safeguards which have not yet been implemented to any appreciable extent, despite assurances from the then Home Secretary, Douglas Hurd.

Kevin Weaver's trial opened in March 1988 at the Bristol Guildhall, where his pleas of guilty to four counts of manslaughter were accepted by the prosecution. On the

25th of the month Weaver was ordered to be detained indefinitely at Broadmoor special hospital.

WEBER, Adolph On the evening of 10 November 1904 the home of Julius Weber and his family in Auburn, California, burst into flames and was burned to the ground. The family consisted of Weber and his wife, an eighteen-year-old daughter, Bertha, and two sons, Adolph, aged twenty, and eight-year-old Earl. In what seemed an extraordinary sequence of events, at the exact time the fire started Adolph Weber bought a new pair of trousers at a nearby store and then ran back to the burning house where he broke a window with his fist and threw the old trousers into the flames. In doing so he cut his hand badly.

Hoping to be of assistance to any survivors, a neighbour forced an entry into the burning house and was shocked to find the bodies of Mrs Weber and Bertha in a room which at that time had not been damaged by the fire; they had both suffered bullet wounds and an attempt had been made to set light to their clothes. Little Earl, an invalid, was still alive despite savage blows to the head with a blunt instrument, but died soon afterwards. Julius Weber's body was found on the following day in a different part of the house; he too had been shot.

An inquest held on 12 November returned a verdict of wilful murder against Adolph Weber and he was immediately placed under arrest. The case for his guilt grew with the discovery of a bloodstained revolver under the floor of a barn on the Weber property. The gun had been fired recently, and attached to the bloody butt was hair, later matched with Earl Weber's. A check into the pedigree of the weapon turned up a pawnbroker who identified it as one he sold to Adolph Weber about four months before the murders. And those trousers that Adolph had been so anxious to get rid of? Uncharred fragments recovered from the fire showed evidence of bloodstains.

Adolph Weber pleaded not guilty when his trial opened on 6 February 1905, but on 22 February the jury returned a verdict of guilty anyway, with a recommendation for the death penalty. Following several appeals and a stay of execution so that an investigation could be held into his sanity, Weber, showing the same complete indifference to his situation as he had throughout his trial, went to the gallows on 27 September 1906.

WENTZ, Grant F. Shortly after eight o'clock on the morning of 25 November 1939, a waitress employed at the Old Barn Inn, Salt Lake City, Utah arrived for work at what she expected to be an empty building. The thirty-three-year-old proprietor, Grant F. Wentz, had left a message at the woman's home warning her that he and his family would be away for the day but that she should report in for work as usual. As she walked into the building, she was immediately aware of a strong smell of gas. Puzzled, the waitress hurried upstairs to the owner's living quarters and was horrified to see the bloodstained body of five-year-old Marie Wentz lying on a settee in the living room. The woman ran screaming from the building. An autopsy later revealed the child had been bludgeoned and bore marks consistent with strangulation with a cord or wire.

In a front bedroom of the apartment police subsequently found the body of Mrs Afton Wentz, the wife of the owner, incongruously tucked up in bed. As in the case of the child, her head had been battered and her throat bore marks of a thin ligature which had been removed. In each of the rooms and the hallway the gas jets had been fully turned on. There was evidence of further tragedy in a second bedroom where the bludgeoned and strangled bodies of the two other Wentz children, Darlene, aged six, and Barth, four, were found. The grisly search continued through into the kitchen which revealed the body of Grant Wentz, a .22-calibre rifle lying beside him.

To the experienced eyes of the detective team this looked like a classic case of murder followed by suicide; an opinion which was confirmed when the pathologist reported that Grant Wentz had been dead for a much shorter time than the rest of the family. It was not difficult for officers to piece together the motive behind so barbarous an act of mass murder because they were soon able to establish that Grant Wentz had recently been depressed over the Old Barn's lack of success resulting in his inability to pay outstanding bills. A bloodstained hammer and pieces of heavy wire cut from a radio aerial were found close to the restaurant, and tests proved them to be the murder weapons. The official verdict on the tragedy was that Grant Wentz had murdered his family and then committed suicide. However, it remains a mystery why Grant Wentz, and we must assume it was him, took the trouble of turning on all the gas taps before killing himself.

WESBECKER, Joseph T. Forty-seven-year-old Joe Wesbecker was twice married and had a history of mental problems which had led to his employers, Standard Gravure Corporation of Louisville, Kentucky, to grant him disability leave. Other employees might have seen this as a generous gesture made by a caring employer; not so Joe Wesbecker. It simply intensified his resentment against Standard Gravure who he believed to have been the cause of his problems to start with. It was Wesbecker's firm belief it was being kept in a stressful job and exposed to a harmful industrial chemical that had led to his blackouts, fits of anger and mental confusion.

For seven months Joe Wesbecker brooded on the best way of revenging himself on the people whom he considered, quite wrongly as it happened, to have ruined his life. On the morning of 14 September 1989, he went to the Standard Gravure plant armed with an AK47 assault rifle and an assortment of hand-guns. He took the elevator to the executive office complex and, as the doors parted on the third floor, opened fire into the lobby, killing the receptionist and wounding several other members of staff. Wesbecker passed through the offices, shooting at anyone in his line of fire. When he arrived in the pressroom, where he had been employed, Joe Wesbecker dropped the AK47 to the floor, took out a 9mm pistol, and killed himself. Within the space of approximately nine minutes he had loosed off hundreds of shots killing seven people and wounding twelve others. It was ironical that none of the dead and wounded were in any of those positions of authority so despised by Wesbecker; in fact, many were the same fellow-workers with whom he had shared his discontent over the previous months.

WHITMAN, Charles Charles Whitman lived in terror of his own mental condition. 'I've been having fears and violent impulses,' he wrote in a memo. 'After my death I wish an autopsy to be performed to see if there's any mental disorder.' Finishing the memo with the words 'Life is not worth living', Whitman left his home at 906 Jewell Street in Austin, Texas, and drove to the home of his mother Margaret, who had separated from her husband on grounds of his habitual violence. At Mrs Whitman's apartment at 1515 Guadalupe Street there was a brief struggle before Charlie stabbed his mother in the chest and killed her with a pistol shot to the back of the head.

Back home, Whitman walked into the bedroom and stabbed his wife three times in the chest as she slept. That was at 3 a.m. on the morning of 1 August 1966; six hours later Whitman was out shopping, with a .30 M-1 carbine, a 12-gauge shotgun, several hundred rounds of ammunition, and a foldaway trolley on his shopping list. He packed a trunk with tinned food, water, tools, a radio and all the other accoutrements of a survival kit, an arsenal of seven guns, three knives and 1,000 rounds of ammunition, and drove his Chevrolet to the campus of the University of Texas – to the 307 ft-high tower of the administration offices.

Charlie Whitman, in his grey overalls, passed himself off as a maintenance man to gain access to the tower, and swiftly ascended to the twenty-seventh floor. Here he clubbed receptionist Edna Townsley to the floor with a rifle butt, before wheeling his heavy trunk on the foldaway trolley out to the observation deck. No sooner had he done so than a group of visitors got out of the lift. Whitman fired three rapid blasts from his sawn-off shotgun, killing Marguerite Lamport and teenager Mark Gabour and seriously injuring Mark's mother and brother. He barricaded the door, shot Mrs Townsley in the head, and went out on to the observation gallery.

The sniping began at 11.45 a.m. Alex Hernandez was the first victim, shot through the leg. Three more students fell in quick succession, before traffic cop Billy Speed picked up the first reports of a gunman on the roof. He pulled in to the campus and was moving in on the tower when Whitman felled him with a single shot.

Over the next fifteen or twenty minutes the gunfire was heavy and deadly. Whitman was an ex-Marine sharpshooter, and most of his victims were hit in or around the heart. Claudia Rutt was strolling up one of the malls when she clutched at her chest and fell, crying 'Help me!' As her boyfriend Paul Sonntag reached down to the girl he too was shot, both victims dying instantly. Harry Walchuk was a good two hundred yards away, browsing at a newsstand, when he was hit in the throat and collapsed on to the magazine rack.

Attempts to get a shot at Whitman from a light aircraft and from a helicopter proved abortive, but three policemen on the ground managed to dash from cover to cover across the plaza to the tower. Here they picked up Allen Crum, an experienced ex-serviceman, deputized him on the spot and gave him a rifle. The four men took the lift to the twenty-sixth floor, and inched their way up to the gunman's lair. Crum encountered the quarry first, loosing off a rifle shot which sent Whitman scurrying back; back into the line of fire of officer Ramiro Martinez. The sniper managed one wild shot before Martinez emptied the magazine of his pistol into his body. As Whitman fell Houston McCoy shot him twice with a shotgun; he was down, but still moving and still armed. Officer Martinez finished Charles Whitman off with a shot to the head at point-blank range. It was 1.20 p.m.

Whitman's killing spree left fifteen dead and thirty injured, some of them permanently scarred or disabled. As to his self-diagnosed mental illness, an autopsy revealed a small tumour in the back of his brain, but medical authorities have been unable to agree whether this was benign or malignant.

WILLIAMS, John   The following is condensed from an account of the Ratcliffe Highway murders by Thomas De Quincey, part of his celebrated essay 'On Murder as a Fine Art':

Ratcliffe Highway is a public thoroughfare in the most chaotic quarter of eastern, or nautical, London. Into this perilous region it was that, on a Saturday night in December [1811], Mr Williams forced his way through the crowded street, bound on business. John Williams was a man of middle stature, slenderly built, rather thin, but wiry, tolerably muscular, and clear of all superfluous flesh; his hair was of the most extraordinary and vivid colour, viz., a bright yellow, something between an orange and a yellow colour. He seems to have laid it down as a maxim that the best person to murder was a friend, and Marr was the name of that unhappy man. Marr's position in life was this: he kept a little hosier's shop. At this time he was a stout, fresh-coloured young man of twenty-seven. The household of Marr is as follows: First, there is himself, second stands his pretty and amiable wife, anxious (if at all) only on account of her darling infant. For, thirdly, there is a baby eight months old. Fourthly, there is a stoutish boy, an apprentice, say thirteen years old; fifthly, and lastly, is a servant girl, a grown-up young woman. To this young woman it was that Marr called aloud to go out and purchase some oysters. Precisely as she emerged from the shop-door, she noticed, by the light of the lamps, a man's figure. This was Williams.

Mary (returned from her errand) rang, and at the same time very gently knocked. Yet how is this? To her astonishment – but with the astonishment came creeping over her an icy horror – no stir or murmur was heard. Still as death she was, and during that dreadful stillness dreadful footsteps were heard advancing along the little narrow passage to the door. Mary began now to ring the bell and to ply the knocker with unintermitting violence. The next door neighbour was roused. A brick wall, nine or ten feet high, divided his premises from those of Marr, but over this he vaulted, and saw that Marr's back door stood wide open. Probably the murderer had passed through it one half-minute before. Rapidly the brave man passed onwards to the shop, and there before him beheld the carnage of the night stretched out on the floor, and the narrow premises so floated with gore, that it was hardly possible to escape the pollution of blood in picking out a path to the front door.

This bloodbath, in which the Marr couple, their baby and the young apprentice were butchered to death with razor and mallet, was on 7 December. On the 18th another multiple murder was committed, this time at the King's Arms in what is now Garnet Street. John Turner, lodging in the house, raised the alarm with a passing watchman:

On looking round the cellar, the first object that attracted their attention was the body of Mr Williamson (the landlord), which lay at the foot of the stairs, with a violent contusion of the head, his throat dreadfully cut, and an iron crow by his side. They proceeded upstairs to the parlour, where they found Mrs Williamson also dead, with her skull and throat cut, and near her the body of the servant-woman, her throat cut in a most shocking manner.

A sailor's maul found at the scene of the latest outrage led police to the Pear Tree tavern in Cinnamon Street where they arrested John Williams on suspicion. Remanded to Coldbath Fields prison, Williams hanged himself from a beam in his cell on 28 December.

On the last day of this fatal year the remains of this sanguinary assassin were privately removed, at eleven o'clock at night. The procession advanced slowly up Ratcliffe Highway, accompanied by an immense concourse of persons; when the cart came opposite the late Mr Marr's house a halt was made for nearly a quarter of an hour. The procession then advanced to St George's Turnpike, where the new road is intersected by Cannon Street; here a grave, about six feet deep, had been prepared. The body was taken from the platform and lowered into the grave, immediately after a stake was driven through it*; and, the pit being covered, this solemn ceremony concluded.

WILSON, John Gleeson   Ann Henrichson was in the habit of letting off apartments when her husband, master of the good ship *Duncan*, was away on voyage. A card announcing vacancies was displayed in the window of her house at 20 Leveson Street (now Grenville Street), Liverpool, and attracted the attention of Mr John Gleeson Wilson. Following a brief enquiry and investigation he agreed to take the back parlour and front top bedroom. This was on Tuesday 27 March 1849. The next morning Wilson paid a boy to deliver a letter addressed to himself at the house in Leveson Street, saying that it was 'from his master'.

Some time later that same morning a delivery boy by the name of Roebuck called at the house and, getting no reply, peeped through the keyhole. What he saw was the feet and legs of a woman lying in the passage. Looking through the parlour window young Roebuck spied the servant, Mary Parr, in a similar position, one of the Henrichson boys sprawled alongside. Neighbours were summoned to effect an entry, and found Mary dying but still alive. Wilson, she recalled, had attacked her with a pair of firetongs; he had smashed the skull of the eldest boy with thirty blows from a poker. The three-year-old was found in the scullery, his throat cut from ear to ear with a large carving knife. According to Mary Parr, Mrs Henrichson had, at this very

* This was a customary precaution to prevent the restless souls of suicides from rising.

moment, returned from shopping and had been attacked in the hall, where she now lay breathing her last; her jewellery box and chest of drawers had been thoroughly ransacked.

John Wilson was seen about various parts of Liverpool from around noon that day. He was seen beside a pond, at Toxteth Park, washing his boots and trousers; and at the pawnshop of Mr Tunstall at 207 London Road, where he offered a gold watch for sale; he was seen at Mr Finn's shop in Great Homer Street, where he bought and put on a pair of black trousers. He gave his old trousers to a paviour named Worthington, who found they were wet and spotted with blood.

The carelessness, the sheer stupidity of John Wilson is seemingly endless: he paid his landlady in Porter Street with silver from Mrs Henrichson's purse; he was wearing her gold watch, which he tried to sell later to a Mr Samuel, in business in Great Howard Street, whose suspicions were aroused. Samuel sent Wilson to his shop in Dale Street to collect a receipt, meanwhile calling the police. Wilson was arrested on suspicion.

He appeared before Mr Justice Pattison, charged only with the murder of Mary Parr. The defence was the rather shallow one that if plunder had been the objective of the crime, why had it been necessary to murder the infants? And if it was murder for its own sake, why flaunt the looted property? The jury evidently decided that John Wilson was idiotic enough to confound this and any other recourse to logic, for after consulting a mere three minutes, and without bothering to leave the box, they returned a verdict of guilty.

John Gleeson Wilson was publicly hanged outside Kirkdale Gaol on 15 September 1849. A crowd of 30,000 cheered him on his way.

WOO BOM-KON   On 26 April 1982, twenty-seven-year-old policeman Woo Bom-Kon went on an eight-hour orgy of violence, killing fifty-three people, including his girlfriend, and wounding thirty-six in villages of the Kyongsang-Namdo province of South Korea.

Woo, a former member of the Korean Marine Corps had

got drunk after a row with his girlfriend and went berserk. He armed himself with two Korean War vintage M2 carbines and broke into the unguarded police armoury while all the other officers were attending a neighbourhood association meeting. Here Woo stole several hand-grenades before going on a rampage through the villages, shooting indiscriminately and detonating the grenades. Eye-witnesses said the mutilated bodies of the dead littered the streets of the settlements along with the wounded who were screaming out for help. A telephone operator on duty at the post office in the village of Uriyong was later found shot dead at her switchboard, the telephone still gripped in her hand. When the police were finally mobilized they followed Woo, but lost him under cover of darkness. By this time he had backtracked towards his home village, where, two miles from the police station where he was based, Woo Bom-Kon blew himself up with his last grenade.

The incident raised serious security questions for the South Korean government, and there were even calls for ministerial resignations. The main element of controversy was that the carnage had clearly been allowed to escalate due to the non-availability of the police at the time of the shootings. It was also remarked that a general lack of discipline within the police force and insufficient safeguards to check the mental stability of applicants were also contributing factors.

Y

YAMAGUCHI, Tsuneo On 22 February 1951 a man who identified himself as Tsuneo Yamaguchi rushed into the Tsukiji police station in Tokyo and claimed he had just seen a dead body. The corpse in question was that of the son of Yamaguchi's employer at the Happo-tei restaurant, and it was lying in a pool of blood at the apartment adjoining the restaurant.

Police officers who went to investigate found not only the body of the eleven-year-old boy, but also his ten-year-old sister and their parents Mr and Mrs Ichiro Iwamoto. All the victims appeared to have been struck on the head with an axe, and although there were copious bloodstains there was little evidence of a struggle. The bodies, except that of the boy, had been covered with a blanket, and the fact that the drawers of a desk had been pulled out and cupboards ransacked, indicated that robbery had been the motive.

Meanwhile, back at the police station Yamaguchi was making a statement. He said that a girl who had been working at the restaurant for only a day had been on the premises the previous night, but now seemed to have vanished. Yamaguchi claimed to have heard the girl, who had given her name as Shigeko Ohta, talking that night to a man who she later claimed was her brother. Nothing else worth speaking of occurred until Yamaguchi got up at around 9.00 a.m. and found the body. Although they said nothing at the time, officers were puzzled as to why Yamaguchi, who lived in at the premises, had not heard any sounds of a scuffle during the night.

That evening, following massive publicity about the murders, a Tokyo bank manager reported that a girl matching the description of the missing waitress had attempted to draw money on a pass book belonging to Ichiro Iwamoto; the bank had refused payment. Yamaguchi, meanwhile, was stressing how earnestly he wanted to help the police catch the murderer, and he spent a considerable amount of time assisting a police artist to compile a picture of the young woman. He also gave interviews to the press, freely volunteering his own theories as to the possible identity of the killer.

On 5 March a policeman named Katsuyoshi Oshima reported that he had overheard two men discussing the artist's impression and commenting that it looked just like a girl who worked at the Shinjuku Hotel. Two days later detectives thought they had made a breakthrough when an informant told them that a young woman had left two parcels with him and that, when she had failed to collect them, he had looked inside and found a bloodstained blouse. However, when the girl was traced she was able to offer a watertight alibi for the night of the killings, and convincingly proved that the blood on her clothing was the result of a nose-bleed.

Policeman Oshima was still going on about the girl at the Shinjuku Hotel, and despite a general lack of interest, he was told to follow it up if he wanted to. Oshima learned that a girl named Tsuyaki Nishino had been employed at the hotel, but had inexplicably left on the same day that the new waitress was taken on at the Happo-tei restaurant. When the officer finally caught up with her, the woman admitted that she was the waitress at the Happo-tei but insisted she had nothing to do with the murders nor, as she did not read the newspapers, did she even know about them. She admitted that she and Tsuneo Yamaguchi had been lovers and that he had threatened her with her life if she refused to draw cash on the pass book he had stolen from their employer. When the bank refused her, Nishino became frightened and that was why she had fled.

Tsuneo Yamaguchi was arrested and, after a prolonged

session of questioning, promised to make a full confession the following day when he was less tired. During the search before he was locked in a cell a phial of cyanide was found on Yamaguchi's person and removed. However, during the night, he was found dead, having taken cyanide from a second, undiscovered, phial.

Z

ZEHETNER, Felix On 9 September 1990, Felix Zehetner was enjoying himself at a barbecue in Vienna. The problem was that he was enjoying himself a little too much; in truth, he was enjoying himself *far* too much, eventually becoming so drunk and objectionable that the host had him thrown out.

Twenty-two-year-old Zehetner stumbled home much the worse for schnaps and a bruised ego. From its hiding place in his bedroom, Zehetner took out his Smith & Wesson pistol and, as they provided the nearest targets on which to focus his anger and frustration, shot his parents, killing his fifty-one-year-old father and severely wounding his mother. Felix Zehetner then returned to the barbecue, forced his way in and, without a word, opened fire on the revellers, killing four and wounding sixteen. The party's host, who had been Zehetner's prime target died and his twenty-three-year-old sister was critically wounded when a bullet pierced her lung.

Police were called and confronted Felix Zehetner in a brief shoot-out, during the course of which he seriously wounded two officers before killing himself with a bullet to the head.

ZEIGLER, William 'Tommy' At around 9.15 p.m. on Christmas Eve 1975, the telephone rang at the home of Theodore Van Deventer, a West Orange County, Florida, judge; when he answered it a voice said: 'It's Tommy Zeigler. I'm hurt.' It so happened that the chief of police,

Don Ficke, was at the judge's house at the time and when he took over the call, Zeigler told him he was at the family store and had been shot. The police chief summoned a team of officers and they drove straight to the Zeigler furniture store down at 1010 South Dillard Street where they found the shop in darkness and Zeigler wounded, his face spattered with blood and his clothing caked with dried blood. Before he was removed to hospital in an ambulance, William 'Tommy' Zeigler was able to tell Chief Ficke: 'It was Charlie Mays.' By this time the police had restored the power supply which had been turned off at the main switch. The light revealed blood everywhere – and four bodies.

Zeigler's mother-in-law, Virginia Edwards, was lying near the front of the shop; she had been shot in the chest and head. His wife Eunice had been shot in the back of the head, apparently as she entered the kitchen area. Father-in-law Perry Edwards' body lay by some linoleum racks, battered and shot through the head. Finally there was Charlie Mays, a local black community leader; he had also been shot and bludgeoned.

The police at first concluded that the motive for the killings was robbery. Tommy Zeigler's wound proved to be less serious than it looked and police were able to interview him in hospital on the day following the shooting. According to his statement, Zeigler had returned to the store just after seven in the evening and found Ed Williams, who did part-time carpentry work for the business, waiting outside the building; they had gone in together by the back entrance. Suddenly he was attacked from behind by at least two men, one of whom was bigger than himself, and black. During the fight which followed Zeigler pulled out a gun and tried to fire it at his assailant – whether he succeeded or not Zeigler could not remember. Then he himself was shot and as he fell he heard a voice say: 'Mays has been hit. Kill him.' Luckily they did not, but instead fled from the premises leaving Tommy to make his call for help.

Police put out a call for the apprehension of Ed Williams, but before he could be brought in he surrendered himself. Williams agreed that he had been at the store with Zeigler;

they had met outside as his boss had said, but Zeigler had gone in through the front entrance while Williams was told to make his way around the back. Williams did as he was told, but when he got into the back of the shop Tommy Zeigler had tried to shoot him; luckily the gun had jammed and the handyman made off as fast as his legs would carry him.

Forensic tests later established that the bullets which killed Mr and Mrs Edwards had come from a .38 which had recently been bought by Zeigler, and all twenty bullets which had been fired during the incident in the store that night had come from one or other of the eight guns later found there – all of them owned by Tommy Zeigler. For good measure it was discovered that two months previously Tommy Zeigler had taken out two insurance policies on his wife's life, each for $520,000. An unexpected bonus arrived at police headquarters in the person of a man who claimed that Zeigler had asked him to test-fire some guns and had also tried to bribe him to throw the main electrical switch at the store on the night of the murders.

On 29 December Tommy Zeigler was charged with two counts of first-degree murder relating to the deaths of Eunice Zeigler and Charles Mays, and two counts of second-degree murder in the deaths of Perry and Virginia Edwards. At the trial a reconstruction of the crime provided by Herbert MacDonell (author of *Bloodstain Pattern Interpretation*, the definitive work on bloodstains) convinced the jury sufficiently to return a verdict of guilty, which they did on 2 July 1976. Although a penalty hearing jury recommended a life sentence, Circuit Judge Maurice M. Paul was feeling less benevolent, and sentenced Zeigler to death. The Florida Supreme Court dismissed his appeal on 12 June 1981, and on 22 March 1982 the United States Supreme Court also refused his appeal. At the time of writing William 'Tommy' Zeigler is still on Death Row in Florida State Prison.

Select Bibliography

ALLEN, Floyd, *et al.*
Memoirs of J. Sidna Allen, F. H. Lamb, Mount Airy, N.C., 1929.

ANDREWS, William, and PIERRE, Dale Selby
Victim, Gary Kinder, Fontana, London, 1983.

ARCHINA, Frank
The Murderer and his Victim, J. M. Macdonald, Thomas, Springfield, Ill., 1961.

AUSTIN, Thomas
The Murder Club Guide to South-West England and Wales, Brian Lane, Harrap, London, 1989.

BALABAN, John
Murder Australian Style, Jim Main, Unicorn Books, Melbourne, 1980.

BARTHOLOMEW, Clifford Cecil
Crimes That Shocked Australia, Alan Sharpe, Currawong Press, Australia, 1982.

BATES, Clyde, *et al.*
Public Justice, Private Mercy, Edmund (Pat) Brown, Weidenfeld & Nicolson, New York, 1989.

BECKETT, Henry
Rope, Knife and Chair (True Crimes), Guy B. H. Logan, Rich & Cowan, London, n.d.
Forty Years of Man-Hunting, Arthur Fowler Neil, Jarrolds, London, 1932.

BIRMINGHAM PUB BOMBINGS
The Birmingham Bombs, Brian Gibson, Barry Rose, Chichester, 1976.
Error of Judgement, Chris Mullin, Chatto & Windus, London, 1986.

BODKIN, John, *et al.*
The Chronicles of Crime, Camden Pelham, T. Miles & Co., London, 1891.

BOOHER, Vernon
The Booher Murder Case, Frank W. Anderson, Gopher Books, Saskatoon, n.d.

BOSTON MASSACRE
The Boston Massacre, Harry Hansen, Hastings House, New York, 1970.

BRAM, Thomas Mead Chambers
Studies in Murder, Edmund Pearson, Macmillan, New York, 1924.

BRYANT, Martin
Suddenly One Sunday, Mike Bingham, HarperCollins, Sydney, 1996.

BURGESS, Richard, *et al.*
Murders on Maungatapu, Frank Clune, Angus & Robertson, Sydney, 1959.
Death Round The Bend, J. Halket Millar, Stiles, Nelson, 1954.
Guilty Wretch That I Am, Ken Byron, Macmillan, Melbourne, 1984.

BURNS, Joseph
Famous New Zealand Murders, Dudley G. Dyne, Collins, Auckland, 1969.

CHARLES, Robert
Carnival of Fury, William Ivy Hair, Louisiana State University Press, Baton Rouge, 1976.

CIUCCI, Vincent
May God Have Mercy On Your Soul, Ed Baumann, Bonus Books, Chicago, 1993.

COLUMBINE HIGH SCHOOL KILLINGS
The Columbine High School Massacre, Isaac Omoike, Baton Rouge, 2000.

COLUMBO, Patricia Ann, and DELUCA, Frank
Mom, Dad, Mike & Pattie, Bonnie Remsberg, Bantam, New York, 1993.

COOK, Robert Raymond
The Work of Justice, J. Pecover, Wolf Willow Press, Edmonton, 1996.

CORDERO, Jose Antonio, *et al.*
Heat, Peter A. Micheels, St Martins Press, New York, 1991.

DANN, Laurie Wasserman
Murder of Innocence, Joel Kaplan, George Papajohn and Eric Zorn, Warner Books, New York, 1990.

D'AUTREMONT BROTHERS
The Chemist of Crime, Eugene B. Block, Cassell, London, 1959.

DEAN, Douglas
Wisconsin Crimes of the Century, Marv Balousek, Robbins, Madison, Wisconsin, 1989.

DeFEO, Ronald
Murder in Amityville, Hans Holzer, Futura, London, 1980.
High Hopes, Gerard Sullivan and Harvey Aronson, Coward, McCann & Geoghegan, New York, 1981.

DE LA ROCHE, Harry
Anyone's Son, Roberta Roesch with Harry De La Roche, Andrews & McMeel, Kansas City, 1979.

DE LEEUW, Huibrecht Jacob
Up For Murder, Benjamin Bennett and F. P. Rousseau, Hutchinson, London, 1934.

DIPENDRA, Crown Prince
Blood Against The Snows, John Gregson, Fourth Estate, London, 2002.

DOMINICI, Gaston
The Dominici Affair, Jean Giono, Museum Press, London, 1956.
The Dominici Affair, Jean Laborde, Collins, London, 1974.
Valley of Silence, Gordon Young, Robert Hale, London, 1955.

DONNELLY MURDERS
The Donnellys Must Die, Orlo Miller, Macmillan of Canada, Toronto, 1962.
The Black Donnellys, Thomas P. Kelley, Signet Books, New York, 1955.
The Donnelly Album, Ray Fazakas, Macmillan of Canada, Toronto, 1977.

EARLY, David F.
The Murderer And His Victim, John M. Macdonald, Thomas, Springfield, Ill., 1961.

EASBY, Thomas
The County Kerchief, Louis Blake Duff, Ryerson Press, Toronto, 1949.

EASTBURN MURDERS
Innocent Victims, Scott Whisnant, Onyx Books, New York, 1993.

ESSEX, Mark James Robert
They Shoot to Kill, Ronald Tobias, Paladin Press, Boulder, Colorado, 1981.
A Terrible Thunder, Peter Hernon, Doubleday, New York, 1978.

FORD, Priscilla
Ladies Who Kill, Tom Kunkl and Paul Einstein, Pinnacle, New York, 1989.

FORD, William S.
Homicide Squad, Frederick L. Collins, Putnam, New York, 1944.

GARCIA, Joseph
Welsh Murders, Peter Fuller and Brian Knapp, Christopher Davies, Llandybie, 1986.

GIBSON, Monk, and POWELL, Felix
Death Penalty for Juveniles, Victor L. Streib, Indiana University Press, Bloomington, 1987.

GONZALEZ, Julio
The Murder Yearbook, Brian Lane, Headline, London, 1992.

GRAHAM, Eric Stanley George
Manhunt, H. A. Willis, Whitcoulls, Christchurch, 1979.

GREENSBORO KILLINGS
Codename GreenKil, Elizabeth Wharton, University of Georgia Press, Athens, Ga., 1987.

GUAY, Albert, *et al.*
Headline Crimes of the Year, Edward D. Radin, Little Brown, Boston, 1952.
Murder, Mayhem and Mystery, Alan Hynd, A. S. Barnes, New York, 1958.

GUILDFORD PUB BOMBINGS
Trial and Error, Robert Kee, Hamish Hamilton, London, 1987.
Time Bomb, Grant McKee and Ros Franey, Bloomsbury, London, 1988.
Double Jeopardy, Ronan Bennett, Penguin, London, 1993.

HALL, Leo
Slaughter of Six (Jam-Session Slayer), W. W. Bride, Superior Books, Toronto, n.d.
One Hundred True Crime Stories, Sam D. Cohen, World Publishing, Cleveland, 1946.

HAMILTON, Thomas
The Public Enquiry into the Shootings at Dunblane Primary School on 13 March 1996, Lord Cullen, Stationery Office, London, 1996.

HEBARD, Harry 'Butch'
Wiscousin Crimes of the Century, Marv Dalousek, Robbins, Madison, Wincousin, 1989.

HEDIN, Tore
Mystery Stranger Than Fiction, Leo Grex, Robert Hale, London, 1979.

HICKS, Albert E.
Celebrated Criminal Cases of America, Thomas S. Duke, Patterson Smith, Montclair, N.J., 1991.
The New York Tombs, Charles Sutton, A. Roman and Co., San Francisco, 1874.

HIRASAWA, Sadamichi
Flowering of the Bamboo, William Triplett, Woodbine House, Kensington, Md., 1985.

HOFFMAN, Victor Ernest
Shell Lake Massacre, Peter Tadman, Gorman & Gorman, Alberta, 1992.

HONA, Henare
Famous New Zealand Murders, Dudley G. Dyne, Collins, Auckland, 1969.

HUBERTY, James
Spree Killers, Art Crockett (ed.), Pinnacle, New York, 1991.

ICE-CREAM WARS
Frightener, Douglas Skelton and Lisa Brownlie, Mainstream, Edinburgh, 1992.
Indictment – Trial By Fire, T. C. Campbell & Reg McKay, Canongate Books, Edinburgh, 2001
The Wilderness Years, T. C. Campbell & Reg McKay, Canongate Books, Edinburgh, 2002.

INGENITO, Ernest
The Mass Murderer, Brad Steiger, Award Books, New York, 1967.

ISAACS, Carl, *et al.*
Blood Echoes, Thomas H. Cook, Onyx Books, New York, 1993.
Brothers in Blood, Clark Howard, St Martins/Marek, New York, 1983.

JAIN, Rattan Bai
They Came To Kill, Leonard Gribble, John Long, London, 1979.

JONES, William
Crimes of Yesteryear, Nigel Green, Sunderland and Hartlepool
    Publishing, Sunderland, 1990.

JOYCE, Myles, *et al.*
Maamtrasna, Jarlath Waldron, Edmund Burke, Dublin, 1992.

KINNAISTER, Charles, *et al.*
The Chronicles of Crime, Camden Pelham, T. Miles and Co.,
    London, 1891.

LEE, John D.
Massacre at Mountain Meadows, William Wise, Crowell, New
    York, 1976.

LIST, John Emil
Thou Shalt Not Kill, Mary S. Ryzuk, Popular Library, New York,
    1990.
Death Sentence, Joe Sharkey, Signet Books, New York, 1990.

LOCK AH TAM
Behind The Bar, A. E. Bowker, Staples Press, London, 1947.

***LOS ANGELES TIMES* BOMBING**
Fallen Angels, Marvin J. Wolf and Katherine Mader, Ballantine,
    New York, 1988.

LUNDGREN, Jeffrey Don, *et al.*
The Kirtland Massacre, Cynthia Stalter Sasse and Peggy Murphy
    Widder, Donald I. Fine, New York, 1991.

M62 BOMBING
Ambushed, Judith Ward, Vermilion, London, 1993.

McCABE, Henry
Memorable Irish Trials, K. E. L. Deale, Constable, London,
    1960.
Irish Murders, Terry Prone, Poolbeg, Dublin, 1992.

McCULLOCH, Thomas Neil, and MONE, Robert Francis
Blood on the Thistle, Douglas Skelton, Mainstream, Edinburgh, 1992.

MacDONALD, Jeffrey R.
Fatal Vision, Joe McGinniss, Putnam, New York, 1983.
I Accuse, Melinda Stephens, American Ideal Publishing, 1987.

McKINLIE, Peter, *et al.*
The Chronicles of Crime, Camden Pelham, T. Miles and Co., London, 1891.

McVEIGH, Timothy
American Terrorist, Lou Michel and Dan Herbeck, Regan Books, New York, 2001.

MAK, Kwan Fai, *et al.*
Death Row, Vol. 1, No. 1, Glenn Hare Publications, Carlsbad, Ca., 1989.

MANSON, Charles
The Manson Murders, Vincent Bugliosi with Curt Gentry, Bodley Head, London, 1975.
The Garbage People, John Gilmore and Ron Kenner, Omega Press, Los Angeles, 1971.

MATUSCHKA, Sylvestre
Gentlemen of the Jury, Hans Habe, Harrap, London, 1967.

MONGE, Luis Jose
Sentenced To Die, Stephen H. Gettinger, Macmillan, New York, 1979.

MOONEY/BILLINGS CASE
The Mooney Case, Richard H. Frost, Stanford Univ. Press, Stanford, Ca., 1968.
Frame-Up, Curt Gentry, Norton, New York, 1967.

MOUNTBATTEN BOMBING
Murder Will Out, Tom Reddy, Gill & Macmillan, Dublin, 1990.

NELSON, Dale Merle
The Limits of Sanity, Larry Still, Bles, London, 1973.

OBERST, Owen
Strange and Mysterious Crimes, anonymous author, Hutchinson, London, n.d.

OHMURA, Ichiro
Murder in Big Cities, Bruce Sanders, Herbert Jenkins, London, 1962.

ORSINI, Felice, *et al.*
Orsini, Michael St John Packe, Little Brown, Boston, 1957.

OWEN, John
Masters of Crime, Guy B. H. Logan, Stanley Paul, London, 1928.

PACKER, Alferd G.
Alferd G. Packer, Cannibal! Victim?, Ervan F. Kushner, Platte'N'Press, Frederick, Co., 1980.
Al Packer, Fred and Jo Mazzulla, Denver, 1968.

PAN AM FLIGHT 103
The Fall of Pan Am 103, Steven Emerson and Brian Duffy, Futura, London, 1988.
On The Trial of Terror, David Leppard, Jonathan Cape, London, 1991.

PHILLIPS, Morgan
The Chronicles of Crime, Camden Pelham, T. Miles and Co., London, 1891.

PORTEOUS, Captain John
Notable Scottish Trials: Trial of Captain Porteous, William Roughead (ed.), Hodge, Glasgow, 1909.

PULAU SENANG MURDERS
Pulau Senang, Alex Josey, Times Books International, Singapore, 1980.

RANSOM, Florence
Inside The C.I.D., Peter Beveridge, Evans, London, 1947.

ROBERTS, Harry, *et al.*
No Answer From Foxtrot Eleven, Tom Tullett, Michael Joseph, London, 1967.

ROTTMAN, Arthur
Famous New Zealand Murders, Dudley G. Dyne, Collins, Auckland, 1969.

RYAN, Michael
Hungerford, One Man's Massacre, Jeremy Josephs, Smith Gryphon, London, 1993.

ST VALENTINE'S DAY MASSACRE
Murders Most Strange, Leonard Gribble, John Long, London, 1959.

SARTIN, Robert
Murder Update, Brian Lane, Robinson, London, 1991.

SAVILLE, William
Nottingham, A Place of Execution, Terry Lambley, Lambley, Nottingham, 1981.

SEGEE, Robert Dale
Crime Stranger Than Fiction, Leonard Gribble, Hale, London, 1981.

SIMMONS, Ronald Gene
Zero At The Bone, Bryce Marshall and Paul Williams, Pocket Star Books, New York, 1991.

SIMPSON, Charles
Charlie Simpson's Apocalypse, Joe Eszterhas, Random House, New York, 1973.

SOVEREIGN, Henry
Twenty Mortal Murders, Orlo Miller, Macmillan of Canada, Toronto, 1978.

SPECK, Richard Franklin
Born To Raise Hell, Jack Altman and Marvin Ziporyn, Zebra Books, New York, 1968.

The Chicago Nurse Murders, George Carpozi, Banner Books, New York, 1967.
The Crime of the Century, Dennis L. Breo and William L. Martin, Bantam Books, New York, 1993.

STACK, James
Famous New Zealand Murders, Dudley G. Dyne, Collins, Auckland, 1969.

STONE, Michael
Stone Cold, Martin Dillon, Hutchinson, London, 1992.

STUELLGENS, Robert Wilhelm
Madly Murderous, John Dunning, Hamlyn, London, 1985.

SWIFT RUNNER
Twenty Mortal Murders, Orlo Miller, Macmillan of Canada, Toronto, 1978.

TOKYO SUBWAY GASSING
Holy Terror – Armageddon in Tokyo, D. W. Brackett, Weatherill, New York, 1996.

TREMAMUNNO, Donato
Compelled To Kill, Leonard Gribble, John Long, London, 1977.

TROPPMANN, Jean-Baptiste
Murder For Profit, William Bolitho, Cape, London, 1934.
Mass Murder, L. C. Douthwaite, John Long, London, 1928.

TYLENOL KILLINGS
Sunday, Bloody Sunday, Drew Mackenzie, Blake, London, 1992.

UNION STATION MASSACRE
Union Station Massacre, Merle Clayton, Bobbs-Merrill, Indianapolis, 1975.

UNRUH, Howard
The Mass Murderer, Brad Steiger, Award Books, New York, 1967.

URICH, Henri
The Deadly Professionals, Leonard Gribble, John Long, London, 1976.

VAN HEERDEN, Cornelius Johannes Petrus
Up For Murder, Benjamin Bennett and F. P. Rousseau, Hutchinson, London, 1934.

VERONICA **MUTINEERS**
Notable British Trials: Trial of the Veronica Mutineers, G. W. Keeton and John Cameron (eds.), Hodge, London, 1952.

WEBER, Adolph
Celebrated Criminal Cases of America, Thomas Duke, Patterson Smith, Montclair, NJ, 1991.

WESBECKER, Joseph T.
Crime Classification Manual, Robert K. Ressler *et al.*, Simon & Schuster, London, 1993.

WHITMAN, Charles
A Sniper in the Tower, Gary M. Lavergne, University of North Texas Press, Denton, 1997.

WILLIAMS, John
The Maul and The Pear Tree, T. A. Critchley and P. D. James, Constable, London, 1971.
On Murder As A Fine Art, Thomas De Quincey, Philip Allan, London, 1925.

WILSON, John Gleeson
Monsters of Crime, Guy B. H. Logan, Mellifont, London, n.d.

ZEIGLER, William
The Evidence Never Lies, Alfred Allan Lewis with Herbert Leon MacDonell, Holt, Rinehart and Winston, New York, 1984.

General Reference Works

Chester, Graham, *Berserk*, Michael O'Mara, London, 1993.

Fox, James Alan & Levin, Jack, *Overkill – Mass Murder and Serial Killing Exposed*, Plenum Press, New York, 1994

Gaute, J. H. H., and Odell, Robin, *The New Murderers' Who's Who*, Harrap, London, 1989.

Gaute, J. H. H., and Odell, Robin, *Murder Whereabouts*, Harrap, London, 1986.

Green, Jonathan, *The Directory of Infamy*, Mills & Boon, London, 1980.

Lasseter, Don, *Going Postal*, Pinnacle Books, New York, 1997

Lane, Brian, *The Murder Yearbook*, Headline, London, 1992.

Lane, Brian, *The Murder Yearbook, 1994 Edition*, Headline, London, 1993.

Levin, Jack, and Fox, James Alan, *Mass Murder*, Plenum Press, New York, 1986.

Lindsay, Philip, *The Mainspring of Murder*, John Long, London, 1958.

Nash, J. Robert, *Bloodletters and Badmen*, Evans, New York, 1973.

Nash, J. Robert, *Murder America*, Harrap, London, 1981.

Nash, J. Robert, *Compendium of World Crime*, Harrap, London, 1983.

Nash, J. Robert, *Look For The Woman*, Harrap, London, 1984.

Nash, J. Robert, *Encyclopedia of World Crime*, Crime Books Inc., Wilmette, 1990.

Nash, J. Robert, *World Encyclopedia of 20th Century Murder*, Headline, 1992.

Newton, Michael, *Mass Murder: An Annotated Bibliography*, Garland, New York, 1988.

O'Brien, Bill, *Agents of Mayhem*, David Bateman, Auckland, 2002

Scott, Sir Harold, *Concise Encyclopedia of Crime and Criminals*, Hawthorn, London, 1961.

Shew, E. Spencer, *A Companion To Murder*, Cassell, London, 1960.

Shew, E. Spencer, *A Second Companion To Murder*, Cassell, London, 1961.

Sifakis, Carl, *The Encyclopedia of American Crime*, Facts on File, New York, 1988.

Wilson, Colin, *A Casebook of Murder*, Leslie Frewin, London, 1969.

Wilson, Colin, *A Criminal History of Mankind*, Granada, London, 1984.

Wilson, Colin, *The Mammoth Book of True Crime*, Robinson, London, 1988.

Wilson, Colin, *The Mammoth Book of True Crime 2*, Robinson, London, 1990.

Wilson, Colin, *Written in Blood*, Equation, Wellingborough, 1989.

Wilson, Colin & Pitman, Pat, *Encyclopedia of Murder*, Barker, London, 1961.

Wilson, Colin & Seaman, Donald, *Encyclopedia of Modern Murder*, Barker, London, 1988.

Monthly Magazines

Master Detective
True Crime
True Detective

Part Works

Crimes and Punishment
Murder Casebook
Real Life Crimes

Alphabetical Index

OKAMOTO, Kozo (Israel)
ORGERON, Paul Harold (USA)
ORSINI, Felice, *et al.* (France)
OWEN, John (England)

PACKER, Alferd (USA)
PAN AM FLIGHT 103 (Scotland)
PHILLIPS, Morgan (England)
PORTEOUS, Captain John (Scotland)
POUGH, James (USA)
PULAU SENANG MURDERS (Singapore)
PULLIAM, Mark (USA)
PURDY, Patrick (USA)

RANSOM, Florence (England)
REYNOLDS, Vernon (Wales)
ROBERTS, HARRY, *et al.* (England)
ROTTMAN, Arthur (New Zealand)
ROUCOULT FAMILY CASE (France)
RUPPERT, James (USA)
RYAN, Michael (England)

SAINT VALENTINE'S DAY MASSACRES (USA)
SARTIN, Robert (England)
SAVILLE, William (England)
SCHLAEPFER, Brian (New Zealand)
SCHWARZ, Bernhard (Germany)
SEEGRIST, Sylvia (USA)
SEGEE, Robert Dale (USA)
SHEARING, David William (Canada)
SHERRILL, Patrick Henry (USA)
SIMANTS, Erwin Charles Herbert (USA)
SIMECECK, James (USA)
SIMMONS, Ronald Gene (USA)
SIMPSON, Charles (USA)
SLAVIN, Patrick, *et al.* (Canada)
SMITH, Robert Benjamin (USA)
SOVEREIGN, Henry (Canada)
SPECK, Richard Franklin (USA)
SPENCER, Brenda (USA)
STACK, James (New Zealand)
STEINHAUSER, Robert (Germany)
STONE, Michael Anthony (Northern Ireland)
STRYDOM, Barend (South Africa)
STUELLGENS, Robert Wilhelm (Germany)
SWIFT RUNNER (Canada)

Geographical Index

(by location of murders)

Wales